THE INDIAN TRIBES
OF NORTH AMERICA

THE INDIAN TRIBES
OF NORTH AMERICA

WITH BIOGRAPHICAL SKETCHES AND
ANECDOTES OF THE PRINCIPAL CHIEFS

THOMAS L. McKENNEY
and
JAMES HALL

EDITED BY

FREDERICK WEBB HODGE

Volume I

ROWMAN AND LITTLEFIELD
TOTOWA, NEW JERSEY

THIS EDITION FIRST PUBLISHED IN THE UNITED STATES 1972
by Rowman and Littlefield, Totowa, New Jersey

ISBN 0 87471 119 3

THIS REPRINT TAKEN FROM THE
1933 EDITION
by John Grant, Edinburgh

This edition published by
kind permission of the copyright holder,
John Grant,
31 George IV Bridge, Edinburgh

Reprinted in Great Britain by
Scolar Press Limited, Menston, Yorkshire

THE INDIAN TRIBES
OF NORTH AMERICA

WAR DANCE OF THE SAUKS AND FOXES

INDIAN TRIBES OF THE UPPER MISSISSIPPI

WAR DANCE OF THE SAUKS AND FOXES

INDIAN TRIBES OF THE UPPER MISSISSIPPI

Explanation of the Plate. By Caleb Atwater, Esq.

1. KEEOKUK, the principal warrior of the Sauks. Shrewd and politic, he possesses great influence in the councils of his nation. Brave, active and enterprising, his warriors implicitly obey his orders. Honourable and high minded, he never begs from the whites. Having met two American soldiers, descending, while he was ascending the Mississippi river, with his warriors, to join us at Prairie du Chien in the summer of 1829, he arrested them as deserters from Fort Crawford, as in fact they were, brought them forward, and delivered them up to the commanding officer at that garrison. Being informed by myself, that he was entitled not only to the thanks of the United States for such an act, but to a pecuniary award, he proudly replied, "that what he had done, was not done with any view to a reward, but from friendship to the United States." He resides near the mouth of Rock River, with his five wives and numerous children.

2. MORGAN, the principal warrior of the Fox, or Musquawkee Indians, resides on the west bank of the Mississippi, a short distance above Dubuque's tomb. He is a brave man and fond of war, but does not possess that versatility of talent belonging to Keeokuk. In the winter of 1828, he went to the country of the Sioux, and killed a woman and her three children, which brought on a war between the Sioux and Foxes.

3. This person represents a prisoner at the stake with his hair so tied up, that his scalp may be taken whenever the moment arrives, rendering it proper to take it.

4. TIAHMA, the principal civil chief of the Foxes, resides at an Indian village, on the western bank of the Mississippi river. He is a sensible, sober, and discreet man, and much respected for his sound judgment and benevolent disposition.

5. The principal civil chief of the Sauks resides on the eastern bank of the Mississippi, near the mouth of Rock river. He is not thirty years old yet, and was raised to his present high station in the spring of 1829, on the demise of his uncle, the former chief.

6. THE IMPROVISATORI—A great wit, whose business it is to take off the warriors at the war dance, when they boast of their exploits. He contrives to ascertain what the subject of the warrior's boasting will be, and he turns it into ridicule, by boasting of having done some mean act, of which the warrior himself has been guilty. His head is adorned with bison hair, dyed red, and the horns of the antelope, very correctly represented by the artist give him a grotesque, and not an inappropriate appearance for the station he fills. He is an amiable man, and greatly esteemed by those who know him best.

7. The musicians, singing a war song, and beating the drum with their war clubs. Quasquawma, one of the persons beating the drum, sits exactly in front of Tiahma, No. 4, and was once a civil chief, but being cheated, as the Indians allege, out of the mineral country by a certain General, acting as a commissioner, Quasquawma was degraded from his rank and Tiahma rules instead. The mineral region was acquired without any consideration from the Sauks and Foxes, and generously given away *by the same commissioner*, to the Chippewas, Ottawas and Pottawattamies. Recently, the same country has been re-purchased from the last mentioned Indians, at an expense of $16,000 per annum, *forever*. Quasquawma joined the United States in the late war with Great Britain.

8. TOM, *a half breed*, as he is called, though, like those Choctaws, who, for mercenary purposes, thus call themselves, he has very little Indian blood in his veins. *Tom*, is a great pet among the whites, speaks *Mississippi French*, and a little English. He, and two or three others in this interesting group, are more muscular than full blooded Indians, and the artist has done them equal and exact justice, in his delineation of their limbs. All the persons represented are singing a war song, and dancing to the tune.

The other figures in the group represent persons in no way remarkable. They are brave men, who strictly obey the principal warriors, Keeokuk and Morgan; are fond of dress, of show, and parade. The figures are spread out so as to show their faces, which are the best miniature likenesses I ever beheld. A few figures show their backs, in order, more fully, to exhibit their dress. Every feather in the picture, is an exact resemblance of the thing itself, and so is each war club, with its looking glass inserted in it. The whole, and every part of this beautiful painting represent the reality itself, in a masterly manner and do great honour to the talent of the artist.

THE INDIAN TRIBES
OF NORTH AMERICA

WITH BIOGRAPHICAL SKETCHES AND ANECDOTES OF THE PRINCIPAL CHIEFS

THOMAS L. McKENNEY

AND

JAMES HALL

A NEW EDITION, EDITED BY

FREDERICK WEBB HODGE

Illustrated with 123 *full-page Plates in Colour (chiefly from the Indian Gallery, formerly in the War Department at Washington), Photogravure Portraits, and two Maps*

VOLUME I

EDINBURGH: JOHN GRANT
31 GEORGE IV. BRIDGE
1933

CONTENTS

v

CONTENTS

Faithfully yours
Tho McKenney

Yours Truly
James Hall

INTRODUCTION

THE desirability of making a permanent record of the features of the more prominent American Indians of the various tribes had its inception about the year 1821, when the administration of Indian Affairs was under the control of the United States War Department, the official immediately in charge being the Superintendent of Indian Trade. The incumbent at the date named was Colonel McKenney, one of the authors of the present work.

Thomas Loraine McKenney, eldest son of William and Anne (Barber) McKenney, sturdy and consistent Quakers, was born on the old family plantation, "Hopewell," in Somerset County, Maryland, March 21, 1785, and died in New York City, February 20, 1859. He attended school at Chestertown, Maryland, married Aditha Gleaves, and while still a young man, settled in Georgetown, District of Columbia, where he became interested in two mercantile establishments, which he disposed of in 1814.[1] Notwithstanding his strict Quaker training, he became adjutant of the First Legion of the Militia of the District of Columbia, and acted in that capacity to a detachment of volunteer

[1] The writer desires to express his indebtedness to Miss Ella Loraine Dorsey, of Washington, grand-niece of Colonel McKenney, for information respecting his family and his early life.

vii

companies in service under the command of Colonel (afterward General) J. Thompson, of Washington, at Piscataway, Maryland, in the summer of 1813, during the war with Great Britain. Later he became one of the aides of Major-General John P. Van Ness, who resigned his commission, thus dissolving McKenney's connection as aide. The latter, however, followed his brigade on foot, and became a private in a company of Georgetown riflemen, under Captain J. I. Stull. Subsequently he was invited by General Walter Smith to become one of his aides, and receiving permission to accept the appointment, continued as a staff officer to the end of the campaign, which resulted in the defeat of the Americans at Bladensburg, near Washington, August 24, 1814, leaving the way open to the capture of the capital and the burning of some of the public buildings by the British forces under General Ross and Admiral Cockburn, on the following day.[1] During this period, McKenney held an interest in the mercantile firm of J(oseph) C. Hall & Co., of Washington City; but in 1816, having been tendered the appointment of the Superintendency of Indian Trade, he relinquished this interest, and entered on his new duties, April 12th of the year named, succeeding General John Mason.

At this time every Indian tribe within the domain of the United States was regarded as if a sovereign power, with which the United States entered into solemn treaty, and the chief interest which the Government manifested in the Indians was for the maintenance of peace and the promotion and regulation of trade. As early as 1776, the

[1] See McKenney, *Narrative of the Battle of Bladensburgh, in a Letter to Henry Banning, Esq.* [n. p.], 1814; also, his *Reply to Kosciusko Armstrong's Assault*, pp. 13, 27 (New York, 1847).

Congress of the Confederation enacted a law for granting licences and regulating trade among the Indians; but it was not until ten years later that the United States entered into regular trade relations with the various tribes by establishing factories, or trading posts, on the frontier, and providing for the appointment of a "Super-intendent of Indian Trade." It was to this office that McKenney was called by President Madison in 1816, and to which he was reappointed by President Monroe in 1820. The position was one of trust and of great responsibility, involving the expenditure of large sums of money for purposes of trade as well as in the distribution of annuities. Goods were purchased in open market in the several cities and shipped to the frontier posts, where they were traded to the Indians, without expectation of profit to the Government, for furs and peltries; these in turn were shipped to the commercial centres and sold. This trade was conducted under McKenney's Superin-tendency for six years; but the large private fur companies meanwhile steadily increased their own trade by the introduction of spirituous liquors, until finally, by Act of Congress of May 6, 1822, the Government trade was brought to an end, and George Graham was appointed to close the affairs of the Superintendency.

McKenney was repeatedly charged with corruption in the administration of his office, especially by Senator Thomas H. Benton, of Missouri, whom McKenney char-acterised as "the legitimate organ" of the Missouri Fur Company; but there is no doubt of McKenney's integrity, while almost his entire life affords ample proof of his sympathy for the Indians. For thirty years he had been an intimate friend of John Ross (*Gûwisguwĭ'*, com-monly Cooweescoowee), the celebrated chief of the

Cherokee, among whom McKenney was known as "White Eagle," in allusion to his strong features and his shock of white hair.

In an examination into his official conduct by the Committee on Indian Affairs of the House of Representatives in 1823, McKenney said:

"My good name was, and yet is, my all. Money is not the god of my idolatry, as those who know me will attest. It had been better for me to-day, perhaps, had I worshipped a little more devotionally at this shrine. My good name I have laboured hard to preserve. I received it as a legacy from parents who died [1] and left me little else with which to combat the roughnesses of this bleak and cheerless world; and the business of my life has been, and I trust will ever be to its close, to preserve that legacy, and to hand it over untarnished to an only son, [2] to whom, although I may have little more to give, it may constitute a source of the most agreeable reflections; and, by a reference to the example which this very inquiry furnishes, he may be induced the more diligently to guard it, and hand it over in perfect purity to his posterity. I am concerned for its preservation. I will not, I could not, disguise it; but I shall expect it to be protected, on this occasion, only on the ground of my having demonstrated that it has been unrighteously assailed." [3]

During his Superintendency, in 1818 or 1819, McKenney

---

[1] McKenney's mother died when he was ten years of age.

[2] The son, William, was still alive, and unmarried, in 1857, after which all trace of him is lost. It may be said here that Colonel McKenney was a devout churchman, becoming a strong Wesleyan after having passed through his experience as a "fighting Quaker."

[3] *American State Papers, Indian Affairs*, II., 424 (Washington, 1834).

addressed a circular to those friendly to the Indian cause, in an endeavour to rescue them "from the sad condition in which they were everywhere known to be." As a direct result of this appeal, Congress in 1819 appropriated $10,000 "for the civilisation of the Indian tribes adjoining the frontier settlements"—the beginning of an educational policy that now involves the expenditure of millions of dollars annually.

After being legislated out of office, in August 1822, McKenney established at the capital a newspaper known as *The Washington Republican and Congressional Examiner*, which continued until July 10, 1824, when it was sold to Peter Force, who conducted it under the name of *The National Journal*. At the outset the paper advocated the election of John C. Calhoun to the Presidency in 1824.

In recognition of the confidence reposed in him by President Monroe and by the Secretary of War, John C. Calhoun, McKenney was next assigned to "the duties of the Bureau of Indian Affairs." This office was not created at this time by Act of Congress, but was organised by the Secretary of War, with the approval of the President, for the better administration of Indian affairs. All the means at the Secretary's disposal which, wrote McKenney, "he could make applicable to my salary, were sixteen hundred dollars. This I declined to accept, upon the ground that it was inadequate to my support, and would not be a just equivalent for the services which I knew the office would require at my hands. He admitted the justice of both—but added, the President would recommend, in his next message to Congress, the organisation of an Indian Department, with a salary equal to that paid to auditors [then $3000], expressing a hope that this would be satisfactory. I finally consented, and on the

11th of March 1824, had assigned to me the duties of the Bureau of Indian Affairs."[1]

Perhaps for the reason that McKenney's appointment had not been made by direct authority of law, the treaties of peace entered into at Washington, August 4, 1824, with the Sauk and Foxes, and with the Iowa, were negotiated by William Clark, "Superintendent of Indian Affairs, and sole commissioner specially appointed for that purpose,"[2] McKenney serving merely as a witness. He witnessed also the treaty with the Choctaw, concluded at Washington, January 20, 1825.

The President was faithful to his promise, and McKenney himself prepared a Bill for the organisation of an Indian Bureau, but it lingered before Congress for several sessions, McKenney meanwhile eking out an existence on his meagre salary until his term of service was terminated. He made an attempt in later years to obtain the promised compensation for what he regarded as his "unrequited labours," but to no avail. In addition to the more practical business of his office, McKenney aided in every way the few students of the period interested in ethnologic and linguistic researches. Among these was Dr C. S. Rafinesque, of Transylvania University, whom he joined, under date of August 22, 1825, in drafting a circular letter asking information respecting the languages of the tribes.

[1] His salary as Superintendent of Indian Trade, at the time the office was abolished, was $2000 per annum—the same as that of the agent for the Creek Indians, who in addition received an allowance for rations.

[2] So reads the preamble to the Sauk and Fox treaty. That with the Iowa reads:—" . . . between William Clark, superintendent of Indian affairs, being specially authorized by the President of the United States thereto."—See *Treaties between the United States of America and the Several Indian Tribes, from* 1778 *to* 1837. Washington, 1837.

"Such were my labors," he later wrote, "so constant and oppressive, and so weighty the responsibilities which devolved on me, as to have very nearly cost me my life. My health gave way under the pressure," and, but for the confidence of President Adams, and of Mr Barbour, the Secretary of War, "I should, in all probability, have died at my post." On June 1, 1826, McKenney started from Georgetown, D.C., on a journey to Lake Superior, for the purpose of negotiating, jointly with Lewis Cass (later Secretary of War), a treaty with the Chippewa Indians, of whom, at that time, the afterward celebrated Henry R. Schoolcraft was agent. This important treaty, by which the copper deposits of Lake Superior were opened to the whites, was successfully carried out on August 5, 1826, at Fond du Lac, and was proclaimed February 7 of the following year.

Another result of McKenney's journey to the Indian country is an illustrated octavo volume bearing the title : *Sketches of a Tour to the Lakes, of the Character and Customs of the Chippeway Indians, and of Incidents connected with the Treaty of Fond du Lac. By Thomas L. McKenney, of the Indian Department, and joint Commissioner with his Excellency Gov. Cass, in negotiating the Treaty. Also, A Vocabulary of the Algic, or Chippeway Language, formed in part, as far as it goes, upon the basis of one furnished by the Hon. Albert Gallatin. . . . Ornamented with Twenty-nine Engravings, of Lake Superior, and other Scenery, Indian Likenesses, Costumes, &c.* Baltimore : published by Fielding Lucas, jun'r, 1827. (8°, 493 + 1 pp., 29 plates.)

The book consists of a series of letters (the first dated Georgetown, D.C., May 31, 1826 ; the last, Baltimore, October 6, 1826) that were addressed to the Honourable

James Barbour, Secretary of War (to whom the volume is dedicated), although the reader is left to surmise the person to whom they were written. In his "To the Reader," McKenney disavows any expectancy at the outset that the letters would be published, but states that he wrote them merely "in compliance with the request of a friend." The letters are interesting, nevertheless, both by reason of the personality of the writer which they reflect, and because of the new light shed on a country then but little known. Writing to Schoolcraft in March 1827, McKenney said: "It is rather a ladies' book. I prefer the sex and their opinions. They are worth ten times as much as we, in all that is enlightened, and amiable, and blissful."[1]

Most of the illustrations with which the volume is "ornamented" are from the pencil of J. O. Lewis, who accompanied McKenney and Cass, and witnessed the treaty of Fond du Lac, and some of whose portraits, copied by King, illustrate the present work.[2] Most of the

[1] Schoolcraft, *Personal Memoirs*, p. 264, 1851. Of the book, Schoolcraft also writes (p. 254):—"In his ' sketches' of his recent tour, he seeks to embody personal and amusing things which daily befell the party—matters upon which he was quite at home. I had mentioned to him, while here, that the time and labour necessary to collect information on Indian topics, of a literary character, imposed a species of research worthy of departmental patronage; that I was quite willing to contribute in this way, and to devote my leisure moments to further researches on the aboriginal history and languages, if the Government would appropriate means to this end. I took the occasion to put these views in writing, and, by way of earnest, enclosed him part of a vocabulary."

[2] Lewis lived in Detroit, where, about 1825, he engraved and published a small map of the city, based on plans for its betterment, drawn up in 1805 and 1806.—See Farmer, *History of Detroit and Wayne County*, p. 33. Detroit and New York, 1890.

illustrations are lithographs, atrociously reproduced ; the few on copper are far more creditable.[1]   McKenney has little to say of Lewis, aside from commending the faithfulness of some of his sketches and his fine singing, which often entertained the party, both afloat and ashore, during their sojourn in the Lake country.   For the appended Chippewa vocabulary, based on the schedule furnished by Albert Gallatin, McKenney acknowledges his indebtedness to Henry R. Schoolcraft, later noted for his great work, in six volumes, on the Indian tribes.

In 1827, McKenney and Cass were again selected as joint commissioners, this time to treat with the Chippewa, Menominee, and Winnebago tribes.   In McKenney's case his political friends, including a dozen senators and representatives in Congress (among the former being William Henry Harrison), made a strong appeal in his behalf, urging the appointment partly on the ground that "he possesses more the confidence of the Indians than any person in the United States who could be so easily employed for this desirable object.   He has perhaps, likewise, equal, if not a superior knowledge of the Indian character and disposition than any person who would likely undertake this work."   The treaty was negotiated at Butte des Morts, Michigan Territory, August 11, 1827, and was proclaimed February 23, 1829.

---

[1] In "the author's own copy," sold by The Anderson Auction Company, New York City, January 28, 1908, "nearly every plate has some pencilled criticism, ' Very good,' ' Excellent,' ' Bad-face ought to be old and deep furrowed,' ' Good except the bow of the canoe,' etc., each of which is signed ' Author.' "   See Rare Americana . . . mainly the Collection formed by Miss Nellie Malcolm, London, England . . . The Anderson Auction Company, 5 West 29th St., New York. [1908.]

By direction of the President, supplementary instructions were issued to McKenney by James Barbour,
Secretary of War, under date of March 28, 1827, directing him to obtain information of the country between the
Great Lakes and the Mississippi, the condition and disposition of the Indian tribes scattered over it, "and
especially to ascertain the disposition of the tribes within
the States, the Chickasaws and Choctaws, and, if practicable, the Cherokees, on the subject of emigration to
lands west of the Mississippi." Another letter of instructions, dated April 10, 1827, directed McKenney to employ
all proper means to procure of the Creeks a cession of
the remaining strip of their land in Georgia. These
missions, very important by reason of the disturbed
condition of the Southern tribes at that time, were successfully accomplished. McKenney held a council with
the Choctaw on October 16; and with agent Crowell
of the Creeks, the treaty with that tribe, resulting in
the cession of their remaining lands in Georgia, was held
at the Creek Agency, November 15 following, and was
proclaimed March 4, 1828.[1]

On his journey through the Creek country, McKenney,
ever ready to embrace an opportunity to advance the
education and civilization of the Indians, adopted two
boys—William Barnard, son of the Creek chief, Timpooche Barnard, and Lee Compere, a Yuchi—whom he
took with him and made members of his household at
"Weston," on the heights of Georgetown. Here the
boys lived with their foster-father, and were educated

[1] See *Reports and Proceedings of Colonel McKenney, on the Subject of his
Recent Tour among the Southern Indians, as submitted to Congress, with a
Message of the President, U.S.* Washington : printed by Gales & Seaton,
1828. (8°, 37 pp.)

under his direction until his term of office came to an end.

In July 1829, the Secretary of War responded to a call made upon him by an association of distinguished citizens (chiefly clergymen and laymen of the Dutch Reformed Church) of New York, for McKenney's presence in that city, and his services in aiding them in the formation of "The Indian Board, for the Emigration, Preservation, and Improvement of the Aborigines of America," an organization that evidently superseded "The American Society for Promoting the Civilization and General Improvement of the Indian Tribes within the United States," organized at Washington about 1822, of whose Committee of Ways and Means McKenney was a member.[1] Of the later organization McKenney was appointed a member of a committee to draft a constitution, and the Honourable Stephen Van Rensselaer was elected president. On August 12, McKenney delivered before the Board an address which appears in *Documents and Proceedings relating to the Formation and Progress of a Board in the City of New York, for the Emigration, Preservation, and Improvement, of the Aborigines of America* (New York : Vanderpool & Cole, printers, 1829 ; 8°, 48 pp.), and is published also, with changes in verbiage, in McKenney's *Memoirs* (pp. 229-248). Neither Association seems to have accomplished anything ; they possibly became exhausted from sheer weight of name.

McKenney had ever been the subject of attack by his political enemies, as has been intimated. The newspapers of the day gave ready circulation to charges against

---

[1] See Jedidiah Morse, *Report to the Secretary of War*, Washington, 1822, App., pp. 284-290.

the Indian commissioner. On one occasion he was accused
of connivance with business firms in illegally supplying
goods for the Indian service, but the charge could not be
substantiated ; at another time he was charged with
extravagance in having Fürst design an Indian medal;
and again we hear of his gross wastefulness of the public
money in paying as much as thirty-three dollars to King
and Ford for a single Indian portrait! Always a
power in Congress, Senator Benton bore no small part in
the abolishment of the Superintendency of Indian Trade,
resulting in the transfer of the traffic with the Indians to
private hands, and the increased debauchery of the native
tribes through the introduction of liquors. McKenney's
strict integrity in the administration of the Indian affairs
made an enemy also of Samuel Houston, later President
of Texas, who had become interested in contracts for
supplying rations to the Southern Indians during their
removal beyond the Mississippi, the difficulty, according
to McKenney's own statement, arising from Houston's
request for his influence in awarding to him the coveted
contracts, which, of course, McKenney indignantly refused.
Another strong opponent was Duff Green, editor of *The
Washington Telegraph*, who lost no opportunity to wield
his sarcastic pen against the "Kickapoo Ambassador," as
McKenney had become known to his enemies after his
successful negotiations as a treaty commissioner.

These affairs had their effect on President Jackson,
who had succeeded John Quincy Adams, March 4, 1829,
and was now the ardent advocate of the "spoils system."
Duff Green was one of Jackson's confidential advisers—
a member of his so-called "kitchen cabinet" — while
Houston had served under him in the Indian wars of
the South; consequently, McKenney's tenure had not

become the most secure after the elevation of Jackson to the Presidency.

Such was the condition of affairs in the summer of 1830, when McKenney obtained leave of absence for the purpose of attending to some personal business connected with the publication of his large work, now in the hands of Samuel F. Bradford, a publisher of Philadelphia. Returning from New York to the latter city in August, McKenney found a letter from the acting Secretary of War, informing him of his dismissal, to take effect on October 1st, on the ground that he was not in harmony with Jackson's views respecting Indian affairs.

To those familiar with the Indian policy of President Jackson, especially with regard to the transfer of the Southern Indians to the territory beyond the Mississippi, it is rather to the credit of our author that his dismissal was based on such grounds.[1] The removal of McKenney, it was later written, "was a marked era in Indian history, as the commencement of that encroaching, arbitrary, and oppressive policy which has cost the country millions of treasure, many thousands of valuable lives, and more reputation than a patriotic American likes to acknowledge," . . .[2]

[1] McKenney later addressed a series of letters, under the pseudonym of "Aristides," to the *Pennsylvania Inquirer*, published at Philadelphia under the editorship of Robert Morris, with the understanding that his name might be divulged in the discretion of the editor when the series (numbering twenty-nine in all) should have been completed. The letters are a vitriolic outburst against the attitude of the President and others toward the Bank of the United States, and were afterward printed in pamphlet form under the title, *Essays on the Spirit of Jacksonism, as exemplified in its Deadly Hostility to the Bank of the United States, and in the Odious Calumnies employed for its Destruction.* By Aristides. . . . Philadelphia: Jesper Harding, printer, 1835. (8°, 151 pp.)

[2] *North American Review*, vol. lxiii., October 1846.

After his dismissal, McKenney requested permission
to take his adopted Yuchi and Creek boys with him to
Philadelphia, but Jackson denied the request, and the
Indians were returned to their people in the South.
William Barnard, the Creek, later became involved in a
murder, and fled to the Seminoles in Florida. Lee
Compere, the Yuchi, was never heard from again.

The fathering of these boys is not the only instance
of McKenney's kindness toward the race to which so
much of his life had been devoted. While chief of Indian
Affairs, his good offices were sought by James Lawrence
McDonald, a Choctaw boy about fourteen years of age,
whom he adopted, and placed under the instruction of
the Reverend James Carnahan, then principal of a classical
school in Georgetown, later president of Princeton College.
McDonald and McKenney's son, William, a boy of
the same age, became warm friends, and McKenney
himself formed a strong attachment for his Indian charge,
who soon became "bent on distinguishing himself."
McKenney gave the boy every advantage of his home,
making no distinction between him and his own son,
in dress or attentions. McDonald outstripped his fellow-
students in Carnahan's academy, where he remained for
three years. On the recommendation of John C. Calhoun,
that the young Indian become a lawyer, McKenney sent
McDonald to Cincinnati, Ohio, where he entered the
office of Judge John McLean, and in a remarkably short
time was admitted to the Bar. He then departed for the
Choctaw country, and became established at Jackson,
Mississippi, where he made a proposal of marriage to a
young white woman, and, being refused, committed suicide
by leaping from a river bluff.

It has been seen that McKenney had already in

contemplation the publication of a large illustrated work on the Indian tribes, but of the successive steps that were taken after 1830 to effect its publication little is known. Toward the close of the year named, McKenney announced by circular that he was about to establish a commercial house, or agency, on a general plan, for supplying articles designed for the Indian trade, and the sale of furs and peltries. Commenting on this, Schoolcraft (*Personal Memoirs*, p. 343, 1851) says : "This appears to me a striking mistake of judgment. The colonel, of all things, is not suited for a merchant." And Schoolcraft was quite correct. We have no evidence that the plan ever materialised ; but with his brother McKenney embarked in at least two other commercial ventures which practically wiped out their fortunes. Meanwhile he turned his attention to the contemplated Indian book.

McKenney's interest in the welfare of the Indians by no means ceased with his official relations. In 1837 we find him at the Seneca village in New York, attending the dedication of a marble slab over the remains of the great Red Jacket. In 1843-44, when the third volume of the *History of the Indian Tribes* was well advanced toward publication, he delivered a series of discourses in New England and the Middle States for the purpose of awakening "in the public mind an interest in behalf of the Indian race, and their destiny ; to give impetus to public opinion in regard to what ought to be done, and done speedily, for their welfare ; and when that opinion should be fully formed, bring it to bear on Congress, in connection with a plan for the preservation and well-being of the remnants of this hapless people." The discourses were enthusiastically received. At Annapolis he addressed the Legislature of Maryland, and by a vote of the House the use of the Capitol at Harrisburg, Pennsylvania, was granted for the same purpose. This series of addresses was published in 1846, under the title : *On the Origin, History, Character, and the Wrongs and Rights of the Indians, with a Plan for the Preservation and Happiness of the Remnants of that Persecuted Race*, forming Volume II. of his *Memoirs, Official and Personal; with Sketches of Travel among the Northern and Southern Indians; Embracing a War Excursion, and Descriptions of Scenes along the Western Border*. New York: Paine & Burgess, 1846 (8°, 136 pp., 13 pl.).[1] The book is dedicated to Mrs Madison, and contains a letter of acceptance in facsimile.

The "war excursion" alluded to in the title of the book refers to the battle of Bladensburg and the capture of Washington City in 1814, which McKenney introduces evidently for the purpose of discussing the causes that led to the resignation of General Armstrong as Secretary of War. This brought forth a *Review of McKenney's "Narrative of the Causes which, in 1814, led to General Armstrong's Resignation of the War Office,"* by Kosciusko Armstrong (New York, 1846), in which the son takes McKenney to task in an attempt to show that the late Secretary had been the victim of a plot; whereupon McKenney, with his usual readiness to enter a controversy when he believed his veracity or judgment to be at stake, issued "A Card" bearing the title, *An Opening Reply to Kosciusko Armstrong's Pamphlet* (sm. 4°, 2 ll. ; dated Lyceum House, Brooklyn, N.Y., Dec. 18, 1846), followed by a *Reply to Kosciusko Armstrong's Assault upon Col.*

[1] A second edition was published in the same year, and in 1854 a third edition was issued under the title: *Sketches of Travels among the Northern and Southern Indians*. New York: Daniel Burgess & Co., 1854.

McKenney's Narrative [etc.] (New York, 1847), which to the reader of to-day is a strong vindication of his attitude in the case, although answered in turn by Armstrong in an *Examination of McKenney's Reply to the "Review"* [etc.] (New York, 1847). These pamphlets shed valuable light on this phase of the War of 1812.

The last published writing by McKenney is "The Winnebago War of 1827," printed, after his death, in the *Report and Collections of the State Historical Society of Wisconsin*, Volume V., part II., pages 178-204 (Madison, 1868). The paper is based on personal information gained during his Tour to the Lakes.

Two years or more before the appearance of the first volume of the Folio Edition, published at Philadelphia in 1836, by Edward C. Biddle, the services of Judge James Hall, of Cincinnati, had been enlisted.

James Hall, son of John and Sarah (Ewing) Hall, was born at Philadelphia, August 19, 1793; and died near Cincinnati, Ohio, July 5, 1868. His grandfather came to Maryland with Lord Baltimore; and his father, James Hall, in 1782 married Sarah Ewing, daughter of the Reverend John Ewing, provost of the University of Pennsylvania. James Hall the elder resided, after his marriage, first in his native State of Maryland, but about 1790 returned to Philadelphia, where he became secretary of the Land Office and United States marshal for the district of Pennsylvania. They lived in Lamberton, New Jersey, in 1801-1805, and again in Maryland until 1811, when they settled in Philadelphia. The wife (born Philadelphia, October 30, 1761; died there, April 8, 1830) was noted for her literary ability, and as a student of religious subjects. Four sons were born of this union: John Elihu (born December 27, 1783; died June 11,

1829), lawyer and author, editor of *The Port-Folio* in Philadelphia from 1817-1827; Harrison (born November 5, 1785; died March 9, 1866), author, and publisher of *The Port-Folio;* James, the subject of the present sketch; and Thomas Mifflin (born February 27, 1798; lost at sea in 1828), naval surgeon.

James Hall the younger received his early training at home, and, reared in a literary atmosphere, it is not surprising that he acquired a taste for letters, and became "the literary venturer on the untried sea of Western literature." He first devoted himself to law, but in 1812, when nineteen years of age, abandoned it to become a volunteer in a company organized in Philadelphia, under the command of Condy Raguet. He served throughout the war with Great Britain, commanding a detachment of his company at Chippewa; and was present at the battle of Lundy's Lane and at the siege of Fort Erie, receiving official commendation for his services. He then became a lieutenant of artillery, and was stationed at Fort Mifflin, Pennsylvania. In 1815 he accompanied Commodore Stephen Decatur on his expedition to Algiers, serving on the United States brig *Enterprise.* Returning in 1816, he was stationed at Newport, Rhode Island, and afterward at Pittsburgh, Pennsylvania, on duty in the Ordnance Department. At this last station, in September 1817, Hall was tried by court-martial for "unofficer-like conduct, disobedience of orders and neglect of duty, and conduct unbecoming an officer and gentleman." He was found guilty on many of the charges, and sentenced to be cashiered; but in consideration of his "fair character in other respects, his brave and meritorious conduct during the late war, and in expectation that his future deportment will merit the lenity now extended to him," the punishment was remitted and he was restored to the ranks, but resigned June 30, 1818.[1] Resuming his studies in law, he was admitted to the Bar in 1818, and two years later descended the Ohio and settled at Shawneetown, Illinois, where he began to practise. In 1821 he was made State's Attorney for a judicial circuit embracing about ten counties in south-eastern Illinois, then a frontier territory overrun by desperadoes and fugitives from justice who terrorised the community. Hall's vigorous prosecution of these criminals restored security and respect for the law, and earned for him the election in 1825 as Judge of the same circuit, an office which he held until the legislative session of 1826-1827 repealed the Act creating it. Removing to Vandalia, then the State capital of Illinois, Hall became associated with Robert Blackwell, State printer, in publishing *The Illinois Intelligencer*, of which Hall became the editor. The Legislature of 1830-1831 elected him State Treasurer, and meanwhile he and Blackwell began the publication of *The Illinois Monthly Magazine*, in octavo form, the first periodical of a literary character issued in the State.

But Hall already had entered on his literary career, having contributed to *The Port-Folio*, published by his brother in Philadelphia, as early as 1820, numerous articles descriptive of the West and its people, which were widely copied. These articles were afterward collected, and with additions were issued in London in 1828 as a volume under the title, *Letters from the West; containing Sketches of Scenery, Manners, and Customs; and Anecdotes connected with the First Settlements of*

---

[1] See *Trial and Defence of First Lieutenant James Hall, of the Ordnance Department, United States Army. Published by Himself*. Pittsburgh: Eichbaum & Johnson, printers, 1820 (xvi. [17] -98 pp., 8°).

the Western Sections of the United States (8°, iv., 385 pp.).

The first number of *The Illinois Monthly Magazine* appeared for October 1830. Owing to the scarcity of labour and materials at Vandalia and the inaccessibility of that frontier town, the second and last volume (concluding September 1832) was published in part at St Louis, and in part at Cincinnati. In January 1833, Judge Hall revived the periodical at the latter place, conducting it under the name, *The Western Monthly Magazine, a continuation of the Illinois Monthly Magazine,* remaining with it in that city (which he now made his home until his death, July 5, 1868) until June 1836, when the editorship passed to the hands of Joseph Reese Fry.

Before this time, Judge Hall issued at Cincinnati the first annual published in the Western States : *The Western Souvenir, a Christmas and New Year's Gift for* 1829 (16°, 324 pp., 7 pl.).

In addition, he wrote the following, some of which are drawn largely from his *Letters from the West* and from his monthly periodicals :—

Legends of the West. Philadelphia : Harrison Hall, 1832 ; second edition, 1833 (16°, 4 p.l., 265 pp.). Published also, with additions, by T. L. Magagnos, New York, 1854 (12°, xvii., 435 pp., pl.).

The Soldier's Bride; and other Tales. Philadelphia : Key & Biddle, 1833 (16°, 9-272 pp.).

The Harpe's Head; a Legend of Kentucky. Philadelphia : Key & Biddle, 1833 (16°, 10-256 pp.). Published also under the title, *Kentucky: A Tale.* London :

printed for A. K. Newman & Co., 1834 (2 vols., 4-230, 2-242 pp.).

Sketches of History, Life and Manners in the West; Containing . . . Descriptions of the Country and Modes of Life, in the Western States and Territories of North America. Cincinnati: Hubbard & Edmands, 1834 (1 vol., 12°). Another edition with the title: *Sketches of History, Life, and Manners in the West.* Philadelphia: Harrison Hall, 1835 (2 vols., 16°, viii., 13-282; 4-276 pp.).

Statistics of the West, at the Close of the Year 1836. Cincinnati: J. A. James & Co., 1836 (12°, xviii., 11-284 pp.). Another edition, 1837. See *Notes on the Western States* (1838), below.[1]

Tales of the Border. Philadelphia: Harrison Hall, 1835 (16°, 2 pl., [9] -276 pp.).

A Memoir of the Public Services of William Henry Harrison, of Ohio. Philadelphia: Key & Biddle, 1836 (16°, 323 pp., portrait).

Notes on the Western States; containing descriptive sketches of their Soil, Climate, Resources, and Scenery. Philadelphia: Harrison Hall, 1838 (16°, xxiii., 13-304 pp.). (Practically the same as his *Statistics of the West*, 1836, 1837.) See also *The West*, 1848.

"Memoir of Thomas Posey, Major-General and Governor of Indiana." (In *The Library of American Biography*, conducted by Jared Sparks, Vol. XIX. (second series, Vol. IX.). Boston, 1846; pp. 359-403.)

---

[1] On the authenticity of this work from a Kentuckian's point of view, see Mann Butler's *An Appeal from the Misrepresentations of James Hall, Respecting the History of Kentucky.* . . . Frankfort, 1837.

The West: Its Commerce and Navigation. Cincinnati: H. W. Derby & Co., 1848 (12°, vii., 328 pp.). (Paper-cover title: "The Commerce and Navigation of the West. Cincinnati: H. W. Derby & Co., 1849.") This work is substantially the same as *Statistics of the West* (1836), and *Notes on the Western States* (1838).

The West: Its Soil, Surface, and Productions. Cincinnati: Derby, Bradley & Co., 1848 (12°, 260 pp.).

The Wilderness and the War Path. New York and London: John Wiley, 1849 (2 p.l., 174 pp.). This work probably first appeared in New York in 1845, and in London in 1846.

The Romance of Western History; or, Sketches of History, Life and Manners, in the West. Cincinnati: Apple-gate & Co., 1857 (12°, iv., 5-420 pp., portrait of author[1]). Republished by Robert Clarke & Co., Cincinnati, 1871.

Legends of the West: Sketches Illustrative of the Habits, Occupations, Privations, Adventures and Sports of the Pioneers of the West. Cincinnati: Robert Clarke & Co., 1874 (8°, 435 pp.).

While in Illinois, Judge Hall married Mary Harrison Posey, daughter of the Revolutionary Major-General, and afterwards Governor of Indiana Territory, whose biography Hall subsequently prepared. Mrs Hall died in 1832. Before the sale of *The Western Monthly Magazine*, Judge Hall became cashier of the Commercial Bank of Cincin-nati, and after its reorganization in 1843, accepted its

[1] Reproduced in the present work.

presidency, which he retained until his death.   In 1839
he married Mrs Mary Louisa Alexander, a daughter of
the Revolutionary soldier, Major Richard Clough Anderson.   The four children of this marriage are : William A.
Hall, James H. Hall, Mrs Thomas H. Wright, and Miss
Kate Longworth Hall.[1]

About the time Hall relinquished the editorship of
The Western Monthly Magazine, i.e., in the winter of
1835-1836, he met George Catlin, the noted Indian painter,
in Cincinnati, where he invited the co-operation of the
latter in the production of the proposed McKenney and
Hall volumes, now seemingly well advanced.   In February
1836, Hall, then in Philadelphia, addressed Catlin on the
same subject, in a letter so interesting in the present connection that it is given here in full :

"PHILADELPHIA, *February* 12, 1836.

"DEAR SIR,—I left home for this place shortly after I
had the pleasure of seeing you, and did not write as I
promised, in consequence of my expectation of meeting
with you at Pittsburgh.   When I got there I was
much disappointed at finding that you had just left
that place, and I then did not know where to write
you, until to-day, when I learned from the papers that

---

[1] For sources of information, consult Hiram W. Beckwith, "The
Illinois and Indiana Indians" (with sketch of Judge James Hall), in
Fergus Historical Series, No. 23, pp. vi-viii (Chicago, 1884).   Thomas
Donaldson, "The George Catlin Indian Gallery," in *Smithsonian Report
for* 1885 (National Museum), (Washington, 1886).   *Historical and Philo-
sophical Society of Ohio : A Partial List of the Books in its Library relating
to the State of Ohio* (Cincinnati, 1893).   Charles T. Greve, *Centennial
History of Cincinnati,* vol. i., p. 808 (1904).

you were at Albany. I now write for the purpose of renewing the proposition which I suggested to you at Cincinnati.

"The work which I am engaged in, in connection with Messrs Key & Biddle, of this city, is a general history of the Indian tribes of North America, to be illustrated with portraits. The portraits are those in the Indian Department at Washington, painted by King. The work will be comprised in twenty numbers, each to contain six portraits, and twenty or thirty pages of letterpress, known as McKenney and Hall's *History of the Indian Tribes of North America*. A portion of the latter will be devoted to a general history of the tribes, and the remainder will be biographies of the distinguished men. My materials for this part of the work are very voluminous, and of the most authentic character, having been collected from a great number of the Indian agents and other gentlemen who are personally acquainted with the Indians. Your collection contains many portraits which it would be very desirable to unite with ours, as they are those of Indians of the more remote tribes; and it has occurred to me that if you should feel disposed to unite with us we could reject from our collection the portraits of the least important persons—say half of them—retaining those only of distinguished men, and add the same number from your collection, or even a larger number, if it should be thought expedient; and the work would then be the most complete and splendid of the kind that has ever been attempted.

"We have already gone to great expense in preparing for this work. Many of the portraits are engraved, and are now undergoing the process of coloring. We have had the type and paper made for the express purpose, of the most expensive kind, and the whole work will be of the most elegant kind.

"Should you think proper to join us, we shall have in our hands a complete monopoly; no other work can compete with that which we could make. We shall begin to print in a few days. As soon as two numbers are complete, an agent may be sent to Europe, where the sale will probably be very extensive.

"Your object, I presume, will be to make money by the exhibition of your gallery, and it will doubtless be a fortune to you. But you could in no way enhance the value of your gallery more than by publishing a part of it in such a work as ours, which would naturally excite the public attention towards it.

"If you feel disposed to join with us, we are willing that you shall become interested in our work, and take such part of the proceeds as shall be considered fair. In this case you would only be asked to contribute the use of such of your portraits as we might agree upon for engraving, say from thirty to fifty, and a few of your landscapes, with such rough notes respecting them as would enable us to write short biographical sketches. My part of the work is to do the writing. Messrs Key & Biddle furnish all the funds, and attend to the labor of publishing, selling, etc.

"In this way we can get up a work from which an immense profit may be realized. Your part of the enterprise will cost you little labor, while the success of the future exhibition of your gallery would be greatly promoted.

"If you think well of this proposal, I would inquire whether it will be in your power to visit Philadelphia? You could then be advised more fully of our plans, and the terms of an arrangement could be agreed upon. Should I have left here before your visit, Messrs Key & Biddle could make every arrangement as well as if I was here. I shall remain here about ten days. I would go to Albany to see you, as I consider this matter of great interest to us both, but I am now confined to the house by indisposition.

" You will oblige me by an early answer.

" Please to present my regards to Mrs. Catlin.

" Very respectfully, your friend and obedient servant,

" JAMES HALL.

" GEORGE CATLIN, Esq."

The offer made to Catlin, as subsequent events show, was not accepted.

As previously mentioned, the actual beginning of a collection of representative Indian portraits, under the auspices of the War Department, was made about the year 1821, during the Secretaryship of John C. Calhoun and the incumbency of McKenney as Superintendent of Indian Trade. These first portraits were doubtless hung in McKenney's office in Georgetown; and after he had assumed charge of the office of Indian Affairs in Washington, there were also displayed at his official quarters what were perhaps the first ethnological collections gathered by an officer of the Government for official exhibition. Among these objects were various relics collected by McKenney on his Tour to the Lakes, including a full Chippewa costume and a British Indian peace medal.

The first portraits of Indian delegates were painted as early as 1821, by Charles Bird King, a man of exemplary character and simple life, who had studied in London for four years under Benjamin West.[1] Whether or not the first of these were the result of personal enterprise, some of them at least were acquired by the War Department for its Indian Gallery. The actual official beginning of his collection was doubtless made during the Secretaryship of Secretary Calhoun, and it was continued when James Barbour (later Minister to the Court of St James) became Secretary of War, March 7, 1825, as is learned from a letter, dated Barboursville, Va., January 26, 1832, in which Barbour writes:

"During my administration of the War Department, many tribes of the North American Indians sent deputations of their head-men, or chiefs, to Washington, for the purpose of transacting business with the Department over which I presided. Col. McKenney, to whom was assigned the Bureau of Indian Affairs, suggested to me the expediency of preserving the likenesses of some of the most distinguished among this most extraordinary race of people. Believing, as I did, that this race was about to become extinct, and that a faithful resemblance of the most remarkable among them would be full of interest in after times, I cordially approved of the measure. This duty was assigned to Mr. King, of Washington, an artist of acknowledged reputation; he executed it with

[1] King met Thomas Sully in London, where the two young artists lodged together in their poverty. King introduced Sully to Benjamin West (Isham, *History of American Painting*, 1905). The writer has learned that much of King's painting was done under the trees of his garden in the rear of his residence on Twelfth Street, in Washington, about where the Columbia Theatre now stands. Miss Dorsey remembers King as a courtly old gentleman, extremely fond of inviting parties of children to his sylvan studio, where they were regaled with toys and other remembrances. For an instance of his remarkable absent-mindedness, see Donaldson in *Smithsonian Report for* 1885, Part II. (National Museum), p. 795, 1886.

fidelity and success, by producing the most *exact* resemblances, including the costume of each." [1]

From 1824 until 1837, King painted many other Indians from life; and also, in 1826 and 1827, copied numerous portraits made among the Indians by James Otto Lewis. The latter had painted at Detroit, for Governor Lewis Cass, in 1823, the portrait of Tenskwau-tawaw, the celebrated "Shawnee Prophet" and brother of Tecumseh; and perhaps in the same year, also at Detroit, a portrait of Black Hawk. Lewis was present at the signing of the treaty of Prairie du Chien, Michigan Territory (now Wisconsin), in August 1825, his name appearing as a witness thereto; and he was likewise a witness to the treaty of Fond du Lac, of Lake Superior, concluded by Cass and McKenney, August 5, 1826,

---

[1] A "Letter from Thomas L. McKenney, Esq., Superintendent of Indian Affairs, to his friend in Baltimore, dated Georgetown, May 15, 1828," sheds some interesting information respecting the origin and cost of the portraits in the Indian Gallery. The letter, published in the *National Intelligencer* of Washington City, reads in part as follows:—

"The price paid to Messrs King and Ford for taking Indian likenesses, with the view of preserving the exterior and appearance of these hapless People, and their costume, etc., is, for each head and about half the body, $20. In full lengths, more, of course, has been given. The average cost of this collection, since 1821, is perhaps $3,000 for *one hundred and sixteen heads*, and the cost for each head, including the full length likenesses, of which latter there are five, is about $33.

"Apart from the great object of preserving in some form, the resemblance of an interesting People, whose original aspect is fast fading away, and will soon be gone; and to whose country we have succeeded, and who are perishing before our presence, and *because of it;* there is another, if of less interest, yet, perhaps of more active influence, and can be seen to be proper by more people, it is presumed, than can comprehend the value to posterity, of being ready with the answer to the question, which it is fair to presume will be asked: ' *What sort of a being was the red man of America ?* ' It is the policy of the thing. Indians are

as previously noted. Lewis was also with Cass and
others at the treaty with the Potawatomi, at the mouth
of the Mississinewa, in Indiana, October 16 of the
latter year, and we find him among the Miami on
the 23rd of the same month. Perhaps about the same
time he visited Fort Wayne, where the portraits of
other noted Indians were painted, and was again with
Cass and McKenney at the Butte des Morts treaty,
on Fox River, Wisconsin, August 11, 1827. Lewis painted
at least eighty-five Indian portraits and scenes, of which
about forty-five portraits were copied, principally by King,
for the Indian Gallery in the War Department. Of the
latter about ten were used as illustrations (some with
slight modifications) in McKenney and Hall's work, while
thirteen other of Lewis's Indian subjects illustrated in the

like other people in many respects—and are not less sensible than we
are, to marks of respect and attention. It is known to you, I presume,
that deputations come on to Washington frequently, on business of deep
interest to their tribes and to the United States. They see this mark of
respect to their people, and respect it. Its effects, as is known to me,
are, in this view of the subject, highly valuable. But it may not be for
me to justify this branch of national policy. I am quite content, any
way. If the Congress, who represent the People, whose servants we are,
think it right to do so, this collection can be sold, at any moment, for
double its original cost. And with it may go, without any regret of
mine, of a personal kind, all the little relics which, in my travels, I have
picked up, and at great trouble brought home with me. It is no fancy
scheme of mine. It was begun by one [evidently John C. Calhoun] who
is more enlightened than I profess to be, and continued by another
[James Barbour] who is also highly qualified to judge of the fitness
of the thing, and of whom no man, who knows him, can feel else than
respect and friendship. I will just add, that our own citizens who visit
Washington, and those who visit it from other countries, unite in commending this grouping of our Indians from the four corners of our
land, as an affair of great interest, and which posterity will be thankful
for."

three volumes are from paintings by other artists. Some of the Lewis pictures were copied for the Indian Gallery by A. Ford in 1826, while other portraits in the Gallery were the work of S. M. Charles (1837), G. Cooke (1837),[1] and Shaw. The date of the latter is not recorded.

As we have already seen, McKenney had in preparation an elaborate work on the Indian tribes, illustrated by means of the paintings in the Indian Gallery, at least as early as 1830. It may therefore seem reasonable to assume that Lewis, anticipating the publication of McKenney's work based more or less directly on his own sketches, endeavoured to forestall it by issuing one of his own. Lewis's *Aboriginal Port-Folio* appeared in 1835, in a series of parts consisting of seventy-two portraits. The lithography is the work of Lehman & Duval, of Philadelphia, and the colour is crudely washed on by hand. If the engravings represent approximately faithful reproductions of Lewis's sketches, the best that can be said of many of the latter is that they could have been little better than caricatures. All the copies of *The Aboriginal Port-Folio* known to the present writer are without title-page or text, the only means of identification being a flimsy paper cover, and an advertisement which prefaced the original parts that formed the

---

[1] Cooke was born in the vicinity of Washington, and resided for a long time at the capital and in Georgetown. He forsook a profitable mercantile business to study art, and spent several years in Genoa, Florence, Rome, and Naples. Returning to America in the early thirties, he established a studio in Broadway, New York, and in 1836 exhibited at King's Gallery in Washington his "Wreck of the Medusa, British Frigate," while in Washington in 1837 he exhibited his paintings for a considerable period in Pennsylvania Avenue, near $4\frac{1}{2}$ Street.

series.[1] The advertisement accompanying the first part is as follows :—

ADVERTISEMENT TO THE FIRST NUMBER OF
THE ABORIGINAL PORT-FOLIO.

In presenting the first Number of the following work to the public, the Publisher will, perhaps, be excused for candidly acknowledging the

---

[1] Yet there is evidence that biographical descriptions accompanied the early numbers at least. Under date of March 4, 1836, Schoolcraft (*Personal Memoirs*, 1851, p. 531) writes :—"Mr J. O. Lewis, of Philadelphia, furnishes me seven numbers of his *Indian Portfolio*. Few artists have had his means of observation of the aboriginal man, in the great panorama of the West, where he has carried his easel. The results are given in this work, with biographical notices of the common events in the lives of the chiefs. Altogether, it is to be regarded as a valuable contribution to this species of knowledge. He has painted the Indian lineaments on the spot, and is entitled to patronage—not as supplying all that is desirable or practicable, perhaps, but as a first and original effort. We should cherish all such efforts."

The lithographed cover bears the title :—"The / Aboriginal Port-Folio. / No. [1 written in.] / [Vignette.] / Philadelphia published [*May* written in] 1835 / by J. O. Lewis. / Lithograph'd by Lehman & Duval No. 8 Bank Alley Philadelphia. / Subscription price $2.00 per Number issued Monthly untill 10 Numbers are complete. / [Copyright notice, 1835.] / Payable on delivery."

The advertisement to the first number is dated Philadelphia, July 20, 1835 ; that of the second number, June 1835 ; while the third number (on the cover of which the "3" and the date "July" are engraved instead of written) bears the same date as the first. In the advertisement to Number 2, Lewis announces his intention to issue an eleventh number, in the form of a biographical and historical sketch, to be distributed gratuitously to subscribers ; and in the advertisement to Number 3 he announces progress in this direction. In the copies of the *Port-Folio* seen by the present writer, no advertisement accompanies the parts following Number 3, and no text anywhere appears.

Fifteen years later there appeared a *Catalogue of the Indian Gallery, painted by J. O. Lewis.* New York : J. O. Lewis, 1850. (8°, 23 pp.) This proposed new Portfolio, however, does not seem to have been published.

consciousness of his own inability to render that full justice in its execution, which the subject from its own importance requires; but as the present is the *first* attempt of the kind in this country, he sincerely trusts, that the judicious and critical will regard it with a favourable and indulgent eye.

The great and constantly recurring disadvantages to which an artist is necessarily subject, while travelling through a wilderness, far removed from the abodes of civilization, and in "pencilling by the way," with the rude materials he may be enabled to pick up in the course of his progress, will, he hopes, secure for him the approbation, not only of the critic, but of the connoisseur:—And when it is recollected, that the time for holding Indian treaties is generally very limited; that the deep-felt anxiety of the artist to possess a large collection must be no small impediment in the way of his bestowing any considerable share of his time and attention on any one production, together with the rapidity with which he is obliged to labor; he confidently believes as they are issued in their original state, that, whatever imperfections may be discoverable, will be kindly ascribed to the proper and inevitable cause.

He would beg leave, moreover, to state, that he had the honor to be employed by the Indian Department expressly for the purpose. As regards the merits of their general character, and the fidelity of the costume, he can with confidence assure the public, that the resemblances of both are faithfully and accurately given.

Copies from the principal *originals* were painted by Mr. King, of Washington, and are now deposited in the War Office. With this brief introduction, the Subscriber respectfully offers the work to the kind patronage of his fellow citizens and the public.

J. O. LEWIS.

Philadelphia, July 20, 1835.

In order that comparison may be made of the portraits in the Lewis *Port-Folio* and those in McKenney and Hall, the following list is given :—

LEWIS.	McKENNEY AND HALL.
1. Waa-na-taa.	Wa-na-ta. I. (different painting).
2. Ma-ko-me-ta.	Mar-ko-me-te. II. (same painting).

Lewis.	McKenney and Hall.
3. Kitch-ee-i-aa-ba (Chippewa).	(= The Good Martin, p. liv, No. 2).
4. Waa-pa-laa.	Wa-pel-la. II. (different).
5. Shing-gaa-ba-w'osin.	Shingaba W'Ossin. I. (different).
6. Cha-co-to (Potawatomi).	......
7. Tshu-gue-ga (Winnebago).	......
8. Ma-che-ka-kat (Menomini).	......
9. Kee-o-kuck (Sauk).	II. (different). See p. liv, No. 17.
10. Shounk-chunk (Winnebago).	......
11. Billy Shane (Shawnee).	......
12. Waa-ba-shaw.	Waapashaw. I. (same).
13. Too-sha-na-gan-ka (Winnebago).	......
14. Men-dow-min (Chippewa).	......
15. Mo-wan-za (Miami).	......
16. Nah-shaw-a-gaa (Potawatomi).	......
17. Prairie du Chien Treaty, 1825.	......
18. Ker-o-menée (Winnebago).	I. (here called Nawkaw, of the Caromanie family ; different portrait).
19. Mi-a-qu-a (Miami).	......
20. Nabu-naa-kee-shick (Chippewa).	......
21. Sun-a-get (Potawatomi).	......
22. Pe-a-jick (Chippewa).	......
23. Little Crow.	I. (different).
24. Brewett (Miami).	......
25. Kaa-nun-der-waaguinse-zoo (Chippewa).	......
26. Caa-taa-ke-mung-ga (Miami).	......
27. Caw-taa-waa-be-ta.	Katawabeda. II. (based on same painting).
28. O'-check-ka (Winnebago).	......
29. Winnebago Squaw (wife of No. 28).	......
30. Na-mas (Chippewa).	......
31. Na-she-mung-ga (Miami).	......
32. Weesh-cub.	I. (different).
33. Cut-taa-tas-tia (Fox Chief).	......
34. Young Miami Chief.	......
35. Pe-schick-ee.	Pee-che-kir. III. (different).

LEWIS.	McKENNEY AND HALL.
36. Miami Chief.	......
37. Pe-che-co (Potawatomi).	......
38. Me-no-quet (Potawatomi).	......
39. Francis Godfroy (Miami).	......
40. She-she-ba (Winnebago).	......
41. Pipe Dance and Tomahawk Dance (Chippewa).	......
42. Kee-o-tuck-kee (Potawatomi).	......
43. Richardville (Miami).	......
44. Chat-o-nis-see (Potawatomi).	......
45. Ash-e-taa-na-quet (Chippewa).	......
46. The Son (Miami).	......
47. Ottawa Chief.	......
48. Mauck-coo-maun (Iowa).	......
49. View of Butte des Morts. (Shows arrival of Cass and McKenney, 1827.)	......
50. Mac-cut-i-mish-e-ca-cu-cac (Black Hawk).	II. (different).
51. Pach-e-po (Potawatomi).	......
52. Waa-kaun-see-kaa (Winnebago).	Wakaun Haka. II. (same, with slight changes).
53. Pen-now-we-ta (Miami).	......
54. Wadt-he-doo-kaana (Winnebago).	......
55. Com-no-sa-qua (Potawatomi).	......
56. Waa-top-e-not.	III. (different).
57. Chippewa Squaws.	I. (middle figure only).
58. Mish-sha-quat (Chippewa).	......
59. O-che-na-shink-kee (Winnebago).	......
60. Chippewa Squaw and Child.	I. (same).
61. Ke-wa-din (Chippewa).	......
62. O-hya-wa-nim-ce-kee.	III. (same).
63. Kee-me-one (Chippewa).	......
64. Ta-ma-kake-toke.	II. (same). (Chippewa Widow.)
65. Sioux Chief.	......
66. Tens-qua-ta-wa.	I. (different).
67. O-wan-ich-koh, or Little Elk (Winnebago).	Hoo-wan-ne-ka, or Little Elk. II. (different).

Lewis.	McKenney and Hall.
68. At-te-conse (Chippewa).	......
69. Wa-kaun.	II. (same).
70. Jack-o-pa.	III. (different).
71. Wa-em-boesh-kaa.	I. (same, reversed).
72. Wa-bin-de-ba, or the White Headed Eagle (Chippewa).	......

From 1837, in which year King and Cooke, especially the former, had been particularly active in painting portraits of Indian delegates to Washington, little seems to have been done toward increasing the collection in the Indian Gallery. In 1849, the office of Indian Affairs, with its collection of paintings, was transferred from the jurisdiction of the War Department to that of the Department of the Interior, the pictures being placed on view in the Patent Office building.

Meanwhile, the Smithsonian Institution, in pursuance of one of the propositions of the programme for its establishment, had formed a gallery of art, for which purpose "the large room in the west wing" (the present "chapel") of the Smithsonian building was set aside in 1852. In March of that year the gallery contained, in the words of Secretary Joseph Henry, "a very interesting series of portraits, mostly full-size, of one hundred and fifty-two [1] North American Indians, with sketches of the scenery of the country they inhabit, deposited by the artist who painted them, Mr J. M. Stanley. These portraits were all taken from life, and are accurate representations of the peculiar features of prominent individuals of forty-three different tribes, inhabiting the south-western prairies,

[1] There were one hundred and fifty-one portraits and scenes in the Indian country, painted between 1842 and 1852, and a portrait of Stanley by A. B. Moore, painted in 1851.—Editor.

New Mexico, California, and Oregon. The faithfulness of the likenesses has been attested by a number of intelligent persons who have visited the Gallery, and have immediately recognised among the portraits those of the individuals with whom they have been personally acquainted. The author devoted to the work of obtaining these pictures ten years of his life, and perseveringly devoted himself to his task in the face of difficulties and dangers which enthusiasm in the pursuit could alone enable him to encounter. The Institution has published a descriptive catalogue of these portraits,[1] which are of interest to the ethnologist as representatives of the peculiar physiognomy, as well as of many of the customs, of the natives of this continent." [2]

J. M. Stanley was born in Canandaigua, New York, in 1814, and at an early age devoted himself to portraiture, afterwards to historical painting. He moved to Detroit in 1835, and in 1842, attracted by the picturesque features of Indian life in the West, visited the Indian Territory, where he painted a series of Seminole, Cherokee, and Wichita portraits, and in June of the following year attended the celebrated council at Tahlequah, in the Cherokee Nation, which continued for four weeks, and was attended by 10,000 Indians, representing seventeen tribes. His painting of this council is still in possession of the Smithsonian Institution. In the same year, Stanley painted portraits of Creeks, Chickasaw, Potawatomi, Stockbridges, Munsee, Ottawa, Chippewa, Delawares, Wea, Shawnee, Osage, Quapaw, Iowa, and Caddo and

---

[1] See *Portraits of North American Indians, with Sketches of Scenery, etc., painted by J. M. Stanley, deposited with the Smithsonian Institution.* Washington, December 1852.

[2] *Smithsonian Report for* 1852, p. 27. Washington, 1853.

affiliated tribes; in 1844 he was again among the
Cherokee, as well as with the Tawakoni, Kichai, and
Comanche. In 1845 he painted "A Buffalo Hunt,"
which also is in possession of the Smithsonian Institution;
and in 1846 visited and painted the Sauk and Foxes,
including the famous Keokuk. In the same year, Stanley
became draughtsman to the advance guard of the "Army
of the West," under Lieutenant-Colonel William H.
Emory, which conducted a reconnaissance from Fort
Leavenworth, Missouri, to San Diego, California, during
the Mexican War. On this expedition Stanley painted
Pima, Maricopa, and Apache Indians in the present
Arizona, as well as numerous scenes *en route*. In the
following two years, we find him among the Shasta of
northern California, and various tribes of Washington
and Oregon, painting portraits and views of the wonderful
scenery of the Columbia River region. In 1851 he painted
some Blackfoot Indian compositions, and in the following year visited the *Pueblo* of Tesuque, in New Mexico,
where he made portraits of five men of that tribe.

The Stanley Collection remained at the Smithsonian
Institution continuously, except for temporary removals
for exhibition elsewhere, the owner from time to time
augmenting it with portraits of individuals belonging to
the Indian deputations which visited Washington, until
by the beginning of the year 1865 it numbered
about two hundred paintings, nearly all of life size.[1]
Meanwhile Secretary Henry, appreciating the need of
recording information respecting the aborigines ere it
became too late, wrote to the Board of Regents of the
Smithsonian Institution: "It is the sacred duty which
this country owes to the civilised world to collect every-

[1] See *Smithsonian Report for* 1855, p. 26; *ibid.*, 1864, p. 119.

thing relative to the history, the manners and customs, the physical peculiarities, and, in short, all that may tend to illustrate the character and history of the original inhabitants of North America."[1] This appeal was made directly in the interest of the Stanley Collection, but the finances of the Government at the critical period immediately preceding the Civil War were not in condition to warrant its purchase. Two years later (in 1859), Stanley, apparently ever hopeful that the Nation would listen to Henry's appeal, asked the Smithsonian Institution for an allowance of one hundred dollars a year to pay the interest on a debt he had incurred to prevent the sacrifice of his paintings by sale.[2] Such is the pitiful story of his poverty while yet the owner of a collection of paintings then valued at $20,000, but which, did they exist to-day, would be well-nigh priceless.

The Indian Gallery formerly in the War Department had remained in the Department of the Interior from 1849 until 1858, when it was transferred in turn to the Smithsonian Institution, there to be displayed with the Gallery of pictures that had been removed to the eastern end of the great hall in the second storey of the Smithsonian building. "These," wrote Henry, "with the Stanley paintings, now form perhaps the most valuable collection in existence of illustrations of the features, costumes, and habits of the aborigines of this country. This Gallery is an object of special interest to all visitors to the national metropolis, and to none more so than to the deputations of Indians frequently called to Washington to transact business with the Government."[3]

A year or two later, the large room in which the

---

[1] *Smithsonian Report for* 1857, p. 36, 1858.
[2] *Ibid.*, 1859, p. 113, 1860.   [3] *Ibid.*, 1858, p. 41, 1859.

paintings were displayed was "furnished with cases to contain the specimens of Indian costume, implements of war, and other articles to illustrate Indian manners and customs, which the Institution has received as presents from different parties."[1] It is not improbable that the small cabinet of objects which McKenney had installed in his office years before may have formed part of this collection, and in its turn have become the nucleus of the present vast collections illustrating the activities of the American aborigines, now in the United States National Museum.

In 1861, King, who was better endowed than Stanley with worldly goods, presented to the Smithsonian Institution a collection of a hundred large engravings from celebrated pictures. In the following year he died at Washington, and thus never knew the fate that befell the original Indian Gallery, to which he had been the chief contributor. On January 15, 1865, a serious fire destroyed a part of the Smithsonian building as well as the entire collection of paintings, except a few by Stanley which were saved and are now for the greater part in possession of the Smithsonian Institution, and a few by King.[2] At the time of the fire, the Stanley Collection numbered about two hundred canvases, nearly all of which were his personal property; those of the Indian Gallery numbered one hundred and forty-seven, half life-size portraits. After the fire, or probably as early as 1863, Stanley returned to his home in Detroit, where he practised his art until his death, April 15, 1872.[3]

[1] *Smithsonian Report for* 1860, p. 53, 1861.

[2] See *Ibid.*, 1864, p. 119 (1865); Donaldson, in *National Museum Report for* 1885, p. 796 (1886).

[3] Besides the paintings burned in the Smithsonian fire, Stanley painted a hundred and fifty others, chiefly Indian scenes and studies.

It is fortunate that we are able to complete fairly well the record of the paintings, with the exception of those added by Stanley to his collection between 1852 and the time of the fire. In the former year the catalogue of his paintings was published, and in 1858 there appeared a list of those in the Indian Gallery formerly in the War Department. The latter list is of sufficient importance to warrant its incorporation here.[1]

CATALOGUE OF INDIAN PAINTINGS BELONG-ING TO THE GOVERNMENT COLLECTION [2]

1. **Sting Ioway.**
2. **Shing-yaw-ba-wus-sen**, *The Figured Stone.* [I.]
3. **Mish-sha-quat**, *The Clear Sky.* Chippeway Chief. Painted by C. B. King, from a drawing by Lewis, 1827. [Lewis, No. 58.]

One of his best-known single paintings is called "The Unveiling of the Conspiracy," portraying the Indian girl informing Gladwin of Pontiac's treachery. Another, "The Trial of Red Jacket," represents that chief in the centre of a group of warriors, on trial for witchcraft. Seven of his works—"Uncas," "Gambling for the Buck," "The Trial of Red Jacket," "Indian Telegraph," "Blackfoot Card-players," "Hunters," and "On the War-path"—have been chromoed; all except the last were produced in Berlin.—Silas Farmer, *History of Detroit and Wayne County*, Detroit and New York, 1890, 3rd ed., pp. 358, 359.

[1] From *An Account of the Smithsonian Institution, its Founder, Building, Operations, etc., prepared from the Reports of Prof. Henry to the Regents, and other Authentic Sources.* By William J. Rhees. Washington: Thomas M'Gill, printer. (Copyright, 1859; pp. 55-58.) Mr Rhees, who had been almost continuously a member of the Smithsonian staff from the year 1852, died at Washington, March 18, 1907. For convenience of comparison, the portraits reproduced in McKenney and Hall are noted by volume in brackets.

[2] "These paintings are arranged on the east and south-east walls of the Picture Gallery."

4. **Pe-a-juk**. A Chippeway. By King, from a drawing by Lewis, 1827. [Lewis, No. 22.]

5. ———

6. **Am-eiquon**, *Wooden Ladle*. By King, from a drawing by Lewis, 1826. [Not in Lewis's *Port-Folio ; cf.* No. 82.]

7. **Mo-nee-kaw**, *He who goes under the ground.*

8. ———

9. **Tu-go-nis-co-te-yeh**, *Black Fox.* Cherokee Chief. King, 1828.

10. **Eesh-tah-hum-leah**, *Sleepy Eye.* Sioux Chief, from the band called Sipsetongs. [I.] [King.]

11. **Moos-e-om-o-nee**, *The Walking Iron.* Wah-pee-ton Sioux. By S. M. Charles, 1837.

12. **La-kee-too-me-ra-sha**, *Little Chief.* Pawnee. King, 1837.

13. **Wah-ro-ne-sah**, *The Surrounder.* Otoe. King, 1837.

14. **Wah-ke-on-taw-kah**, *Big Thunder.* Chief of the Medana Kanton Sioux. King, 1837.

15. **Haw-che-ke-ong-ga**, *He who kills Osages.* Missouri. King, 1837.

16. **O-wan-ick-koh**, *Little Elk.* Winnebago. By A. Ford, from a drawing by Lewis, 1826. [*Cf.* No. 58 ; Lewis, No. 67 ; McK. and H., II.]

17. ———

18. ——— Chippeway Chief. By King, from a drawing by Lewis, 1827.

19. **Ga-de-ge-we**, *Spotted.* Second Chief of the Chippeways, 54 years old. King, 1835.

20. **Waa-kann-see-kaa**, *Rattlesnake.* Winnebago. By Ford, from a drawing by Lewis, 1826. [Lewis, No. 52. See Nos. 61 and 127 below = McK. and H., Wakaun Haka, II.]

21. **Naa-gar-nep**, *The one who sits at the head.* Chippeway Chief. By King, from a drawing by Lewis, 1827. [Not in Lewis.]

22. **General Push-ma-ta-ha.** Choctaw Chief. (See No. 42.) [I.]

23. **Menawee.** A great Warrior and Creek Chief. This chief commanded the party that killed General McIntosh, and was one of the few that saved themselves from the defeat at the Horseshoe, by swimming the river, after being badly wounded in the head. [= Menawa. II.]

24. **Mistepe.** Yoholo-Mico's Son. A Creek. King, 1825. [II. See p. liii, No. 3.]

25. **Naa-she-o-shuck**, *Roaring Thunder.* Sac of Mississippi. Son of Black Hawk. King, 1837.

26. **Yoosto**, *Spring Frog.* [= Tooan Tuh (Dustu, a Cherokee). II.]
27. **Yoholo-Mico.** Creek Chief. King, 1825. [II.]
28. ——— A Creek Warrior.
29. ——— A Chippeway Chief. By King, from a drawing by Lewis, 1827.
30. **I-au-beanu.** A Chippeway. By King, from a drawing by Lewis, 1826. [Not in Lewis. Spelled *I-aw-beance* on the Inman eopy.]
31. **Pah-gue-sah-ah.** Son of Tecumseh. Shaw.
32. **Tah-col-a-quot.** A Sac. [III.]
33. **Keokuk**, *Watchful Fox.* Chiocook Sac. (See Nos. 77 and 144.) [II.]
34. **Paw-a-shick**, *To dash the water off.* A Fox Chief. Cooke, 1837. [= Powasheek. II. See p. liv, No. 13.]
35. **Colonel John Stedman or Stidham.** King, 1825.
36. **Wea-matla.** Seminole War Chief. King, 1826. [= Neamathla. II.]
37. **Kee-sheswa**, *The Sun.* Fox Warrior. King. [II.]
38. **Tah-ro-hou**, *Plenty of Meat.* Ioway. King, 1837. [Tarohon. II.]
39. **Ap-pa-noose-o-ke-maw**, *A Chief when a child.* Sac. Cooke, 1837. [II.]
40. **Ca-ta-ne-cas-sa**, *Black Hoof.* Shawnee Chief. [I.]
41. **Pah-she-pah-how**, *Stabber.* First Chief of the Sankys [Sauk]; a Sac. King. [I.]
42. **General Push-ma-ta-haw.** Choctaw Chief. (See No. 22, and p. liii, No. 6. King.) [I.]
43. ———
44. **Kai-pol-e-quah**, *White-nosed Fox.* A Fox Chief. [II.]
45. **Ke-wa-din**, *The North Wind.* Chippeway Chief. By King, from a drawing by Lewis, 1827. [Lewis, No. 61.]
46. **Wa-cha-mo-ne**, *Partisan.* Ioway. King, 1837. [II.]
47. **Whesh-laub**, *The Sweet.* By King, from a drawing by Lewis, 1826. [Lewis, No. 32; McK. and H., I.]
48. **Tia-mah**, *The bear whose scream makes the rock tremble.* Fox Chief. [II.]
49. **Wau-top-e-not**, *The Eagle's Bill.* Fox. By King, from a drawing by Lewis, 1826. [Lewis, No. 56; McK. and H., III.]
50. **Nahetluc-Hopie**, *Little Doctor.* Creek Chief. King, 1825. The red spots on his dress mark the balls that he received when he was surprised in his hut. The three lower balls were lower than marked in the picture. The paint on the face is commemorative of the same event, as the blood ran from his nostrils and mouth. [III.]

51. **Coosa-Tustenugga.** Creek Chief. King, 1825.
52. **Kee-me-one,** *Rain.* A Chippeway. King, 1827. [Lewis, No. 63.]
53. **Opothle-Yoholo.** Principal Chief of the Creek Deputation to Washington in 1825. King, 1825. [II.]
54. **At-te-coure,** *The Young Reindeer.* Chippeway Chief. By King, from a drawing by Lewis, 1827. [Lewis, No. 68.]
55. **O-tya-wa-nim-ee-hee,** *Yellow Thunder.* Chippeway Chief. By King, from a drawing by Lewis, 1827. [Lewis, No. 62; = O-hya-wa-mince-kee, McK. and H., III.]
56. **A-na-cam-o-gush-ia.** Chippeway Chief from Rainy Lake. By King, from a drawing by Lewis, 1827. [= Anacamegishca. I. Not in Lewis.]
57. **Waa-kawn,** *The Snake.* Winnebago. By Ford, from a drawing by Lewis, 1826. [Lewis, No. 69. McK. and H., II.]
58. **Hoo-wau-nee-kaw,** *Little Elk.* Winnebago Orator of the Car-ray-mau-nee family. [II. See No. 16.]
59. **O-chee-na-shink-kaa,** *The man that stands and strikes.* Winnebago. By Ford, from a drawing by Lewis, 1826. [Lewis, No. 59.]
60. **Pa-she-nine,** *The good marksman.* Chippeway Chief. By King, from a drawing by Lewis, 1827. [Not in Lewis. McK. and H., III.]
61. **Wa-he-kans-he-kai.** Winnebago. By King, from a drawing by Lewis, 1826. [See No. 20. Lewis, No. 52.]
62. **Wadtz-he-doo-kaana.** Chief of the Winnebagos. By Ford, from a drawing by Lewis, 1826. [Lewis, No. 54.]
63. **Mi-co-a-na-pas.** Second Chief of Seminoles; owns 70 slaves. King. [= Micanopy. II.]
64. **No-way-ke-sug-ga,** *He who strikes two at once.* Otoe. King, 1837. [III.]
65. **Wai-kee-chai,** *Crouching Eagle.* Sanky [Sauk] Chief; Fox. King. [II. See p. liii, No. 7.]
66. **Caw-taa-waa-bee-ta,** *The Snagled Tooth.* [Lewis, No. 27; McK. and H., II.]
67. **Yaha-Hajo,** *Mad Wolf.* Creek Chief King, 1825.
68. **Folke-tuste-najo,** *Craggy Black Clay.* Seminole War Chief. King, 1826. [II.]
69. **Johr** [*sic*] **Ridge.** Cherokee Chief. Secretary to the Creek Delegation to Washington, 1825. King. [II.]
70. **Selota.** Creek Chief; a distinguished warrior; fought under General Jackson. King, 1825. [= Selocta. II.]
71. **Tuskie-hu-Tustenugge,** *Little Prince.* Creek Chief. King, 1825.

72. **Jack-o-pa,** *The Six.* Chippeway Chief. By King, from a drawing by Lewis, 1827. [III. Lewis, No. 70.]

73. ———

74. **Le-shaw-loo-la-le-hoo,** *Big Chief.* Pawnee Loup. King, 1837.

75. **Nau-kaw,** *Wood.* Of the Cor-ray-mau-nee family. Principal Chief of Winnebago Deputation; 94 years old. [Lewis, No. 18; McK. and H., II.]

76. **Don Vincente Guerrero.** Former President of the Mexican Republic; a distinguished Chieftain.

77. **Keokuk,** *Watchful Fox.* First Chief of the Sankys [Sauk]. King, 1829. [*Cf.* Lewis, No. 9; Nos. 33 and 144 of this list, and p. liv, No. 17. McK. and H., II.]

78. ———

79. **Pee-che-ker,** *Buffalo.* Chief of Chippeways. [Lewis, No. 33; McK. and H., III.]

80. **Apauli-Tustenugge.** Creek Chief. King, 1825. [III.]

81. **Mou-ka-ush-ka,** *Trembling Earth.* Sioux of Missouri; died in Baltimore, October 25, 1837. Cooke, 1837. [I.]

82. **A-misk-quew,** *The Spoon.* Menomina War Chief. King. [III. See p. liv, No. 16.]

83. ——— A Chippeway Chief. By King, from a drawing by Lewis, 1827.

84. **Oloe,** *Ox.* Mahara [Omaha.]

85. **To-ca-cou,** *He that gives the first wound.* Sioux of Missouri. Cooke, 1837. [I.]

86. **Ha-sa-za,** *Elk's Horn.* Sioux of Missouri. Cooke, 1837.

87. **Ammoi,** *He that comes for something.* Yancton Sioux. King, 1837.

88. **Mah-ne-hah-nah,** *Great Walker.* Ioway Chief. King [1824]. [= Moanahonga. I. See p. liii, No. 5.]

89. **Pes-ke-lecaro.** Chief of the Republican Panis. [II. See p. liv, No. 15.]

90. **Au-pantan-ga,** *Big Elk.* Mohas (Omaha) Chief; a great orator. [= Ongpatonga. I.] (King.)

91. **Man-chousia.** White Plume. Kansas Chief. King. [= Monchonsia. III.]

92. **Terre-ki-tan-ahu.**

93. **Is-ca-ta-pe,** *Wicked Chief.* Great Panis. King.

94. **Chou-cape-otos,** *Half Chief.* King. [= Choucape, Otos half chief. I.]

95. **A-she-au-kou,** *Sunfish.* Sac Chief. King, 1837.

96. **Mar-ko-me-ta,** *Bear's Oil.* [II.]
97. **Rant-che-waime.** [See No. 131. McK. and H., I.]
98. **Red Jacket.** Seneca Chief. King, 1828. (See No. 143.) [I.]
99. **Teus-qua-ta-wa,** *Open Door.* [= Tenskwautawaw. I. *Cf.* Lewis, No. 66. Copy by King.]
100. ——— Cooke.
101. **Ne-o-mou-ne,** *Walking Rain.* Ioway. King, 1837. [II.]
102. **Waa-pua-taa,** *Playing Fox.* Prince of the Foxes. By Ford, from a drawing by Lewis, 1826. [Not in Lewis.]
103. **Nau-che-wing-ga,** *No Heart.* Ioway. King, 1837. [= Notchimine. II. See p. liv, No. 3.]
104. **Pee-mash-ka,** *Fox winding in his course.* Chief of the Foxes. King. [= Peahmuska. I. See p. liv, No. 12.]
105. **Wah-bawn-see,** *Causer of Paleness.* Principal Chief of the Potawotamies. King, 1835. [II. See p. liii, No. 2.]
106. **Wa-pella,** *The Prince.* Fox. King, 1837. [II.]
107. **Holato-mico,** *Blue King.* Seminole War Chief. King, 1826.
108. **We-ke-roo-tau,** *He who exchanges.*
109. **Cor-ba-map-pa,** *Wet Mouth.* Chippeway Chief. By King, from a drawing by Lewis, 1827. [Not in Lewis.]
110. **Ma-hong-ga.** Osage. King, 1830. [= Mohongo. I.]
111. **Heho-tustenugge,** *Deer Warrior.* Seminole Partisan War Chief. King, 1826. [= Itcho Tustennugge. III.]
112. **Es-me-boin** [Essneboin]. Chippeway Chief. By King, from a drawing by Lewis, 1827. [Not in Lewis. See p. lv, No. 7.]
113. **Cut-taa-tase-tia.** Fox. By Ford, from a drawing by Lewis, 1826. [Lewis, No. 33. = Catahecassa, McK. and H., I.]
114. **Pa-nan-se,** *Shedding Elk.* Sac. King, 1827.
115. **Catoouse.** Chippeway Chief. By King, from a drawing by Lewis, 1827. [Not in Lewis. McK. and H., I.]
116. ——— A Sioux Chief. [*Cf.* Lewis, No. 65.]
117. **O-kee-ma-kee-guid,** *The Chief that speaks.* A Chippeway. [King, after Lewis. McK. and H., I.]
118. **Governor Hicks.** Head Chief of the Seminoles. King, 1826.
119. **Waa-na-taa.** Grand Chief of the Sioux. King, 1826. [= Wanata. I.]
120. **Kis-te-kosh,** *One leg off.* Fox Brave. Cooke, 1837. [= Kishkekosh. II.]
121. ——— A Fox Chief. By King, from a drawing by Lewis, 1826. [Not in Lewis.]

122. **Ocan-gee-wack.** Chippeway Chief. By King, from a drawing by Lewis, 1827. [Not in Lewis.]

123. **Kai-kee-kai-maih,** *All fish.* Chief of Sankys [Sauk]. King.

124. **Ochio-Finico** (war name), Charles Connello (English name). Creek Chief. King, 1825. [= Ochefinceco. III.]

125. **She-tah-wah-coe-wah-mene,** *The sparrow that hunts as he walks.* A Sioux. King. [= Little Crow. I.]

126. **Tshi-zhun-kau-kaw,** *He who runs with the deer.* Of the Day-kau-ray family. Winnebago Chief.

127. **Wau-kaun-hah-kaw,** *Snake Skin.* Of the Day-kau-ray family. [Winnebago. = Wakaunhaka. II. See No. 20.]

128. **Artoway, Paddy Carr.** Creek Boy. [II. King.]

129. **No-din,** *Wind.* Chief of Chippeways. King. [= Notin. III.]

130. **Chou-man-i-case.** Otoe Half Chief; husband of Eagle of Delight. King [1821]. [= Shaumonekusse. I. See p. liii., No. 10.]

131. **Rant-che-wai-me, Ma-ha-ka,** *Female Flying Pigeon, Eagle of Delight.* [An error for " Hayne Hudjihini, the Eagle of Delight, wife of Shaumonekusse." (McK. and H., I.) Ranchewaime, or Female Flying Pigeon (see No. 97 and McK. and H., I.), was the wife of Mahaskah the elder. See also p. liv, Nos. 11 and 14.]

132. **Wa-em-boush-haa.** Chippeway from Sandy Lake. [Lewis, No. 71 ; McK. and H., I.]

133. **Much-a-tai-me-she-ka-kaik,** *Black Hawk.* King, 1837. [II. *Cf.* Lewis, No. 50. See p. liii, No. 8.]

134. **Ioway.**

135. **Major Timpoochy Barnard.** A Creek [Yuchi] Chief. King, 1825. [II. See p. liii, No. 9.]

136. **Mauch-coo-maim.** Ioway. By King, from a drawing by Lewis, 1826. [Lewis, No. 48.]

137. **Ki-he-ga-maw-she-she,** *Brave Chief.* Omahaw. King, 1837.

138. **Ledagie.** Creek Chief. King, 1835. [III.]

139. **We-ke-roo-taw.** *He who exchanges.* Otoe. King, 1837.

140. **Kaa-kaa-huxe,** *Little Crow.* By King, from a drawing by Lewis, 1826. [*Cf.* Lewis, No. 23. Not the Little Crow in McK. and H., I. *Cf.* No. 125.]

141. ———

142. **Toma-hake-take,** *The Warrior*[1] *who speaks first.* 1826. [*Cf.* Lewis, No. 64.]

---

[1] Error for *Woman.*

143. **Red Jacket.** Seneca Chief. (See 98, and p. liii, No. 1.) [I.]
144. **Keokuk,** *Watchful Fox;* and **Mu-se-wont,** son of Keokuk, *Long-haired Fox.* King, 1827. [See Nos. 33 and 77. McK. and H., II.]
145. **Chippeway Squaws.** 1826. [See Lewis, No. 57.]
146. **Chippeway Squaw and Child.** By King, from a drawing by Lewis, 1827. [Lewis, No. 60.]
147. **Tschusick.** King, 1827. [I.]

It is further fortunate that all the examples of King's Indian portraiture are not lost. On his death at Washington, March 19, 1862, where he had lived for forty years, the Redwood Library at Newport, Rhode Island (in which city King was born in 1785), was bequeathed a sum of money, a small but choice library, and many engravings and paintings, among the latter being twenty Indian portraits and one Indian composition.[1] Most of the portraits in this collection are copies of those that were in the Indian Gallery, and justify the assertion that King's pictures "were prized for their truthfulness rather than for delicacy of finish." A list is appended, the volumes of McKenney and Hall, in which nearly all of them appear, being given.

1. Red Jacket. (I.)
2. Wabaunsee. (II.)
3. Mistippee. (II.)
4. Nesouaquoit. (I.)
5. Moanahonga. (I.)
6. Pushmataha. (I.)
7. Wakechai. (II.)
8. Black Hawk. (II.)
9. Timpooche Barnard. (II.)
10. Chonmonicase. (= Shaumonekusse. I.)

[1] See *Catalogue of Pictures, Statuary, &c., belonging to the Redwood Library, September* 1, 1885. Numbers 20, 25, 44, 80, 165-170, 174-177, 194-196, 201-203, 219.

11. Hayne Hudjihini. (I.)
12. Peamuska. (I.)
13. Powasheek. (II.)
14. Rantchewaime. (I.)
15. Peskelechaco. (II.)
16. Amiskquew. (III.)
17. Keokuk with the standard of his nation. (Apparently a copy of Lewis's No. 9, reversed.)
18. Chenannoquot. Menominee.
19. An Assiniboin Indian, from the most remote tribe that had ever visited Washington previous to 1838.
20. Indian Chief in dress of ceremony.
21. Indian Girl at her toilet.

In addition to King's Indian portraits in the Redwood Library, a few others are known. Nos. 1 and 2 of the following list are in the Free Museum of Science and Art of the University of Pennsylvania at Philadelphia, and Nos. 3 to 7 are preserved in the United States National Museum at Washington.

1. "Tul-cee Mathla. Seminole War Chief, much distinguished in the late War. Washington, 1826, painted by Charles B. King." [McKenney and Hall, III.]

2. "The Good Martin. Ojibua Chief. C. B. King, 1827." [= No. 98 of the Peabody Museum list.]

3. "Nau-che-ning-ga; or, *No Heart*. Ioway. By C. B. King, 1837." [McKenney and Hall, III. ("Not-chi-mi-ne.") Rhees Catalogue, No. 103.]

4. "Wad-ben-de-ba, *Little Eagle*. Pawnee Squaw. Coppy from Charles King, September 12, 1822."

5. "Loup Pawnee, *Generous Chief*. Pawnee Nation. Coppy from Charles King, September 19, 1822." [= Petalesharro, McK. and H., I.]

6. "Jack-o-pa, *The Six*. Chippeway Chief. Painted by C. B. King, from a drawing by Lewis. Washington, 1827." [See Lewis, No. 70; Rhees *Catalogue*, No. 72; McKenney and Hall, III.]

7. "Es.-sne-boin. Chippeway Chief. Painted by C. B. King, from a
     drawing by Lewis.   Washington, 1827."   [No. 112 of the
     Rhees list.]
8. "Ne-sou-a-quoit. Fox Chief. Painted by King in 1838." Original
     in possession of George D. Smith, bookseller, New York City, in
     1907. (See note 2 under *Nesouaquoit* in this volume, and for
     another portrait of the same Indian, see page liii, No. 4.)

The source of most of the illustrations utilised by
McKenney and Hall is thus recorded with a reasonable
degree of completeness.   A few others, not in possession
of the Government, were used ; to these, reference is made
in the form of notes in connection with the portraits and
biographical sketches.

The negotiations between McKenney and Samuel F.
Bradford, the Philadelphia publisher, in 1830, were not
consummated.   A *Catalogue of One Hundred and Fifteen
Indian Portraits, Representing Eighteen Different Tribes,
Accompanied by a Few Brief Remarks on the Character,
&c. of Most of Them* (8°, 24 pp.), was issued at Philadelphia
under date of April 13, 1836—two months after Hall's
letter to Catlin.[1]

The first copies of the Indian pictures for the new

[1] The *Catalogue,* two editions of which were published under the
same date (one containing descriptions of 101 portraits, the other of 103,
i.e., Nos. 1-101, 117, 119), continues : " More detailed biographies will
appear in the great work on Indian history, by Col. M'Kenney & James
Hall, which work is now in the press of Messrs. Key & Biddle, a specimen
No. of which may be seen in the exhibition room at the Masonic Hall,
in Chestnut street.   Visitors to the Gallery will see on comparing the
likeness of this specimen No. with the portraits, with what fidelity the
portraits are lithograph'd.   The portraits are copies by Inman, from
the celebrated collection in the War Department at Washington,
most of which were taken from life, by King, of that city."   The
letter from former Secretary Barbour, above quoted, appears in this
Catalogue.

work were made probably in 1832, in which year Henry
Inman, then thirty-one years of age, removed from New
York to Philadelphia, where he married, and opened a
studio. In addition to copying the portraits in the Indian
Gallery for the illustration of the forthcoming work, in
conjunction with Childs he engraved one of the plates
(that of Shingaba W'Ossin) appearing in Volume I. Other
individual engravers represented in the first volume were
Corbould and J. W. Gear.

The copies of the portraits made by Inman from those
in the Indian Gallery of the War Department are now in
possession of the Peabody Museum of Archæology and
Ethnology, Harvard University, Cambridge, Mass., and
by the kindness of Professor F. W. Putnam a list of
them has been furnished the writer. These copies were
presented to the Museum in November 1882, by the heirs
of Edmund P. Tileston and Amor Hollingsworth (see
Sixteenth and Seventeenth Reports of the Peabody
Museum, Vol. III., 1884, pp. 189, 199), and a few others
are still in possession of the heirs. Through the courtesy
of Horace E. Ware, Esq., of Boston, who is related to
both families, the firm of Tileston & Hollingsworth,
paper manufacturers of Boston, was established in 1801,
and was succeeded by the sons of the two members in the
'30's. There is current in both families what may be
regarded as stronger than a tradition that in 1857, to
satisfy a debt to the firm, the latter came in possession of
the Inman pictures. It will be seen that Rice & Hart
issued editions of McKenney and Hall immediately preceding this date, in 1854, 1855, and 1856. Unfortunately
many of the Inman pictures are without number, name,
or other data. A few of them bear numbers identical
with those of the Indian Gallery collection, and some

afford information, especially regarding the artists of the originals, which the Rhees list does not supply; but owing to the shifting of the pictures and the frames the original numbers have become greatly confused.[1] Frequent reference to this list of Inman copies will be made in subsequent notes. In the Catalogue of the Peabody Museum the portraits bear numbers 28. 187 to 28. 292. Nos. 28. 255 to 28. 284 are not labelled as to names of the subjects. An additional portrait, that of Nawkaw the Winnebago, bears number 66. 307. This is the Inman copy from King, and was presented to the Museum in 1906 by Mrs Cornelia Dexter.

The work of the engravers for the McKenney and Hall work began to bear fruit in 1833, in which year Key & Biddle, of Philadelphia, copyrighted the first of the plates. Then came the publication of Lewis's *Aboriginal Port-Folio*, in 1835, a year before Volume I. of the first Folio Edition of McKenney and Hall was issued at Philadelphia by Edward C. Biddle. Other copyrights were procured by Key & Biddle in 1836 (in which year Hall made his unsuccessful attempt to obtain the use of the Catlin Collection), and by Edward C. Biddle in the year following. In 1837 also, Edward C. Biddle reissued Volume I. (or at least some copies bear that date), and in the same year it appeared in London with the imprint of J[ames] M. Campbell, apparently of the firm of Burns & Campbell, who copyrighted the portrait of Pushmataha appearing in this volume.[2] Volume II.

---

[1] Since this was written, Mr Charles C. Willoughby, of the Peabody Museum, has traced the original Indian Gallery numbers faintly written in pencil on the backs of fifteen of the portraits.

[2] " Under the energetic management of Mr James M. Campbell, the publisher in England, a large edition is sold in that country. As a

first appeared in Philadelphia in 1838, with Frederick W. Greenough (Biddle's successor) as publisher, who reissued Volume I. in the same year. In 1842 the publication passed to Daniel Rice and James G. Clark, who republished Volume I. (without date, and which appeared in London with the imprint of Charles Gilpin, 5 Bishopsgate Without), and Volume II. (1842), and issued Volume III. (1844).[1] Most of the plates in the second volume were copyrighted in 1838 by Greenough; the remainder between the years 1841 and 1844 (although the title-page bears date 1842), by either James G. Clark or J. T. Bowen. All but one of the plates in Volume III. bear the Clark copyright notice (1842-1843); the exception is that of Bowen (1842). At the lithographic establishment of the latter, most of the plates for the whole work were made. . A few of the earlier portraits were lithographed by Lehman & Duval, the engravers of the Lewis *Port-Folio*. The entire work was issued in twenty parts.

The Folio Edition having been pronounced, according to the publishers, "by the learned and polished both of Europe and America, to be one of the most valuable and interesting productions of the present age," a new edition

proof of the patronage it receives, it is enough to state, that the entire work, the plates, coloring, and letterpress, are executed anew in London for the British market, and that there is encouragement for an extensive sale on the continent."—*North American Review*, July 1838, p. 148. Some copies of Vol. II. and Vol. III. also bear the Philadelphia and London imprint, without date.

[1] Volume III. is said to have been published also by Frederick W. Greenough, thus forming a set with this publisher's imprint: Vol. I. (1838), pp. 4, 206 (1); Vol. II. (1838), pp. 237 (1); Vol. III. (1844), pp. (2) 196 (2), facsimiles 18, (1). 120 plates and portraits. See Sabin, *Dictionary of Books relating to America;* Rich, *Bibliotheca Americana Nova*, II., 1801-1844 (London, 1846, pp. 306, 307).

in three royal octavo volumes was published at Philadelphia in 1842-1844 (Volumes I. and II. in 1842,
Volume III. in 1844), by D. Rice & A. N. Hart, successors
to Rice & Clark, and reissued by the same firm in
1848.

The octavo edition was again reissued at Philadelphia
by J. T. Bowen in 1848-1850 (Volume I., 1848 ; Volume
II., 1849 ; Volume III., 1850) ; by F. Rice in 1854 ;
by D. Rice & A. N. Hart in 1854, 1855, 1856, and 1858 ;
by Rice, Rutter, & Co., in 1865, 1868 (in which latter
year it appeared also in London, in two volumes), and
1870, and by D. Rice in 1872-1874 (2 volumes roy. 8vo
and 1 volume of 120 plates folio).

On the title-pages of some of the octavo editions (as
1848, 1850, 1856, and 1865), McKenney's name alone
appears as author ; and he likewise refers to himself as
"author of *The History of the Indian Tribes of North
America*," on the title-page of his *Memoirs*, published
in 1846.

McKenney appears also as the sole author of a
four-volume edition, without date or copyright notice,
but which, from its allusion to the recent Smithsonian
fire, must have been published not long after January
1865. This edition consists of two imperial volumes
of text (450 and 541 pp.), and two folio volumes containing eighty plates only. Volume II. of the text
contains a single plate—the portrait of Billy Bowlegs,
a Seminole Chief. The title-page of the volumes of
text reads :—

History / of the / Indian Tribes / of / North America, /
with biographical sketches and anecdotes / of the / principal
chiefs. / Embellished with / Eighty Portraits from the
Indian Gallery / in the War Department, Washington. /

By Thomas L. McKenney, / late of the Indian Department, Washington. / Two vols. plates.—Two vols. text. /
Vol. I. [-Vol. II.]—Text.

Philadelphia : / Published by D. Rice & Co., / 508
Minor Street.

The folio volumes of plates of this edition bear the
same title, somewhat rearranged, and with the exception
of a change in the eighth line, which reads : "Embellished
with 80 Authentic Colored Portraits / Copied from the
Indian Gallery, / Recently Destroyed by Fire, / in the /
Smithsonian Institute at Washington." And, below :
"Two Folio Volumes of Illustrations, and two Imperial
Volumes / of Biographies and General History. / Volume
I. [-Volume II.]—Plates."

It is not the intention to present a complete bibliography of McKenney and Hall's *History of the Indian
Tribes,* which would involve treatment of the variation in
the number and placement of the plates in the several
editions. The number of the plates ranges from fifty (in
an undated two-volume Philadelphia edition not mentioned above) to one hundred and twenty. In successive
editions the frontispieces especially are changed, either by
the substitution of entirely new plates, or by the transfer
of illustrations from the body of the work. All the
illustrations in the various editions are included in
the present publication with the exception of one,
bearing the title "Prairie on Fire (the Escape),"
which appears in Volume III. of the octavo edition
of 1848, as a substitute for the much more valuable
"Encampment of Piekann Indians" appearing in the
same volume of the Folio Edition, and reproduced in
Volume III. of the present work. The "Prairie on

Fire" is worthless as an illustration, and is therefore omitted.

The value of the great work of McKenney and Hall lies chiefly in the fact that it records the features of numerous Indians prominent in the history of the American Commonwealth, faithfully reproduced from portraits painted from life, by far the most of which were subsequently destroyed; and also in the fact that the data for many of the biographical notices were obtained during the lifetime of the individuals, and are now the only source of information respecting them. As has been seen, the portraits for the greater part were painted either in the native wilds during the trying times of the civilisation of the West, or at Washington, while the subjects were representing their respective tribes before the Government. Considering the remarkable changes that have taken place in the Indians in recent years, the value of a series of coloured portraits showing their native costumes, facial painting, hairdressing. ornaments, etc., cannot be overestimated. Had it not been for our authors' assurance of success in so vast an undertaking, comparatively little would now be extant to illustrate the appearance of the Indians as they were three-quarters of a century ago, when they were in a condition that has passed forever.

So much cannot be said of the "Essay on the History of the North American Indians," prepared by James Hall, and forming a prominent part of Volume III. Considerable material of historical value is incorporated in this essay, but as the author was not an ethnologist, and as, indeed, ethnology as a science had scarcely reached its beginning at that time, his statements regarding the customs and beliefs of the Indians must usually be taken with allowance. The essay, like the biographical sketches, is nevertheless reproduced verbatim except when otherwise noted, and when necessary, to prevent the reader from drawing erroneous conclusions, or for the purpose of affording additional information, explanatory notes are given.

F. W. HODGE.

WAR DANCE

DANCING is among the most prominent of the aboriginal ceremonies. There is no tribe in which it is not practised. The Indians have their War Dance and their Peace Dance, their Dance of Mourning for the Dead, their Begging Dance, their Pipe Dance, their Green Corn Dance, and their *Wabana*.[1] Each of these is distinguished by some peculiarity appropriate to the occasion, though to a stranger they appear much alike, except the last. In the war dance the actors are distinguished by a more free use of red and black paint, except in mimic representations in time of peace, when the colours are not so closely adhered to; in the peace dance by a display of white and green; in that for the dead by black; and generally in the other dances, except the *Wabana*, black prevails, mingled with other colours.

The paint, in all the dances, is put on according to the fancy of each individual. A line is sometimes drawn dividing the body, from the forehead, and from the back of the head downwards, on either side of which different figures are drawn, representing beasts, birds, fish, snakes, etc. Frequently the hand is smeared with paint and pressed on either cheek, the breast, and the sides. It rarely happens that two of a group are painted alike.

The music consists of a monotonous thumping with sticks upon a rude drum, accompanied by the voices of the dancers, and mingled with the rattling of gourds containing pebbles, and the jingling of small bells and pieces of tin, worn as ornaments.

The *Wabana* is an offering to the devil, and, like some others, the Green Corn Dance for example, winds up with a feast.

The picture which we have selected as a frontispiece for the first number of our series, is an accurate representation of one of the War Dances of the Winnebagoes,* drawn by Rhinedesbacher,[2] a young Swiss artist, who resided for some years on the frontier, and attained a happy facility in sketching both the Indians and the wild animals of that region. This drawing is considered as one of his best efforts, and is valuable not so much as a specimen of art, in which respect it is in some particulars defective, as on account of the correct impression which it conveys of the scene intended to be represented. It was drawn on the spot as the scene was actually exhibited. The actors are persons of some note, and the faces are faithful likenesses.

The War Dances are pantomimic representations of the incidents of border warfare, and, although by no means attractive in themselves, become highly picturesque when contemplated in connection with their significant meaning. The persons engaged are warriors, the leaders of the tribe, and the great men of the day ; and the allusions are to the heroic deeds or subtle stratagems of themselves, or their ancestors, or to some danger that threatens, or some act of violence about to be perpetrated.

The dances of the Indians are not designed to be graceful amusements, nor healthful exercises, and bear no

---

* The person from whom we received the painting of the War Dance stated it to be a representation of a war dance of the Sauks and Foxes. This was an error, which we now correct.

resemblance to the elegant and joyous scenes of the ball-room. The music, the lights, the women, and above all the charms thrown about the hilarious exhibition by the courtesy and gallantry of the parties—all these are wanting in the War Dance, in which the warriors only engage. It is a ceremony, not a recreation, and is conducted with the seriousness belonging to an important public duty. The music is a monotonous beating upon a rude drum, without melody or tune; the movements exhibit neither grace nor agility, and the dancers pass round in a circle with their bodies uncouthly bent forward, as they appear in the print, uttering low, dismal, syllabic sounds, which they repeat with but little perceptible variation throughout the exhibition. The songs are, in fact, short, disjointed sentences, which allude to some victory, or appeal to the passion of revenge, and the object of which is to keep alive the recollection of injury, and excite the hatred of the tribe against their enemies. From the monotony of most of these dances there are, of course, exceptions. Sometimes the excitement of a recent event gives unwonted life and spirit to the ceremony; and occasionally an individual, throwing talent and originality into the representation, dramatises a scene with wonderful force and truth. Keokuk,[3] the chief of the Saukies, is considered a great dancer, because he brings his fine oratorical talents to bear on such occasions, and counterfeits, with singular energy and fidelity, the different passions to which he refers in his recitative, while Shaumonekussee,[4] the celebrated Oto chief, threw a rich fund of humour into these displays, and enacted many practical jokes, to the infinite delight of the spectators. Sometimes the dance is suspended as it were, for a few moments, and a prominent actor in it addresses his companions in a short speech, when the dance is renewed with increased activity. But

it seems to be chiefly by their expressive countenances, and
significant gestures, that they convey ideas on these
occasions, and produce an interest in the savage assemblage of spectators, who, like most other human beings,
are ready to applaud whatever is done by their chiefs and
leading men.

NOTES

1. From the Chippewa *wâban*, "it is twilight" (in the morning);
plural, *waiabang*. *Biwâban*, "daylight is approaching." Baraga, *Dictionary of the Otchipwe Language*, Montreal, 1878, p. 390. For an account of
the dance, see McKenney, *Tour to the Lakes*, 1827, pp. 206, 322.

2. His name correctly appears as "Rindisbacher" on the engraving,
which appears as the frontispiece in the folio edition only. The original
oil-painting is owned by Mr Fred. B. M'Guire, director of the Corcoran
Gallery of Art, Washington, D.C., who received it from the estate of his
father, James C. M'Guire, a noted collector of pictures, who bequeathed
to the Corcoran Gallery, among others, a fine portrait of Colonel
McKenney, by Charles Loring Elliott. It may be added that in the
same gallery are two specimens of Charles B. King's work—portraits of
Henry Clay and John C. Calhoun, both painted in 1822, and a painting
by J. M. Stanley, "The Disputed Shot." This Rindisbacher may have
been related to one Peter Rindesbacher (note the slight difference in
the orthography), a prominent member of Lord Selkirk's Red River
colony, and one of its seniors in age. See Gen. A. L. Chetlain's "The Red
River Colony," in *Harper's Magazine* for December 1878, pp. 48-49, with
portrait. A lithograph of the same War Dance picture appears as a
frontispiece to Volume II. of Charles Augustus Murray's *Travels in North
America during* 1834, 1835, *and* 1836, London, 1839. The same artist
painted the "Buffalo Hunt," which forms the frontispiece of Volume II.
of the present work.

3. See Volume II.

4. See page 156 of this volume.

RED JACKET

(A SENECA WAR CHIEF)

THE Seneca tribe was the most important of the celebrated confederacy, known in the early history of the American colonies as the Iroquois, or Five Nations.[1] They were a powerful and warlike people, and acquired a great ascendancy over the surrounding tribes, as well by their prowess as by the systematic skill with which their affairs seem to have been conducted. Their hunting grounds, and principal residence, were in the fertile lands, now embraced in the western limits of the State of New York—a country whose prolific soil and majestic forests, whose limpid streams and chains of picturesque lakes, and whose vicinity to the shores of Erie and Ontario, must have rendered it in its savage state the paradise of the native hunter. Surrounded by all that could render the wilderness attractive, by the greatest luxuriance of Nature, and by the most pleasing, as well as the most sublime scenery, and inheriting proud recollections of power and conquest, these tribes were among the foremost in resisting the intrusion of the whites, and the most tardy to surrender their independence. Instead of receding before the European race, as its rapidly accumulating population pressed upon their borders, they tenaciously maintained their ground, and when forced to make cessions of territory to the whites, reserved large tracts for their own use, which they continued to occupy. The swelling tide has passed over and settled around them; and a little remnant of that once proud and fierce people, remains broken and dispirited, in the heart of a civilised country, mourning over the ruins of savage grandeur, yet spurning the richer blessings enjoyed by the civilised man and the Christian. A few have embraced our religion, and learned our arts; but the greater part have dwindled away under the blasting effects of idleness, intemperance, and superstition.[2]

Red Jacket was the *last of the Senecas:* there are many left who may boast the aboriginal name and lineage, but with him expired all that had remained of the spirit of the tribe. In the following notice of that eminent man we pursue, chiefly, the narrative furnished us by a distinguished gentleman, whose information on this subject is as authentic as his ability to do it justice is unquestionable.

That is a truly affecting and highly poetical conception of an American poetess, which traces the memorials of the aborigines of America, in the beautiful nomenclature, which they have indelibly impressed on the scenery of our country. Our mountains have become their enduring monuments; and their epitaph is inscribed, in the lucid language of Nature, on our majestic rivers.

> " Ye say that all have passed away,
>   The noble race and brave—
> That their light canoes have vanished
>   From off the crested wave;
> That 'mid the forests where they roamed,
>   There rings no hunter's shout;
> But their name is on your waters,
>   Ye may not wash it out.

" Ye say their cone-like cabins
    That clustered o'er the vale,
Have disappeared as withered leaves
    Before the autumn gale :
But their memory liveth on your hills,
    Their baptism on your shore ;
Your ever rolling rivers speak,
    Their dialect of yore."

These associations are well fitted to excite sentiments of deeper emotion than poetic tenderness, and of more painful and practical effect. They stand, the landmarks of our broken vows and unatoned oppression ; and they not only stare us in the face from every hill and every stream, that bears those expressive names, but they hold up before all nations, and before God, the memorials of our injustice.

There is, or was, an Indian artist, self-taught, who, in a rude but most graphic drawing, exhibited upon canvas the events of a treaty between the white men and an Indian tribe. The scene was laid at the moment of settling the terms of a compact, after the proposals of our Government had been weighed, and well-nigh rejected by the Indians. The two prominent figures in the front ground were an Indian chief, attired in his peculiar costume, standing in a hestitating posture, with a hand half extended towards a scroll hanging partly unrolled from the hand of the other figure. The latter was an American officer in full dress, offering with one hand the unsigned treaty to the reluctant savage, while with the other he presents a musket and bayonet to his breast. This picture was exhibited some years ago near Lewiston, New York, as the production of a man of the Tuscarora tribe, named *Cusick*.[3] It was an affecting appeal from the Indian to the white man ; for although, in point of fact, the Indians have never been compelled, by direct force, to part with their lands, yet we have triumphed over them by our superior power and intelligence, and there is a moral truth in the picture, which represents the savage as yielding from fear, that which his judgment, and his attachments, would have withheld.[4]

We do not design to intimate that our colonial and national transactions with the Indians have been uniformly, or even habitually unjust. On the contrary, the treaties of Penn, and of Washington, and some of those of the Puritans, to name no others, are honourable to those who presided at their structure and execution; and teach us how important it is to be just and magnanimous in public, as well as in personal acts. Nor do we at all believe that migrating tribes, small in number, and of very unsettled habits of life, have any right to appropriate to themselves as hunting grounds and battlefields, those large domains which God designed to be reclaimed from the wilderness, and which under the culture of civilised man are adapted to sustain millions of human beings, and to be made subservient to the noblest purposes of human thought and industry. Nor can we in justice charge, exclusively, upon the white population, the corrupting influence of their intercourse with the Indian tribes. There is to be presupposed no little vice and bad propensity on the part of the savages, evinced in the facility with which they became the willing captives, and ultimate victims of that "knowledge of evil," which our people have imparted to them. The treachery also of the Indian tribes, on our defenceless frontiers, their untamable ferocity, their brutal mode of warfare, and their systematic indulgence of the principle of revenge, have too often assumed the most terrific forms of wickedness and destruction towards our confiding emigrants. It is difficult to decide between

RED JACKET
A Seneca War Chief

parties thus placed in positions of antagonism, involving a long series of mutual aggressions, inexcusable on either side, upon any exact principle of rectitude, yet palliated on both by counterbalancing provocation. So far as our Government has been concerned, the system of intercourse with the Indians has been founded in benevolence, and marked by a forbearing temper; but that policy has been thwarted by individual avarice, and perverted by unfaithful or injudicious administration. After all, however, the burthen of guilt must be conceded to lie upon the party having all the advantages of power, civilisation, and Christianity, whose position placed them in paternal relation towards these scattered children of the forest. All the controlling interests of the tribes tended to instil in them sentiments of fear, of dependence, of peace, and even of friendship, towards their more powerful neighbours; and it has chiefly been when we have chafed them to madness by incessant and unnecessary encroachment, and by unjust treaties, or when they have been seduced from their fidelity by the enemies of our country, that they have been so unwise as to provoke our resentment by open hostility. These wars have uniformly terminated in new demands on our part, in ever-growing accessions from their continually diminishing soil, until the small *reservations*, which they have been permitted to retain in the bosom of our territory, are scarcely large enough to support the living, or hide the dead, of these miserable remnants of once powerful tribes.[5]

It is not our purpose, however, to argue the grave questions growing out of our relations with this interesting race; but only to make that brief reference to them, which seems unavoidably connected with the biographical sketch we are about to give, of a chief who was uniformly, through life, the able advocate of the rights of his tribe, and the fearless opposer of all encroachment—one who was not awed by the white man's power, nor seduced by his professions of friendship.

From the best information we can obtain, it appears probable that this celebrated chief was born about A.D. 1756, at the place formerly called "Old Castle," now embraced in the town of Seneca, Ontario County, in the State of New York, and three miles west of the present beautiful village of Geneva. His Indian name was *Sa-go-you-wat-ha*, or *Keeper awake*, which, with the usual appropriateness of the native nomenclature, indicates the vigilance of his character.[6] He acquired the more familiar name, which he bore through life among white men, in the following manner. During the war of the revolution, the Seneca tribe fought under the British standard. Though he had scarcely reached the years of manhood, he engaged in the war, was much distinguished by his activity and intelligence, and attracted the attention of the British officers. One of them presented him with a richly embroidered scarlet jacket, which he took great pride in wearing. When this was worn out, he was presented with another; and he continued to wear this peculiar dress until it became a mark of distinction, and gave him the name by which he was afterwards best known. As lately as the treaty of 1794, Captain Parish,[7] to whose kindness we are indebted for some of these details, presented him with another red jacket, to perpetuate a name to which he was so much attached.

When but seventeen years old, the abilities of Red Jacket, especially his activity in the chase, and his remarkably tenacious memory, attracted the esteem and admiration of his tribe; and he was frequently employed during the war of the revolution, as a *runner* to carry despatches. In that contest he took little or no part as a warrior; and it would appear that like his celebrated predecessors in rhetorical fame, Demosthenes and Cicero, he better understood how to rouse his countrymen to war than to lead them to victory. The warlike chief, Cornplanter,[8] boldly charged him with want of courage, and his conduct on one occasion at least seems to have fully justified the charge. During the expedition of the American General Sullivan against the Indians in 1779,[9] a stand was attempted to be made against him by Cornplanter, on the beach of the Canandaigua Lake. On the approach of the American army, a small number of the Indians, among whom was Red Jacket, began to retreat. Cornplanter exerted himself to rally them. He threw himself before Red Jacket, and endeavoured to prevail on him to fight, in vain; when the indignant chief, turning to the young wife of the recreant warrior, exclaimed, "Leave that man, he is a coward."

There is no small evidence of the transcendent abilities of this distinguished individual, to be found in the fact of his rising into the highest rank among his people, though believed by them to be destitute of the virtue which they hold in the greatest estimation. The savage admires those qualities which are peculiar to his mode of life, and are most practically useful in the vicissitudes to which it is incident. Courage, strength, swiftness, and cunning are indispensably necessary in the constantly recurring scenes of the battle and the chase; while the most patient fortitude is required in the endurance of the pain, hunger, and exposure to all extremes of climate, to which the Indian is continually subjected. Ignorant and uncultivated, they have few intellectual wants or endowments, and place but little value upon any display of genius, which is not combined with the art of the warrior. To this rule, eloquence forms an exception. Where there is any

government, however rude, there must be occasional
assemblies of the people ; where war and peace are made,
the chiefs of the contending parties will meet in council ;
and on such occasions the sagacious councillor, and able
orator, will rise above him whose powers are merely
physical. But under any circumstances, courage is so
essential, in a barbarous community, where battle and
violence are continually occurring, where the right of the
strongest is the paramount law, and where life itself must
be supported by its exposure in procuring the means of
subsistence, that we can scarcely imagine how a coward
can be respected among savages, or how an individual
without courage can rise to superior sway among such
fierce spirits.

But though not distinguished as a warrior, it seems
that Red Jacket was not destitute of bravery ; for on a
subsequent occasion, the stain affixed upon his character,
on the occasion alluded to, was wiped away by his good
conduct in the field. The true causes, however, of his
great influence in his tribe, were his transcendent talents,
and the circumstances under which he lived. In times of
public calamity the abilities of great men are appreciated,
and called into action. Red Jacket came upon the theatre
of active life, when the power of his tribe had declined,
and its extinction was threatened. The white man was
advancing upon them with gigantic strides. The red
warrior had appealed, ineffectually, to arms ; his cunning
had been foiled and his strength overpowered ; his foes,
superior in prowess, were countless in number ; and he
had thrown down the tomahawk in despair. It was then
that Red Jacket stood forward as a patriot, defending his
nation with fearless eloquence, and denouncing its enemies
in strains of fierce invective, or bitter sarcasm. He
became their counsellor, their negotiator, and their orator.

Whatever may have been his conduct in the field, he now evinced a moral courage, as cool and sagacious as it was undaunted, and which showed a mind of too high an order to be influenced by the base sentiment of fear. The relations of the Senecas with the American people, introduced questions of a new and highly interesting character, having reference to the purchase of their lands, and the introduction of Christianity and the arts. The Indians were asked not only to sell their country, but to embrace a new religion, to change their occupations and domestic habits, and to adopt a novel system of thought and action. Strange as these propositions must have seemed in themselves, they were rendered the more unpalatable when dictated by the stronger party, and accompanied by occasional acts of oppression.

It was at this crisis that Red Jacket stood forward, the intrepid defender of his country, its customs, and its religion, and the unwavering opponent of all innovation. He yielded nothing to persuasion, to bribery, or to menace, and never, to his last hour, remitted his exertions, in what he considered the noblest purpose of his life.

An intelligent gentleman, who knew this chief intimately, in peace and war, for more than thirty years, speaks of him in the following terms: "Red Jacket was a *perfect Indian* in every respect—in costume,* in his

* NOTE BY McKENNEY AND HALL.—The portrait represents him in a blue coat. He wore this coat when he sat to King of Washington. He rarely dressed himself otherwise than in the costume of his tribe. He made an exception on this occasion.

NOTE BY THE EDITOR.—The accompanying portrait was painted by Charles Bird King in 1828, and a copy, by the same artist, is in possession of the Redwood Library of Newport, Rhode Island, while the Inman (?) copy is in the Peabody Museum of Harvard University (original numbers, 5 and 96; museum number, 28. 187). The copy is not accredited to Inman, but it is fair to assume that it was made by contempt of the dress of the white men, in his hatred and opposition to the missionaries, and in his attachment to,

him.   See further on.   Another portrait of Red Jacket (19 × 29), painted from life by Robert Walter Weir at New York City in the same year, is in the collection of the New York Historical Society, having been presented in 1893 by Mr Winthrop Chanler.   Another Weir portrait of Red Jacket, or rather a copy of the last, bearing date 1828, is in possession of the Long Island Historical Society of Brooklyn, New York, having been presented to it by Mr John E. Schumaker in 1864. George Catlin painted a full-length, life-size portrait of him at Table Rock, Niagara Falls, in 1829, and forms No. 263 of his *Descriptive Catalogue* (London, 1840), and plate 205 (pages 104-106) of Volume II. of his *Notes of Eight Years' Travels* (10th ed., London, 1866).   Still another portrait of this famous Indian (22 × 30), by an unknown painter (Henry Inman ?), was presented to the Pennsylvania Historical Society in 1855. The following interesting note regarding the portraits of Red Jacket is extracted from *The Life and Times of Red Jacket, or Sa-go-ye-wat-ha*, by William L. Stone (New York and London, 1841), pages 374-376 :—

"There are no portraits of Red Jacket extant, taken in early life, or even when in the prime of his manhood, although many efforts were made by the artists of New York and Philadelphia, and also by other gentlemen, during his visits to those cities, to induce him to sit.   His reply to all importunities upon the subject, for many years, was, that when Red Jacket died, all that appertained to him should die with him. He wished nothing to remain.   But this purpose was changed in the autumn of 1820, through the interposition of the blacksmith of the tribe, and he was induced to sit to Mr Mathies, a self-taught artist, residing at Rochester.   Indeed, his reluctance was readily overcome by an appeal to his vanity—Mr Mathies having assured him that his only motive was to obtain a likeness to be placed by the side of the portraits of other great men of the United States.   He sat three times to Mathies, and the picture is said to be very good.   The Rubicon having been passed, there was less difficulty in prevailing upon him to favour other artists ; among them was the distinguished delineator of Indians, Mr George Catlin, who painted him twice.   Henry Inman also made a sketch of him—a head only—which is thought very spirited.   But the picture by Mr Robert W. Weir, taken in 1828, at the request of Doctor John W. Francis, of New York, is of far the highest order of merit, and has become the standard likeness of 'the last of the Seneca orators.'   An acquaintance of several years, and the reception of some trifling presents and veneration for, the ancient customs and traditions of his tribe. He had a contempt for the English language,

from Doctor Francis, had enabled the latter to induce a promise from the old chief to sit, on his next visit to New York. This happened in the year last mentioned; when, with his interpreter, Jemison, he very promptly repaired to the painting-room of Mr Weir. 'For this purpose he dressed himself in the costume which he deemed most appropriate to his character, decorated with his brilliant overcovering and belt, his tomahawk, and Washington medal. For the whole period of nearly two hours, on four or five successive days, he was as punctual to the arrangements of the artist as any individual could be. He chose a large arm-chair for his convenience, while his interpreter, as well as himself, was occupied, for the most part, in surveying the different objects which decorated the artist's room. He had a party of several Senecas with him, who, adopting the horizontal position, in different parts of the room, regaled themselves with the fumes of tobacco to their utmost gratification. Red Jacket occasionally united in this relaxation; but was so deeply absorbed in attention to the work of the painter as to think, perhaps, of no other subject. At times he manifested extreme pleasure, as the outlines of the picture were filled up. The drawing of his costume, which he seemed to prize, as peculiarly appropriate, and the distant view of the Falls of Niagara—scenery at no great distance from his residence at the reservation—forced him into an indistinct utterance of his satisfaction. When his medal appeared complete in the picture, he addressed his interpreter, accompanied by striking gestures; and when his noble front was finished, he sprang upon his feet with great alacrity, and seizing the artist by the hand, exclaimed, with great energy, "Good! good!" The painting being finished, he parted with Mr Weir with a satisfaction apparently equal to that which he doubtless, on some occasions, had felt on effecting an Indian treaty. Red Jacket must have been beyond his seventieth year when the painting was made. He exhibited in his countenance somewhat of the traces of time and trial on his constitution. Nevertheless, he was of a tall and erect form, and walked with a firm gait. His characteristics are preserved by the artist to admiration; and his majestic form exhibits an attitude surpassing every other that I have ever seen of the human skull. As a specimen for the craniologist, Red Jacket need not yield his pretensions to those of the most asute philosopher. He will live long by the painting of Weir, the poetry of Halleck, and the fame of his own deeds.'"

and disdained to use any other than his own. He was
the finest specimen of the Indian character I ever knew,
and sustained it with more dignity than any other chief.
He was the second in authority in his tribe. As an
orator he was unequalled by any Indian I ever saw.
His language was beautiful and figurative, as the Indian
language [10] always is, and delivered with the greatest ease
and fluency. His gesticulation was easy, graceful, and
natural. His voice was distinct and clear, and he always
spoke with great animation. His memory was very
strong. I have acted as interpreter to most of his
speeches, to which no translation could do adequate
justice."

Another gentleman, who had much official and
personal intercourse with the Seneca orator, writes thus :
"You have no doubt been well informed as to the
strenuous opposition of Red Jacket, to all improvement in
the arts of civilised life, and more especially to all innovations upon the religion of the Indians—or as they
generally term it, the religion of their fathers. His
speeches upon this and other points, which have been
published, were obtained through the medium of illiterate
interpreters, and present us with nothing more than
ragged and disjointed sketches of the originals. In a
private conversation between Red Jacket, Colonel Chapin [11]
and myself, in 1824, I asked him why he was so much
opposed to the establishment of missionaries among his
people. The question seemed to awaken in the sage old
chief feelings of surprise, and after a moment's reflection
he replied, with a sarcastic smile, and an emphasis
peculiar to himself, 'Because they do us no good. If they
are not useful to the white people, why do they send
them among the Indians; if they are useful to the white
people, and do them good, why do they not keep them

at home? They are surely bad enough to need the labour of every one who can make them better. These men know we do not understand their religion. We cannot read their book; they tell us different stories about what it contains, and we believe they make the book talk to suit themselves. If we had no money, no land, and no country, to be cheated out of, these black coats would not trouble themselves about our good hereafter. The Great Spirit will not punish us for what we do not know. He will do justice to his red children. These black coats talk to the Great Spirit, and ask for light, that we may see as they do, when they are blind themselves, and quarrel about the light which guides them. These things we do not understand, and the light they give us makes the straight and plain path trod by our fathers dark and dreary. The black coats tell us to work and raise corn; they do nothing themselves and would starve to death if somebody did not feed them. All they do is to pray to the Great Spirit; but that will not make corn or potatoes grow; if it will, why do they beg from us, and from the white people? The red men knew nothing of trouble until it came from the white man; as soon as they crossed the great waters they wanted our country, and in return have always been ready to teach us how to quarrel about their religion. Red Jacket can never be the friend of such men. The Indians can never be civilised; they are not like white men. If they were raised among the white people, and learned to work, and to read, as they do, it would only make their situation worse. They would be treated no better than negroes. We are few and weak, but may for a long time be happy, if we hold fast to our country and the religion of our fathers.'"

It is much to be regretted that a more detailed account

of this great man cannot be given. The nature of his life and attachments, threw his history out of the view, and beyond the reach of white men. It was part of his national policy to have as little intercourse as possible with civilised persons, and he met our country only amid the intrigues and excitement of treaties, or in the degradation of that vice of civilised society, which makes white men savages, and savages brutes. Enough, however, has been preserved to show that he was an extraordinary man.

Perhaps the most remarkable attribute of his character was commanding eloquence. A notable illustration of the power of his eloquence was given at a council, held at Buffalo Creek, in New York. Cornplanter, who was at that period chief of the Senecas, was mainly instrumental in making the treaty of Fort Stanwix, in 1784.[12] His agency in this affair, operated unfavourably upon his character, and weakened his influence with his tribe. Perceiving that Red Jacket was availing himself of his loss of popularity, he resolved on counteracting him. To do this effectually, he ordained one of his brothers a prophet, and set him to work to *pow-wow* against his rival, and his followers. The plan consummated, Red Jacket was assailed in the midst of the tribe, by all those arts that are known to be so powerful over the superstition of the Indian. The council was full—and was, no doubt, convened mainly for this object. Of this occurrence De Witt Clinton says: "At this crisis, Red Jacket well knew that the future colour of his life depended upon the powers of his mind. He spoke in his defence for near three hours—the iron brow of superstition relented under the magic of his eloquence. He declared the Prophet an impostor, and a cheat—he prevailed—the Indians divided, and a small majority appeared in his favour. Perhaps the annals of history cannot furnish a more conspicuous instance of the power and triumph of oratory in a barbarous nation, devoted to superstition, and looking up to the accuser as a delegated minister of the Almighty." Of the power which he exerted over the minds of those who heard him, it has been justly remarked, that no one ignorant of the dialect in which he spoke can adequately judge. He wisely, as well as proudly, chose to speak through an interpreter, who was often an illiterate person, or sometimes an Indian, who could hardly be expected to do that justice to the orator of the forest, which the learned are scarcely able to render to each other. Especially, would such reporters fail to catch even the spirit of an animated harangue, as it fell rich and fervid from the lips of an injured patriot, standing amid the ruins of his little state, rebuking on the one hand his degenerate tribe, and on the other repelling the encroachments of an absorbing power. The speeches which have been reported as his are, for the most part, miserable failures, either made up for the occasion in the prosecution of some mercenary, or sinister purpose, or unfaithfully rendered into puerile periods by an ignorant native.

There are several interesting anecdotes of Red Jacket, which should be preserved as illustrations of the peculiar points of his character and opinions, as well as of his ready eloquence. We shall relate a few which are undoubtedly authentic.

In a council which was held with the Senecas by Governor Tompkins of New York, a contest arose between that gentleman and Red Jacket, as to a fact connected with a treaty of many years' standing. The American agent stated one thing, the Indian chief corrected him, and insisted that the reverse of his assertion was true. But, it was rejoined, "you have forgotten—we have it written down on paper." "The paper then tells a lie," was the confident answer; "I have it written here," continued the chief, placing his hand with great dignity upon his brow. "You Yankees are born with a feather between your fingers; but your paper does not speak the truth. The Indian keeps his knowledge here—this is the book the Great Spirit gave us—it does not lie!" A reference was immediately made to the treaty in question, when to the astonishment of all present, and to the triumph of the tawny statesman, the document confirmed every word he had uttered.

About the year 1820, Count D., a young French nobleman, who was making a tour in America, visited the town of Buffalo. Hearing of the fame of Red Jacket, and learning that his residence was but seven miles distant, he sent him word that he was desirous to see him, and that he hoped that the chief would visit him at Buffalo, the next day. Red Jacket received the message with much contempt, and replied, "Tell the *young* man that if he wishes to see the *old chief*, he may find him with his nation, where other strangers pay their respects to him; and Red Jacket will be glad to see him." The Count sent back his messenger, to say that he was fatigued by his journey, and could not go to the Seneca village; that he had come all the way from France to see Red Jacket, and after having put himself to so much trouble to see so great a man, the latter could not refuse to meet him at Buffalo. "Tell him," said the sarcastic chief, "that it is very strange he should come so far to see me, and then stop short within seven miles of my residence." The retort was richly merited. The Count visited him at his wigwam, and *then* Red Jacket accepted an invitation to dine with the foreign traveller at his lodgings in Buffalo. The young nobleman declared that he considered Red Jacket a greater wonder than the Falls of Niagara. This remark was the more striking, as it was made within view of the great cataract. But it was just. He who made the world, and filled it with wonders, has declared man to be the crowning work of the whole creation.

It happened during the revolutionary war, that a treaty was held with the Indians, at which Lafayette was present. The object was to unite the various tribes in amity with America. The majority of the chiefs were friendly, but there was much opposition made to it, more especially by a young warrior, who declared that when an alliance was entered into with America he should consider the sun of his country had set for ever. In his travels through the Indian country, when last in America,[18] it happened at a large assemblage of chiefs, that Lafayette referred to the treaty in question, and turning to Red Jacket, said, "Pray tell me if you can, what has become of that daring youth who so decidedly opposed all our propositions for peace and amity? Does he still live; and what is his condition?" "I, myself, am the man," replied Red Jacket; "the decided enemy of the Americans, so long as the hope of opposing them successfully remained, but now their true and faithful ally until death."

During the war between Great Britain and the United States, which commenced in 1812, Red Jacket was disposed to remain neutral, but was overruled by his tribe, and at last engaged heartily on our side, in consequence of an argument which occurred to his own mind. The lands of his tribe border upon the frontier between the United States and Canada. "If the British succeed," he said, "they will take our country from us; if the Americans drive them back, *they* will claim our land by right of conquest." He fought through the whole war, displayed the most undaunted intrepidity, and completely redeemed his character from the suspicion of that unmanly weakness with which he had been charged in early life; while in no instance did he exhibit the ferocity of the savage, or disgrace himself by any act of outrage towards a prisoner or a fallen enemy. His, therefore, was that true moral courage, which results from self-respect and the sense of duty, and which is a more noble and more active principle, than that mere animal instinct which renders many men insensible to danger. Opposed to war, not ambitious of martial fame, and unskilled in military affairs, he went to battle from principle, and met its perils with the spirit of a veteran warrior, while he shrunk from its cruelties with the sensibility of a man, and a philosopher.

Red Jacket was the foe of the white man. His nation was his God; her honour, preservation, and liberty, his religion. He hated the missionary of the Cross, because he feared some secret design upon the lands, the peace, or the independence of the Senecas. He never understood Christianity. Its sublime disinterestedness exceeded his conceptions. He was a keen observer of human nature; and saw that among white, and red men, sordid interest was equally the spring of action. He, therefore, naturally enough suspected every stranger who came to his tribe of some design on their little and dearly prized domains; and felt towards the Christian missionary as the Trojan priestess did towards the wooden horse of the Greeks. He saw too, that the same influence which tended to reduce his wandering tribe to civilised habits, must necessarily change his whole system of policy. He wished to preserve the integrity of his tribe by keeping the Indians and white men apart, while the direct tendency of the missionary system was to blend them in one society, and to bring them under a common religion and government. While it annihilated paganism, it dissolved the nationality of the tribe. In the wilderness, far from white men, the Indians might rove in pursuit of game, and remain a distinct people. But the district of land reserved for the Senecas was not as large as the smallest county in New York, and was now surrounded by an ever-growing population impatient to possess their lands, and restricting their hunting grounds, by bringing the arts of husbandry up to the line of demarcation. The deer, the buffalo, and the elk were gone. On Red Jacket's system, his people should have followed them; but he chose to remain, and yet refused to adopt those arts and institutions, which alone could preserve his tribe from an early and ignominious extinction.

It must also be stated in fairness, that the missionaries are not always men fitted for their work. Many of them have been destitute of the talents and information requisite in so arduous an enterprise; some have been bigoted and over-zealous, and others have wanted temper and patience. Ignorant of the aboriginal languages, and obliged to rely upon interpreters to whom religion was an occult science, they doubtless often conveyed very different impressions from those which they intended. "What have you said to them?" inquired a missionary once, of the interpreter who had been expounding his sermon. "I told them you have a message to them from the Great Spirit," was the reply. "I said no such thing," cried the missionary; "Tell them I am come to speak of God, the only living and True God, and of the life that is to be hereafter—well, what have you said?" "That you will tell them about Manito[14] and the land of spirits." "Worse and worse!" exclaimed the embarrassed preacher; and such is doubtless the history of many sermons which have been delivered to the bewildered heathen.

There is another cause which has seldom failed to

operate in opposition to any fair experiment in reference to the civilisation of the Indians. The frontiers are always infested by a class of adventurers, whose plans of speculation are best promoted by the ignorance of the Indian; who, therefore, steadily thwart every benevolent attempt to enlighten the savage; and who are as ingenious as they are busy, in framing insinuations to the discredit of those engaged in benevolent designs towards this unhappy race.

Whatever was the policy of Red Jacket, or the reasons on which it was founded, he was the steady, skilful, and potent foe of missions in his tribe, which became divided into two factions, one of which was called the *Christian*, and the other the *Pagan*, party. The Christian party in 1827 outnumbered the Pagan—and Red Jacket was formally, and by a vote of the council, displaced from the office of Chief of the Senecas, which he had held ever since his triumph over Cornplanter. He was greatly affected by this decision, and made a journey to Washington to lay his griefs before his Great Father. His first call on arriving at Washington was on Colonel McKenney, who was in charge of the Bureau of Indian Affairs. That officer was well informed, through his agent, of all that had passed among the Senecas, and of the decision of the council, and the cause of it, displacing Red Jacket. After the customary shaking of hands, Red Jacket spoke, saying, "I have a talk for my Father." "Tell him," answered Colonel McKenney, "I have one for him. I will make it, and will then listen to him." Colonel McKenney narrated all that had passed between the two parties, taking care not to omit the minute incidents that had combined to produce the open rupture that had taken place. He sought to convince Red Jacket that a spirit of forbearance on his part, and a yielding to the Christian party the right, which he claimed for himself, to believe as he pleased on the subject of religion, would have prevented the mortifying result of his expulsion from office and power. At the conclusion of this talk, during which Red Jacket never took his keen and searching eye off the speaker, he turned to the interpreter, saying, with his finger pointing in the direction of his people, and of his home, "Our Father has got a long eye!" He then proceeded to vindicate himself, and his cause, and to pour out upon the black coats the phials of his wrath. It was finally arranged, however, that he was to go home, and there, in a council that was directed to be convened for the purpose, express his willingness to bury the hatchet, and leave it to those who might choose to be Christians to adopt the ceremonies of that religion, whilst for himself, and those who thought like him, he claimed the privilege to follow the faith of his fathers. Whereupon, and as had been promised him at Washington, the council unanimously replaced him in the office of chief, which he held till his death, which happened soon after. It is due to him to state, that a cause, which has retarded the progress of Christianity in all lands lying adjacent to Christian nations, naturally influenced his mind. He saw many individuals in Christendom who were worse than Pagans. He did not know that few of these professed to be Christians, and that a still smaller number practised the precepts of our religion; but judging them in the mass, he saw little that was desirable in the moral character of the whites, and nothing inviting in their faith. It was with these views, that Red Jacket, in council, in reply to the proposal to establish a mission among his people, said with inimitable severity and shrewdness, "Your talk is fair and good. But I propose this. Go, try your hand in the town of Buffalo, for one year. They need missionaries, if you can do what you say. If in that time you shall have done them any good, and made them any better, then we will let you come among our people."

A gentleman, who saw Red Jacket in 1820, describes him as being then apparently sixty years old. He was dressed with much taste, in the Indian costume throughout, but had not a savage look. His form was erect, and not large; and his face noble. He wore a blue dress, the upper garment cut after the fashion of a hunting shirt; with blue leggings, very neat moccasins, a *red jacket*, and a girdle of red about his waist. His eye was fine, his forehead lofty and capacious, and his bearing calm and dignified. Previous to entering into any conversation with our informant, who had been introduced to him under the most favourable auspices, he inquired, "What are you, a gambler, (meaning a land speculator,) a sheriff, or a black coat?" Upon ascertaining that the interview was not sought for any specific object, other than that of seeing and conversing with himself, he became easy and affable, and delivered his sentiments freely on the subject which had divided his tribe, and disturbed himself, for many years. "He said that he had no doubt that Christianity was good for white people, but that the red men were a different race, and required a different religion. He believed that Jesus Christ was a good man, and that the whites should all be sent to hell for killing him; but the red men having no hand in his death, were clear of that crime. The Saviour was not sent to them, the atonement not made for them, nor the Bible given to them, and, therefore, the Christian religion was not intended for them. If the Great Spirit had intended they should be Christians, he would have made his revelation to them as well as to the whites; and not having made it, it was clearly his will that they should continue in the faith of their fathers."

The whole life of the Seneca chief was spent in vain endeavours to preserve the independence of his tribe, and in active opposition as well as to the plans of civilisation proposed by the benevolent, as to the attempts at encroachment on the part of the mercenary. His views remained unchanged and his mental powers unimpaired, to the last. The only weakness, incident to the degenerate condition of his tribe, into which he permitted himself to fall, was that of intoxication. Like all Indians, he loved ardent spirits, and although his ordinary habits were temperate, he occasionally gave himself up to the dreadful temptation, and spent several days in succession in continual drinking.

The circumstances attending his decease were striking, and we shall relate them in the language of one who witnessed the facts which he states. For some months previous to his death, time had made such ravages on his constitution as to render him fully sensible of his approaching dissolution. To that event he often adverted, and always in the language of philosophic calmness. He visited successively all his most intimate friends at their cabins, and conversed with them, upon the condition of the nation, in the most impressive and affecting manner. He told them that he was passing away, and his counsels would soon be heard no more. He ran over the history of his people from the most remote period to which his knowledge extended, and pointed out, as few could, the wrongs, the privations, and the loss of character, which almost of themselves constituted that history. "I am about to leave you," said he, "and when I am gone, and my warnings shall be no longer heard, or regarded, the craft and avarice of the white man will prevail. Many winters have I breasted the storm, but I am an aged tree, and can stand no longer. My leaves are fallen, my branches are withered, and I am shaken by every breeze. Soon my aged trunk will be prostrate and the foot of the exulting foe of the Indian may be placed upon it in safety ; for I leave none who will be able to avenge such an indignity. Think not I mourn for myself. I go to join the spirits of my fathers, where age cannot come ; but my heart fails, when I think of my people, who are soon to be scattered and forgotten." These several interviews were all concluded with detailed instructions respecting his domestic affairs and his funeral.

There had long been a missionary among the Senecas, who was sustained by a party among the natives, while Red Jacket denounced "the man in dark dress," and deprecated the feud by which his nation was distracted. In his dying injunctions to those around him, he repeated his wishes respecting his interment : "Bury me," said he, "by the side of my former wife ; and let my funeral be according to the customs of our nation. Let me be dressed and equipped as my fathers were, that their spirits may rejoice in my coming. Be sure that my grave be not made by a white man ; let them not pursue me there !" He died on the 20th of January, 1830, at his residence near Buffalo.[15] With him fell the spirit of his people. They gazed upon his fallen form, and mused upon his prophetic warnings, until their hearts grew heavy with grief. The neighbouring missionary, with a disregard for the feelings of the bereaved, and the injunctions of the dead, for which it is difficult to account, assembled his party, took possession of the body, and conveyed it to their meeting house. The immediate friends of Red Jacket, amazed at the transaction, abandoned the preparations they were making for the funeral rites, and followed the body in silence to the place of worship, where a service was performed, which, considering the opinions of the deceased, was as idle as it was indecorous. They were then told, from the sacred desk, that, if they had anything to say, they had now an opportunity. Incredulity and scorn were pictured on the face of the Indians, and no reply was made except by a chief called Green Blanket, who briefly remarked, "This house was built for the white man, the friends of Red Jacket cannot be heard in it." Notwithstanding this touching appeal, and the dying injunctions of the Seneca chief, his remains were taken to the grave prepared by the whites, and interred. Some of the Indians followed the corpse, but the more immediate friends of Red Jacket took a last view of their lifeless chief, in the sanctuary of that religion which he had always opposed, and hastened from a scene which overwhelmed them with humiliation and sorrow. Thus early did the foot of the white man trample on the dust of the great chief, in accordance with his own prophetic declaration.[16]

The medal which Red Jacket wore, and which is faithfully copied in the portrait before the reader, he prized above all price. It was a personal present, made in 1792, from General Washington.[17] He was never known to be without it. He had studied and comprehended the character of Washington, and placed upon this gift a value corresponding with his exalted opinion of the donor.[18]

NOTES

1. After the admission of the Tuscarora tribe into the Iroquois confederacy in 1728, it became known to the English as the Six Nations.

2. In 1906 there were 2742 Seneca in New York State, and 383 in Indian Territory.

3. This was, perhaps, the treaty between the Oneida, Tuscarora, and Stockbridges, concluded at Oneida, New York, December 2, 1794, of which treaty "Kanatjogh, or Nicholas Cusick," war-chief of the Tuscarora, was one of the signers. Nicholas died near Lewiston, New York, in 1840, aged about eighty-two years. His son David, the historian of the tribe, died shortly after. James, another son, became a Baptist minister in 1838, and was a leader in temperance work. He went to the Indian territory with other emigrants, most of whom died, and being ill himself, he returned in three years. Being blamed for their deaths, he became unpopular and went to Canada, where he preached until his death.

4. For the best presentation of the Indians' beliefs respecting land tenure, and of their ideas concerning land cessions, see Dr George Bird Grinnell's "Tenure of Land among Indians," in *American Anthropologist*, N. S., IX., No. 1, Lancaster, Pa., 1907.

5. The facts are here generally well summarised. For an able account of the policy of the various Governments having dealings with the Indians of North America, see the Introduction, by Cyrus Thomas, to C. C. Royce's "Indian Land Cessions in the United States," in the *Eighteenth Annual Report of the Bureau of American Ethnology*, Washington, 1899.

6. Red Jacket's original name was *Otetiani*, "Always ready"; but when he was elevated to a chiefship, he was given the name *Shagoie'hwät'hä'*, which, according to Mr J. N. B. Hewitt, signifies, "He causes them to be awake." See also Horatio Hale in "Obsequies of Red Jacket at Buffalo, October 9th, 1884" (*Transactions of the Buffalo Historical Society*, Vol. III., Buffalo, 1885), app. 12, p. 71.

7. The treaty with the Six Nations, concluded at Canandaigua, New York, November 11, 1794. Of this treaty Jasper Parish was a witness.

8. See page 174 of this volume.

9. Consult *Journals of the Military Expedition of General John Sullivan against the Six Nations of Indians in* 1779, prepared by Frederick Cook, Secretary of State, Auburn, New York, 1887; Mary Cheney Elwood, *An Episode of the Sullivan Campaign and its Sequel*, Rochester, New York, 1904; George H. Harris, *Aboriginal Occupation of the Lower Genesee Country*, Rochester, 1884.

10. The author falls into the prevalent error of implying that the Indians speak a common tongue. In North America, north of Mexico, alone there were more than fifty stock languages, with at least three times as many mutually unintelligible dialects.

11. "General Israel Chapin, long the Superintendent of Indian Affairs for the Northern Department, died early in the spring of 1795" (Stone, *Life and Times of Red Jacket*, 1841, page 145).

12. The treaty of Fort Stanwix, New York, was concluded, October 22, 1784, between the Six Nations and the United States. Cornplanter

(see page 174 of this volume) signed under the name Keyenthoghke, in behalf of the Seneca tribe.

13. In 1824-1825.

14. The mysterious and unknown potencies and powers of life and of the universe, adopted by the whites to express the idea of God, " Great Spirit."

15. According to Stone, he died " at his residence, near the church and mission-house at the Seneca village." For an account of the subsequent removal of the remains, and the obsequies attending their reburial at Forest Lawn, Buffalo, New York, in 1884, see " Obsequies of Red Jacket," above cited, note 6.

16. Regarding this account of his death and burial, Stone (pages 393-395) makes the following important statement :—
" The management of his funeral was committed by himself to his wife's son-in-law, William Jones. He himself had not a near kinsman in the world. His friends of the Wolf-clan, to which he belonged, determined that his remains should be carried to the church in which they worshipped, and buried in the ground belonging to the Christian party. The funeral was numerously attended, not only by his own race, but by the white people, who gathered from the adjacent country. Among the latter were some of the leaders of the infidel white men, who had acted in concert with the deceased in his opposition to Christianity. These latter came with high expectations of beholding a splendid pagan funeral, accompanied by the howlings of women, and all the barbarous rites and ceremonies incident to savage funerals in the days when ' darkness brooded ' over the wilds of the continent. Great, therefore, was their disappointment on finding themselves in the train of a Christian funeral, attended by its simple and solemn observances." *

17. This medal, of solid silver, measuring $6\frac{3}{4}''$ by $4\frac{3}{4}''$, was presented by Washington to Red Jacket at Philadelphia, having been engraved at the United States Mint in that city. The obverse represents Washington in uniform presenting a pipe to an Indian, who is smoking it ; near the feet of the Indian is a tomahawk ; behind him some pine trees ; in the distance a man ploughing ; in exergue, *George Washington President* 1792. Reverse, arms and crest of the United States on the

---

* " My authority for the preceding account of the last days of Red Jacket's life, including the last council summoned by him, and his funeral, is the Rev. Mr Harris, with whom I have had repeated and full conversations upon the subject, and whose report, written at the time, and published in the *Missionary Herald*, Vol. XXVI., I have consulted. Very grievous misrepresentations in regard to the conduct of this gentleman at the death and funeral of the chief were sent abroad by the disappointed white pagans, referred to in the text, some of which unfortunately found their way into the sketch published in the Indian Biography of Colonel McKenney. [After some extracts from McKenney and Hall bearing on this point, Stone adds :] Now all this is very well told, and with good dramatic effect. But, like most other dramatic compositions, it is an entire fiction."

breast of an eagle, in the right talon of which is an olive branch, in the left a sheaf of arrows, in its beak a ribbon with the motto *E Pluribus Unum;* above, a glory breaking through the clouds, and surrounded by thirteen stars. The medal descended to General Eli S. Parker, and is now in possession of the Buffalo Historical Society.

18. The foregoing biography of Red Jacket is attributed by Stone (page 18, note) to the Reverend John Breckenridge, D.D. In addition to the works above cited, consult Elizabeth Seelye and E. Eggleston, *Brant and Red Jacket,* New York [1879]; J. N. Hubbard, *An Account of Sa-go-ye-wat-ha, or Red Jacket, and his People,* Albany, 1886.

KISHKALWA

(A SHAWNEE CHIEF)

KISHKALWA [1] is nominally and legally the head chief of the Shawanoe [2] nation, but is too far advanced in life to take any active part in its affairs. He is believed to be between eighty-six and ninety years of age, and is living, with a daughter, upon the Kansas River, although his band have settled in the neighbourhood of the Sabine. The family of this chief is numerous and very distinguished; he is one of seven brothers, all renowned warriors, one of whom was the celebrated Black Hoof, [3] who died in 1831, at the advanced age of from ninety-five to one hundred years.

This chief was about seventeen years of age when he engaged, for the first time, in a war party; and on that occasion he made himself conspicuous for his bravery. The expedition was of a character which strikingly illustrates the history of savage life. The Shawanese were a warlike tribe, that roved through the whole of the territory north-west of the Ohio, and were continually engaged in hostilities, at first with the English, and subsequently with their descendants, while they maintained friendly relations with the French. The latter occupied Fort Massac, [4] a military station, on the northern shore of the Ohio, not far above its junction with the Mississippi; and were at variance with the Chickasaws, who lost no opportunity to do them an injury. Among other strata-

gems which were practised by these Indians, was one that
was frequently adopted by all the tribes, and in which the
savages were very successful.   A party of warriors
disguised in the skins of deer, or of bears, would appear
creeping upon the shore of the river opposite the fort.
The width of the stream was so great as to render it quite
possible to practise the deception with good effect, even if
the imitation of the animals had been less perfect than it
really was.   But the Indians, accustomed to notice the
habits of the brute creation, and versed in all the strategy
of sylvan sport, and border war, played their parts with
admirable fidelity to nature.   Sometimes the French saw
a number of bears issuing from the forest which clothed
the bank, and walking sluggishly over the narrow margin
of sand that fringed the river; and sometimes a herd of
deer was seen, half-disclosed among the bushes, as if
reclining in the shade, and gazing upon the placid stream.
The ardent Frenchmen, unsuspicious of danger, would
cross the river hastily in pursuit of the supposed game and
fall into an ambuscade prepared by the Chickasaws.   The
Shawanese heard of several massacres which occurred in
this manner, and determined to avenge their friends.   A
war party proceeded secretly to the neighbourhood of the
fort, and waited for the appearance of the counterfeit
game, which they knew could not impose upon them, however it had deceived the Europeans.   It was not long before
the trick which had often proved successful was again
attempted ; the mimic animals appeared upon the shore ;
the French soldiers, apprised of the plan of their allies,
busied themselves in preparing a boat as if to cross
the river, while the Shawanese having made a circuit
through the woods, and passed the river at a distant
point, threw themselves into the rear of the enemy.   The
Chickasaws were surprised and defeated with great los

On such expeditions, the *medicine bag*, supposed to possess supernatural virtues, is carried, during the march from home, by the leader of the enterprise, whose station is in the van of the party; but on the return, this mysterious bag is borne by the warrior who has acquired the greatest distinction during that expedition, or, in some cases, by him who killed the first enemy, and the person thus honoured marches foremost. The young Kishkalwa, on this occasion, returned in the proud station of bearer of the medicine bag.

Another adventure occurred a year or two afterwards, the recital of which will serve to throw some light, as well on the character of Kishkalwa, as on the peculiarities of the Indian. The beautiful and fertile country, which now forms the State of Kentucky, was not, previous to its occupation by the whites, inhabited by any tribe of Indians, but was a common hunting ground, and battle field, for the various surrounding tribes, whose fierce conflicts gave to this lovely region the name of "The dark and bloody ground."[5] The Indian who ventured among those forests, was prepared alike for the chase, and for war. The daring spirit of the young Kishkalwa led him into Kentucky, to hunt the buffalo, then abundant on the southern shore of the Ohio; but before he had succeeded in getting any game, he was discovered, and pursued, by a party of hostile Indians. Being alone, resistance would have been unavailing, and his only hope of escape was in flight. While running with great speed through the woods, a vestment which constituted his only article of clothing,[6] became entangled in the bushes, and was torn off; but as the pursuit was very hot, he had not time to recover it. Having reached the river opposite Fort Massac, he tied his gun to his head with his long hair, and swam across. Among the Shawanese it is highly disreputable in a warrior to throw away his arms or clothing, when in flight from an enemy, as the act indicates cowardice, and supplies a trophy to the pursuer. "None," they say, "but an Osage, will thus disencumber himself, that he may run the faster from his foes." When Kishkalwa, therefore, arrived in safety among his friends, who had seen his pursuers following him to the water's edge, they no sooner noticed the absence of the garment, than a number of jokes were passed at his expense. He explained the manner of the loss, and the urgency of the case, but his companions perceiving that he was annoyed, affected not to be satisfied, and deplored with mock gravity, that so fine a young man should be so destitute of activity as to be obliged to throw away his clothes in order to outrun his enemies.

As the accusation implied a want of courage, Kishkalwa said that he would show that he was no coward. Accordingly he set off, a few days afterwards, *alone*, in search of some enemy on whom he could prove his prowess. In the forest of Kentucky, late in the night, he discovered a fire, by which slept two Indians, who were easily distinguished as belonging to a hostile tribe. He approached near to them with a stealthy tread, then crouching like the panther, waited according to the custom of the Indian, until the first indications of the approaching dawn of day; when taking a deliberate aim he shot one of his foemen, and rushing upon the other, despatched him instantly with the tomahawk. This exploit gained him great credit; although it would seem characterised only by the lowest species of cunning, and to be destitute of all the higher attributes of warfare, it was, according to the notions of the savage, not only in exceedingly good taste, but a fine specimen of courage and military talent; for the Indian awards the highest honour to the success which is gained at the least expense, and considers every stratagem meritorious which leads to the desired result. Still his companions continued to jeer him upon the loss of a garment in the former adventure. Nettled by these jokes, and determined to retrieve his reputation, he secretly raised a party of four or five young men, whom he led on another expedition. They were successful, and returned with seventeen scalps.

Those who imagine that the apparent apathy of the Indian character indicates the entire absence of a propensity for mirth, will be surprised to learn that the remarkable success which attended the arms of Kishkalwa, failed to blunt the point of that unhappy jest, which had become a source of serious inconvenience to this great warrior. The pertinacity with which his companions continued to allude to this subject evinces, on their part, a strong perception of the ludicrous and a relish for coarse raillery, which balanced even their decided admiration of warlike qualities, while the extreme sensitiveness of Kishkalwa shows how highly the Indian prizes his honour. Successful as he had been, he conceived it necessary that the blood of his enemies should continue to flow, to blot out a stain affixed upon him in the mere wantonness of boisterous humour. He now took the field in a more imposing manner; and having raised a party of twenty-five warriors, went forth in pursuit of the enemies of his tribe, travelling only in the night, and lying in ambush during the day. They proceeded down the southern shore of the Ohio and Mississippi, until they reached the Iron Banks, near which they came upon an encampment of hostile Indians, consisting of one hundred and fifty men, women, and children. Kishkalwa halted his party, and having reconnoitred the enemy, directed the mode of attack. His men were so stationed as to surround the camp, and remained concealed until the dawn of day, when, at a signal given, the dreadful war-whoop was uttered by the whole in concert, and the assailants rushed in. The astonished enemy, believing themselves hemmed in by superior numbers, fled in every direction; thirty-three men were killed, and seventeen women and children taken prisoners. Kishkalwa returned in triumph with his captives and the scalps of the slain. On his arrival, many of the tribe who had lost their relatives in battle, clamorously demanded vengeance upon the prisoners; but Kishkalwa declared that not a drop of their blood should be spilt. He consented to the adoption of the captives into the families of those who had been killed in battle, and success-fully protected these unfortunates from injury. Among them was a beautiful young woman, whom Kishkalwa pre-sented to the chief, to be his wife, on condition that orders should be given, prohibiting the repetition of the jest which had so long galled his pride. The proclamation was accord-ingly made, in the manner in which all public acts are announced in the Indian villages, by a crier who passed about, declaring in a loud voice that Kishkalwa having proved that he could not have thrown away his clothes out of fear, no one was permitted thereafter to repeat or allude to that event. The reader will decide, whether this warrior's success or his judicious present to the chief contributed most to relieve him from so annoying a dilemma.

Whatever might have been the effect upon his private character, or social intercourse, these successful expeditions, in which not a single life had been lost, established the reputation of Kishkalwa, as a brave, skilful, and fortunate warrior, and he was soon after raised to the dignity of principal brave, or war chief. It may be proper to remark here, that, to this day, nothing so vexes the old chief, as an allusion to the story which distressed him so much in his youth, and that, although more than half a century has passed since the occurrence, it would not be safe in any, but an intimate friend, to mention it in his presence.

This chief took part in the great battle at Point Pleasant,[7] between the Virginians under General Lewis, and a large Indian force, consisting of Shawanese, Delawares, Mingoes, and other tribes ; but unwilling to be again embroiled with the Americans, towards whom he was well disposed, or to take any part in the contest which was about to be commenced between Great Britain and her colonies, he removed with a part of the tribe, called the Sawekela band,[8] to the south, in 1774, and settled among the Creeks. This band returned again to the shores of the Ohio, in 1790, but took no part in the war of 1794, nor in that of 1812, nor has this portion of the tribe ever been engaged against the Americans since the decisive battle of Point Pleasant.

During the last war, a part of the Sauk and Fox nations, who had been in the habit of trading with the British, were removed from Illinois to the interior of Missouri, at their own request, that they might not be within the reach of British influence. But restless by nature, unable to remain neutral in time of war, and receiving no encouragement to join the Americans, who from principle declined employing the savages, they took up the hatchet against us, and after committing some depredations, fled to Canada. The alarm created by these hostilities, in which the Weas and Piankeshaws were believed to participate, induced the Governor of the Missouri Territory to call out the militia, and to request the assistance of the Shawanoe and Delaware Indians. A party of sixty-six warriors was accordingly raised by Kishkalwa, and the other chiefs, and placed under the command of General Dodge.[9]

The Sauks and Foxes having fled before the arrival of

the militia, a small fort was surrounded in which it was
supposed that the Weas and Piankeshaws were concealed;
but in the morning it was found that they too had retreated.   They were pursued, overtaken, and made
prisoners.   The object of General Dodge, in their capture,
was to protect and not to injure them.   The inhabitants
of the frontier are at all times quick to take umbrage at
any supposed hostility on the part of the Indians, against
whom they have long been accustomed to entertain a
mingled feeling of fear and hatred; and believing that the
party now in their power had been equally as guilty as the
Sauks and Foxes, the militia were excited to such a state
of indignation, that they could with difficulty be restrained
from the perpetration of what they supposed to be a just
revenge.   General Dodge, with a decision that did him
honour as a man and a soldier, immediately placed the
captives under the protection of a disciplined volunteer
company from St Louis, and of the Indians under Kishkalwa.   This resolute conduct had the desired effect;
and no further molestation was offered to the unfortunate
prisoners, who were trembling with dread.   We have the
testimony of a gentleman who was himself a volunteer in
this expedition, that a finer set of men was seldom seen
than the band of Shawanese and Delawares to which this
anecdote has reference, and that their whole conduct
during this campaign was most orderly, decorous, and
proper.

Disappointed in the desired objects of their vengeance,
the militia set fire to the fort which had been abandoned
by the Weas and Piankeshaws, and gave vent to the
wantonness of their excited feelings by shooting a few
dogs of the Indians that lingered about the premises.   One
of these faithful creatures was caught by a soldier, who so
far forgot himself in the fury of the moment, as to throw

KISH-KAL-WA
A Shawnee Chief

the animal into the fire, from which it escaped, howling
with pain. Some of the bystanders laughed; but Kishkalwa, perceiving that an Indian boy joined in the merri-
ment, instantly checked him, and explained in a few words
the impropriety of making sport of the miseries of a
helpless brute.

The last military adventure in which Kishkalwa
engaged, was in a war undertaken by the Cherokees,
Delawares, and Shawanese, against the Osages, in 1818.
In a battle which was fought, and which resulted in the
defeat of the Osages, this chief is represented as having
displayed his usual bravery and prudence, although he
must then have been burthened by the weight of upwards
of eighty years. In attacking their enemies, it is customary
with the Osages to rush to the onset with great impetuosity,
uttering the savage yell with deafening concert, and
endeavouring to win the battle by the terrors attending
the first blow; but failing in this object they usually
abandon the contest. All the Indian tribes, indeed, act
upon this system, to a greater or less extent, seeking
victory by cunning rather than force, and avoiding the
hazard of a battle which must be contested upon equal
terms. Kishkalwa, aware of this trait in the character of
his race, and knowing that the Osages pursued this mode
of warfare more invariably than his own followers, exhorted
them to stand firmly, and resist the first attack; "Do not
heed their shouts," said he; "they are but the yells of
cowardly wolves, who, as soon as they come near enough
to look you in the eye, will flee; while if you turn your
backs on them, they will devour you." This counsel
evinced the sagacity of one who had observed human
nature, and could adapt his own measures to the circumstances in which he was placed. The result verified his
prediction. The Osages, twice as numerous as the party

of Kishkalwa, rushed to the attack with their usual impetuosity, and with loud shouts; but failing in making an impression in the first onset, recoiled before the steady firmness of their opponents, and fled in confusion, suffering great loss in killed and prisoners.

Kishkalwa visited Washington in 1825, as one of a delegation of chiefs, accompanied by Colonel Menard,[10] a highly respectable agent of the Indian Department, to whom we are indebted for the details included in the foregoing biographical sketch.

We have said that this chief was the brother of Black Hoof; but we are not certain that they might not have been cousins-german, as the term *brother* is applied among the Indians to this degree of relationship.

NOTES

1. In Volume I. of the folio edition of 1838 the accompanying portrait of "Kish-kallo-wa" is accredited to King. It does not appear, however, in Rhees's *Catalogue of Indian Paintings belonging to the Government Collection* (1859), and no trace of the original has been found. The Inman copy, in the Peabody Museum (original number, 14; museum number, 28. 189), bears the information that it is after King. Kishkalwa was a signer of the treaty with the Shawnee held at St Louis, Missouri, November 7, 1825, in which year he also visited Washington, when, no doubt, his portrait was painted.

2. The Shawanoe, or Shawanese, now better known as the Shawnee, are a tribe of the Algonquian family. Their remnant reside in Oklahoma, where they number about 800. See note 8.

3. This is Catahecassa, whose biography appears on page 235 of this volume.

4. Near the present Metropolis City, Massac County, Illinois. For details, consult Coues, *Expeditions of Zebulon Montgomery Pike*, II., 656-657, note, 1895.

5. This has led to the popular belief that the name Kentucky bears the same meaning; on the contrary, the word signifies "place of coonti," according to information furnished Mr J. N. B. Hewitt. *Coonti* is a cycadaceous plant (*Zamia integrifolia*), or the breadstuff obtained from it.

6. His breech-cloth, no doubt.

7. At the mouth of the Great Kanawha, in the present West Virginia, October 10, 1774. The leader of the Shawnee on this occasion was Cornstalk, and the battle has been regarded as the greatest that had taken place between the Indians and the colonists up to that time. Gen. Andrew Lewis (1720-1781) is the officer alluded to.

8. This band, properly called Hathawekela, formed the principal division of the Shawnee. With others they removed to Missouri about 1793, thence into Arkansas, and, about 1832, to Texas, where they settled on Sabine River, until driven out by the Texas Government. The Hathawekela form part of the so-called "Absentee Shawnees," because they were absent from the more recent treaties with the rest of the tribe.

9. Major (afterward General) Henry Dodge (1782-1867), a noted Indian fighter, for whose services Congress voted a sword. President Jackson appointed him Governor of Wisconsin Territory and Superintendent of Indian Affairs in 1836, which office he held until 1841, when he was elected delegate to Congress, serving two terms. In 1846 he again served as Governor of Wisconsin; and, after its admission to the Union, was one of its first senators, serving from 1846 until 1857.

10. Pierre Menard, a sub-Indian agent, who witnessed the Shawnee treaty of 1825, above referred to.

MOHONGO

(AN OSAGE WOMAN)

OF the early life of this female we know nothing; and, perhaps, little could be gathered that would be worthy of record. She is interesting on account of the dignity and beauty of her countenance, and the singular nature of her adventures since her marriage. She was one of a party of seven of her tribe, who were decoyed from the borders of Missouri by an adventurer whose intention was to exhibit them in Europe, for the purpose of gain. He was a Frenchman, and was assisted in his design by a half-breed Indian, who acted as interpreter between him and the deluded victims of his mercenary deception. The Indians were allured from home by the assurance that curiosity and respect for the Indian character would make them so welcome in Europe, that they would be received with distinguished marks of respect, and loaded with valuable presents. It is not probable that they understood that they were to be shown for money, or that they had any knowledge of the nature of such exhibitions; but it is obvious that their own views were mercenary, and that they were incited to travel by the alleged value of the presents which would probably be made them.

Whether any other arguments were used to induce these untutored savages to embark in an enterprise so foreign from their timid and reserved habits, we have been

unable to discover.   It is only known that the individual
who seduced them from their native plains assumed the
character and dress of an American officer, and by this
deception gained their confidence; and it is more than
probable that, as they only knew him under this disguise,
they were deceived into the belief that he was acting under
the sanction of the Government.   Whatever may have been
the pretence, it was a cruel deception; and it would be
curious to know what were the feelings and the reflections
of those wild savages, accustomed to roam uncontrolled
through the deep forests, and over the boundless plains,
when they found themselves among the habitations of an
enlightened people, the objects of intense curiosity, and
the prisoners of a mercenary keeper.   The delusion under
which they commenced their journey was probably not
dispelled previous to their arrival at New York; those
with whom they met on the way supposed them to be
proceeding to Washington, on a visit to the President;
and as the Indians were ignorant of our language, it is not
surprising that this singular device escaped detection.

At New York the party embarked for Europe.   They
visited Holland, Germany, and some other parts of the
continent, and at last came to the French metropolis.
Here the imposture was detected.   The pretended
American officer had been at Paris before; he was
recognised by his creditors, stripped of his borrowed
character, and thrown into prison; while the wandering
savages were so fortunate as to find a protector in
Lafayette, whose affection for America was so great that
the native of our land, even though an illiterate Indian,
was ever sure of a welcome under his hospitable roof.
He supplied them with money, and caused arrangements
to be made for their passage to the United States.   During
the voyage they were attacked by the smallpox, and three

of them died. Among the victims was the husband of
Mohongo, who was now left to carry back to her people,
with the varied tale of her adventures, the bitter story of
her bereavement.

The party landed at Norfolk, in Virginia, whence they
were sent to Washington City. They were kindly received
at the seat of Government, where directions were given
for their hospitable entertainment during their stay, and
for their safe conveyance to the Osage villages. They
reached their forest home in safety, and have done us the
justice to acknowledge that, although they suffered much
from the treachery of one of our race, who allured them
from the wigwams of their tribe, they were indebted to
the white man for many acts of kindness and sympathy
during their novel and adventurous journey. They profess
to have been on the whole gratified with the expedition.

The likeness which we have copied was taken at
Washington, by order of the War Department, while
Mohongo remained in that city. It is a faithful and
striking representation of the original; and the contemplation of it, to one acquainted with the Indian character,
gives rise to a train of thought which it may be well to
notice. The ordinary expression of the countenance of
the Indian woman is subdued and unmeaning; that of
Mohongo is lighted up with intelligence. It is joyous as
well as reflective. It is possible that this difference may
be accidental; and that Mohongo adventured upon her
perilous journey *in consequence* of possessing a mind of
more than common vigour, or a buoyancy of spirit, not
usual among her tribe. But we incline to a different
theory. The Indian woman is rather the servant than the
companion of man. She is a favourite and confidential
servant, who is treated with kindness, but who is still an
inferior. The life of the untamed savage affords little

range for the powers of reflection ; his train of thought is neither varied nor extensive ; and as the females are confined to domestic duties, neither meddling in public affairs, nor mingling in that which we would call society, the exercise of their mental powers must be extremely limited. The Indian village affords but few diversions, and still fewer of the operations of industry, of business, or of ingenuity. The mind of the warrior is bent on war, or on the chase, while the almost undivided attention of the female is devoted to the procuring and preparation of food. In the moments of leisure, when the eye would roam abroad, and the mind unbend itself in the play of its powers of observation, a monotonous scenery is ever present. They have their mountains and plains, their woods and rivers, unchanged from year to year ; and the blue sky above them subjected only to the varieties of storm and sunshine. Is it strange that the countenance of the Indian woman should be vacant, and her demeanour subdued ?

Mohongo travelled in company with her husband. Constantly in his society, sharing with him the perils, the vicissitudes, and the emotions incident to the novel scenes into which they were thrown, and released from the drudgery of menial occupation, she must have risen to something like the station of an equal. Perhaps when circumstances of embarrassment, or perplexing objects of curiosity, were presented, the superior tact and flexibility of the female mind became apparent, and her companions learned to place a higher estimation upon her character than is usually awarded by the Indian to the weaker sex. Escaped from servile labour, she had leisure to think. New objects were continually placed before her eye ; admiration and curiosity were often awakened in her mind ; its latent faculties were excited, and that beautiful system of association which forms the train of rational thought became connected and developed.   Mohongo was no longer the drudge of a savage hunter, but his friend.   Such are the inferences which seem to be fairly deducible, when contrasting the agreeable expression of this countenance with the stolid lineaments of other females of the same race.   If our theory be correct, the example before us affords a significant and beautiful illustration of the beneficent effects of civilisation upon the human mind.

NOTE

The name of this Osage woman, as interpreted by Miss Alice C. Fletcher, is possibly the Osage form of the Omaha *Mihunga*, signifying " woman leader, or chief."   Fortunately, we are able to add some interesting data regarding this woman and her companions, from contemporary brochures, which bear the following titles :—

Six indiens rouges de la tribu des grands Osages, arrivés du Missouri au Havre, le 27 Juillet 1827, sur la navire Américain New-England, cap. Hunt.   Troisième   Edition   [etc.].   Paris: Delaunay,   Libraire   [etc.], 1827. (8°, 36 pp., 1 pl.)

Histoire de la tribu des Osages, peuplade sauvage de l'Amérique Septentrionale, dans l'état du Missouri, l'un des États-Unis d'Amérique ; écrite d'après les six Osage actuellement à Paris.   Par P[aul] V[issier], [etc.]. Paris : Chez Charles Béchet, Libraire [etc.], 1827.   (8°, 92 pp.)

It is gathered from these accounts that, accompanied by David Delaunay, a native of France, who, it is said, had been a colonel in the service of the United States, and who had lived in St Louis for twenty-five years, together with M. Tesson, a resident of St Louis, and M. Loise, their interpreter, the party left St Louis in 1827, and proceeded down the Mississippi, on the steamboat *Commerce*, to New Orleans.   (One David Delaunay was an associate-justice in the Court of Quarter Sessions at St Louis, according to Thwaites, *Original Journals of Lewis and Clark*, Vol. I., 22, 1904.)   The Indian members of the party were Kihegashugah, Kishagashugah, or Little Chief, his wife Mohongo or Myhangah, and his cousin Grétomih ; Washingsabba, Washingasbha, or   Black   Spirit, Marcharthitahtoongah,   or   the   Orator,   and   Minkchatahooh.   The plate in the brochure first mentioned consists of a portrait group of the six Osages.   Sailing from New Orleans, the party arrived at Havre, July 27, 1827, and later went to Paris, everywhere being the objects of marked attention and curiosity.   They were

MO-HON-GO
An Osage Woman

showered with gifts, entertained by people of prominence, and on August 21 were received at St Cloud by Charles X. It is said that Kihegashugah was inspired to visit France, because an ancestor had been there during the reign of Louis XIV. In addition to the above writings, see Miss Fletcher's note in *American Anthropologist*, II., 395, New York, 1900, and David I. Bushnell, jr., in the same journal, X., 6, 1908. As Mohongo's infant is not mentioned in the accounts noted, it is probable that it was born before the return of the Indians to America, thus constituting the seventh member of the party. In the Rhees *Catalogue of the Indian Gallery*, Mohongo's portrait by King is numbered 110, and was painted in 1830, or the third year after the party left their Western home. A portrait of "Cah-he-ga-shín-ga, the Little Chief" (apparently the same name as Kihegashugah), was painted by George Catlin in 1834.

Osage, the name of the tribe to which these Indians belonged, is the French trader's corruption of *Wa-zhahez*, their designation for themselves. They belong to the Siouan family, and, when first known to history, lived in the present Missouri, whence they moved into Kansas, and subsequently were assigned a reservation in Oklahoma, where they numbered 1994 in 1906. They are credited with a fund of more than $8,300,000, which, together with pasturage leases, yields them an annual income of about $550,000. They thus constitute one of the wealthiest communities in the world.

SHINGABA W'OSSIN

(OR, IMAGE STONE)

SHINGABA W'OSSIN, or *Image Stone*,[1] was a Chippeway, and first chief of his band. In summer he lived on the banks of the St Mary's, at the outlet of Lake Superior—in winter he retired with his band to his hunting grounds. Fish was his food in summer; in winter he subsisted on the carcasses of animals, whose fur was the great object of his winter's toils, it being the medium of exchange with the traders for blankets, strouds, calico, ammunition, vermilion, etc., and such articles of necessity or of ornament as he and his people required.

Shingaba W'Ossin was one of the most influential men in the Chippeway nation. He was deservedly esteemed, not only by the Indians, but by the whites also, for his good sense, and respectful and conciliating deportment. In his person he was tall, well-proportioned, and of a commanding and dignified aspect. In council he was remarkable for a deliberate and thoughtful manner; in social intercourse no less so for his cheerfulness. He was disposed to be familiar, yet never descended to frivolity. He was of the totem of the Crane, the ancient badge of the chiefs of this once powerful band.[2]

War is the chief glory of the Indian. He who dissuades from war is usually regarded as a coward; but Shingaba W'Ossin was the uniform advocate of peace, yet his

50

bravery was never questioned. Perhaps his exemption
from the imputation of cowardice was owing to his having,
when but a youth, joined several war parties against the
Sioux, those natural and implacable enemies of his people,
to reach whom he had to travel at least five hundred
miles. He is said to have distinguished himself at the
great battle on the St Croix, which terminated the feud
between the Chippeways and the Foxes. In that battle
he fought under the northern Alaric, *Waab-Ojeeg*.

We hope to be excused for introducing, in this place,
some remarks upon this extraordinary chieftain, especially
as the few incidents we shall use are from our own work,
published in 1827.[3]

We made our voyage up Lake Superior in 1826. So
late as that, the name of Waab-Ojeeg was never spoken
but in connection with some tradition exemplifying his
great powers as a chief and warrior. He was a man of
discretion, and far in advance of his people in those
energies of the mind which command respect, wherever
and in whomsoever they are found. He was, like Pontiac
and Tecumthe, exceedingly jealous of the white man.
This jealousy was manifested when the hand of his
daughter, *O-shaw-ous-go-day-way-gua*, was solicited by
Mr Johnson, the accomplished Irish gentleman, who
resided so many years after at the Sault de St Mary,[4] and
who was not better known for his intelligence and polished
manners than for his hospitality. He lived long enough
to merit and receive the appellation of *Patriarch of the
Sault*. This gentleman was a native of Dublin or Belfast,
in Ireland. In the course of his travels he arrived at
Montreal, when he determined to ascend the great chain
of lakes to the head waters of Lake Superior. On
arriving at Michael's Island he heard of Waab-Ojeeg,
whose village lay across the strait which divides the island

from the main. He made him a visit. Being well received he remained some time, formed an attachment to his daughter, and solicited permission to marry her. Waab-Ojeeg replied to his request thus :—"White man, I have noticed your behaviour. It has been correct. But, white man, *your colour is deceitful.* Of you, may I expect better things? You say you are going to return to Montreal—go; and if you return I shall be satisfied of your sincerity, and will give you my daughter." Mr Johnson, being honest in his professions, went to Montreal and returned, when the chief fulfilled his promise. The amiable, excellent, and accomplished Mrs Schoolcraft, wife of Henry R. Schoolcraft, Esq., so favourably known as a tourist and mineralogist, and a family of as interesting children as we met with in our travels, are the fruits of this marriage.[5]

Waab-Ojeeg used to stimulate his warriors to battle by singing a favourite war song. Doubtless Shingaba W'Ossin, on the memorable occasion referred to, felt the stirring influence of this song. We received the following translation of it from Mr Johnson, to whom the Chippeway language was quite familiar :—

"On that day when our heroes lay low, lay low,
  On that day when our heroes lay low ;
  I fought by their side, and thought ere I died,
  Just vengeance to take on the foe, the foe,
  Just vengeance to take on the foe.

"On that day when our chieftains lay dead, lay dead,
  On that day when our chieftains lay dead ;
  I fought hand to hand, at the head of my band,
  And here on my breast have I bled, have I bled,
  And here on my breast have I bled.

"Our chiefs shall return no more, no more,
  Our chiefs shall return no more ;

And their brothers in war, who can't show scar for scar,
Like women their fates shall deplore, deplore,
Like women their fates shall deplore.

" Fine winters in hunting we'll spend, we'll spend,
Fine winters in hunting we'll spend ;
Then our youth grown to men, to the war lead again,
And our days like our fathers we'll end, we'll end,
And our days like our fathers we'll end." [6]

It is not surprising that, under such a leader, Shingaba W'Ossin should acquire fame sufficient to make good his claims to bravery in after life. Thus fortified at the point where the Indian no less than the white man is peculiarly sensitive, he could counsel his band to cultivate peace, and attend to the more important concerns of hunting, without the danger of losing his influence over them. " If my hunters," he would say, "will not take the game, but will leave the chase and join the war parties, our women and children must suffer. If the game is not trapped, where will be our packs of furs ? And if we have no furs, how shall we get blankets ? Then when winter comes again we shall perish ! It is time enough to fight when the war drum sounds near you—when your enemies approach—then it is I shall expect to see you painted for war, and to hear your whoops resound in the mountains ; and then you will see me at your head with my arm bared—

'Just vengeance to take on the foe.'"

Besides thus wisely counselling his people to live in peace, and follow the chase, he gave much of his time to attending the public councils convened under the authority of our Government. These councils, in those regions especially, had for their principal object the adjustment of boundaries between the tribes—encroachments upon each

other's territory being a principal cause of war.   Councils
of pacification were held in 1825 at Prairie du Chien, on
the Upper Mississippi; at the Fond du Lac Superior in
1826; and at the Butte des Morts, on the Fox River of
Lake Michigan, in 1827.   Shingaba W'Ossin attended
each of these councils, and signed the treaties.[7]   We were
present at the two last, and witnessed the good conduct
and extraordinary influence of the subject of this brief
memoir.   At the council of Fond du Lac, Shingaba
W'Ossin was the first to respond to the commissioners.
He spoke as follows :—

"*My relations*—Our fathers have spoken to us about
the line made at the Prairie.   With this I and my band
are satisfied.   You who live on the line are most interested.   To you I leave the subject.   The line was left
unfinished last summer, but will be finished this.

"*My relations*—The land to be provided for my half-
breeds I will select.   I leave it to you to provide your
reserves for your own.

"*My friends*—Our fathers have come here to establish
a school at the Sault.   Our great father over the hills
(meaning the President of the United States) has said
this would be well.   I am willing.   It may be a good
thing for those who wish to send their children.

"*My brothers*—Our fathers have not come here to speak
hard words to us.   Do not think so.   They have brought
us bread to eat, clothing to wear, and tobacco to smoke.

"*My brothers*—Take notice.   Our great father has been
at much trouble to make us live as one family, and to make
our path clear.   The morning was cloudy.   The Great
Spirit has scattered those clouds.   So have our difficulties
passed away.

"*My friends*—Our fathers have come here to embrace
their children.   Listen to what they say.   It will be good

for you. If you have any copper on your lands, I advise you to sell it. It is of no use to us. They can make articles out of it for our use. If anyone has any knowledge on this subject, I ask him to bring it to light.

"*My brothers*—Let us determine soon. We, as well as our fathers, are anxious to go home." [8]

This talk was taken down as it was interpreted, and in the words of the interpreter. A good deal of the speaker's style is no doubt lost. Critics tell us that Pope, in his admirable translation of Homer, has failed to show the father of poetry to his readers in his original costume. It is not surprising, therefore, that an Indian interpreter should make the Indian talk like a white man. There is enough in this address of the old chief, however, to show that he was a man of sense and discretion. A few explanatory remarks may make this more apparent. The "line," to which he referred, was the proposed boundary between the Sioux and Chippeways. He and his band, living five hundred miles from it, were not so immediately interested as were those bands who bordered it. Hence, although he and his band were satisfied with it, he referred it to his "relations," who were more immediately concerned, and whose peace and lives depended upon its suitable and harmonious adjustment, to decide for themselves.

The next subject was one of great importance to the whole Chippeway nation. It had for some time engaged the attention of Shingaba W'Ossin; and the proposition originated with him. It was, that reservations of land should be laid off in the most genial and productive situations, and assigned to the half-breeds, to be cultivated by them. The wisdom and humanity of the measure will appear when the reader is informed that almost the whole country of the Chippeways is sterile, and that scarcely any vegetables do or can grow in it. The soil is cold and

barren; and winter pervades so much of the year, that if
seed of any kind be sown, except in the most favourable
situations, the frosts overtake and destroy the hoped for
increase before it arrives at maturity.   The Chippeways
suffer greatly by reason of their climate, and when, from
any cause, they fail in their hunts, many of them perish
with cold and of starvation.   The frequent recurrence of
this calamity led Shingaba W'Ossin to consider how
it might be provided against.   He saw the military
gardens at the Sault, and those of Mr Johnson, producing,
by the culture that was bestowed upon them, large crops
of potatoes and other roots.   It occurred to him, that if
the half-breeds of his nation could be induced to profit by
such examples, they might husband away these products
of the earth, and when the dreaded famine should threaten
them, they could retire to the neighbourhood of those
provisions and be preserved.   In pursuance of his
earnest entreaties, and seeing in the plan everything to
recommend it, and nothing to oppose it, the commissioners
inserted an article in the treaty making the provision, and
accompanied it with a schedule of the names of those
half-breeds that were given in by the chiefs of the various
bands, and who it was intended should engage in this new
employment.   The persons to whom it was proposed to
make these grants were prohibited the privilege of conveying the same, without the permission of the President
of the United States.

This article in the treaty was not ratified by the
Senate.   So the old chief was saved the trouble of
selecting situations for the half breeds of his band; as
were his "relations," to whom he left it to "provide
reserves" for theirs.[9]

Shingaba W'Ossin was the patron of the school that
has since been established at the Sault for the education

SHIN-GA-BA W'OSSIN, *or* IMAGE STONE
A Chippeway Chief

of Indian children, and advised that the thousand dollar
annuity, the only annuity the tribe receives, should be
appropriated for its support.   It was accordingly done.
He was not an advocate for school knowledge in his own
family, but remarked that some of the Chippeways might
profit by it.   In this he gave proof of his disinterestedness.

The largest mass of virgin copper of which we
have any knowledge, is in the Chippeway country.   It is
supposed to weigh from twenty-five hundred to three
thousand pounds.   The existence of this mass, and the
fact that pieces of copper were brought in by the Indians
who assembled from many parts of their country to attend
the council, induced the belief that the country abounded
in this metal.   The commissioners endeavoured to obtain
all the knowledge they could on this subject, and their
inquiries were responded to by Shingaba W'Ossin in the
manner as indicated in his talk.

It may not be out of place to remark, that this huge
specimen of virgin copper lies about thirty-five miles
above the mouth of the Ontanagon of Lake Superior;
and on the west bank of that river, a few paces only
above low-water mark.   An intelligent gentleman, who
accompanied a party sent by the commissioners from the
Fond du Lac for the purpose of disengaging this specimen
of copper from its bed, and transporting it down the lakes
to the Erie Canal, and thence to New York and Washington, says :—" It consists of pure copper, ramified in every
direction through a mass of stone (mostly serpentine,
intermixed with calcareous spar), in veins of one to three
inches in diameter; and in some parts exhibiting masses
of pure metal of one hundred pounds weight."

It was found impossible, owing to "the channel of the
river being intercepted by ridges of sandstone, forming

three cataracts, with a descent in all of about seventy feet," to remove this great natural curiosity. Specimens were broken from it, some of which we ascertained were nearly as pure as a silver dollar, losing in fusion a residuum of only one part in twenty-seven. Evidences were disclosed, in prying this rock of copper from its position, confirming the history of the past, which records the efforts of companies to extract wealth from the mines that were supposed to abound there. These evidences consisted in chisels, axes, and various implements which are used in mining. It is highly probable that this copper rock may have once been of larger dimensions—since those who worked at it no doubt took away specimens, as have all persons who have since visited.[11]

It was in reference to the wish of the commissioners to obtain every possible information respecting the existence of copper in the Chippeway country, that Shingaba W'Ossin was induced to say—"If anyone has any knowledge on this subject, I ask him to bring it to light." In doing this, as will be seen in the sequel, he placed himself above the *superstitions* of his people, who regard this mass of copper as a *manitou*.

Being weatherbound at the portage of Point Kewewena, we had an opportunity of observing the habits of Shingaba W'Ossin, and occasionally to hear him talk. During this time the old chief made frequent visits to our tent, always in company with a young Indian who attended him. At this time he was a good deal concerned about a blindness which threatened him. He spoke principally of this, but never without saying something in favour of his attendant. Among other things, he said— "Father, I have not the eyes I once had. I am now old. I think soon this great world will be hid from me. But the Great Spirit is good. I want you, father, to hear me.

This young man is eyes to me, and hands too. Will you not be good to him?" At each visit, however, inflamed as were the old chief's eyes, he would, like other Indians, be most grateful for a little whisky; and like them too, when he tasted a little, he wanted more. It is impossible to conceive the ratio with which their wants increase, after a first taste. The effects are maddening. Often, to enjoy a repetition of the beverage, have instances occurred in which life itself has been taken, when it stood between the Indian and this cherished object of his delight. Shingaba W'Ossin would indulge in the use of this destructive beverage occasionally; but even when most under its influence he was harmless—so generally had the kindly feelings taken possession of him. On the occasion referred to, we found him to be gentle, obliging, and free from all asperities of manner or temper. He was then in his sixty-third year, and used to assist in the management of his canoe, and in all the business connected with the prosecution of his voyage. He kept company with us to the Fond du Lac; not always, however, encamping where we did. The old man and his party partook of our refreshments; and when he would meet with any of his people who had been taking fish, he never failed to procure some, and always divided his good luck with us—appearing happy to have something to offer in return for our attentions to him.

Shingaba W'Ossin's father was named *Maid-O-Saligee*. He was the chief and chronicler of his tribe. With him died much of their traditionary information. He was also noted for the tales which he related for the amusement of the young. But he was a voluptuary. He married four wives, three of whom were sisters. By these wives he had twenty children. Each of the male children, in time, deemed himself a legitimate chief, and attached to himself some followers. Political divisions were the consequence.

The harmony of the band was thus destroyed, and the posterity of the ancient chief scattered along the waters of the St Mary's.

The superior intellect of Shingaba W'Ossin, in these times of contention for the supremacy, became manifest. He secured the respect and confidence of his band, and was at last acknowledged as the *nittum*,[12] or first man. His band became more and more attached to him, until on all hands the choice was admitted to be well ordered, and that he upon whom it had fallen merited the distinction. Having secured the general confidence, he counselled his charge in all their trials, and enabled them to overcome many difficulties, whilst by his kindness and general benevolence of character, he made himself beloved. He was on all occasions the organ for expressing the wants and wishes of his people, and through him also they received both presents and advice from the officers and agents of our Government.

During the late war, in 1813, Shingaba W'Ossin went to York, in Canada, and had an interview with Proctor and Tecumthe.[13] Nothing is known of the object or result of this interview, except that one of his brothers joined the British, and fought and fell in the battle of the Thames, in Upper Canada. His death was deeply lamented by Shingaba W'Ossin—so much so as to induce the belief that he counselled, or at least acquiesced in, his joining the British standard.[14]

NOTES

1. The name is strictly *Shingabäwasin*, signifying "Reclining human figure of a stone," according to information kindly furnished by Dr William Jones, a leading authority on the central Algonquian languages, of which Chippeway, or Ojibwa, is one. These "image stones," or *shingaba-wossins*, are described and illustrated by Schoolcraft, *Western Scenes and Reminiscences*, Auburn, 1853, pp. 291-293.

2. That is, he was a member of the Ojeejok or Crane gens.

3. The reference is to McKenney's *Sketches of a Tour to the Lakes*, Baltimore, 1827. See the Introduction to the present work.

4. Sault de Sainte Marie, in the present Chippeway county, northern peninsula of Michigan.

5. Schoolcraft's wife was Jane Johnston (not Johnson), an accomplished woman, who had been educated in Europe. See Schoolcraft's *Personal Memoirs*, Philadelphia, 1851, p. xl., and McKenney's *Tour*, op. cit.

6. From McKenney's *Tour*, pp. 189-190.

7. "Shingaubaywassin" signed also the treaty of Sault de Sainte Marie, concluded June 16, 1820. At the "Prairie des Chiens" treaty of August 19, 1825, his name is signed "Shinguaba × W'Ossin, 1st chief of the Chippeway nation, Sault St Marie."

8. From McKenney's *Tour*, p. 459. Regarding the treaty, see the Introduction.

9. For the Fond du Lac treaty, as finally ratified (February 7, 1827), see *Treaties between the United States and the Several Indian Tribes, from 1778 to 1837*, Washington, 1837, p. 396.

10. This huge copper bowlder is now in the National Museum at Washington. For an account of its history, see Charles Moore, "The Ontonagon Copper Bowlder in the U. S. National Museum," *National Museum Report for* 1895, Washington, 1897.

11. There is no doubt that the copper deposits of the Lake Superior region were worked by the Indians in prehistoric times, and that they formed the chief source of supply to the Indians of the central part of the United States, who made extensive use of this metal for implements and ornaments.

12. *Nitam*, "first," "the first one."—Baraga, *Dictionary of the Otchipwe Language*, 1878. See note 2, 346.

13. Brigadier-General Henry A. Proctor, in command of the British forces at the battle of the Thames, October 5, 1813, in which Tecumthe, or Tecumseh, the famous Shawnee, was killed.

14. The accompanying portrait of this chief was painted originally by J. O. Lewis during the period of the Treaty of Fond du Lac in 1826. It forms the frontispiece of McKenney's *Sketches of a Tour to the Lakes*. Another portrait by the same artist, and quite different in dress and pose, appears in Lewis's *Port-folio*, 1835. In Rhees's *Catalogue* of the Government collection, the name is given as "Shing-yaw-ba-wus-sen, The Figured Stone," but neither the artist nor the date is given. The copy in the Indian Gallery was probably by King. The copy in the Peabody Museum (original number, 57; museum number, 28. 190) furnishes no information respecting either the original artist or the copyist, but there is little doubt that the copy was made by Inman.

PUSHMATAHA

(A CHOCTAW WARRIOR)

THIS individual[1] was a distinguished warrior of the Choctaw nation,[2] and a fair specimen of the talents and propensities of the modern Indian. It will have been noticed, by those who have paid attention to Indian history, that the savage character is always seen in a modified aspect among those of the tribes who reside in juxtaposition with the whites. We are not prepared to say that it is either elevated or softened by this relation; but it is certainly changed. The strong hereditary bias of the wild and untamed rover of the forest remains in prominent development, while some of the arts, and many of the vices of the civilised man, are engrafted upon them. The Choctaws have had their principal residence in that part of the country east of the Mississippi River which now forms the State of Mississippi, and have had intercourse with the European race from the time of the discovery of that region by the French, nearly two centuries ago. In 1820, that tribe was supposed to consist of a population of twenty-five thousand souls. They have always maintained friendly relations with the American people, and have permitted our missionaries to reside among them; some of them have addicted themselves to agriculture, and a few of their females have intermarried with the white traders.

Pushmataha was born about the year 1764, and at the age of twenty was a captain, or a war chief, and a great hunter. In the latter occupation he often passed to the western side of the Mississippi, to hunt the buffalo, upon the wide plains lying towards our southern frontier. On one occasion, while hunting on the Red River with a party of Choctaws, he was attacked by a number of Indians of a tribe called the Callageheahs,[3] near the Spanish line, and totally defeated. He made his own escape, alone, to a Spanish settlement, where he arrived nearly starved; having, while on the way given a little horse, that he found grazing on the plains, for a single fish. He remained with the Spaniards five years, employing himself as a hunter, brooding over the plans of vengeance which he afterwards executed, and probably collecting the information necessary to the success of his scheme. Wandering back to the Choctaw country, alone, he came by stealth, in the night, to a little village of the enemies by whom he had been defeated, suddenly rushed in upon them, killed seven of the inhabitants, and set fire to the lodges, which were entirely consumed before the surviving occupants recovered from their alarm.

After this feat he remained in his own nation about six years, increasing his reputation as a hunter, and engaging occasionally in the affairs of the tribe. He then raised a party of his own friends, and led them to seek a further revenge for the defeat which still rankled in his bosom. Again he surprised one of their towns upon Red River, and killed two or three of their warriors without any loss on his own side. But engaging in an extensive hunt, his absence from home was protracted to the term of eight months. Resting from this expedition but ten days, he prevailed on another party of Choctaw warriors to follow his adventurous steps in a new enterprise against

the same enemy, and was again victorious, bringing home
six of the scalps of his foes without losing a man. On
this occasion he was absent seven or eight months. In
one year afterwards he raised a new party, led them
against the foe whom he had so often stricken, and was
once more successful.[4]

Some time before the war of 1812, a party of Creek
Indians, who had been engaged in a hunting expedition,
came to the Choctaw country, and burned the house of
Pushmataha, who was in the neighbourhood intently
occupied in playing ball, a game at which he was very
expert. He was too great a man to submit to such an
injury, and, as usual, immediate retaliation ensued. He
led a party of Choctaws into the Creek country, killed
several of that nation, and committed as great destruction
of their property as was practicable in his rapid march;
and he continued from time to time, until the breaking
out of the war between the United States and Great
Britain, to prosecute the hostilities growing out of this
feud with relentless vigour; assailing the Creeks frequently
with small parties, by surprise, and committing indis-
criminate devastation upon the property or people of that
tribe. Such are the quarrels of great men; and such
have been the border wars of rude nations from the
earliest times.

In the war that succeeded, he was always the first to
lead a party against the British or their Indian allies; and
he did much injury to the Creeks and Seminoles during
that contest. His military prowess and success gained
for him the honorary title which he seems to have well
deserved; and he was usually called *General* Pushmataha.

This chief was not descended from any distinguished
family, but was raised to command, when a young man, in
consequence of his talents and prowess. He was always

poor, and when not engaged in war, followed the chase with ardour and success. He was brave and generous; kind to those who were necessitous, and hospitable to the stranger. The eagerness with which he sought to revenge himself upon his enemies, affords no evidence of ferocity of character; but is in strict conformity with the Indian code of honour, which sanctions such deeds as nobly meritorious.

It is curious to observe the singular mixture of great and mean qualities in the character of a barbarous people. The same man who is distinguished in war, and in the council, is often the subject of anecdotes which reflect little credit on his character in private life. We shall repeat the few incidents which have reached us, in the public and private history of Pushmataha.

He attended a council held in 1823 near the residence of Major Pitchlynn,[5] a wealthy trader among the Choctaws, and at a distance of eighty miles from his own habitation. The business was closed on the third of July, and on the following day, the anniversary of our independence, a dinner was given by Major Pitchlynn to Col. Ward, the agent of the Government of the United States, and the principal chiefs who were present. When the guests were about to depart, it was observed that General Pushmataha had no horse; and as he was getting to be too old to prosecute so long a journey on foot, the Government agent suggested to Mr Pitchlynn the propriety of presenting him a horse. This was readily agreed to, on the condition that the chief would promise not to exchange the horse for whisky; and the old warrior, mounted upon a fine young animal, went upon his way rejoicing. It was not long before he visited the Agency, on foot, and it was discovered that he had lost his horse in betting at ball-play. "But did you not promise Mr Pitchlynn," said the agent, "that you would

not sell his horse?" "I did so, in the presence of yourself
and many others," replied the chief; "but I did not
promise that I would not risk the horse on a game of
ball."

It is said that during the late war, General Pushmataha, having joined our Southern army with some of
his warriors, was arrested by the commanding general for
striking a soldier with his sword. When asked by the
commander why he had committed this act of violence,
he replied that the soldier had been rude to his wife, and
that he had only given him a blow or two with the side of
his sword to teach him better manners—"But if it had
been you, general, instead of a private soldier," continued
he, "I should have used the sharp edge of my sword in
defence of my wife, who has come so far to visit a great
warrior like myself."

At a time when a guard of eight or ten men was
kept at the Agency, one of the soldiers having become
intoxicated, was ordered to be confined; and as there was
no guard house, the temporary arrest was effected by
tying the offender. Pushmataha seeing the man in this
situation, inquired the cause, and on being informed,
exclaimed, "Is that all?" and immediately untied the unfortunate soldier, remarking coolly, "many good warriors
get drunk."

At a meeting of business at the Agency, at which
several American gentlemen, and some of the chief men
of the Choctaw nation were present, the conversation
turned upon the Indian custom of marrying a plurality of
wives. Pushmataha remarked that he had two wives,
and intended to have always the same number. Being
asked if he did not think the practice wrong, the chief
replied, "No; is it not right that every woman should be
married—and how can that be, when there are more

women than men, unless some men marry more than one ? When our Great Father the President caused the Indians to be counted last year, it was found that the women were most numerous, and if one man could have but one wife, some women would have no husband."

In 1824, this chief was at the City of Washington, as one of a deputation sent to visit the President, for the purpose of brightening the chain of friendship between the American people and the Choctaws. The venerable Lafayette, then upon his memorable and triumphal tour through the United States, was at the same metropolis, and the Choctaw chiefs came to pay him their respects. Several of them made speeches, and among the rest, Pushmataha addressed him in these words : "Nearly fifty snows have melted since you drew the sword as a companion of Washington. With him you fought the enemies of America. You mingled your blood with that of the enemy, and proved yourself a warrior. After you finished that war, you returned to your own country ; and now you are come back to revisit a land where you are honoured by a numerous and powerful people. You see everywhere the children of those by whose side you went to battle crowding around you, and shaking your hand as the hand of a father. We have heard these things told in our distant villages, and our hearts longed to see you. We have come, we have taken you by the hand, and are satisfied. This is the first time we have seen you ; it will probably be the last. We have no more to say. The earth will part us for ever."

The old warrior pronounced these words with an affecting solemnity of voice and manner. He seemed to feel a presentiment of the brevity of his own life. The concluding remark of his speech was prophetic. In a few days he was no more. He was taken sick at Washington, and died in a strange land.   When he found that his end was approaching, he called his companions around him, and desired them to raise him up, to bring his arms, and to decorate him with all his ornaments, that his death might be that of a man.   He was particularly anxious that his interment should be accompanied with military honours, and when a promise was kindly given that his wishes should be fulfilled, he became cheerful, and conversed with composure until the moment when he expired without a groan.   In conversation with his Indian friends shortly before his death, he said : "I shall die, but you will return to our brethren.   As you go along the paths, you will see the flowers, and hear the birds sing, but Pushmataha will see them and hear them no more.   When you shall come to your home, they will ask you, '*Where is Pushmataha?*' and you will say to them, '*He is no more.*' They will hear the tidings like the sound of the fall of a mighty oak in the stillness of the woods."

The only speech made by Pushmataha, on the occasion of his visit to Washington, was the following.   It was intended by him to be an opening address, which, had he lived, he would doubtless have followed by another more like himself.   We took it down as he spoke it.[6]   The person addressed was the Secretary of War.

"*Father*—I have been here some time.   I have not talked—have been sick.   You shall hear me talk to-day. I belong to another district.   You have no doubt heard of me—*I am Pushmataha.*

"*Father*—When in my own country, I often looked towards this Council House, and wanted to come here.   I am in trouble.   I will tell my distresses.   I feel like a small child, not half as high as its father, who comes up to look in his father's face, hanging in the bend of his arm, to tell him his troubles.   So, Father, I hang in the bend of your arm, and look in your face, and now hear me speak.

"*Father*—When I was in my own country, I heard there were men appointed to talk to us. I would not speak there; I chose to come here, and speak in this beloved house. I can boast, and say, and tell the truth that none of my fathers or grandfathers, nor any Choctaw, ever drew bows against the United States. They have always been friendly. We have held the hands of the United States so long, that our nails are long like birds' claws; and there is no danger of their slipping out.

"*Father*—I have come to speak. My nation has always listened to the applications of the white people. They have given of their country till it is very small. I repeat the same about the land east of the Tombigby. I came here when a young man to see my Father Jefferson. He told me if ever we got in trouble we must run and tell him. I am come. This is a friendly talk; it is like a man who meets another and says, How do you do? Another will talk further." [7]

The celebrated John Randolph, in a speech upon the floor of the Senate, alluded thus to the forest chieftain whose brief memoirs we have attempted to sketch: "Sir, in a late visit to the public graveyard,[8] my attention was arrested by the simple monument of the Choctaw Chief Pushmataha. He was, I have been told by those who knew him, one of nature's nobility; a man who would have adorned any society. He lies quietly by the side of our statesmen and high magistrates in the region—for there is one such—where the red man and the white man are on a level. On the sides of the plain shaft that marks his place of burial, I read these words: '*Pushmataha, a Choctaw Chief, lies here. This monument to his memory is erected by his brother chiefs, who were associated with him in a delegation from their nation, in the year* 1824, *to the*

Government of the United States. Pushmataha was a warrior of great distinction. He was wise in council, eloquent in an extraordinary degree; and on all occasions, and under all circumstances, the white man's friend. He died in Washington, on the 24th of December, 1824, of the croup, in the 60th year of his age.'"   Among his last words were the following : "When I am gone, let the big guns be fired over me."

. The chief had five children.   His oldest son died at the age of 21, after having completed an excellent English education.   The others were young at the time of the decease of their father.   A medal has been sent by the President to the oldest surviving son, as a testimony of respect for the memory of a warrior whose attachment to our Government was steady and unshaken throughout his life.

The day after the funeral of Pushmataha, the deputation visited the officer in charge of the Bureau of Indian Affairs.[9] The countenances of the chiefs wore a gloom which such a loss was well calculated to create.   Over the face of one of the deputation, however, was a cloud darker than the rest, and the expression of his face told a tale of deeper sorrow. Ask that young man, said the officer in charge of the Bureau, what is the matter with him ?   The answer was, "*I am sorry.*" Ask him what makes him sorry ?   The loss, the answer was expected to be, of our beloved chief— But no—it was, "*I am sorry it was not me.*"   Ask him to explain what he means by being sorry that it was not him.   The ceremonies of the funeral, the reader will bear in mind, were very imposing. The old chief had said, "When I am gone, let the big guns be fired over me"; and they were fired.   Beside the discharge of minute guns on the Capitol Hill, and from the ground contiguous to the place of interment, there was an immense concourse of citizens, a long train of carriages, cavalry, military, bands of music, the whole procession extending at least a mile in length; and there were thousands lining the ways, and filling the doors and windows, and then the military honours at the grave, combined to produce in this young chief's mind a feeling of regret that he had not been himself the subject of these honours—Hence his reply—"*I am sorry it was not me*"; and so he explained himself.[10]

NOTES

1. The full original form of his name is *Apushimataha,* or *Apushimalhtaha,* "which name, no doubt, was given to the future *mingo* [chief] in his babyhood, from some trivial circumstance, the memory of which has long since been lost. *Apushi im alhtaha,* literally translated, is 'The sapling is ready, or finished for him.' The statement made in Brewer's *Alabama,* p. 16, note, that *Pushmataha* means, 'He has won all the honours of his race,' is not worth a second's consideration."—Halbert in *Transactions Alabama Historical Society,* Vol. II., 108, 1898.

2. The Choctaw are a tribe of the Muskhogean family. Their early habitat was the territory now included in southern and central Mississippi, and extending for some distance eastward from Tombigbee River into Georgia. Soon after the middle of the eighteenth century, some of their bands settled beyond the Mississippi River, in Louisiana and Texas, and most of the remainder, beginning in 1832 (having ceded their lands in the south), departed for Indian Territory, where lands had been set aside for them. Here they still live, their population numbering 17,529 in 1906, exclusive of 1550 "Choctaw by intermarriage," and 5378 negroes, who were formerly slaves. The Choctaw have made marked progress in civilisation, constituting one of the Five Civilised Tribes.

3. These were the Cherokee. The locality referred to is the Texas border.

4. Early in the nineteenth century Pushmataha became *mingo,* or chief, of the Okla Hannali, or the Six Towns district of the Choctaw. His influence extended also over the Potato-eating People and the Long People, as the north-eastern and western divisions of the Choctaw were called.—Halbert in *Transactions Alabama Historical Society,* II., 109, 1898.

5. Evidently the father of Peter P. Pitchlynn, born in the present Noxubee County, Mississippi, January 30, 1806; died in Washington, D.C., in January, 1881, and was buried in the graveyard (Congressional Cemetery) where lie the remains of Pushmataha. Dickens refers to him in his *American Notes*. See also Charles Lanman, *Recollections of Curious Characters and Pleasant Places*, Edinburgh, 1881, pp. 67-94.

6. The occasion was the treaty with the Choctaw and the United States, concluded at Washington, January 20, 1825. McKenney was a witness to this treaty. The tenth article reads: "The chief, Puck-she-nubbee [Pushmataha], one of the members of the delegation, having died on his journey to see the President, and Robert Cole being recommended by the delegation as his successor, it is hereby agreed, that the said Robert Cole shall receive the medal which appertains to the office of chief, and, also, an annuity from the United States of one hundred and fifty dollars during his natural life, as was received by his predecessor."

7. Much has been written about the oratory of this celebrated chief, but inasmuch as Pushmataha knew no English himself, and as none of the other members of the Choctaw delegation were educated men, the flowery speeches attributed to this Indian, as well as to many others, must be taken with considerable allowance. Mr H. S. Halbert (*Transactions Alabama Historical Society*, Vol. II., p. 114, 1898) regards "the dying talk of Pushmataha," given by McKenney and Hall, as a piece of pure fiction, and presents good reasons for his assertion.

8. The Congressional Cemetery at Washington.

9. This officer was Thomas L. McKenney.

10. The accompanying portrait of Pushmataha was painted by Charles B. King, probably at the time of the visit to Washington that ended with Pushmataha's death in 1824. The subject was evidently a favourite one with this artist, as two portraits of the celebrated Choctaw hung in the Indian Gallery (numbers 22 and 42 of the Rhees list), while another, representing him as wearing a hat adorned in front with three ostrich plumes, is among the King collection (number 201) in the Redwood Library at Newport, Rhode Island. The Inman copy is preserved in the Peabody Museum (No. 28. 188).

The following notice of Pushmataha appeared in *The National Journal*, Washington, December 28, 1824 :—

"Died, at his lodgings at Tennison's, on Thursday night last, at about 12 o'clock, in his sixtieth year, Push-ma-ta-ha, one of the Choctaw Delegation, now at Washington, on business with the Government. The best attendance and best medical skill were employed to save him, but in vain. He died of the croup, and was ill but a day. He was buried on Saturday with military honours, which were performed by the Marine Corps, by direction the Hon. the Secretary of the Navy, assisted by Captain Mauro's and Captain Dyer's companies of volunteers : Christian ceremonies by the Rev. Mr Hawley. The procession was large (at least two thousand), and highly respectable. General Jackson, who knew and appreciated the services of this Chief, paid his last respects to his memory, as did also many members of both Houses of

PUSH-MA-TA-HA
A Choctaw Warrior

Congress, and members of the Government, some of whom attended him, though so distant, to the grave.

"Push-ma-ta-ha was an extraordinary man. He was one of the three great Chiefs of his nation, and had attained that distinction by his powers of oratory and military prowess. Nature had impressed him with the stamp of greatness, and he was himself even in death. 'I am told,' he said (in his native tongue, for he spoke no English), 'that I am better. It is a mistake. I shall die—and at about 12 o'clock to-night. It has always been in my heart that I should die in the land of strangers.' He then gave some directions respecting his family, and the disposition of his affairs, and concluded by saying : 'When I am dead, let the big guns be fired over me.' His request was respected. He had won this high distinction by his uniform attachment to the people and cause of the United States, and by the scars he had received, and the blood he had shed in seconding our power on our borders, when it was exerted to save our citizens from the hostile of his own race, and the combined hostility of the enemy with them, and especially in the late war. He even foiled Tecumseh — though not with the sword. He saw his opportunity, and seized it ; he knew his means, and he employed them. He triumphed over that master-spirit, broke the spell in which he was attempting to bind his nation, and turned the sword of his people upon our enemies. *It was by the powers of his oratory.* Every arm fell when Push-ma-ta-ha had spoken. Every hostile spirit was hushed; and the Choctaw nation, powerful as it was, were united to us. He put himself at the head of 500 warriors, and entered our service—was in twenty-four battles—served under the eye of General Jackson in his Pensacola campaign, and won the admiration of even this veteran. Push-ma-ta-ha remembered his leader in death. 'I want,' said he, 'to see General Jackson.' But it was late at night, and the knowledge of this wish was not conveyed. To the writer of this hasty notice, General Jackson said, when informed of it the next day, 'I deeply regret it. Had it been midnight, I would have risen and gone to see him.'

"Push-ma-ta-ha, though uneducated himself, saw the necessity of improving his people, and demonstrated his attachment to civilization by giving $2000 of his annuity, for fifteen years, towards the support of the school system.

"Push-ma-ta-ha sleeps with the great and the venerated of our land. He lies in the same enclosure with our Clintons and Gerrys. When the tidings of his death shall reach his people, they will be like the fall of the noblest tree in their forest, which had long furnished them with shelter and shade ; every ear will listen to the echoes occasioned by its fall, and all hearts will mourn the mighty ruin. But let them remember, though he 'died in the land of strangers,' that he was respected and treated like a friend, and that the 'big guns' were fired over him, not barely in compliance with his last request, but out of respect for his services, and to show that his attachment to our people, and his efforts in our cause, were not forgotten.

"It was the boast of Push-ma-ta-ha that *his hand was white.*' 'It has never been stained,' said he, 'by the blood of Americans. But it is *red* with that of their enemies.' 'I am an American,' said he, the other day, to the writer of this. 'My skin is red, but my heart is white.' He was asked, about ten weeks ago, how he was? He threw his eyes upward, and, with a most devotional and grateful look, spoke: 'He says,' said his interpreter, 'he feels that the Great Spirit loves him to-day. He is so well that he feels *happy.*'

"On his way to Washington he met an old acquaintance going to the land of his achievements in war. 'You have come in a path, so far,' said Push-ma-ta-ha, 'which is straight, and the green grass and flowers border it. The trees are all leafy, and the birds sing amidst their branches. You are going where the paths are all crooked, and where the land is desolate and white with the bones of my enemies.'

"Did time permit, even with the barren resources which are at hand, it would be easy to illustrate the extraordinary sayings of this man. He was of Nature's construction in intellect and prowess. And when she turns off a favourite, as in Shakespeare, art only fetters, and its adventitious aids are spurned as beneath the attention of the mind which is rich and powerful in its own resources."

For additional information, consult Halbert, *op. cit.*, and Lanman, *Recollections of Curious Characters*, Edinburgh, 1881.

TENSKWAUTAWAW

(OR, THE PROPHET)

THIS individual is a person of slender abilities, who acquired great celebrity from the circumstances in which he happened to be placed, and from his connection with the distinguished Tecumthe, his brother. Of the latter, unfortunately, no portrait was ever taken; and, as the two brothers acted in concert in the most important events of their lives, we shall embrace what we have to say of both, in the present article.[1]

We have received, through the politeness of a friend, a narrative of the history of these celebrated Indians, dictated by the Prophet himself, and accurately written down at the moment. It is valuable as a curious piece of auto-biography, coming from an unlettered savage, of a race remarkable for tenacity of memory, and for the fidelity with which they preserve and transmit their traditions among themselves; while it is to be received with great allowance, in consequence of the habit of exaggeration which marks the communications of that people to strangers. In their intercourse with each other, truth is esteemed and practised; but, with the exception of a few high-minded men, little reliance is to be placed upon any statement made by an Indian to a white man. The same code which inculcates an inviolable faith among themselves, justifies any deception towards an enemy, or one of an alien race, for which a sufficient motive may be held out. We know, too, that barbarous nations in all ages have evinced a decided propensity for the marvellous, which has been especially indulged in tracing the pedigree of a family, or the origin of a nation.   With this prefatory caution, we proceed to give the story of Tenskwautawaw, as related by himself—compiled, however, in our own language, from the loose memoranda of the original transcriber.

His paternal grandfather was a Creek, who, at a period which is not defined in the manuscript before us, went to one of the southern cities, either Savannah or Charleston, to hold a council with the English governor, whose daughter was present at some of the interviews.   This young lady had conceived a violent admiration for the Indian char-acter; and, having determined to bestow herself upon some "warlike lord" of the forest, she took this occasion to communicate her partiality to her father.   The next morning, in the council, the governor inquired of the Indians which of them was the most expert hunter; and the grandfather of Tecumthe, then a young and handsome man, who sat modestly in a retired part of the room, was pointed out to him.   When the council broke up for the day, the governor asked his daughter if she was really so partial to the Indians as to prefer selecting a husband from among them, and finding that she persisted in this singular predilection, he directed her attention to the young Creek warrior, for whom, at first sight, she avowed a decided attachment.   On the following morning the governor announced to the Creeks that his daughter was disposed to marry one of their number; and, having pointed out the individual, added that his consent would be given.   The chiefs, at first, very naturally, doubted whether the governor was in earnest; but, upon his assuring them that he was sincere, they advised the young man to embrace the lady and her offer. He was not so ungallant as to refuse; and, having consented to the fortune that was thus buckled on him, was immediately taken to another apartment, where he was disrobed of his Indian costume by a train of black servants, washed, and clad in a new suit, and the marriage ceremony was immediately performed.

At the close of the council the Creeks returned home, but the young hunter remained with his wife. He amused himself in hunting, in which he was very successful, and was accustomed to take a couple of black servants with him, who seldom failed to bring in large quantities of game. He lived among the whites until his wife had borne him two daughters and a son. Upon the birth of the latter, the governor went to see his grandson, and was so well pleased that he called his friends together, and caused thirty guns to be fired. When the boy was seven or eight years old the father died, and the governor took charge of the child, who was often visited by the Creeks. At the age of ten or twelve he was permitted to accompany the Indians to their nation, where he spent some time; and, two years after, he again made a long visit to the Creeks, who then, with a few Shawnees, lived on a river called Pauseekoalaakee, and began to adopt their dress and customs. They gave him an Indian name, Pukeshinwau, which means, *Something that drops down;* and, after learning their language, he became so much attached to the Indian mode of life, that when the governor sent for him he refused to return. He married a Creek woman, but afterwards discarded her, and united himself with Methoataaskee, a Shawnees, who was the mother of Tecumthe, and our narrator, the Prophet. The oldest son by this marriage was Cheeseekau; and, six years afterwards, a daughter was born, who was called Menewaulaakoosee; then a son, called Sauawaseekau, soon after whose birth, the Shawnees determined to remove to other hunting grounds. His wife, being unwilling to separate from her tribe, Pukeshinwau accompanied them, after first paying a visit to his grandfather. At parting, the governor gave him a written paper, and told him, that upon showing it at any time to the Americans, they would grant any request which he might make—but that he need not show it to French traders, as it would only vex them, and make them exclaim, *Sacre Dieu!* His family, with about half the Shawnees, then removed to old Chillicothe[2]; the other half divided again, a part remaining with the Creeks and the remainder going beyond the Mississippi. Tecumthe was born on the journey. Pukeshinwau was killed at the battle of Point Pleasant, in the autumn of 1774,[3] and the Prophet was born the following winter.[4]

The fourth child of this family was Tecumthe—the fifth, Nehaaseemoo, a boy—and the sixth, the Prophet, whose name was, originally, Laulewaasikaw, but was changed when he assumed his character of Prophet, to Tenskwautawaw, or the *Open Door*.[5] Tecumthe was ten years older than the Prophet; the latter was one of three brothers born at a birth, one of whom died immediately after birth, while the other, whose name was Kumskaukau, lived until a few years ago.[6] The eldest brother had a daughter, who, as well as a daughter of Tecumthe, is living beyond the Mississippi. No other descendant of the family remains, except a son of Tecumthe, who now lives with the Prophet.

Fabulous as the account of the origin of this family undoubtedly is, the Prophet's information as to the names and ages of his brothers and sisters may be relied upon as accurate, and as affording a complete refutation of the common report, which represents

Tenskwautawaw and Tecumthe as the offspring of the same birth.

The early life of the Prophet was not distinguished by any important event, nor would his name ever have been known to fame, but for his connection with his distinguished brother. Tecumthe was a person of commanding talents, who gave early indications of a genius of a superior order. While a boy he was a leader among his playmates, and was in the habit of arranging them in parties for the purpose of fighting sham battles. At this early age his vigilance, as well as his courage, is said to have been remarkably developed in his whole deportment. One only exception is reported to have occurred, in which this leader, like the no less illustrious Red Jacket, stained his youthful character by an act of pusillanimity. At the age of fifteen he went, for the first time, into battle, under the charge of his elder brother, and at the commencement of the engagement ran off, completely panic stricken. This event, which may be considered as remarkable, in the life of an individual so conspicuous through his whole after career for daring intrepidity, occurred on the banks of Mad River, near the present site of Dayton.[7] But Tecumthe possessed too much pride, and too strong a mind, to remain long under the disgrace incurred by a momentary weakness, and he shortly afterwards distinguished himself in an attack on some boats descending the Ohio. A prisoner, taken on this occasion, was burnt, with all the horrid ceremonies attendant upon this dreadful exhibition of savage ferocity; and Tecumthe, shocked at a scene so unbecoming the character of the warrior, expressed his abhorrence in terms so strong and eloquent, that the whole party came to the resolution that they would discontinue the practice of torturing prisoners at the stake. A more striking proof of the genius of Tecumthe could not be given ; it must have required no small degree of independence and strength of mind, to enable an Indian to arrive at a conclusion so entirely at variance with all the established usages of his people ; nor could he have impressed others with his own novel opinions without the exertion of great powers of argument.   He remained firm in the benevolent resolution thus early formed ; but we are unable to say how far his example conduced to the extirpation of the horrid rite to which we have alluded, and which is now seldom, if at all, practised.   Colonel Crawford, who was burned in 1782, is the last victim to the savage propensity for revenge who is known to have suffered this cruel death.[8]

Tecumthe seems to have been connected with his own tribe by slender ties, or to have had a mind so constituted as to raise him above the partialities and prejudices of clanship, which are usually so deeply rooted in the Indian breast.   Throughout his life he was always acting in concert with tribes other than his own.   In 1789, he removed, with a party of Kickapoos, to the Cherokee country ; and, shortly after, joined the Creeks, who were then engaged in hostilities with the whites.   In these wars Tecumthe became distinguished, often leading war parties—sometimes attacked in his camp, but always acquitting himself with ability.   On one occasion, when surrounded in a swamp by superior numbers, he relieved himself by a masterly charge on the whites ; through whose ranks he cut his way with desperate courage.   He returned to Ohio immediately after Harmar's defeat,[9] in 1791 ; he headed a party sent out to watch the movements of St Clair, while organising his army, and is supposed to have participated in the active and bloody scenes which eventuated in the destruction of that ill-starred expedition.[10]

In 1792, Tecumthe, with ten men, was attacked by twenty-eight whites, under the command of the celebrated Simon Kenton,[11] and, after a spirited engagement, the latter were defeated; and, in 1793, he was again successful in repelling an attack by a party of whites whose numbers were superior to his own.

The celebrated victory of General Wayne,[12] in which a large body of Indians, well organised and skilfully led, was most signally defeated, took place in 1794, and produced an entire change in the relations then existing between the American people and the aborigines, by crushing the power of the latter at a single blow, and dispersing the elements of a powerful coalition of the tribes. In that battle Tecumthe led a party, and was with the advance which met the attack of the infantry, and bore the brunt of the severest fighting. When the Indians, completely overpowered, were compelled to retreat, Tecumthe, with two or three others, rushed on a small party of their enemies who had a fieldpiece in charge, drove them from the gun, and cutting loose the horses, mounted them, and fled to the main body of the Indians.

In 1795, Tecumthe again raised a war party, and, for the first time, styled himself a chief, although he was never regularly raised to that dignity; and in the following year he resided in Ohio, near Piqua. Two years afterwards, he joined the Delawares, in Indiana, on White River, and continued to reside with them for seven years.

About the year 1806, this highly gifted warrior began to exhibit the initial movements of his great plan for expelling the whites from the valley of the Mississippi. The Indians had, for a long series of years, witnessed with anxiety the encroachments of a population superior to themselves in address, in war, and in all the arts of civil life, until, having been driven beyond the Alleghany Ridge, they fancied that Nature had interposed an impassable barrier between them and their oppressors. They were not, however, suffered to repose long in this imaginary security. A race of hardy men, led on step by step in the pursuit of game and in the search of fertile lands, pursued the footsteps of the savage through the fastnesses of the mountains, and explored those broad and prolific plains, which had been spoken of before in reports supposed to be partly fabulous, but which were now found to surpass in extent and in the magnificence of their scenery and vegetation all that travellers had written, or the most credulous had imagined. Individuals and colonies began to emigrate, and the Indians saw that again they were to be dispossessed of their choicest hunting grounds. Wars followed, the history of which we have not room to relate —wars of the most unsparing character, fought with scenes of hardy and romantic valour, and with the most heartrending incidents of domestic distress. The vicis-situdes of these hostilities were such as alternately to flatter and alarm each party ; but as year after year rolled away, the truth became rapidly developed, that the red men were dwindling and receding, while the descendants of the Europeans were increasing in numbers, and pressing forward with gigantic footsteps. Coalitions of the tribes began to be formed, but they were feebly organised, and briefly united. A common cause roused all the tribes to hostility, and the whole frontier presented scenes of violence. Harmar, St Clair, and other gallant leaders, sent to defend the settlements, were driven back by the irritated savages, who refused to treat on any condition than that which should establish a boundary to any farther advance of the whites. Their first hope was to exclude the latter from the valley of the Mississippi ; but driven from this position by the rapid settlement of Western Pennsylvania and Virginia, they assumed the Ohio River as their boundary, and proposed to make peace with General Wayne, on his agreeing to that stream as a permanent line between the red and white men. After their defeat by that veteran leader, all negotiation for a permanent boundary ceased, the tribes dispersed, each to fight its own wars, and to strike for plunder or revenge, as opportunity might offer.

Tecumthe seems to have been at this time the only Indian who had the genius to conceive, and the perseverance to attempt, an extended scheme of warfare against the encroachment of the whites. His plan embraced a general union of all the Indians against all white men, and proposed the entire expulsion of the latter from the valley of the Mississippi. He passed from tribe to tribe urging the necessity of a combination which should make a common cause; and burying, for a time, all feuds among themselves, wage a general war against the invader who was expelling them, all alike, from their hunting grounds, and who would not cease to drive them towards the setting sun until the last remnant of their race should be hurled into the great ocean of the West. This great warrior had the sagacity to perceive that the traffic with the whites, by creating new and artificial wants among the Indians, exerted a powerful influence in rendering the latter dependent on the former; and he pointed out to them in forcible language, the impossibility of carrying on a successful war while they depended on their enemies for the supply of articles which habit was rendering necessary to their existence. He showed the pernicious influence of ardent spirits, the great instrument of savage degradation and destruction; but he also explained, that in using the guns, ammunition, knives, blankets, cloth, and other articles manufactured by the whites, they had raised up enemies in their own wants and appetites more efficient than the troops of their oppressors. He urged them to return to the simple habits of their fathers—to reject all superfluous ornaments, to dress in skins, and to use such weapons as they could fabricate, or wrest by force from the enemy; and, setting the example, he lived an abstemious life, and sternly rejected the use of articles purchased from the traders.

Tecumthe was not only bold and eloquent, but sagacious and subtle; and he determined to appeal to the prejudices as well as the reason of his race. The Indians are very superstitious; vague as their notions are respecting the Deity, they believe in the existence of a *Great Spirit*, to whom they look up with great fear and reverence; and artful men have, from time to time, appeared among them, who have swayed their credulous minds by means of pretended revelations from Heaven.[13] Seizing upon this trait of the Indian character, the crafty projector of this great revolution prepared his brother Tenskwautawaw, or Ellsquatawa (for the name is pronounced both ways), to assume the character of a Prophet; and, about the year 1806, the latter began to have dreams, and to deliver predictions. His name, which, previous to this time, was Olliwachica,[14] was changed to that by which he was afterwards generally known, and which signifies *"the open door"*—by which it was intended to represent him as *the way*, or door, which had been opened for the deliverance of the red people.

Instead of confining these intrigues to their own tribe, a village was established on the Wabash, which soon became known as the *Prophet's town*,[15] and was for many years the chief scene of the plots formed against the peace of the frontier. Here the Prophet denounced the white

man, and invoked the malediction of the Great Spirit
upon the recreant Indian who should live in friendly
intercourse with the hated race.   Individuals from
different tribes in that region—Miamis, Weas, Pianka-
shaws, Kickapoos, Delawares, and Shawnees collected
around him, and were prepared to execute his commands.
The Indians thus assembled were by no means the most
reputable or efficient of their respective tribes, but were
the young, the loose, the idle—and here, as in the case
in civilised societies, those who had least to lose were
foremost in jeoparding the blood and property of the
whole people.   The chiefs held back, and either opposed
the Prophet or stood uncommitted.   They had, doubtless,
intelligence enough to know that he was an impostor;
nor were they disposed to encourage the brothers in assum-
ing to be leaders, and in the acquisition of authority which
threatened to rival their own.   Indeed, all that portion
of the surrounding tribes which might be termed the
aristocratic, the chiefs and their relatives, the aged men
and distinguished warriors, stood aloof from a conspiracy
which seemed desperate and hopeless, while the younger
warriors listened with credulity to the Prophet, and were
kindled into ardour by the eloquence of Tecumthe.   The
latter continued to travel from tribe to tribe, pursuing
the darling object of his life with incessant labour,
commanding respect by the dignity and manliness of his
character, and winning adherents by the boldness of his
public addresses, as well as by the subtlety with which in
secret he appealed to individual interest or passion.

This state of things continued for several years.   Most
of the Indian tribes were ostensibly at peace with the
United States; but the tribes, though unanimous in their
hatred against the white people, were divided in opinion
as to the proper policy to be pursued, and distracted by

intestine conflicts.   The more prudent deprecated an open rupture with our Government, which would deprive them of their annuities, their traffic, and the presents which flowed in upon them periodically, while the great mass thirsted for revenge and plunder.   The British authorities in Canada, alarmed at the rapid spread of our settlements, dispersed their agents along the frontier, and industriously fomented these jealousies.   Small parties of Indians scoured the country, committing thefts and murders—unacknowledged by their tribes, but undoubtedly approved, if not expressly sanctioned, at their council fires.

The Indiana Territory, having been recently organised, and Governor Harrison [16] being invested with the office of Superintendent of Indian Affairs, it became his duty to hold frequent treaties with the Indians; and on these occasions Tecumthe and the Prophet were prominent men.   The latter is described as the most graceful and agreeable of Indian orators; he was easy, subtle, and insinuating — not powerful, but persuasive in argument; and it was remarked that he never spoke when Tecumthe was present.   He was the instrument, and Tecumthe the master-spirit, the bold warrior, the able, eloquent, fearless speaker, who, in any assembly of his own race, awed all around him by the energy of his character, and stood forward as the leading individual.

The ground assumed by these brothers was, that all previous treaties between the Indians and the American Government were invalid, having been made without authority.   They asserted that the lands inhabited by the Indians belonged to all the tribes indiscriminately—that the Great Spirit had given them to *the Indians* for hunting grounds—that each tribe had a right to certain tracts of country so long as they occupied them, but no longer—that if one tribe moved away another might take possession; and they contended for a kind of entail, which prevented any tribe from alienating that to which he had only a present possessory right. They insisted, therefore, that no tribe had authority to transfer any soil to the whites without the assent of all; and that, consequently, all the treaties that had been made were void.[17] It was in support of these plausible propositions that Tecumthe made his best speeches, and showed especially his knowledge of human nature by his artful appeals to the prejudices of the Indians. He was, when he pleased to be so, a great demagogue; and when he condescended to court the people, was eminently successful. In his public harangues he acted on this principle; and while he was ostensible in addressing the Governor of Indiana, or the chiefs who sat in council, his speeches, highly inflammatory yet well digested, were all in fact directed to the multitude. It was on such an occasion that, in ridiculing the idea of selling a country, he broke out in the exclamation—" Sell a country! why not sell the air, the clouds, and the great sea, as well as the earth? Did not the Great Spirit make them all for the use of his children?"

We select the following passages from the *Memoirs of General Harrison :*—[18]

"In 1809, Governor Harrison purchased from the Delawares, Miamis, and Pottawatimies, a large tract of country on both sides of the Wabash, and extending up that river about sixty miles above Vincennes.[19] Tecumthe was absent, and his brother, not feeling himself interested, made no opposition to the treaty; but the former, on his return, expressed great dissatisfaction, and threatened some of the chiefs with death who had made the treaty. Governor Harrison, hearing of his displeasure, despatched a messenger to invite him to come to Vincennes, and to assure him 'that any claims he might have to the lands which had been ceded, were not affected by the treaty; that he might come to Vincennes and exhibit his pretensions, and if they were found to be valid, the land would be either given up, or an ample compensation made for it.'

"Having no confidence in the faith of Tecumthe, the governor directed that he should not bring with him more than thirty warriors; but he came with four hundred, completely armed. The people of Vincennes were in great alarm, nor was the governor without apprehension that treachery was intended. This suspicion was not diminished by the conduct of the chief, who, on the morning after his arrival, refused to hold the council at the place appointed, under an affected belief that treachery was intended on our side.

"A large portico in front of the governor's house had been prepared for the purpose, with seats as well for the Indians as for the citizens who were expected to attend. When Tecumthe came from his camp, with about forty of his warriors, he stood off, and on being invited by the governor, through an interpreter, to take his seat, refused, observing that he wished the council to be held under the shade of some trees in front of the house. When it was objected that it would be troublesome to remove the seats, he replied, 'that it would only be necessary to remove those intended for the whites — that the red men were accustomed to sit upon the earth, which was their mother, and that they were always happy to recline upon her bosom.'

"At this council, held on the 12th of August, 1810, Tecumthe delivered a speech, of which we find the following report, containing the sentiments uttered, but in a language very different from that of the Indian orator :—

"'I have made myself what I am; and I would that I could make the red people as great as the conceptions of

TENS-KWAU-TA-WAW, *or* THE PROPHET

my mind, when I think of the Great Spirit that rules over all. I would not then come to Governor Harrison to ask him to tear the treaty; but I would say to him, Brother, you have liberty to return to your own country. Once there was no white man in all this country: then it belonged to red men, children of the same parents, placed on it by the Great Spirit to keep it, to travel over it, to eat its fruits, and fill it with the same race—once a happy race, but now made miserable by the white people, who are never contented, but always encroaching. They have driven us from the great salt water, forced us over the mountains, and would shortly push us into the lakes—but we are determined to go no farther. The only way to stop this evil, is for all the red men to unite in claiming a common and equal right in the land, as it was at first, and should be now—for it never was divided, but belongs to all. No tribe has a right to sell, even to each other, much less to strangers, who demand all, and will take no less. The white people have no right to take the land from the Indians who had it first—it is theirs. They may sell, but all must join. Any sale not made by all, is not good. The late sale is bad—it was made by a part only. Part do not know how to sell. It requires all to make a bargain for all.'

"Governor Harrison, in his reply, said, ' That the white people, when they arrived upon this continent, had found the Miamis in the occupation of all the country of the Wabash; and at that time the Shawnees were residents of Georgia, from which they were driven by the Creeks. That the lands had been purchased from the Miamis, who were the true and original owners of it. That it was ridiculous to assert that all the Indians were one nation; for if such had been the intention of the Great Spirit, he would not have put six different tongues into their heads, but would have taught them all to speak one language. That the Miamis had found it for their interest to sell a part of their lands, and receive for them a further annuity in addition to what they had long enjoyed, and the benefit of which they had experienced, from the punctuality with which the *seventeen fires* complied with their engagements; and that the Shawnees had no right to come from a distant country to control the Miamis in the disposal of their own property.'

"The interpreter had scarcely finished the explanation of these remarks, when Tecumthe fiercely exclaimed, 'It is false!' and giving a signal to his warriors, they sprang upon their feet, from the green grass on which they were sitting, and seized their war-clubs. The governor and the small train that surrounded him were now in imminent danger. He was attended by a few citizens, who were unarmed. A military guard of twelve men, who had been stationed near him, and whose presence was considered rather as an honorary than a defensive measure —being exposed, as it was thought unnecessarily, to the heat of the sun in a sultry August day, had been humanely directed by the governor to remove to a shaded spot at some distance. But the governor, retaining his presence of mind, rose and placed his hand upon his sword, at the same time directing those of his friends and suite who were about him to stand upon their guard. Tecumthe addressed the Indians in a passionate tone, and with violent gesticulations. Major G. R. C. Floyd, of the U.S. army, who stood near the governor, drew his dirk; Winnemak,[20] a friendly chief, cocked his pistol, and Mr Winans, a Methodist preacher, ran to the governor's house, seized a gun, and placed himself in the door to defend the family. For a few moments all expected a bloody rencounter. The guard was ordered up, and would instantly have fired upon the Indians, had it not been for the cool-ness of Governor Harrison, who restrained them. He then calmly but authoritatively told Tecumthe, that 'he was a bad man—that he would have no further talk with him—that he must now return to his camp, and take his departure from the settlements immediately.'

"The next morning, Tecumthe having reflected on the impropriety of his conduct, and finding that he had to deal with a man as bold and vigilant as himself, who was not to be daunted by his audacious turbulence, nor circum-vented by his specious manœuvres, apologised for the affront he had offered, and begged that the council might be renewed. To this the governor consented, suppressing any feeling of resentment which he might naturally have felt, and determined to leave no exertion untried to carry into effect the pacific views of the Government. It was agreed that each party should have the same attendance as on the previous day; but the governor took the pre-caution to place himself in an attitude to command respect, and to protect the inhabitants of Vincennes from violence, by ordering two companies of militia to be placed on duty within the village.

"Tecumthe presented himself with the same undaunted bearing which always marked him as a superior man; but he was now dignified and collected, and showed no dis-position to resume his former insolent deportment. He disclaimed having entertained any intention of attacking the governor, but said he had been advised by white men to do as he had done. Two white men—British emissaries undoubtedly—had visited him at his place of residence, had told him that half the white people were opposed to the governor, and willing to relinquish the land, and urged him to advise the tribes not to receive pay for it, alleging that the governor would soon be recalled, and a good man put in his place, who would give up the land to the Indians. The governor inquired whether he would forcibly oppose the survey of the purchase. He replied, that he was determined to adhere to the *old boundary*. Then arose a Wyandot, a Kickapoo, a Pottawatimie, an Ottawa, and a Winnebago chief, each declaring his determination to stand by Tecumthe. The governor then said, that the words of Tecumthe should be reported to the President, who would take measures to enforce the treaty; and the council ended.

"The governor, still anxious to conciliate the haughty savage, paid him a visit next day at his own camp. He was received with kindness and attention—his uniform courtesy and inflexible firmness having won the respect of the rude warriors of the forest. They conversed for some time, but Tecumthe obstinately adhered to all his former positions; and when Governor Harrison told him that he was sure the President would not yield to his pretensions, the chief replied: 'Well, as the great chief is to determine the matter, I hope the Great Spirit will put sense enough into his head to induce him to direct you to give up this land. It is true, he is so far off, he will not be injured by the war. He may sit still in his town, and drink his wine, while you and I will have to fight it out.'"

The two brothers who thus acted in concert, though, perhaps, well fitted to act together in the prosecution of a great plan, were widely different in character. Tecumthe was bold and sagacious—a successful warrior, a fluent orator, a shrewd, cool-headed, able man in every situation in which he was placed. His mind was expansive and generous. He detested the white man, but it was with a kind of benevolent hatred, based on an ardent love for his own race, and which rather aimed at the elevation of the one than the destruction of the other. He had sworn eternal vengeance against the enemies of his race, and he held himself bound to observe towards them no courtesy, to consent to no measure of conciliation, until the purposes to which he had devoted himself should be accomplished. He was full of enthusiasm and fertile of expedient. Though his whole career was one struggle against adverse circumstances, he was never discouraged, but sustained himself with a presence of mind and an equability of temper which showed the real greatness of his character.

The following remarkable circumstance may serve to illustrate the penetration, decision, and boldness of this warrior chief:—He had been down south, to Florida, and succeeded in instigating the Seminoles in particular, and portions of other tribes, to unite in the war on the side of the British.[21] He gave out, that a vessel, on a certain day, commanded by red coats, would be off Florida, filled with guns and ammunition, and supplies for the use of the Indians. That no mistake might happen in regard to the day on which the Indians were to strike, he prepared bundles of sticks—each bundle containing the number of sticks corresponding to the number of days that were to intervene between the day on which they were received, and the day of the general onset. The Indian practice is, to throw away a stick every morning—they make, therefore, no mistake in the time. These sticks Tecumthe caused to be painted red. It was from this circumstance that, in the former Seminole war, these Indians were called "Red Sticks."[22] In all this business of mustering the tribes, Tecumthe used great caution. He supposed inquiry would be made as to the object of his visit. That his plans might not be suspected, he directed the Indians to reply to any questions that might be asked about him, by saying that he had counselled them to cultivate the ground, abstain from ardent spirits, and live in peace with the white people. On his return from Florida, he went among the Creeks, in Alabama, urging them to unite with the Seminoles. Arriving at Tuckhabatchee, a Creek town on the Tallapoosa River, he made his way to the lodge of the chief called the *Big Warrior.*[28] He explained his object; delivered his war talk —presented a bundle of sticks—gave a piece of wampum and a war hatchet; all which the Big Warrior took. When Tecumthe, reading the spirit and intentions of the Big Warrior, looked him in the eye, and pointing his finger towards his face, said—"Your blood is white. You have taken my talk, and the sticks, and the wampum, and the hatchet, but you do not mean to fight. I know the reason. You do not believe the Great Spirit has sent me. You shall know. I leave Tuckhabatchee directly—and shall go straight to Detroit. When I arrive there, I will stamp on the ground with my foot, and shake down every house in Tuckhabatchee." So saying, he turned, and left the Big Warrior in utter amazement, at both his manner and his threat, and pursued his journey. The Indians were struck no less with his conduct than was the Big Warrior, and began to dread the arrival of the day when the threatened calamity would befall them. They met often, and talked over this matter—and counted the days carefully, to know the day when Tecumthe would reach Detroit. The morning they had fixed upon as the day of his arrival at last came. A mighty rumbling was heard—the Indians all ran out of their houses—the earth began to shake; when, at last, sure enough, every house in Tuckhabatchee was shaken down! The exclamation was in every mouth, "Tecumthe has got to Detroit." The effect was electric. The message he had delivered to the Big Warrior was believed, and many of the Indians took their rifles and prepared for the war.

The reader will not be surprised to learn that an earthquake had produced all this; but he will be, doubtless, that it should happen on the very day on which Tecumthe arrived at Detroit, and in exact fulfilment of his threat. It was the famous earthquake of New Madrid, on the Mississippi. We received the foregoing from the lips of the Indians, when we were at Tuckhabatchee in 1827, and near the residence of the Big Warrior.[24] The anecdote may, therefore, be relied on. Tecumthe's object, doubtless, was, on seeing that he had failed by the usual appeal to the passions, and hopes, and war spirit of the Indians, to alarm their fears, little dreaming himself that on the day named his threat would be executed with such punctuality and terrible fidelity.

Tecumthe was temperate in his diet, used no ardent spirits, and did not indulge in any kind of excess. Although several times married, he had but one wife at a time, and treated her with uniform kindness and fidelity; and he never evinced any desire to accumulate property, or to gratify any sordid passion. Colonel John Johnston, of Piqua, who knew him well, says: "He was sober and abstemious; never indulging in the use of liquors, nor catering to excess; fluent in conversation, and a great public speaker. He despised dress, and all effeminacy of manners; he was disinterested, hospitable, generous, and humane— the resolute and indefatigable advocate of the rights and independence of the Indians." Stephen Ruddle, a Kentuckian, who was captured by the Indians in childhood, and lived in the family of Tecumthe, says of him, "His talents, rectitude of deportment and friendly disposition, commanded the respect and regard of all about him"; and Governor Cass, in speaking of his oratory, says, "It was the utterance of a great mind, roused by the strongest motives of which human nature is susceptible, and developing a power and a labour of reason which commanded the admiration of the civilised as justly as the confidence and pride of the savage."

The Prophet possessed neither the talents nor the frankness of his brother. As a speaker, he was fluent, smooth, and plausible, and was pronounced by Governor Harrison the most graceful and accomplished orator he had seen among the Indians; but he was sensual, cruel, weak, and timid. Availing himself of the superstitious awe inspired by supposed intercourse with the Great Spirit, he lived in idleness, supported by the presents brought him by his deluded followers. The Indians allow polygamy,[25] but deem it highly discreditable in anyone to marry more wives than he can support; and a prudent warrior always regulates the number of his family by his capacity to provide food. Neglecting this rule of propriety, the Prophet had an unusual number of wives, while he made no effort to procure a support for his household, and meanly exacted a subsistence from those who dreaded his displeasure. An impostor in everything, he seems to have exhibited neither honesty nor dignity of character in any relation of life.

We have not room to detail all the political and military events in which these brothers were engaged, and which have been related in the histories of the times. An account of the battle of Tippecanoe, which took place in 1811, and of the intrigues which led to an engagement so honourable to our arms, would alone fill more space than is allotted to this article.[26] On the part of the Indians it was a fierce and desperate assault, and the defence of the American general was one of the most brilliant and successful in the annals of Indian warfare; but Tecumthe was not engaged in it, and the Prophet, who issued orders from a safe position, beyond the reach of any chance of personal exposure, performed no part honourable to himself or important to the result. He added cowardice to the degrading traits which had already distinguished his character, and from that time his influence decreased. At the close of the war, in 1814, he had ceased to have any reputation among the Indians.

The latter part of the career of Tecumthe was as brilliant as it was unfortunate. He sustained his high reputation for talent, courage, and good faith without achieving any advantage for the unhappy race to whose advancement he had devoted his whole life. In the war between the United States and Great Britain, which commenced in 1812, he was an active ally of the latter, and accompanied their armies at the head of large bodies of Indians. He fought gallantly in several engagements, and fell gloriously in the battle of the Thames, where he is supposed, with reason, to have fallen in a personal conflict with Colonel Richard M. Johnson, of Kentucky.[27]

One other trait in the character of this great man deserves to be especially noticed. Though nurtured in the forest, and accustomed through life to scenes of bloodshed, he was humane. While a mere boy, he courageously rescued a woman from the cruelty of her husband, who was beating her, and declared that no man was worthy of the name of a warrior who could raise his hand in anger against a woman. He treated his prisoners with uniform kindness; and, on several occasions, rescued our countrymen from the hands of his enraged followers.

The Prophet is living west of the Mississippi, in obscurity.[28]

NOTES

1. For Tecumthe, see the following :—Benj. Drake, *Life of Tecumseh and of his Brother the Prophet*, Cincinnati, 1852; Edward Eggleston and Lillie E. Seelye, *Tecumseh and the Shawnee Prophet*, New York, 1878; also, *The Shawnee Prophet, or The Story of Tecumseh*, London (n.d.); Lossing, *The American Revolution and the War of* 1812, Vol. III., 1875 ;

Schoolcraft, *Indian Tribes*, Vol. IV., p. 259, 1854; Catlin, *Letters and Notes*, Vol. II., pp. 117-118, London, 1844; Mooney in *Fourteenth Report of the Bureau of Ethnology*, Washington, 1896, p. 670 *et seq.*; F. Moore, *American Eloquence*, Vol. II., 1864; *Wisconsin Historical Society Collections*, Vol. IV., 1859; James A. Green, "Tecumseh," in *Great Men and Famous Women*, edited by Charles F. Horne, New York, 1894.

The only known portrait of Tecumthe is a pencil sketch made by Pierre Le Dru, a young French trader, at Vincennes, Indiana, in 1808. Forty years later Lossing found it at Quebec, in possession of Le Dru's son, who permitted him to copy it. The likeness appears in Lossing's *American Revolution*, above cited, which is the source of many subsequent copies.

The painter of the accompanying portrait of Tenskwautawaw would have remained unknown, but for the information accompanying the Inman copy in the Peabody Museum (original numbers, 20 and 99; museum number, 28. 192), which accredits the original to King. In the museum list the name is spelled " Els-kwau-ta-waw." No date is given. According to the Rhees *Catalogue*, this portrait was number 99 of the Indian Gallery. The portrait is quite distinct from that by Lewis, painted at Detroit in 1823, at the instance of Governor Lewis Cass. In the Lewis *Port-folio* the latter bears the title, "Tens-qua-ta-wa, or the one that opens the door."

2. In the present State of Ohio.

3. See note 7, p. 43.

4. Regarding the ancestry and birth of Tecumseh and the Prophet, little reliance is now placed in the story as here recorded. Eggleston and Seelye say, and their statement is regarded as authoritative:—

"There are always curious contradictions in the accounts of an event that reach us only through the traditions of Indians and frontier men. Tecumseh was born, according to some accounts, in 1768, and according to others, in 1771, some say near Chillicothe, though Tecumseh is reported to have said his birth occurred near the old Indian village of Piqua. There is a story that he and his brother, the Prophet, were twins, and even that a third brother was born at the same time; though, according to one account, the Prophet and a twin brother were some years younger than Tecumseh. It seems more likely that the earlier date, 1768, was that of Tecumseh's, and the latter, 1771, the date of the Prophet's birth, who was perhaps a twin. There can be little doubt that Tecumseh was born at the old Indian village of Piqua, or Pickaway, on the Mad River, near the Miami.

"There is likewise great contradictoriness in the accounts given of the family history. It would be easy to believe, from Tecumseh's superior mind, that there was white blood in his family. There is, however, pretty good evidence that the family was of pure Shawnee extraction. The assertions of some, that he had both Anglo-Saxon and Creek blood in his veins, seem to be entirely founded on a boast of Lauliwasikau, the

Prophet, who excelled more in bragging than he did in battle, and who was more voluble than truthful. The story is interesting to us as a small novel of the Prophet's own invention, rather than for any probable historical basis."

5. His original name was properly *Lalawéthika* ("Laulewaasikaw," on p. 78), signifying, in the Shawnee language, a rattle or similar instrument. *Tenskwatawa* is from *skwaté*, "a door," and *thénui*, "to be open." He is frequently called Elskwatawa (see Mooney, *op. cit.*, p. 674).

6. That is, a few years prior to 1836.

7. Tecumthe was born on Mad River, at the "Old Piqua Town," south-west of the present Springfield, Ohio. See note 4.

8. Colonel William Crawford was born in Berkeley County, Virginia, in 1732. He became a surveyor and a companion of Washington, and, like the latter, served under Braddock in the expedition to Fort Duquesne, Pennsylvania, continuing in service until 1761. He served also in the Pontiac war of 1763-64, and in 1767 settled in western Pennsylvania, where he purchased land, and became a justice of the peace. He fought in the Revolution, resigning in 1781 after winning a colonelcy, and retiring to his home. At the request of Washington and Irvine, in 1782, Crawford assumed command of an expedition against the Wyandot and Delaware Indians on the Muskingum in Ohio. After a two days' fight, the soldiers found themselves surrounded by the Indians, and in cutting their way out the former became separated, and Crawford fell into the hands of the savages. After being held a prisoner for several days, he was burned to death on June 11th, at a point about ten miles north-west of the present Upper Sandusky, Ohio. See Hill, "Crawford's Campaign," in *Magazine of Western History*, Cleveland, Ohio, May, 1885.

9. General Josiah Harmar (born in Philadelphia in 1753, died there August 20, 1813) led this expedition against the Miami Indians. He resigned his commission in 1792, and became Adjutant-General of Pennsylvania, which office he held until 1799.

10. General Arthur St Clair was born in Thurso, Caithness, Scotland, in 1734; died at Greensburg, Pennsylvania, August 31, 1818. He was Governor of the North-West Territory from 1789 until 1802. He made a treaty with the Indians at Fort Harmar, Ohio, in 1789, and in the following year established the seat of justice of the territory at Cincinnati, which town he named in honour of the Society of the Cincinnati, of which he was president for Pennsylvania from 1783 until 1789. In March 1791, St Clair was appointed commander-in-chief of the army then operating against the Indians, and although suffering so severely from gout that he had to be borne on a litter, moved toward the savages on the Wabash and the Miami, in Ohio. On November 4 he was surprised near the Miami villages, in western central Ohio, not

far from the Indiana line, suffering defeat. His actions were criticised, and Washington refusing a court of inquiry, he resigned his General's commission in March 1792; but Congress later ordered a committee of inquiry, which fully exonerated him. See St Clair's *Narrative of the Manner in which the Campaign against the Indians in the Year* 1791 *was Conducted*, Philadelphia, 1812; William H. Smith, *Life and Public Services of Arthur St Clair*, Cincinnati, 1882.

11. Kenton (born in Virginia, April 3, 1755; died in Logan County, Ohio, April 29, 1836) was of Scotch-Irish descent. Being involved in a difficulty growing out of a love affair, during which he believed he had killed his opponent, he fled beyond the Alleghanies, where he formed a friendship with several adventurers then living in Ohio. He served as a spy against the Indians for several years, and once saved the life of the celebrated pioneer, Daniel Boone. He served under General George Rogers Clark during the revolutionary period, and in 1778 was captured by the Indians and delivered to the British commandant at Detroit; but escaped in July 1779, and in 1782 again commanded a company under Clark. Learning that the man he supposed he had killed was still alive in Virginia, he went to his old home in 1782; but soon returned with his father's family, and settled near Maysville, Kentucky. Kenton served with the rank of major under General Anthony Wayne in 1793-94, became Brigadier-General of the Ohio Militia in 1805, and fought in the battle of the Thames, Canada (in which Tecumthe was killed), in 1813. During his absence his lands were taken by settlers, reducing him to great poverty, but Congress afterward granted him a pension of $240 a year.

12. Anthony Wayne was born in Easttown, Chester County, Pennsylvania, January 1, 1745; died at Presque Isle (Erie), Pennsylvania, December 15, 1796. He was educated at the Philadelphia Academy, became a surveyor, and when twenty years of age was sent to Nova Scotia, on the recommendation of Benjamin Franklin, as the representative of a wealthy corporation. Two years later, in 1767, he was married and settled on a farm in his native county, but continued to follow his profession, and held several local offices. In 1774 he served as a provincial deputy, to consider the disturbing relations between Great Britain and the colonies, and also as a member of the Pennsylvania Convention to discuss similar questions. During 1774-75, he was representative from Chester County to the Pennsylvania Colonial Legislature, and in 1775 was a member of the Committee of Safety. Meanwhile, he devoted himself to the study of the art of war, and raised a regiment of troops, receiving the commission of Colonel, January 3, 1776. Having been sent to reinforce the northern army, he met the British at Three Rivers, but was wounded and compelled to withdraw his troops, concentrating them at Ticonderoga, over which he was given charge. On February 21, 1777, he became a Brigadier-General, and joined Washington's army in New Jersey. He was actively engaged against the British during the following summer, his bravery and good conduct being publicly testified to by Washington. Wayne was successively engaged at the Brandywine, at Warren Tavern, and near Paoli, where the left wing of his division was compelled to retreat, but afterward joined the other wing not far away. Charges against Wayne's action on this occasion led to his demand for a court of inquiry, which acquitted him " with the highest honour." He took a prominent part in the battle of Germantown; in the winter of 1777-78 he did much to relieve the suffering of the troops at Valley Forge, and in March successfully raided the British lines, capturing horses, cattle, and other material. It was through him that the victory of Monmouth was made possible after retreat had been ordered. During the summer of 1779 he commanded a corps of light infantry, which captured the strongly fortified and important Stony Point on the Hudson, July 15-16, in which he was wounded in the head. So important was this victory regarded that Congress voted Wayne a gold medal and the thanks of the nation, and his native State conferred a similar honour. He quelled a mutiny of 1300 Pennsylvania troops in January 1781, to the satisfaction of the troops, and to the advantage of the Government. Sent by Washington to join Lafayette, then operating against Cornwallis in Virginia, Wayne met the entire British army at Jamestown Ford, and by Lafayette's orders attacked the enemy at Green Springs, July 6, thus disconcerting a projected movement by the British before himself falling back. This action demonstrated Wayne's great ability as a General, in that he turned an almost positive defeat into a success. He was actively engaged in the investment and capture of Yorktown, October 6-14, and, after the surrender of Cornwallis, joined Greene in the South. On June 23-24, 1782, Wayne's force was surrounded by a numerous body of Creek Indians under a British officer, who for a brief time held possession of his artillery; but Wayne succeeded in recovering it by a furious attack with swords and bayonets, which compelled the Indians to flee. His last military service was to take possession of Charleston, South Carolina, after its evacuation by the British, December 14, 1782. The brevet rank of Major-General was conferred on him in October 1783.

Returning to Pennsylvania, Wayne resumed his civil life ; in 1784 he was elected to the General Assembly, and served in the Convention that ratified the Federal Constitution. Subsequently, Wayne settled in Georgia, on a tract of land granted him by the State in recognition of his military services, and became a delegate to the Convention that framed the State Constitution in 1787. He was elected to represent Georgia in Congress in 1791, but served only five months, his seat being contested and declared vacant in March 1792. A new election was ordered, but he declined to be a candidate. On Washington's recommendation, Wayne was nominated to be General-in-Chief of the United States army, and was confirmed in that office in April 1792. As several of the Indian tribes of the North-West Territory refused to cease hostilities after the peace of 1783, and attempts by Generals Harmar and St Clair to subjugate them having failed, Wayne collected an adequate and selected force, drilled them for more than a year for the special service for which they were required, and in the autumn of 1793 marched into the North-West, and near Greenville, Ohio, built a stockade, which he called Fort Recovery. Pushing on through the wilderness to the Maumee River in the following summer, Wayne built another post, Fort Adams, at the mouth of the Auglaize, and in August went down the Maumee with a thousand men and encamped at a British post at the foot of the Maumee rapids, called Fort Miami. Here Wayne offered the Indians peace if they would lay down their arms; and, on their refusal, advanced to Fallen Timbers, where, on August 20, the Indians were attacked, and after a severe fight were defeated. Almost all the dead warriors were found with British arms. After laying the country waste, he moved to the mouth of St Joseph and St Mary's Rivers, in the present Indiana, where he built a strong fortification, which he called Fort Wayne. He spent the winter at Greenville, Ohio, where, on August 3, 1795, was signed one of the most important treaties held up to that time, the twelve participating tribes agreeing to lasting peace, and to the cession to the United States of about two-thirds of the present state of Ohio and a portion of Indiana. Returning to Pennsylvania, Wayne was appointed sole commissioner to treat with the Indians, and to take possession of all the forts that had been held by the British, but died from an attack of gout while descending Lake Erie from Detroit.

Wayne's unexpected successes in perilous expeditions won for him the appellation of "Mad Anthony," although Washington referred to him as a prudent officer; and on account of his attention to dress, the sobriquet "Dandy Wayne" was also applied to him. To the Indians he was known as "The Black Snake," and after their defeat in 1794, as "Wind" and "Tornado." His body was removed in 1809 from Presque Isle to Radnor, in his native county. See Armstrong, "Life of Anthony Wayne," in Sparks's *American Biography; Orderly Book of the Northern Army at Fort Ticonderoga and Mount Independence*, Albany, 1859; Appleton's *Cyclopædia of American Biography*.

13. The general statement in regard to the belief of the Indians in a "Great Spirit" equivalent to "God," is a popular fallacy. To the Indian every object had a spirit, or shade, but it is improbable that any Indians realised a spirit greater than all the rest prior to the teachings of the missionaries.

14. Properly Lalawéthika. See note 5.

15. In the northern part of the present Tippecanoe County, Indiana.

16. William Henry Harrison, ninth President of the United States. Indiana territory, organised in 1800, then included the area now comprising the states of Indiana, Illinois, Michigan, and Wisconsin, and a part of Minnesota.

17. This, in brief, is exactly the attitude of the Indians in regard to the tenure of land. There was no individual ownership, and when the tribes first ceded their lands to the Government, it was in the belief that the transfer was for the temporary use of the whites. The Indian had no idea whatsoever of title in fee. See Grinnell in *American Anthropologist*, Vol. IX., No. 1, 1907.

18. *A Memoir of the Public Services of William Henry Harrison, of Ohio*, by James Hall (one of the authors of the present work), Philadelphia, 1836.

19. The purchase was made under the provisions of the treaty held at Fort Wayne, September 30, 1809.

20. "Winemac" was a Potawatomi, and one of the signers of the treaty that aroused Tecumthe's indignation.

21. Tecumthe first had an interview with Harrison in July 1811, and started on this southern trip the next day. He was among the Choctaw in Mississippi in the late summer or early fall of the year named.

22. The settlements of the Creeks and the Seminole were divided into "red towns" and "white towns," or war and peace towns respectively. In the former all wars were declared; in the latter peace was negotiated, and no human blood was allowed to be shed. When war was declared, a red painted pole was erected in the public square, around which the warriors assembled, hence the name "Red Sticks." Baton Rouge, the capital of Louisiana, derived its name from a similar pole erected to define the boundary between the Huma and the Bayougoula tribes.

23. This was Menawa, whose biography and portrait appear in Volume II.

24. During McKenney's journey to the South in the autumn of 1827, for the purpose of conducting negotiations with the Choctaw and the Creeks. See the Introduction. The New Madrid earthquake occurred in 1811.

25. This statement is by no means true of all Indians.

26. See Hall's *Memoir of Harrison*, above cited; also Drake's *Tecumseh*.

27. On this point, see McKenney's *Memoirs*, 1846, Vol. I., p. 181, in which the author aims to support a conclusion that has not been fully substantiated.

28. The date of his death is not known.

ESHTAHUMBAH

(OR, SLEEPY EYES)

WE have but little to say of this individual, whose name, when translated, signifies *Sleepy Eyes*, and is expressive of the character of his countenance. He is one of the hereditary chiefs of the Teton tribe, of the Dacotah nation. In person, he is large and well-proportioned, and has rather a dignified appearance. He is a good-natured, plausible person, but has never been distinguished either in war or as a hunter.

The word Teton means *boaster*, and has been given to this tribe in consequence of the habit of bragging, which is said to prevail among them. They dwell in skin lodges, which are easily removed, and are constantly roving over the vast plains between the St Peter and the Missouri. They trade on both rivers, and are very hostile to white men, whom they insult and rob when they find them on the prairies, where such acts may be safely perpetrated. But all the tribes who live in contact with our frontier have become so conscious of the power of the American Government, as to be cautious in their depredations upon our citizens; and acts of violence are growing every day less numerous upon our borders. The Tetons are fierce, rapacious, and untamable; but are not considered braver than the other Sioux tribes.

ESH-TAH-HUM-LEAH, *or* SLEEPY EYES
A Sioux Chief

NOTE

His name appears as "Eesh-tah-hum-leah (the sleepy eye)" in a list of Indians "now at the seat of Government," in the *National Journal* of Washington City, copied by *Niles' Register* for July 31, 1824. He is mentioned in connection with "She-tah-wah-coe-wah-mene," better known as Little Crow (see p. 125), as one of the "Nacatas, or Sieux— the amiable people." The painter of the portrait, as well as the date, is omitted from the Rhees *Catalogue* of the Government collection; but this lack is supplied by the Inman copy in the Peabody Museum (original numbers, 10 and 43; museum number, 28. 192), which attributes it to King, without date. The name appears as "Esh-tak-hum-leah, Sleepy Eye," in the museum list. The picture (No. 10), according to the Rhees *Catalogue*, bore the title "Eesh-tah-hum-leah, Sleepy Eye. Sioux Chief, from the band called Sipsetongs [Sissetongs]." The subject of the sketch, therefore, belonged to quite another branch of the Dakota, or Sioux. He was born on Minnesota River, near the site of the present Mankato, in Brown County, Minnesota. He died in Roberts county, South Dakota; but his remains, many years after his death, were disinterred and removed to the town in Minnesota that now bears his name, where they were reburied, and a stately monument erected by citizens. The native name of this Indian is doubtless derived from *ishta*, "eye," and *hba*, "dreamy," "sleepy," "drowsy," the *h* in the latter term being a guttural. The last part of the name (*leah*), as given in earlier editions of McKenney and Hall, is hence a misprint of *bah*. Moreover, the name Teton, also, does not signify "boasters" (an error derived from Long's *Second Expedition*, Vol. I., 378, 1824), but is a contraction of *Titoŋwaŋ*, which means "prairie dwellers." The Sisseton and Wahpeton are under the Sisseton Agency, South Dakota, and together numbered 1950 in 1906.

The name of the subject of this sketch was signed to the treaties of Prairie du Chien, August 19, 1825, as "Sleepy Eyes," and July 15, 1830, as "Ete-tahken-bah, Sleeping eyes"; and St Peters, November 30, 1836, as "Ese-tah-ken-bah, or the sleepy eyes." A treaty held at Traverse des Sioux, July 23, 1851, was signed by "Sleepy Eyes young," probably a son. The Sisseton band of which Ishtahba was chief, was known as Chansdachikana, and lived below Lake Traverse, Minnesota. See S. R. Riggs, *Forty Years with the Sioux*, 85, 1880; Heard, *History of the Sioux War*, 1863.

WAAPASHAW

(A SIOUX CHIEF)

THIS distinguished man is head chief of the Keoxa tribe, of the Dacotah nation. His father was a great warrior; the present chief is a wise and prudent man, who holds his station by hereditary tenure, while he sustains himself in the estimation of his people by his talents. He devotes a portion of his time to agriculture. The name by which this tribe is distinguished signifies "relationship overlooked"; because, in their marriages, they unite between nearer relations than the other Sioux; first cousins, uncles and nieces, and even brothers and sisters, intermarry.[1]

We extract from the account of *Long's Second Expedition*, an anecdote in reference to a curious and much vexed question, in which the name of this chief is honourably mentioned. It is a matter of some doubt to what extent the practice of cannibalism has prevailed among the North American Indians. It is certain that some of the tribes have been guilty of this outrage upon decency; it is probable that most of them have participated in it; but we are inclined to believe that there is no evidence of the eating of human flesh by our Indians, from choice, as an article of food; but that they have devoured the flesh of victims sacrificed in their war feasts in obedience to some principle of revenge, or of superstition. The Dacotahs repel the imputation of cannibalism with great horror;

they assert that they have never been guilty of it, but charge their neighbours with the crime. The following incident is in the work to which we have referred, stated on the authority of Renville, an interpreter, to have taken place at Fort Meigs,[2] in 1813.

"The fort was besieged by General Proctor, at the head of the British army, attended by a corps of about three thousand Indians, consisting of Dacotahs, Potawa-tomis, Miamis, Ottowas, Wolves,[3] Hurons, Winnebagoes, Shawnees, Sauks, Foxes, Menominies, etc. They had all shared in the battle, except the Dacotahs, who had not yet engaged against the Americans, and who were then on their way to Quebec. While Renville was seated, one afternoon, with Wapasha and Chetanwakoamane,[4] a deputation came to invite them to meet the other Indians, the object of the meeting not being stated; the two chiefs complied with the request. Shortly after, Frazier (an interpreter), came and informed Renville that the Indians were engaged in eating an American, and invited him to walk over to the place. He went thither, and found the human flesh cut up, and portioned out into dishes, one for each nation of Indians. In every dish, in addition to the flesh, there was corn. At that moment they called upon the bravest man in each nation, to come and take a portion of the heart and head; one warrior from each nation was allowed a fragment of this choice morsel. In the group of Indians present, there was a brave Dacotah, the nephew of Chetanwakoamane, known by the name of the 'Grand Chasseur.' They invited him to step forward and take his share; and among others a Winnebago addressed him, and told him that they had collected their friends to partake of a meal prepared with the flesh of one of that nation that had done them so much injury. Before the Sioux warrior had time to reply, his uncle arose, and bade his nephew rise and depart thence; he then addressed himself to the Indians: 'My friends,' said he, 'we came here, not to eat the Americans, but to wage war against them; that will suffice for us; and could we even do that if left to our own forces? We are poor and destitute, while they possess the means of supplying themselves with all that they require; we ought not therefore to do such things.' His comrade, Wapasha, added, 'We thought that you, who live near to white men, were wiser and more refined than we are who live at a distance; but it must indeed be otherwise if you do such deeds.' They then rose and departed."[5]

It appears that on this occasion human flesh was not resorted to for want of provisions, as the camp was plentifully supplied; nor did fondness for this species of food lead to the dreadful repast, which seems to have been regarded with a natural aversion. The Dacotahs speak of that case in terms of the most decided reprobation. But one instance of cannibalism is known to have occurred among them; when, during a famine, three women, urged by a necessity which few could have controlled, partook of the flesh of a man who had died of hunger; but, two of them dying shortly after, the Indians attributed their decease to this fatal meal. The third lived in degradation, induced by this single act; the nation regard her with horror, and suppose, that a state of corpulence into which she has grown, has been induced by that food, which they predict will eventually prove fatal to her.[6]

During the war between the United States and Great Britain, which commenced in 1812, the British took possession of the outpost which had been established at Prairie du Chien,[7] for the convenience of our intercourse with the Indians, but afterwards abandoned it. The little village, consisting of a few houses, occupied by French

WAA-PA-SHAW
A Sioux Chief

Canadians, was left defenceless, and the Winnebago Indians, a fierce and restless tribe, who occupied the surrounding country, seemed disposed to create a quarrel, which might afford them an opportunity for plunder. Although the whites had long been established there, and had lived in amity with them, they came to the village, took some articles of private property by force, and threatened to massacre the inhabitants, and plunder the town. The alarmed villagers, intimately acquainted with the reckless and desperate character of their neighbours, and aware of their own danger, immediately despatched a messenger to Waapashaw, at his residence on the opposite shore of the Mississippi, not far above Prairie du Chien.[8] His interposition was claimed on account of his great influence, as well in his own tribe as among his neighbours; he was at peace with the surrounding Indians, and with the whites; and there was, between his own band and the Winnebagoes, a long-standing friendship. These tribes had intermarried, and there were then at Prairie du Chien many individuals, the offspring of these marriages, who stood in an equal degree of relationship to both, and some of whom were nearly allied to Waapashaw. Obeying the request, he went down to the village immediately, attended by but one person. The inhabitants, seeing him thus, without the imposing train of warriors by which they had expected to have seen him followed, gave themselves up as lost; justly apprehending that the Winnebagoes, ascertaining that no force would be opposed to them, would now put their sanguinary threats into execution. To an intimation of their fears, and an earnest appeal which they made to him, the chief, with the characteristic taciturnity of his race, gave no reply, but sent his attendant to the Winnebagoes with a message, requiring them to meet him in

council, during that day, at an hour and place which he
appointed. In the meanwhile he remained silent and
reserved, apparently wrapped in deep thought.

The Indian chief is careful of his reputation, and
never appears in public without the preparation which is
necessary to the dignity of his personal appearance, and
the success of any intellectual effort he may be called
upon to make. His face is skilfully painted, and his
person studiously decorated; his passions are subdued,
his plans matured, and his thoughts carefully arranged,
so that when he speaks he neither hazards his own fame
nor jeopards the interest of the tribe. At the appointed
hour the Winnebago chiefs assembled, and Waapashaw
seated himself among them; the warriors formed a circle
around their leaders, and the individuals of less consequence occupied the still more distant places. A few
minutes were passed in silence; then Waapashaw arose,
and placing himself in an attitude of studied, though
apparently careless, dignity, looked round upon the
chiefs with a menacing look. His countenance was fierce
and terrible; and cold and stern were the faces upon
which his piercing eye was bent. He plucked a single
hair from his head—held it up before them—and then
spoke in a grave and resolute tone: "Winnebagoes! do
you see this hair? Look at it. You threaten to massacre
the white people at the Prairie. They are your friends
and mine. You wish to drink their blood. Is that your
purpose? Dare to lay a finger upon one of them, and I
will blow you from the face of the earth, as I now"—
suiting the action to the word—"blow this hair with my
breath, where none can find it." Not a head was turned
at the close of this startling and unexpected annunciation;
not a muscle was seen to move—the keen, black, and
snake-like eyes of that circle of dusky warriors remained

fixed upon the speaker, who, after casting around a look of cool defiance, turned upon his heel and left the council, without waiting for a reply. The insolent savages, who had been vapouring about the village in the most arrogant and insulting manner, hastily broke up the council, and retired quietly to their camp. Not a single Winnebago was to be seen next morning in the vicinity of the village. They knew that the Sioux chief had the power to exterminate them, and that his threats of vengeance were no idle words, uttered by a forked tongue; and, taking counsel from wisdom, they prudently avoided the conduct which would have provoked his resentment.

The Keoxa tribe have two villages on the Mississippi, one near Lake Pepin, and the other at the Iowa River ; and they hunt on both banks of the Great River.[9]

NOTES

1. This noted Indian, known to the French as La Feuille (The Leaf), was at least the second known chief of his name. Pike, who met him in the fall of 1805, makes frequent allusion to him. Commenting on this Indian, Dr Elliott Coues says (*The Explorations of Zebulon Montgomery Pike*, Vol. I., 1895, p. 43):—

"La Feuille is a name which Pike rarely, and only by accident, spells correctly. But in writings of the period it was extremely variable, being found even as Lefei, Lefoi, Lefoy, La Fye, etc. This French term commonly appears in English as The Leaf, sometimes Falling Leaf, and is conjecturally a translation of the native name of the hereditary chiefs of the Kioxa (Kiyuksa) band of Sioux. [S. R. Riggs, *Gram. and Dict. of the Dakota Lang.*, 224, 1851, says :—'. . . the hereditary name of the Dakota chief at the lowest village on the Mississippi, commonly pronounced by the Dakotas Wápaṡa [ṡ = *sh*]; and as the name of a county in Minnesota written, with some want of judgment and taste, Wabashaw.'] This has usually been rendered Wabasha or Wapasha, and explained as derived from *wapa*, leaf, and *sha*, red. In one place Long has Wauppaushaw. In Riggs and Pond's Dakota dictionary the name is given as Wápahasha, and etymologized as from *wapaha*, a standard, and *sha*, red. In *Minn. Hist. Coll.*, I., 2nd ed., 1872, p. 370, J. Fletcher Williams surmises the origination of the name in the chieftainship of the Warpekutes, otherwise Leaf Shooters—though why the tribe was so called, and whether the English term is a proper version of the aboriginal name, seem never to have been satisfactorily shown. Such forms of the chief's name as Wabashaw and Wapashaw, etc., are common, besides which there are some odd and rare ones; e.g., Beltrami, II., p. 180, has: 'The Great Wabiscihouwa, who is regarded as the Ulysses of the whole nation.' Three chiefs named Wabasha are known to us in history. Wabasha I. was famous during the Revolutionary war. Wabasha II. was his son, and the latter is the one of whom Pike, Long, Beltrami, and many others speak. He was already a great chief in Pike's time, who grew in credit and renown with years. He was seen in 1820 by General Henry Whiting, who describes him as a small man, with a patch over one eye, who, nevertheless, impressed every one with respect, and whose profile was said to resemble that of the illustrious Condé. 'While with us at Prairie du Chien,' says Whiting, 'he never moved, or was seen, without his pipe-bearer. His people treated him with reverence. Unlike all other speakers in council, he spoke sitting, con- sidering, it was said, that he was called upon to stand only in the presence of his great father at Washington, or his representatives at St Louis.' He was not a warrior, believing that Indians could prosper only at peace with one another and with the whites, and declared that he had never been at war with the latter, though many of his young men, against his advice, had been led astray in the war of 1812. His son, Wabasha III., resided at the village below Lake Pepin until 1853, and in 1872 was living on the Niobrara Reservation."

Pike regarded Wabasha as chief of the entire Sioux or Dakota nation, and in consequence of his importance granted him a commission and a flag; but he was in fact chief only of the Kiyuksa (Kioxa) band of the Mdewakanton Sioux (a sub-tribe of the Santee), which occupied two villages: one on the Mississippi below Lake Pepin, at the present Winona, Minnesota; the other on upper Iowa River, at its mouth, on the south side, and, therefore, in the north-eastern corner of Iowa. In 1823 the Kiyuksa numbered about 400. After the Sioux war in 1862, they were removed to the Missouri River, and are now on the Niobrara Reservation in Nebraska, but are no longer officially recognised as distinct from the other Santee. The name Kiyuksa does not signify "relationship overlooked" (a definition copied from Long), but "to break in two one's own," "to break or violate," the band having been so designated because its members broke the marriage law by taking wives within prohibited degrees of relationship.

The original of the accompanying portrait was painted at Prairie du Chien, Wisconsin, by J. O. Lewis (who recorded the name in the form Waa-ba-shaw) on the occasion of the treaty held at that place, August 19, 1825. The Inman copy, "after King," in the Peabody Museum, bears original number, 99; and museum number, 28. 193.

The importance of this chief may be judged by the fact that his name ("Wa-ba-sha, or the leaf") appears first among twenty-six Sioux signers of that treaty. He was the first signer also, on behalf of the "Sioux of the Mississippi," of another treaty made at Prairie du Chien, July 15, 1830, his name appearing as "Wabishaw, or red leaf." George Catlin painted his portrait in 1835 (see Catlin's *North American Indians*, Vol. II., p. 132, London, 1866) as "Wá-a-pa-shaw, head chief of the Keoxa tribe of the Dacotah nation." Catlin adds that he was a very distinguished man; blind in one eye; since dead (Catlin, *Catalogue*, 1840, No. 90). The latter statement seems to be substantiated by the treaty of September 10, 1836, which is signed by "Sau-tabe-say, Wa-ba-shaw's son"; while the loss of one eye is suggested by the Lewis portrait, which shows the subject wearing a triangular blind of cloth. For information respecting Wabasha I., see E. D. Neill, *History of Minnesota*, 1858, and the *Collections of the Minnesota Historical Society.*

2. Fort Meigs, on the Maumee River, below Toledo, Ohio.

3. The Munsee, or Wolf, division of the Delawares.

4. *Chetañ wakan mañi*, or Little Crow (see p. 125), chief of the Kapozha division of the Mdewakanton Sioux.

5. The extract is from Stephen H. Long's *Narrative of a Second Expedition to the Source of St Peter's River*, compiled by William H. Keating, Vol. I., 1824, p. 394.

"Frazier the interpreter," referred to, was James Frazer, trader at Prairie du Chien, whom Pike alludes to as "a young gentleman, clerk to Mr Blakely of Montreal; he was born in Vermont, but has latterly resided in Canada" (Coues ed., Vol. I., p. 40). Coues believed him to be a relative of Robert Frazer, Frazier, Fraser, etc., who accompanied Lewis and Clark. The occasion of the cannibalism referred to is thus described by Rev. Edward D. Neill in "A Sketch of Joseph Renville" (*Minnesota Historical Society Collections*, Vol. I., p. 199, reprint 1872):—
"In 1813 he was at the siege of Fort Meigs. One afternoon, while he was seated with Wabasha and the renowned Petit Corbeau, the grandfather of the present chief of the Kaposia band, an Indian presented himself, and told the chiefs that they were wanted by the head men of the other nations that were there congregated. When they arrived at the rendezvous, they were surprised to find that the Winnebagoes had taken an American captive, and after roasting him, had apportioned his body in as many dishes as there were nations, and had invited them to participate in the feast. Both the chiefs and Renville were indignant at this inhumanity, and Col. Dickson [a British officer] being informed of the fact, the Winnebago who was the author of the outrage was turned out of camp."

6. Cannibalism has been a not uncommon practice among the American tribes, and while the custom of eating human flesh has been usually ceremonial or religious in character, it is also known to have been practised during stress of hunger, as well as, indeed, from choice. The term "cannibal" is a Spanish corruption of the Indian tribal name *Carib*. In its principal form, cannibalism was a war ceremony, the

belief being that the estimable qualities of an enemy, which centered chiefly in the heart, would be imparted to those who partook of that organ of the slain warrior.   In other instances other parts of the body were eaten, and sometimes even women and children participated in the gruesome feast.   Some of the Iroquois tribes compelled their prisoners to swallow pieces of their own flesh.   The custom of consuming human flesh was so characteristic of the Mohawk, Attacapa, and Tonkawa tribes, that they were generally known among their neighbours by names which mean "man-eaters."

7. Fort Shelby, later Fort Crawford, at the present Prairie du Chien, Crawford County, Wisconsin.   For an account of the capture in 1814, see Neill, *History of Minnesota*, p. 283 *et seq.*, 1858 ; *Collections of the State Historical Society of Wisconsin*, Vol. II., 122 *et seq.*, 220, 1856 ; *Ibid.*, III., 270-279, 1857.   A part of Wabasha's band participated in the capture.

8. The distance from Prairie du Chien to Winona is about 100 miles in an air line.

9. See note 1.

METAKOOSEGA

(OR, PURE TOBACCO)

METAKOOSEGA, or *Pure Tobacco*,[1] is one of the *Lac du Flambeau* band of the Chippeway, or, more properly, Ojibway nation,[2] and resides on the borders of Trout Lake. This man was one of a war party, raised in 1824, to go against the Sioux. They descended the Chippeway River to the Mississippi, and unfortunately fell in with a trader named Findley, from Prairie du Chien, whom, together with the crew of his boat, they murdered.[3]

It is provided, by our treaties with the Indian tribes, that, upon the commission of such outrages, the offenders shall be given up by their tribes, to be tried and punished under our laws; and the practice of our Government has been to insist upon a rigid observance of this regulation. When the usual demand was made for the murderers of Findley, twenty-nine of the party voluntarily surrendered themselves to the agent at the Sault de Ste Marie. They were examined, seven of them committed for trial, and confined at Mackinaw, and the remainder discharged. At the ensuing term of the court, the judge of the district declined trying the prisoners, in consequence of some objection which had been raised against his jurisdiction; and, during the following winter, they cut their way out of the log jail and escaped.

In the mission of Governor Cass and Colonel McKenney

to the Upper Lakes, in 1826, it was made part of their
duty to ascertain and demand the real perpetrators of the
aggression on the party of Mr Findley. This has always
been a difficult and delicate subject in the relations of our
Government with the Indians, in consequence of the very
wide difference between their moral code and our own.
They admit the obligation of the *lex talionis* to its fullest
extent, but they cannot understand that any other than
the injured party has a right to claim the penalty. Had
any of the near relatives of Mr Findley, for instance, gone
to the Lac du Flambeau, to revenge themselves upon his
murderers, they would have been considered as in the
praiseworthy performance of an act of duty, and would
have been permitted to put the guilty parties to death, *if
they could*—and none would have interfered, either to aid
or prevent them. But they view the interference of the
Government with jealousy; and, while on the one hand,
they often refuse obstinately to betray the offender, or
shield him by evasion and delay, they as often, on the
other, when their fears of the resentment of our Government become awakened, deliver up some innocent party,
who volunteers his life as a peace offering, to satisfy what
they deem a kind of national thirst for the blood of one
of the tribe which has insulted us.

The following extract from Colonel McKenney's account
of this transaction will be interesting :—" The council
met ; when, according to arrangement, I made the demand
for the surrender of the murderers. This being done, and
there being one Indian present belonging to the Lac du
Flambeau band, and who was of the party who committed
the murder, he was called up, and formally examined. He
is clearly innocent. Indeed his presence here demonstrates
that fact. It was in proof, that he dissuaded the murderers
from committing the act. We told him, if he had been

META-KOOSEGA, *or* PURE TOBACCO
A Chippeway Warrior

guilty, we would have taken him with us, and tried him by our laws; and if, on proof, he had turned out to have had a hand in the bloody act, he should have been hanged. During the examination, his brother came up to the table, greatly agitated. He showed great anxiety, and said he knew the murderers had *upbraided* his brother because he would not join them. Another Indian declared *he knew* he was innocent. The governor said, 'Will you put your hand on your breast, and say that in the presence of the Great Spirit?' The moment the interpreter put this question, the Indian looked him full in the face, and answered, '*Am I a dog that I should lie?*' This reply is somewhat remarkable, not only on account of its resemblance to the scriptural expression—'Is thy servant a dog?' etc.—but because there is hardly anything on which an Indian sets so high a value as his dog. This is proverbial; yet he is constantly referred to as an object of contempt! Indians never swear—I mean until they learn it of their white brothers—and their most degrading epithet is to call their opponents *dogs*. Here is a strange union of respect and contempt." [4]

Metakoosega was implicated in the murder, but did not surrender himself. He is a tall, well-made man, with a stern countenance; and is a *jossekeed*,[5] or medicine worker, much respected by his band for his supposed skill in necromancy.

NOTES

1. The proper name of this chief is doubtless *Mitakosige*, "I smoke pure tobacco" (*i.e.*, without any admixture of bark or of other plants), or *Métakosiged*, "He who smokes pure tobacco." The name is signed "Maytaukooseegay" to the treaty of Fond du Lac, Lake Superior, August 5, 1826. The painting was evidently made by Lewis, who, it will be remembered (see the Introduction), was present on this occasion, and witnessed the treaty. This portrait, however, does not appear in

the Lewis *Port-folio*, nor does the name appear in the list of portraits in the Indian Gallery of the War Department, although it should be said that the names of all the subjects are not included. That the portrait did exist in the Indian Gallery, however, and that it was a copy by King, is attested by the Inman copy, "after King," in the Peabody Museum, which bears original number, 81 ; and museum number, 28. 194.

H. R. Schoolcraft, the ethnologist, came into close contact with this Indian while agent at Sault Ste Marie, Michigan. He says : "This man resides the greater part of the time on the Canadian side of the [St Mary's] river, but hunts often on the American shore. He resided many years ago with a French family at St Mary, and has imbibed some-thing of the French taste and manners, always wearing an ornamental hat, and making a bow on entering and leaving the office. He has been in the regular habit of visiting me from the year 1822, and generally applies for what is termed *nwappo* [i.e., *nawâpon*, 'provisions for a journey'] on setting out for his fall and winter hunts. His elder wife, for he has two, is a Sioux slave, taken in youth" (*Personal Memoirs*, 124, 1851; entry for November 7, 1826). Again : "Me-ta-koos-se-ga, *i.e.*, Smoking-weed, or Pure Tobacco, who was living with two wives, a mother and her daughter. He complained that a young woman whom he had brought up had left his lodge, and taken shelter with the family of the widow of a Canadian. It appears that the old fellow had been making advances to this girl to become his third wife, and that she had fled from his lodge to avoid his importunities" (*Ibid.*, p. 124 ; entry for October 17, 1822). One of the wives, probably the elder, was named Margaret. The Sioux captive had lived with the Chippeway for thirty years. Metakoosega seems to have been an inveterate beggar, often visiting the agent himself, or sending a wife under pretence that he was incapacitated, in quest of provisions. On one occasion—the third in three weeks—Schoolcraft accused him of laziness and of investing too freely in liquor. Giving him some tobacco and good advice, the Indian was told to go home and smoke upon the agent's words (p. 253).

2. The term Chippeway, or Chippewa, is the popular adaptation of the tribal name *Ojibway*, meaning "to roast till puckered up," referring to the puckered seam on their moccasins. The Lac du Flambeau band of this important tribe, called Wáswágaming ("Lake of Torches"), within the tribe, lived on Trout Lake, in the present Vilas County, northern Wisconsin, until, by treaty of September 30, 1854, they ceded their lands to the United States, and were assigned a reservation of 26,356 acres, a short distance south-westward, where they now number 810 souls.

3. John L. Findley (or Findlay) was a sutler's clerk at Fort Craw-ford, Prairie du Chien, in 1816, but was discharged. He later went to Mackinaw, procured a stock of goods, and set up a trading establishment at Prairie du Chien, but failed, his business being assigned to Joseph Rolette, a trader and close bargainer. In 1819 he was clerk of court. Findlay married Miss Hurtileese, a quarter-blood Sioux, half-sister of

Mrs Rolette. The circumstances of the killing here mentioned vary in details, but from the best accounts Findley, in July 1824, in company with a Frenchman named Depouse, a Canadian named Barrette, and one other, went up the Mississippi in a canoe, landing on the shore of Lake Pepin, where they met a party of Chippewa, led by Nubobeence, or Little Broth (or, according to another account, Kewaynokwut of the Lac Vieux Desert band of Ojibwa), on their way to fight the Sioux. According to the Nubobeence story, that chief had lost a favourite child by sickness, and he became bent on shedding the blood of the hereditary enemies of his people, in order to assuage his grief. The narrator of the Kewaynokwut account relates that that Indian, while very ill, made a vow that if he recovered he would lead a party against the Sioux, and that this excursion was the result. Very likely both accounts are correct. The Canadian thought he recognised in the party an Indian who had stolen a horse from him during the previous winter, and the white men, being in liquor, provoked a quarrel, which resulted in the killing of the entire party, and the theft of their goods. On the other hand, it is said that the Ojibway party, consisting of twenty-nine warriors, discovered the camp of the white men on a foggy morning when all were asleep. Finding that they were not Sioux, they began to pillage the camp, first killing all but Findley, who was near his canoe. He was at length pursued by an Indian named Little Thunder, who shot him, then waded into the water, cut off his head, and took the scalp. The affair created great excitement, and the murderers surrendered on June 22, 1825. Nubobeence and The Little Eddy, another member of the party, were living respectively at Ontonagan and La Pointe as late as 1852. See *Minnesota Historical Society Collections*, V., 1885 ; *Wisconsin Historical Society Collections*, II., 1856 ; Neill, *History of Minnesota*, 1858 ; Schoolcraft, *Personal Memoirs*, pp. 198-199, 210-211, 1851.

4. The account of this episode is extracted, with slight changes, from McKenney's *Sketches of a Tour to the Lakes*, pp. 324-325, Baltimore, 1827.

5. *Tchéssakid*, "he who performs juggling" : "Indian juggler."—Baraga, *Otchipwe Dictionary*.

WESHCUBB

(OR, THE SWEET)

WESHCUBB, *The Sweet*, is a chief of Red Lake, north
of the sources of the Mississippi.[1] He is the son of *Le
Sucre*, a chief who is mentioned by General Pike, in his
narrative of his voyage up the Mississippi, in 1806. The
similarity of the names of the father and son, would seem
to indicate the existence of some family trait of character,
which was designed to be described by their respective
names, which have reached us in English and French
translations. The father died on Lake Superior, while on
his return home from a visit to Michilimackinac. The
son is represented as worthy of the place he holds in the
estimation of his tribe. He is considered a just and good
man, but has never evinced much capacity, nor shown a
disposition to lead war parties. The family is noted for a
singular freak of the son of Weshcubb, who feigned, or
fancied himself, a woman, and assumed the female dress
and employments. The cause of this transformation, so
especially remarkable in a savage, who considers the
woman an inferior being, and in the son of a chief, who
can aspire to the office of his father, if worthy, but not
otherwise, is not known. It might have been suggested
by a dream, or induced by monomania, or by some bodily
infirmity.[2] He, however, joined war parties, and after

120

WESH-CUBB, *or* THE SWEET
A Chippeway Chief

serving in seven expeditions, was at last killed by the
enemy.

NOTES

1. Properly *Wishkub* (the vowels here, as elsewhere, have the continental values), signifying "sweet (something)." The original portrait
was painted by Lewis at Prairie du Chien in 1825, and was copied, with
considerable change, by King in the following year. See the Introduction, Lewis list, p. xxxix., No. 32 ("Weesh-cub"), and the Indian
Gallery list, p. xlviii., No. 47 ("Whesh-laub"). The Inman copy, preserved in the Peabody Museum (original number, 74; museum number,
28. 195), attributes the original to King. It bears no date.

The name of this Indian was signed to the Prairie du Chien treaty
of August 19, 1825, but not to that of Fond du Lac in the year following.
He was certainly not, as McKenney and Hall state, so distinguished as
his father, the head-chief the Red Lake band of Chippeway when Lieut.
Zebulon Montgomery Pike visited them in 1806. The Sweet, the elder,
Pike describes as "a venerable old man," who delivered to him a speech
at Leech Lake, Minnesota, February 16, 1806, politely declining Pike's
invitation to visit General Wilkinson at St Louis :—"I have heard and
understood the words of our great father. It overjoys me to see you
make peace among us. I should have accompanied you had my family
been present, and would have gone to see my father, the great war-
chief. This medal I hold in my hands I received from the English
chiefs. I willingly deliver it up to you. Wabasha's calumet, with
which I am presented, I receive with all my heart. Be assured that I
will use my very best endeavours to keep my young men quiet. There
is my calumet. I send it to my father, the great war-chief. What does
it signify that I should go to see him? Will not my pipe answer the
same purpose?" Pike spells his name "Wiscoup," and refers to him
also by both his English and his French names. Indeed, he was
generally known as Le Sucre.

Another interesting anecdote reflecting the character of Wishkub
the elder is related by Warren in 1852 ("History of the Ojibways," *Minn.
Hist. Soc. Coll.*, V., 376, 1885), referring to the period of the war of
1812 :—

"About the same time that Keesh-ke-mun so firmly withstood the
inducements and threats of the British officers at Fort Howard, We-esh-
coob, the war-chief of the Pillagers, with a party of his people from
Leech Lake, happened to be present at the Island of Michilimackinac.
He was vainly urged by the British agents to join their arms with his
band of warriors, who were noted as being the bravest of the Ojibway
tribe. At a council held within the fort, this chief was asked, for
the last time, by the British commandant, to array himself under their

flag. We-esh-coob, in more decided terms than ever, refused, and his words so exasperated the commandant that he rose from his seat, and forgot himself so far as to say to the Pillagers:—

"'I thought you were men, but I see that you are but women, not fit even to wear the breech-cloth. Go back to your homes. I do not wish the assistance of women. Go, put on the clothing which more befits you, and remain quiet in your villages.'

"As he delivered this violent speech, he was proceeding to leave the council room, when We-esh-coob, having quietly listened to the interpretation thereof, rose to his feet, and approaching the angry Englishman, he put his hand on his epaulette and gently held him back. 'Wait,' said he, 'you have spoken; now let me speak. You say that we should not wear the breech-cloth, but the dress of women.' Then pointing to the opposite shore of the lake, towards the site of the old English fort which the Ojibways had taken in 1763, We-esh-coob exclaimed:—

"'Englishman! have you already forgotten that we once made you cry like children? yonder! Who was the woman then?

"'Englishman! you have said that we are women. If you doubt our manhood, you have young men here in your strong house. I have also young men. You must come out on some open place, and we will fight. You will better know whether we are fit or not to wear the breech-cloth.

"'Englishman! you have said words which the ears of We-esh-coob have never before heard,' and throwing down his blanket in great excitement, he pointed to different scars on his naked body, and exclaimed: 'I thought I carried about me the marks which proved my manhood.'

"The English officer, whose irritation had somewhat abated during the delivery of this answer, grasped the unusually excited Indian by the hand, and requested the interpreter to beg him to forget his hasty words. Peace and goodwill were thus restored, but this bitter taunt tended greatly to strengthen the minds of the Ojibways against the agents who were continually engaged amongst them to draw them into the war."

The Red Lake Chippeway at this time were estimated at 1020; their present population (including the Pembina band) is 1360. Their reservation, in north-western Minnesota, comprises more than half a million acres.

2. On January 2, 1801, Wiskub, or Weshcubb, junior, visited Alexander Henry, who had established a trading-post in the Red River valley, a short distance from Little Park River, Minnesota. Henry (*Manuscript Journals of Alexander Henry and of David Thompson*, 1799-1814, edited by Elliott Coues, New York, 1897, I., pp. 164-165) describes the offspring of the great warrior as follows:—

"Berdash [*i.e.*, bardash, a catamite], a son of Sucrie, arrived from the Assiniboine, where he had been with a young man to carry tobacco concerning the war. This person is a curious compound between a man and a woman. He is a man both as to members and courage, but pretends to be womanish, and dresses as such. His walk and mode of sitting, his manners, occupations, and language are those of a woman. His father, who is a great chief amongst the Saulteurs, cannot persuade him to act like a man. About a month ago, in a drinking-match, he got into a quarrel, and had one of his eyes knocked out with a club. He is very troublesome when drunk. He is very fleet, and a few years ago was reckoned the best runner among the Saulteurs. Both his speed and his courage were tested some years ago on the Schian River, when Monsieur Reaume attempted to make peace between the two nations, and Berdash accompanied a party of Saulteurs to the Sioux camp. They at first appeared reconciled to each other through the intercession of the whites; but on the return of the Saulteurs, the Sioux pursued them. Both parties were on foot, and the Sioux have the name of being extraordinarily swift. The Saulteurs imprudently dispersed in the plains, and several were killed; but the party with Berdash escaped without any accident, in the following manner: One of them had got from the Sioux a bow, but only a few arrows. On starting and finding themselves pursued, they ran a considerable distance, until they perceived the Sioux were gaining fast upon them, when Berdash took the bow and arrows from his comrades, and told them to run as fast as possible, without minding him, as he feared no danger. He then faced the enemy, and began to let fly his arrows. This checked their course, and they returned the compliment with interest; but it was so far off that only a chance arrow could have hurt him, as they had nearly spent their strength when they fell near him. His own arrows were soon expended, but he lost no time in gathering up those that fell near him, and thus he had a continual supply. Seeing his friends some distance ahead, and the Sioux moving to surround him, he turned and ran full speed to join his comrades, the Sioux after him. When the latter approached too near, Berdash again stopped and faced them with his bow and arrows, and kept them at bay. Thus did he continue to manœuvre until they reached a spot of strong wood, which the Sioux dared not enter."

John Tanner, the captive, gives the following account of the peculiarities of this Indian (*Narrative of the Captivity of John Tanner*, New York, 1830, pp. 105-106):—

"Some time in the course of this winter, there came to our lodge one of the sons of the celebrated Ojibbeway chief, called Wesh-ko-bug (the sweet), who lived at Leech Lake. This man was one of those who make themselves women, and are called women by the Indians. There are several of this sort among most, if not all, Indian tribes; they are commonly called A-go-kwa, a word which is expressive of their condition. This creature, called Czaw-wen-dib (the yellow head), was now near fifty years old, and had lived with many husbands. I do not know whether she had seen me, or only heard of me, but she soon let me know she had come a long distance to see me, and with the hope of living with me. She often offered herself to me, but not being discouraged with one refusal, she repeated her disgusting advances, until I was almost driven from the lodge. Old Net-no-kwa was perfectly well acquainted with her character, and only laughed at the embarrassment and shame which I evinced whenever she addressed me. She seemed rather to countenance and encourage the Yellow Head in remaining at our lodge. The latter was very expert in the various employments of the women, to which all her time was given. At length, despairing of success in her addresses to me, or being too much pinched by hunger, which was commonly felt in our lodge, she disappeared, and was absent three or four days. I began to hope I should be no more troubled with her, when she came back loaded with dry meat. She stated that she had found the band of Wa-ge-to-tah-gun, and that that chief had sent by her an invitation for us to join him. He had heard of the niggardly conduct of Wah-zhe-kwaw-maish-koon towards us, and had sent the A-go-kwa to say to me, 'My nephew, I do not wish you to stay there to look at the meat that another kills, but is too mean to give you.' I was glad enough of this invitation, and started immediately. At the first encampment, as I was doing something by the fire, I heard the A-go-kwa at no great distance in the woods, whistling to call me. Approaching the place, I found she had her eyes on game of some kind, and presently I discovered a moose. I shot him twice in succession, and twice he fell at the report of the gun ; but it is probable that I shot too high, for at last he escaped. The old woman reproved me severely for this, telling me she feared that I should never be a good hunter. But before night the next day, we arrived at Wa-ge-to-te's lodge, where we ate as much as we wished. Here, also, I found myself relieved from the persecutions of the A-go-kwa, which had become intolerable. Wa-ge-to-te, who had two wives, married her. This introduction of a new inmate into the family of Wa-ge-to-te occasioned some laughter, and produced some ludicrous incidents, but was attended with less uneasiness and quarrelling than would have been the bringing in of a new wife of the female sex."

Those who desire to pursue the subject may consult Krafft-Ebing, *Psychopathia Sexualis, with Especial Reference to Contrary Sexual Instinct,* translated by Charles Gilbert Chaddock, Philadelphia and London, 1894.

LITTLE CROW

(A SIOUX CHIEF)

The name of this individual is, in his own language, *Chatonwahtooamany*, or the "Sparrowhawk that comes to you walking." The French gave him the name of *Petit Corbeau*, and the English appellation, placed at the head of this sketch, is a translation from the latter.[1]

He visited Washington City in 1824, and was, at that time, head chief of the *Kahpozhay* band of the *Munday-wahkanton*, and a person of some consideration. He claims to be, and perhaps is, by hereditary right, the head chief of the whole Sioux nation; but he has fallen into disrepute, and is at this time without any influence, even in his own band. He resides at a distance from his band, on or near the western shore of Lake Superior; is cunning, artful, and treacherous; is not much distinguished as a warrior, but is very successful as a hunter, especially of beaver.[2] The name Kahpozhay, or Kapoja, as others understand it, signifies *light*, and is applied to this band to indicate that they are more active than the other branches of the Sioux or Dacotah family.

Soon after peace was declared between the United States and Great Britain, in 1815, the Sioux were invited by the commanding officer at Drummond's island[3] to visit that post. On their arrival, the Indians were informed by the officer, that he had sent for them to thank them in the name of His Majesty, for the aid they had rendered the British during the late war and for the bravery they had displayed on several occasions, as well as to communicate the intelligence of the peace which had been declared between the great belligerent parties. He concluded by pointing to a large pile of goods that lay heaped upon the floor, which, he told them, were intended as presents for themselves. The Little Crow replied, that his people had been prevailed upon by the British to make war upon a people whom they scarcely knew, and who had never done them any harm. "Now," continued he, "after we have fought for you, endured many hardships, lost some of our people, and awakened the vengeance of a powerful nation, our neighbours, you make a peace for yourselves, and leave us to get such terms as we can. You no longer need our services, and offer us these goods as a compensation for having deserted us. But, no—we will not take them; we hold them and yourselves in equal contempt." So saying, he spurned the articles of merchandise with his foot, and walked away. This conduct was the more remarkable, from its inconsistency with the gravity and decorum with which the chiefs usually deport themselves on public occasions. The Indians, however, who were not so sensitive in regard to the injury supposed to have been done them, received the goods.

The Little Crow has a son named Big Thunder, who is a fierce and terrible fellow. A few years ago [in 1819 or 1820] the father and son took a long journey to the north-west, in search, as they pretended, of knowledge. They visited the British settlement at Pembina,[4] and attended a great meeting at Lake Traverse,[5] at which fifteen hundred warriors are said to have been present, from the Assiniboin, Mandan, Minnetaree, Ioway, and other tribes, as

well as from each of the tribes of the Dacotah nation.   On
this solemn occasion the various speakers all addressed the
Little Crow by the title of "Father"; thus, according to
their rules of etiquette, in the observance of which they
are exceedingly tenacious, acknowledging him to be
superior by hereditary right to all other Dacotah chiefs,
and the Dacotah nation as superior to their own.   The
festivities, which lasted almost a fortnight, consisted of
dances, songs, and repasts; the principal feast was celebrated on the 25th June; and, as the buffalo were abundant
at that season, a great number were killed.[6]

The Kahpozhay band have but one village, which is
on the Mississippi River, below the mouth of the St
Peter's.[7]

NOTES

1. Strictly, the name is *Chetañ-wakan-mañi*, and signifies in the Dakota
language, "The sacred pigeon-hawk which comes walking." Little
Crow was one of several hereditary chiefs of the Kapozha band who bore
this common dynastic name, all of them more or less distinguished.
(For additional information, see the *Collections of the Minnesota Historical
Society; Collections of the State Historical Society of Wisconsin; South
Dakota Historical Collections*, Vol. II., 1904; Neill, *History of Minnesota*,
1858; *Pike's Expeditions*, Coues ed., 1895.) The Little Crow here
described, who may be designated Little Crow II., was born about
1770, and died about 1827, being succeeded by his son, generally
called Wamde Tanka, "Big Eagle," who accidentally died as the result
of a gunshot wound, when he was succeeded by his son Taoyatiduta,
"His Red People," who was the "Little Crow" at the time of the
Sioux outbreak in 1862, and was killed at its close. The occasion of
the visit of Little Crow II. to Washington in 1824 is noted in *Niles'
Register* for July 31 of that year, copied from the *National Journal* of
Washington, the name appearing as "She-tah-wah-coe-wah-mene (the
Sparrow that hunts as he walks"). It was probably at this time that
the accompanying portrait was painted by King (No. 125 of the Govern-
ment collection; see Introduction, p. lii.). Little Crow II. signed the
treaties of Prairie du Chien, August 19, 1825 (on which occasion
Lewis painted his portrait, No. 23 of the Lewis *Port-folio*), and July 15,

1830 ("Tchataqua Manie, or little crow"). He was not chief of the
entire Sioux nation, except through appointment by Lieutenant Pike.
The Inman copy of Little Crow's portrait, "after King," is preserved
in the Peabody Museum (original number, 29; museum number, 28.
196). It is without date.

The name Kapozha means "not encumbered with much baggage,"
and this is the sense in which McKenney and Hall, following Long,
here employ the term "light." This band, like the Kiyuksa, belonged
to the Mdewakanton division of the Sioux, although a branch of the
Sisseton was also designated Kapozha. Their village, known as Kaposia,
and often called Little Crow's Village, was on the east bank of the
Mississippi, below the mouth of Minnesota River, on the site of the
present St Paul, Minnesota. It was visited in 1820 by the party of Lewis
Cass, including Henry R. Schoolcraft, the latter describing it as consisting
of "twelve large lodges, which are said to give shelter to two hundred
souls. . . . The chief was among the first to greet us. He is a
man below the common size, but brawny and well proportioned; and,
although above fifty years of age, retains the look and vigour of forty.
He invited us to his lodge—a spacious building about sixty feet by
thirty, substantially constructed of logs and bark. . . ."—Schoolcraft, *Summary Narrative of an Exploratory Expedition to the Sources of the
Mississippi River in* 1820, pp. 160-161, Philadelphia, 1855.

James Doty, the secretary to Governor Cass, adds: "There is a great
deal of fire in his eyes, which are black and piercing. His nose is
prominent and has an aquiline curve, his forehead falling a little from
the facial angle, and his whole countenance animated and expressive
of a shrewd mind."—*Wisconsin Historical Society Collections*, XIII., p. 212.

The Kapozha are now on the Santee Reservation in Nebraska, but
are no longer officially recognised as a separate band.

2. A beaver-trapping episode that well displays Little Crow's
magnanimity is interestingly related by Schoolcraft (*op. cit.*, pp. 157-
158):—

"It is related that the chief, Little Crow, going out to the confines
of the Chippeway territory, to examine his beaver-traps, discovered an
individual of that tribe in the act of taking a beaver from the trap. As
he was himself unperceived, the tribes being at war, and the offence an
extreme one, a summary punishment would have been justified by Indian
law. But the Sioux chief decided differently: 'Take no alarm,' said he,
approaching the offender; 'I come to present you the trap, of which I
see you stand in need. Take my gun also, as I see you have none of
your own, and return to the land of your countrymen; and linger not
here, lest some of my young men should discover your footsteps.'"

3. In Lake Erie, in the extreme eastern part of the northern
peninsula of Michigan.

4. Probably Pembina in the present North Dakota. The name means
"cranberry."

LITTLE CROW
A Sioux Chief

5. The present Lake Traverse, on the boundary of Minnesota and South Dakota.

6. This information is derived from Long's *Expedition to the Source of St Peter's River,* Vol. I., pp. 383-384, Philadelphia, 1824. Big Thunder was possibly one of the two boys, sons of Little Crow, killed by the Chippeway while on a war expedition on St Croix River in 1841. See Sibley's "Recollections," in *Minnesota Historical Society Collections,* Vol. III., p. 251.

7. See note 1.

SEQUOYAH, OR GEORGE GUESS

(THE INVENTOR OF THE CHEROKEE ALPHABET)

THE portrait of this remarkable individual is one of great interest.[1] It presents a mild, engaging countenance, entirely destitute of that wild and fierce expression which almost invariably marks the features, or characterises the expression, of the American Indians and their descendants. It exhibits no trace of the ferocity of the savage; it wants alike the vigilant eye of the warrior and the apathy of the less intellectual of that race. The contour of the face, and the whole style of the expression, as well as the dress, are decidedly Asiatic, and might be triumphantly cited in evidence of the Oriental origin of our tribes by those who maintain that plausible theory. It is not merely intelligent and thoughtful, but there is an almost feminine refinement and a luxurious softness about it which might characterise the features of an Eastern sage, accustomed to ease and indolence, but are little indicative of an American origin, or of a mind formed among the wilds of our western frontier.

At an early period in the settlement of our colonies, the Cherokees received with hospitality the white men who went among them as traders; and having learned the value of articles of European fabric, became in some measure dependent upon this traffic. Like other Indians, they engaged in hostilities against us when it suited their

180

convenience, or when stimulated by caprice or the love of plunder. But as our settlements approached, and finally surrounded them, they were alike induced by policy, and compelled by their situation, to desist from their predatory mode of life, and became comparatively inoffensive neighbours to the whites. The larger number continued to subsist by hunting, while a few engaged in agriculture. Inhabiting a fertile country, in a southern climate, within the limits of Georgia, their local position held out strong temptations to white men to settle among them as traders, and many availed themselves of these advantages. With the present object of carrying on a profitable traffic, and the ulterior view of acquiring titles to large bodies of land, they took up their residence among the Indians, and intermarried with the females of that race. Some of these were prudent, energetic men, who made themselves respected, and acquired influence, which enabled them to rank as head-men, and to transmit the authority of chiefs to their descendants. Many of them became planters, and grew wealthy in horses and cattle, and in negro slaves, which they purchased in the southern states. The only art, however, which they introduced, was that of agriculture ; and this but few of the Indians had the industry to learn and practise, further than in the rude cultivation of small fields of corn by the women.

In this condition they were found by the missionaries who were sent to establish schools, and to introduce the gospel. The half-breeds had now become numerous ; many of them were persons of influence, using with equal facility the respective tongues of their civilised and savage ancestors, and desirous of procuring for their children the advantages they had but partially enjoyed themselves. By them the missionaries were favourably received, their exertions encouraged, and their schools sustained ; but the great mass of the Cherokees were as little improved by these as other portions of the race have been by similar attempts.

Sequoyah, or, as he is commonly called, George Guess, is the son of a white man, named Gist, and of a woman who was of the mixed blood. The latter was perfectly untaught and illiterate, having been reared in the wigwam in the laborious and servile habits of the Indian women. She soon became either a widow or a neglected wife, for in the infancy of George we hear nothing of the father, while the mother is known to have lived alone, managing her little property and maintaining herself by her own exertions. That she was a woman of some capacity, is evident from the undeviating affection for herself with which she inspired her son, and the influence she exercised over him, for the Indians have naturally but little respect for their female relations, and are early taught to despise the character and the occupations of women. Sequoyah seems to have had no relish for the rude sports of the Indian boys, for when quite young he would often stroll off alone into the woods, and employ himself in building little houses with sticks, evincing thus early an ingenuity which directed itself towards mechanical labours. At length, while yet a small boy, he went to work of his own accord, and built a milk-house for his mother. Her property consisted chiefly in horses and cattle, that roamed in the woods, and of which she owned a considerable number. To these he next turned his attention, and became expert in milking the cows, straining the milk, and putting it away with all the care and neatness of an experienced dairyman. He took care of the cattle and horses, and when he grew to a sufficient size, would break the colts to the saddle and harness. Their farm comprised only about eight acres of cleared ground, which he planted in corn, and cultivated with the hoe. His mother was much pleased with the skill and industry of her son, while her neighbours regarded him as a youth of uncommon capacity and steadiness. In addition to her rustic employments, the active mother opened a small traffic with the hunters, and Sequoyah, now a hardy stripling, would accompany these rough men to the woods, to make selections of skins, and bring them home. While thus engaged he became himself an expert hunter; and thus added by his own exertions to the slender income of his mother. When we recollect that men who live on a thinly populated frontier, and especially savages, incline to athletic exercises, to loose habits, and to predatory lives, we recognise in these pursuits of the young Sequoyah the indications of a pacific disposition, and of a mind elevated above the sphere in which he was placed. Under more favourable circumstances he would have risen to a high rank among intellectual men.

The tribe to which he belonged, being in the habit of wearing silver ornaments, such as bracelets, arm-bands, and brooches, it occurred to the inventive mind of Sequoyah to endeavour to manufacture them; and without any instruction he commenced the labours of a silversmith, and soon became an expert artisan. In his intercourse with white men he had become aware that they possessed an art by means of which a name could be impressed upon a hard substance, so as to be comprehended at a glance, by any who were acquainted with this singular invention; and being desirous of identifying his own work, he requested Charles Hicks,[2] afterwards a chief of the Cherokees, to write his name. Hicks, who was a half-blood, and had been taught to write, complied with his desire, but spelt the name George Guess, in conformity with its usual pronunciation, and this has continued to be the mode of writing it.   Guess now made a *die*, containing a *facsimile* of his name, as written by Hicks, with which he stamped his name upon the articles which he fabricated.

He continued to employ himself in this business for some years, and in the meanwhile turned his attention to the art of drawing.   He made sketches of horses, cattle, deer, houses, and other familiar objects, which at first were as rude as those which the Indians draw upon their dressed skins, but which improved so rapidly as to present, at length, very tolerable resemblances of the figures intended to be copied.   He had, probably, at this time never seen a picture or an engraving, but was led to these exercises by the stirrings of an innate propensity for the imitative arts.   He became extremely popular.   Amiable, accommodating, and unassuming, he displayed an industry uncommon among his people, and a genius which elevated him in their eyes into a prodigy.   They flocked to him from the neighbourhood, and from distant settlements, to witness his skill, and to give him employment; and the untaught Indian gazed with astonishment at one of his own race who had spontaneously caught the spirit, and was rivalling the ingenuity of the civilised man.   The females especially were attracted by his manners and his skill, and lavished upon him an admiration which distinguished him as the chief favourite of those who are ever quick-sighted in discovering the excellent qualities of the other sex.

These attentions were succeeded by their usual consequences.   Genius is generally united with ambition, which loves applause, and is open to flattery.   Guess was still young, and easily seduced by adulation.   His circle of acquaintance became enlarged, the young men courted his friendship, and much of his time was occupied in receiving

visits, and discharging the duties of hospitality. On the
frontier there is but one mode of evincing friendship or
repaying civility—drinking is the universal pledge of
cordiality, and Guess considered it necessary to regale his
visitors with ardent spirits. At first his practice was to
place the bottle before his friends, and leave them to
enjoy it, under some plea of business or disinclination.
An innate dread of intemperance, or a love of industry,
preserved him for some time from the seductive example
of his revelling companions. But his caution subsided by
degrees, and he was at last prevailed upon to join in the
bacchanalian orgies provided by the fruits of his own
industry. His laborious habits thus broken in upon, soon
became undermined, his liberality increased, and the
number of his friends was rapidly enlarged. He would
now purchase a keg of whisky at a time, and, retiring
with his companions to a secluded place in the woods,
became a willing party to those boisterous scenes of mad
intoxication which form the sole object and the entire
sum of an Indian revel. The common effect of drinking,
upon the savage, is to increase his ferocity, and sharpen
his brutal appetite for blood; the social and enlivening
influence ascribed to the cup by the Anacreontic song,
forms no part of his experience. Drunkenness, and not
companionship, is the purpose in view, and his deep
potations, imbibed in gloomy silence, stir up the latent
passions that he is trained to conceal, but not to subdue.
In this respect, as in most others, Sequoyah differed from
his race. The inebriating draught, while it stupefied his
intellect, warmed and expanded his benevolence, and made
him the best-natured of sots. Under its influence he gave
advice to his comrades, urging them to forgive injuries, to
live in peace, and to abstain from giving offence to the
whites or to each other. When his companions grew

quarrelsome, he would sing songs to amuse them, and while thus musically employed would often fall asleep.

Guess was in a fair way of becoming an idle, a harmless, and a useless vagabond; but there was a redeeming virtue in his mind, which enabled it to react against temptation. His vigorous intellect foresaw the evil tendencies of idleness and dissipation, and becoming weary of a life so uncongenial with his natural disposition, he all at once gave up drinking, and took up the trade of a blacksmith. Here, as in other cases, he was his own instructor, and his first task was to make for himself a pair of bellows; having effected which, he proceeded to make hoes, axes, and other of the most simple implements of agriculture. Before he went to work, in the year 1820, he paid a visit to some friends residing at a Cherokee village on the Tennessee River, during which a conversation occurred on the subject of the art of writing. The Indians, keen and quick-sighted with regard to all the prominent points of difference between themselves and the whites, had not failed to remark with great curiosity and surprise, the fact that what was written by one person was understood by another, to whom it was delivered, at any distance of time or place. This mode of communicating thoughts, or of recording facts, has always been the subject of much inquiry among them; the more intelligent have sometimes attempted to detect the imposition, if any existed, by showing the same writing to different persons; but finding the result to be uniform, have become satisfied that the white men possess a faculty unknown to the Indians, and which they suppose to be the effect of sorcery, or some other supernatural cause. In the conversation alluded to, great stress was laid on this power of the white man—on his ability to put his thoughts on paper, and send them afar off to speak for him, as if he who wrote them was

SE-QUO-YAH, *or* **GEORGE GUESS**
Inventor of the Cherokee Alphabet

present. There was a general expression of astonishment at the ingenuity of the whites, or rather at their possession of what most of those engaged in the conversation considered as a distinct faculty, or sense, and the drift of the discussion turned upon the inquiry whether it was a faculty of the mind, a gift of the Great Spirit, or a mere imposture. Guess, who had listened in silence, at length remarked, that he did not regard it as being so very extraordinary. He considered it an art, and not a gift of the Great Spirit, and he believed he could invent a plan by which the red men could do the same thing. He had heard of a man who had made marks on a rock, which other white men interpreted, and he thought he could also make marks which would be intelligible. He then took up a whetstone, and began to scratch figures on it with a pin, remarking that he could teach the Cherokees to talk on paper like white men. The company laughed heartily, and Guess remained silent during the remainder of the evening. The subject that had been discussed was one upon which he had long and seriously reflected, and he listened with interest to every conversation which elicited new facts, or drew out the opinions of other men. The next morning he again employed himself in making marks upon the whetstone, and repeated that he was satisfied he could invent characters, by the use of which the Cherokees could learn to read.

Full of this idea, he returned to his own home, at Will's town,[3] in Will's valley, on the southern waters of the Coosa River, procured paper, which he made into a book, and commenced making characters. His reflections on the subject had led him to the conclusion that the letters used in writing represented certain words or ideas, and being uniform, would always convey to the reader the same idea intended by the writer—provided the system of characters which had been taught to each was the same. His project, therefore, was to invent characters which should represent words; but after proceeding laboriously for a considerable time, in prosecution of this plan, he found that it would require too many characters, and that it would be difficult to give the requisite variety to so great a number, or to commit them to memory after they should be invented. But his time was not wasted; the dawn of a great discovery was breaking upon his vision; and although he now saw the light but dimly, he was satisfied that it was rapidly increasing. He had imagined the idea of an alphabet, and convinced himself of the practicability of framing one to suit his own language. If it be asked why he did not apply to a white man to be taught the use of the alphabet already in existence, rather than resort to the hopeless task of inventing another, we reply, that he probably acted upon the same principle which had induced him to construct, instead of buying a pair of bellows, and had led him to teach himself the art of the blacksmith in preference to applying to others for instruction. Had he sought information, it is not certain he could have obtained it, for he was surrounded by Indians as illiterate as himself, and by whites who were but little better informed; and he was possessed, besides, of that self-reliance which renders genius available, and which enabled him to appeal with confidence to the resources of his own mind. He now conceived the plan of making characters to represent sounds, out of which words might be compounded—a system in which single letters should stand for syllables. Acting upon this idea, with his usual perseverance, he worked diligently until he had invented eighty-six characters, and then considered that he had completely attained his object.

While thus engaged, he was visited by one of his

intimate friends, who told him he came to beg him to quit his design, which had made him a laughing-stock to his people, who began to consider him a fool. Sequoyah replied that he was acting upon his own responsibility, and as that which he had undertaken was a personal matter, which would make fools of none besides himself, he should persevere.

Being confirmed in the belief that his eighty-six characters, with their combinations, embraced the whole Cherokee language, he taught them to his little daughter, *Ahyokah*, then about six years of age. After this he made a visit to Colonel Lowrey,[4] to whom, although his residence was but three miles distant, he had never mentioned the design which had engaged his constant attention for about three years. But this gentleman had learned, from the tell-tale voice of rumour, the manner in which his ingenious neighbour was employed, had regretted the supposed misapplication of his time, and participated in the general sentiment of derision with which the whole community regarded the labours of the once popular artisan, but now despised alphabet maker. "Well," said Colonel Lowrey, "I suppose you have been engaged in making marks." "Yes," replied Guess; "when a talk is made, and put down, it is good to look at it afterwards." Colonel Lowrey suggested that Guess might have deceived himself, and that, having a good memory, he might recollect what he had intended to write, and suppose he was reading it from the paper. "Not so," rejoined Guess; "I read it."

The next day Colonel Lowrey rode over to the house of Guess, when the latter requested his little daughter to repeat the alphabet. The child, without hesitation, recited the characters, giving to each the sound which the inventor had assigned to it, and performing the task with such ease and rapidity that the astonished visitor, at its conclusion, uttered the common expression—"Yoh!" with which the Cherokees express surprise.   Unwilling, however, to yield too ready an assent to that which he had ridiculed, he added, "It sounds like Muscogee, or the Creek language"; meaning to convey the idea that the sounds did not resemble the Cherokee.   Still there was something strange in it.   He could not permit himself to believe that an illiterate Indian had invented an alphabet, and perhaps was not sufficiently skilled in philology to bestow a very careful investigation upon the subject.   But his attention was arrested; he made some further inquiry, and began to doubt whether Sequoyah was the deluded schemer which others thought him.

The truth was, that the most complete success had attended this extraordinary attempt, and George Guess was the Cadmus of his race.   Without advice, assistance, or encouragement—ignorant alike of books and of the various arts by which knowledge is disseminated—with no prompter but his own genius, and no guide but the light of reason, he had formed an alphabet for a rude dialect, which, until then, had been an unwritten tongue! It is only necessary to state, in general, that, subsequently, the invention of Guess was adopted by intelligent individuals engaged in the benevolent attempt to civilise the Cherokees, and it was determined to prepare types for the purpose of printing books in that tongue.   Experience demonstrated that Guess had proved himself successful, and he is now justly esteemed the Cadmus of his race.   The conception and execution are wholly his own.   Some of the characters are in form like ours of the English alphabet; they were copied from an old spelling book that fell in his way, but have none of the powers or sounds of the letters thus copied.   The

following are the characters systematically arranged with
the sounds :

D a		R e	T i	ꝝ o	Ꝍ u	i y
Ꞩ ga Ꙩ ka		ᴘ ge	y gi	ᴀ go	ᴊ gu	ᴇ gv
ᴕ hə		ᴘ he	Ꙗ hi	ꜰ ho	г hu	Ꙋ hv
w la		ᴅ le	ᴘ li	ᴳ lo	ᴍ lu	ᴀ lv
Ꙗ ma		ᴄ₁ me	ʙ mi	Ꙩ mo	ʏ mu	
⊖ na ᴜ hꞐa ᴄ nah	ᴧ ne	h ni	ᴢ no	ᴀ nu	Ꝍ nv
ᴣ qua		Ꙩ que	Ꙋ qui	Ꙍ quo	Ꙍ quu	ᴇ quv

ᴔ s ᴗ sv	4 se	Ꞗ si	Ɫ so	Ꙋ su	ʀ sv
ᴜ dw w ta	ꙅ de ᴢ te	ᴧ di ᴧ tih ᴧ do	s du	ꙉ dv
ᴧ dla ᴄ tla	ʟ tle	ᴄ tli	Ꙋ tlo	Ꙋ tlu	ᴘ tlv
ᴳ tsa	ᴧ tse	ɪᴄ tsi	ᴋ tso	ᴊ tsu	ᴄᴄ tsv
ᴄ wa	ꙍ we	⊖ wi	Ꙍ wo	ꙅ wu	ᴇ wv
ᴔ ya	ꙅ ye	Ꝝ yi	h yo	ᴳ yu	ʙ yv

SOUNDS REPRESENTED BY VOWELS

a as *a*   in *father*,   or short as *a* in *rival*,
e as *a*   in *hate*,   or short as *e* in *met*,
i as *i*   in *pique*,   or short as *i* in *pit*,
o as *aw* in *law*,   or short as *o* in *not*,
u as *oo* in *fool*,   or short as *u* in *pull*,
v as *u*   in *but*, nasalised.

CONSONANT SOUNDS

g nearly as in English, but approaching to k.   d nearly as in
English, but approaching to t.   h, k, l, m, n, q, s, t, w, y, as in
English.

Syllables beginning with g, except Ꞩ , have sometimes the power
of k ; ᴧ, s, Ꝍ, are sometimes sounded to, tu, tv ; and syllables written
with tl, except ᴄ , sometimes vary to dl.

Guess completed his work in 1821.   Several of his
maternal uncles were at that time distinguished men

among the Cherokees. Among them was *Keahatahee*,[5] who presided over the beloved town, *Echota*,[6] the town of refuge, and who was one of two chiefs who were killed by a party of fourteen people, while under the protection of a white flag, at that celebrated place. One of these persons observed to him, soon after he had made his discovery, that he had been taught by the Great Spirit. Guess replied, that he had taught himself. He had the good sense not to arrogate to himself any extraordinary merit, in a discovery which he considered as the result of an application of plain principles. Having accomplished the great design, he began to instruct others, and after teaching many to read and write, and establishing his reputation, he left the Cherokee nation in 1822, and went on a visit to Arkansas, where he taught those of his tribe who had emigrated to that country. Shortly after, and before his return home, a correspondence was opened between the Cherokees of the west and those of the east of the Mississippi, in the Cherokee language. In 1823, he determined to emigrate to the west of the Mississippi. In the autumn of the same year, the General Council of the Cherokee nation passed a resolution, awarding to Guess a silver medal, in token of their regard for his genius, and of their gratitude for the eminent service he rendered to his people. The medal, which was made at Washington City, bore on one side two pipes, on the other a head, with this inscription— "Presented to George Gist, by the General Council of the Cherokee nation, for his ingenuity in the invention of the Cherokee Alphabet." The inscription was the same on both sides, except that on one it was in English, and on the other in Cherokee, and in the characters invented by Guess. It was intended that this medal should be presented at a council, but two of the chiefs dying, John Ross, who was now the principal chief, being desirous of the honour and gratification of making the presentation, and not knowing when Guess might return to the nation, sent it to him with a written address.

Guess has never since revisited that portion of his nation which remains upon their ancient hunting grounds, east of the Mississippi. In 1828, he was deputed as one of a delegation from the western Cherokees, to visit the President of the United States, at Washington, when the likeness which we have copied was taken.

The name which this individual derived from his father was, as we have seen, George Gist; his Indian name, given him by his mother, or her tribe, is Sequoyah; but we have chosen to use chiefly in this article, that by which he is popularly known—George Guess.[7]

NOTES

1. The portrait was painted by King at Washington in 1828, but it did not form a part of the collection in the Indian Gallery at Washington, or, rather, it is not mentioned in the Rhees list given in our Introduction. Sequoyah was a member of the deputation of his tribe which negotiated the treaty of May 6, 1828, four of the signers affixing their names "in the characters now in use among them, as discovered by George Guess." Mr Emmet Starr of Claremore, Oklahoma, informs us that the portrait of Sequoyah in the Cherokee capitol at Tahlequah was painted about fifteen years ago by Mrs W. A. Duncan from the Inman copy in McKenney and Hall.

2. Charles R. Hicks, a Moravian convert of mixed blood, and at that time the most influential man in the Cherokee nation, was elected chief at New Echota, Georgia, July 26, 1827, with John Ross (see Vol. III.) as assistant chief. Hicks introduced coffee among the Cherokee tribe. See Mooney, "Myths of the Cherokee," in *Nineteenth Report of the Bureau of American Ethnology*, 1900.

3. Willstown, so called from a half-breed chief known to the whites as Red-headed Will, below Fort Payne, in De Kalb County, Alabama.— Mooney.

4. Major George Lowrey, known as *Agi'lĭ*, "He is Rising," a cousin of Sequoyah, and assistant chief of the Cherokee nation about 1840.— Mooney.

5. The meaning of the name is not known, but the ending *tahee* is no doubt intended for *dihĭ*, "killer," a frequent ending in Cherokee warriors' names.

6. "Itsă'tĭ—commonly spelled Echota, Chota, Chote, etc.—a name occurring in several places in the old Cherokee country: the meaning is lost. The most important settlement of this name, frequently distinguished as Great Echota, was on the south side of the Little Tennessee River, a short distance below Citico Creek, in Monroe County, Tennessee. It was the ancient capital and sacred 'peace town' of the Nation. Little Echota was on Sautee (*i.e.* Itsâ'tĭ) Creek, a head stream of the Chattahoochee, west of Clarkesville, Georgia. New Echota, the capital of the Nation for some years before the Removal, was established at a spot originally known as Gănsa'gĭ, at the junction of the Oostanaula and Conasauga Rivers, in Gordon County, Georgia. It was sometimes called Newtown. The old Macedonia mission, on Soco Creek, of the North Carolina Reservation, is also known as Itsâ'tĭ to the Cherokee, as was also the great Nacoochee mound."—Mooney, *op. cit.*, p. 523.

"The year 1793 began with a series of attacks all along the Tennessee frontier. As before, most of the depredation was by Chickamaugas and Creeks, with some stray Shawano from the north. The Cherokee from the towns on Little Tennessee remained peaceable, but their temper was sorely tried by a regrettable circumstance which occurred in June. While a number of friendly chiefs were assembled for a conference at Echota, on the express request of the President, a party of men under command of a Captain John Beard suddenly attacked them, killing about fifteen Indians, including several chiefs and two women, one of them being the wife of Hanging-maw (Ushwâ'li-gûtă), principal chief of the Nation, who was himself wounded. The murderers then fled, leaving others to suffer the consequences. Two hundred warriors at once took up arms to revenge their loss, and only the most earnest appeal from the deputy-governor could restrain them from swift retaliation. While the chief, whose wife was thus murdered and himself wounded, forebore to revenge himself, in order not to bring war upon his people, the Secretary of War was obliged to report, 'to my great pain, I find to punish Beard by law just now is out of the question.' Beard was in fact arrested, but the trial was a farce, and he was acquitted."—*Ibid.*, p. 74.

7. Much has been written on this noteworthy Indian. For the most authentic information regarding him and his invention, see Mooney, *op. cit.;* J. C. Pilling, *Bibliography of the Iroquoian Languages*, 1888; George E. Foster, *Se-quo-yah, the American Cadmus and Modern Moses*, 1885; Phillips in *Harper's Magazine*, September 1870; Royce in *Fifth Annual Report of the Bureau of Ethnology*, 1888; and the writings cited in these works. To these the following is added, by way of resurrecting an interesting newspaper note of the period (*New York Mirror*, June 17, 1826), showing the uses to which Sequoyah's alphabet was first put:—

" 'It is now but two or three years since the discovery was made, and reading and writing have already become so general among the Cherokees, that they not only carry on a correspondence by letters between the different points of their territory, but are also in the habit of taking receipts and giving promissory notes in affairs of trade.' The gentleman from whom we received this information told us that it is now common, in travelling the lands of the tribes, to see directions for the different paths inscribed on the trees."

A still earlier notice appeared in *The Columbian Star* of Washington City, March 26, 1825, as follows :—

"The Cherokee language is now reduced to a system. Mr George Guess, a Cherokee who does not understand the English, has invented alphabetical characters, consisting of 86, each being a sound or syllable. In this way the Indians now correspond with their Arkansas brethren with facility. The Legislature, in consideration of the benefit which Mr Guess has conferred on the Nation, by reducing and forming the language into a system, resolved that a silver medal, bearing a suitable inscription, be procured and presented to him, as a testimonial of their gratitude to him for his useful discovery."

Regarding Sequoyah's last years, Mooney (*op. cit.*, p. 147) says :—

"Sequoyah, who had occupied a prominent position in the affairs of the Old Settlers, and assisted much in the reorganization of the Nation, had become seized with a desire to make linguistic investigations among the remote tribes, very probably with a view of devising a universal Indian alphabet. His mind dwelt also on the old tradition of a lost band of Cherokee living somewhere toward the western mountains. In 1841 and 1842, with a few Cherokee companions, and with his provisions and papers loaded in an ox cart, he made several journeys into the West, received everywhere with kindness by even the wildest tribes. Disappointed in his philologic results, he started out in 1843 in quest of the lost Cherokee, who were believed to be somewhere in Northern Mexico ; but, being now an old man and worn out by hardship, he sank under the effort and died—alone and unattended, it is said—near the village of San Fernando [in Chihuahua ?], Mexico, in August of that year. Rumours having come of his helpless condition, a party had been sent out from the Nation to bring him back, but arrived too late to find him alive. A pension of three hundred dollars, previously voted to him by the Nation, was continued to his widow—the only literary pension in the United States. Besides a wife, he left two sons and a daughter. Sequoyah district of the Cherokee Nation was named in his honour, and the great trees of California (*Sequoia gigantea*) [for the preservation of which the Sequoia National Park in California has been set apart by the Nation] also preserve his memory."

Had the Indian Territory been admitted into the Union as a State independent of Oklahoma, there is little doubt that it also would have borne Sequoyah's name.

NAWKAW

(OR, WOOD)

THE countenance of this chief is prepossessing, and indicative of his true character. He was a firm, sagacious man, of
upright deportment and pacific disposition, who filled his
station with dignity, and commanded respect by his fidelity
to his engagements. His name is less expressive than most
of those which are borne by Indians of reputation—the word
Nawkaw signifying *wood*. He was of the Winnebago tribe,
and of the *Caromanie* or Walking Turtle family, which is of
the highest distinction. The name Caromanie, among the
Winnebagoes, implies rank and dignity, conveys the idea of
sovereignty, and is, therefore, highly respected; for this
people, like all other savages, have an inherent veneration
for hereditary greatness.

This chief was the head of his tribe, who inhabited a
broad and beautiful country, lying between the Mississippi
and Lake Michigan, and spread out in plains of great extent,
fertility, and magnificence. His residence was at the Big
Green Lake, which is situated between Green Bay and
Fort Winnebago, and is about thirty miles from the
latter.[1] Although a warrior by profession, the successful
leader in many a fight, he was a person of excellent disposition, who preferred and courted peace; and his upright
conduct, in connection with his military talents, caused

him to be respected and beloved. His conduct was patriarchal, and his sway that of the parent rather than the master.

In the recent war between the United States and the Sauks and Foxes,[2] it was feared that the Winnebagoes, inhabiting the country immediately north of the hostile Indians, would unite with them, and forming a powerful combination, would devastate the defenceless frontier before our Government could adopt measures for its relief. The opportunity was a tempting one to a savage tribe naturally disposed to war, and always prepared for its most sudden exigencies; and many of the Winnebagoes were eager to rush into the contest. But the policy of Nawkaw was decidedly pacific, and his conduct was consistent with his judgment and his professions. To keep his followers from temptation, as well as to place them under the eye of an agent of our Government, he encamped with them near the Agency, under the charge of Mr Kinzie,[3] expressing on all occasions his disapprobation of the war, and his determination to avoid all connection with those engaged in it. The Indian tribes are often divided into parties, having their respective leaders, who alone can control their partisans in times of excitement. On this occasion, the more respectable and by far the most numerous part of the Sauk and Fox nation, headed by Keokuk,[4] the proper chief, remained at peace, while a faction, called *the British band*, was led headlong into a disastrous war by Black Hawk, a warrior having no lawful rank, and his coadjutor, the Prophet, while among the Winnebagoes a similar division occurred; a few restless and unprincipled individuals giving loose to their propensity for blood and plunder by joining the war parties, while the great body of the tribe remained at peace, under the influence of their venerable chief.

Having narrated, in the historical part of this work, the interesting story of the surrender of Red Bird, we shall only advert to that circumstance here for the purpose of remarking that Nawkaw took an active and a judicious part in that melancholy and singular affair.   He exerted his influence to have the murderers arrested and delivered up to the officers of our Government ; but, having thus discharged his duty, he was equally diligent in his endeavours to obtain for them the pardon of the President.   For this purpose he visited Washington in 1829 [1828], accompanied by fifteen of his chief men ; and it was at that time that the portrait which we have copied was taken.   He is represented in the attitude of addressing the President, and in the act of extending towards him his calumet at the conclusion of his speech.

The intercession of Nawkaw was successful ; the clemency of the President was extended to the wretched men then lying captive in the prison at Prairie du Chien— but unfortunately too late.[5]   The Indian, accustomed to unlimited freedom, languishes in confinement.   The Red Bird[6] was a high-spirited warrior, unused to restraint, and habituated to roam over boundless plains, with a step as unfettered as that of the wild horse of the prairie.   The want of exercise and the privations of imprisonment destroyed his health, broke his spirit, and hurried him to a premature grave.   He died before the news of his pardon reached him.

We shall conclude this article with a few anecdotes of Nawkaw and his companions.   In conducting these persons to Washington, it was deemed proper to lead them through some of the principal cities, where they might witness the highest evidences of our wealth, power, and civilisation.   Their conductors were Major Forsyth and Mr Kinzie,[7] the latter of whom speaks the languages of the north-western tribes with fluency, and to him we are indebted for these facts.

While at New York, the Winnebago deputies attended, by invitation, a balloon ascension at the Battery.[8] At this beautiful spot, where the magnificence of a city on the one hand, and a splendid view of one of the noblest harbours in the world on the other, combine to form a landscape of unrivalled grandeur, thousands of spectators were assembled to witness the exploit of the aeronaut, and to behold the impression which would be made upon the savage mind by so novel an exhibition. The chiefs and warriors were provided with suitable places, and many an eye was turned in anxious scrutiny upon their imperturbable countenances, as they gazed in silence upon the balloon ascending into the upper atmosphere. At length Nawkaw was asked what he thought of the aeronauts. He replied coolly—" I think they are fools to trifle in that way with their lives—what good does it do ? Being asked if he had ever before seen so many people assembled at one time, he answered : " We have more in our smallest villages."

While at Washington they were lodged at a public hotel, and regaled in the most plentiful and sumptuous manner ; notwithstanding which, when about to leave the city, Nawkaw complained of the quality of the food placed upon his table. Such a remark from an Indian, whose cookery is the most unartificial imaginable, and whose notions of neatness are far from being refined, was considered singular ; and on inquiry being made, it turned out that a piece of roast beef which had been taken from the table untouched, was placed a second time before these fastidious gentlemen, who, on their native prairies, would have devoured it raw, but who now considered their dignity infringed by such a procedure. Being asked if the beef was not good enough, he replied, that there were plenty of turkeys and chickens to be had, and he chose them in preference.

On their way home, at the first place at which they stopped to dine, after leaving Baltimore, they sat down at a well-furnished table. A fine roasted turkey at the head of the board attracted their attention, but keeping that in reserve, they commenced upon a chicken-pie. While thus engaged, a stranger entered, and taking his seat at the head of the table, called for a plate. The Indians became alarmed for the turkey, cast significant glances at each other, and eyed the object of their desire with renewed eagerness. They inquired of each other, in subdued accents, what was to be done—their plates being well supplied, they could not ask to be helped again, yet the turkey was in imminent jeopardy. The stranger was evidently hungry, and he looked like a man who would not trifle with his knife and fork. Luckily, however, he was not yet supplied with these necessary implements; there was a moment still left to be improved, and the red gentlemen, having cleared their plates, occupied it by dividing among them an apple-pie, which quickly vanished. A clean plate, knife, and fork were now placed before the stranger, who was about to help himself, when to his astonishment and utter discomfiture, one of the Indians rose, stepped to the head of the table, and adroitly fixing his fork in the turkey bore it off to his companions, who very gravely, and without appearing to take the least notice of the details of the exploit, commenced dividing the spoil, while the stranger, recovering from his surprise, broke out into a loud laugh, in which the Indians joined.

As the party receded from the capital, the fare became more coarse, and the red men began to sigh for the fat poultry and rich joints that were left behind them. And

now another idea occurred to their minds. Having
noticed that payment was made regularly for every meal,
they inquired if *all* the meals they ate were paid for, and
being answered in the affirmative, each Indian, on rising
from the table, loaded himself with the fragments of the
feast, until nothing remained. When they observed that
this conduct was noticed, they defended it by remarking
that the provisions were all paid for.

It has been well said that there is but a step between
the sublime and the ridiculous; and this aphorism is
strikingly illustrated in the conduct of savages or uneducated men. The Indian has some heroic traits of
character; he is brave, patient under fatigue or privation,
often generous, and sometimes tenacious of the point of
honour to an extreme which has scarcely a parallel,
except in the records of chivalry. In all that relates to war
or the council they are systematic, and the leading men
exhibit much dignity and consistency of character. As
hunters they are keen, skilful, and diligent; as warriors,
bold, sagacious, and persevering. But when the Indian is
taken from this limited circle of duties and thrown into
contact with the white man, in social intercourse, his want
of versatility, and deficiency of intellectual resources, often
degrade him at once into meanness and puerility. For a
time he may disguise himself in his habitual gravity, and his
native shrewdness and presence of mind may enable him
to parry any attempts to pry into his thoughts, or throw
him off his guard, but the sequel inevitably betrays the
paucity of the savage mind. Thus the chiefs and warriors
of whom we have spoken were, some of them, distinguished warriors, and others eminent in council; but when
thrown out of their proper sphere, and brought into
familiar contact with strangers, they become the subjects
of anecdotes such as we have related, and which, except

the first one, would be too trifling for repetition, were they not illustrative of the peculiarities to which we have adverted.

When at Washington, in 1829 [1828], Nawkaw, in speaking of his own age, called himself *ninety-four* winters old. He died in 1833, at the advanced age of ninety-eight, and was succeeded in his rank and honours by his nephew, who was worthy to inherit them. The latter is a person of temperate habits, who abstains entirely from the use of ardent spirits. He also is a *Caromanie*, and has assumed the name of his uncle.[9]

Nawkaw was a man of large stature and fine presence. He was six feet tall, and well made. His person was erect, his muscles finely developed, and his appearance such as indicated activity and great strength. Like many of his race, he was remarkably fond of dress ; and even in the last days of his protracted life, devoted the most sedulous care to the decoration of his person. His portrait affords ample evidence of his taste ; the head-dress, the ear-rings, and the painted face show that the labours of the toilet had not been performed without a full share of the time and study due to a matter of so much importance ; while the three medals, presented to him at different times, as the head of his tribe and as tokens of respect for himself, are indicative of his rank, and are worn with as much pride and as much propriety as the Orders of nobility which decorate the nobles of Europe.

The memory of this distinguished chief and respectable man is cherished by his people, and his deeds are recounted in their songs. He was one of those rulers whose wisdom, courage, and parental sway endear them to their people while living, and whose precepts retain the force of laws after their decease.[10]

NAW-KAW, *or* **WOOD**
A Winnebago Chief

NOTES

1. This Winnebago village was on the south side of Green Lake, in the present Green Lake County, Wisconsin. Fort Winnebago was on the site of Portage, Columbia County. By treaty of Fort Armstrong, Rock Island, Illinois, September 15, 1832, the Winnebago ceded these lands to the United States.

2. That is, the Black Hawk War of 1832. See the Black Hawk biography in Vol. II.

3. See note 7.

4. For Keokuk, see Vol. II.

5. The first portrait of Nawkaw was painted by Lewis at the treaty of Butte des Morts, Wisconsin, August 11, 1827 (in which the name appears as "Karry-Man-nee, walking turtle"), not at Green Bay, as engraved on the Lewis plate (No. 18 of his *Port-folio*), as the Green Bay treaty was not negotiated until a year later. The Indian Gallery portrait of Nawkaw (No. 75 of the collection) was the work of King; it undoubtedly was painted while Nawkaw and his deputation were in Washington in the autumn of 1828. The Inman copy is preserved in the Peabody Museum, to which it was presented in 1906 by Mrs Cornelia Dexter (museum number, 66. 307).

6. For Red Bird, see Vol. II. Red Bird died in prison at Prairie du Chien, February 16, 1828. His alleged accomplices in the Gagnier and Lipcap murder—Wekau and Chickhonsic—were sentenced to be hanged on December 26, 1828, but were pardoned by President Adams, November 3, 1828, at the instance of Nawkaw and his followers. See note 8. Consult McKenney, "The Winnebago War of 1827," in *Wisconsin Historical Society Collections*, Vol. V., p. 202, with note by L. C. Draper.

7. Thomas Forsyth, an Indian trader, and until 1830 the agent for the Winnebago tribe; and John H. Kinzie, an employee of the American Fur Company at Prairie du Chien, Wisconsin, afterward at Mackinaw, and in 1832 a sub-agent for the Winnebago. His wife, Juliette A., was the author of *Wau-Bun*, first published in 1856, a book of prime importance to the history and ethnology of this period of Wisconsin. Kinzie's father, a Scotchman, whose original name was John M'Kenzie, was the founder of Chicago, in which city he died in 1828.

8. The party reached New York City, October 19, 1828. After arriving in Washington, the Winnebago agreed to give a war dance in the grounds of the President's House on November 15, at which the volunteer militia of the District of Columbia were ordered to attend. The exhibition was postponed several times on account of the weather, but was finally held November 28th, "much to the amusement of a large concourse of spectators," according to contemporary newspapers. The Indians took leave of the President next day.

9. The nephew's original name is said to have been "Maukeeki-shunka, or shaking of the earth." He died at Dexterville, Iowa, in or after 1848 (*Wisconsin Historical Society Collections*, XII., 408). Authorities conflict respecting the date of the elder Nawkaw's death. Draper (*Wisconsin Historical Society Collections*, V., 181, note, 1868) says:— " Naw-Kaw, or *Car-a-mau-nee*, or *The Walking Turtle*, went on a mission with TECUMSEH in 1809 to the New York Indians, and served with that chief during the campaign of 1813, and was present at his death at the Thames. . . . He was still living as late as 1840." Draper thus evidently confuses Nawkaw with his nephew. Mrs Kinzie (*Wau-Bun*, p. 73, 1873), speaking of the period beginning with the autumn of 1830, says:—"There was Naw-kaw, or Kar-ray-mau-nee, 'the Walking Turtle,' now the principal chief of the nation, a stalwart Indian, with a broad, pleasant countenance, the great peculiarity of which was an immense under lip, hanging nearly to his chin." As Mrs Kinzie does not refer to his extreme age, and as the accompanying portrait gives no suggestion of an abnormal lip, but rather bears out McKenney's descrip-tion of a man of "fine presence," the nephew is here doubtless referred to by her. More definite information respecting the death of Nawkaw is given by Catlin, who painted his portrait in 1836 (*Illustrations of the Manners, Customs, and Condition of the North American Indians*, 10th ed., II., p. 146, London, 1866). Writing in 1838, he says:—"In plate 254 will be seen the portrait of an old chief, who died a few years since, and who was for many years the head chief of the tribe, by the name of Naw-kaw (*wood*). This man has been much distinguished in his time for his eloquence ; and he desired me to paint him in the attitude of an orator addressing his people." In *A Descriptive Catalogue of Catlin's Indian Gallery* . . . *Exhibiting at the Egyptian Hall, Piccadilly*, in 1840, the portrait of this Indian is entered as follows : " 209. *Náw-káw*, Wood ; formerly the Head Chief [of the Win-ne-ba'-goes], with his war-club on his arm (dead)." Quoting from an earlier catalogue, apparently, Thomas Donaldson (*Smithsonian Institution Report for* 1885, Pt. II., p. 128) gives the year 1836 as that in which the picture was made. This would seem to be sufficient evidence that Nawkaw died soon after Catlin painted his portrait.

10. Much additional information respecting Nawkaw's career is con-tained in the *Collections of the State Historical Society of Wisconsin*. This, with other data, has been summarised by Publius V. Lawson in *The Wisconsin Archeologist*, Vol. VI., No. 3, pp. 150-152, Milwaukee, June 1907 ; but, unfortunately, the summary contains numerous errors, and apparently confuses at least two chiefs of the same name. Regarding Nawkaw's career in the war of 1812, and his presence at the time of Tecumseh's death, consult Beckwith, "The Illinois and Indiana Indians," *Fergus Historical Series*, No. 27, p. 139, Chicago, 1884 ; Atwater, *Tour to*

Prairie du Chien, 119, 1850; Atwater, *History of Ohio*, 2nd ed., 236, 1838. Respecting the name of this chief, Atwater says: " Carrymaunee (Walking Turtle), a Winnebago chief, carries a large tortoise, fully extended and beautifully painted, perfect in all its limbs, on his back as he marches onward at the head of the Turtle tribe."

It should be added that Nawkaw the elder signed the treaties of St Louis, June 3, 1816 (as " Onunaka, or Karamanu "); Prairie du Chien, August 19, 1825 (as " Carimine, the turtle that walks "); Butte des Morts, August 11, 1827 (as " Karry-Man-nee, walking turtle "); Green Bay, August 25, 1828 as (" Nan-kaw, or wood "); and Prairie du Chien, August 1, 1829 (as " Nau-kaw-kary-maunie, wood "). The treaty of Fort Armstrong, Rock Island, Illinois, September 15, 1832—the year before Nawkaw's death, according to McKenney and Hall—was signed on the part of the " Prairie du Chien deputation " of the Winnebago, by " Tshee-o-nuzh-ee-kaw, war chief (Kar-ray-mau-nee)," Nawkaw seemingly being incapacitated at the time.

SHAUMONEKUSSE, OR L'IETAN

(AN OTO HALF-CHIEF[1])

IN the progress of our work we have found no small
difficulty in settling the orthography of proper names.
Not only are the Indian languages unwritten, but the
interpreters, through whom most of our information is
necessarily communicated, are illiterate persons, who
arbitrarily affix to words the pronunciation which suits
their own fancy, or which accords best with their own
national or local idiom. Thus the Indians who call themselves Saukies[2] are denominated Sacs by the French, and
Sauks by the Americans; and the names of many of the
chiefs are given with such variations by different travellers,
that it is sometimes difficult to recognise them. The
names which are attached to the portraits in this work
are, with a few exceptions, those which we found written
upon them in the gallery at the War Office, and which
were dictated by the persons who attended the chiefs as
interpreters, in their visit to Washington. Whether they
have been changed in copying, we cannot say; but some of
them are evidently incorrect. We have, however, in most
cases, left them unaltered, preferring to make our correc-
tions in the biographical notices, rather than alter that
which may have been written on authority better than our
own. Whether the individual now before us should be
called *Chonmonicase* or *Shaumonekusse,* is a question which

156

CHON-MON-I-CASE, *or* L'IETAN
An Oto Half-Chief

we suppose will never excite as much curiosity as has been awakened by the rival claims for the birthplace of Homer; we have, however, taken some pains to arrive at the proper reading, and have adopted the latter, on the authority of the writers of *Long's First Expedition to the Rocky Mountains*,[3] in which we place implicit confidence.

Shaumonekusse was distinguished early in life as a daring, active, and successful warrior. We are not aware of his having any hereditary claims to the chieftainship of his tribe, to which he has risen gradually by his own merits.[4] He is a person of deep penetration, and is capable of acting with much duplicity on any occasion when he may consider it politic to conceal his real views. Having had intercourse with the traders, from his infancy, he has acquired an intimate knowledge of the character of the white men, and has studied to turn this acquisition to advantage. The Otoes have always maintained friendly relations with the American people, and it was, therefore, not difficult for this chief to cultivate the good opinion of such of our countrymen as visited the distant shores of the Upper Missouri.

The Otoes and the Missouris are remnants of numerous and warlike nations which once roamed over these boundless plains, the monarchs of all they surveyed, but which are now so greatly reduced, that the whole number of the warriors in both tribes together is not more than two hundred.[5] Being united by the closest friendship, they have cast their lots in union, and act together as one people; and small as is their aggregated force, they have sustained themselves with such uniform bravery and good conduct as to command the respect of the tribes around them. They are more indebted to Shaumonekusse than to any other individual for the high reputation they have maintained, as he is not only one of the boldest of their warriors, but is very expert and politic in the management of their affairs.

He is more commonly known to the whites by the name of *Ietan,* or, as the French traders denominate him, *L'Ietan,* a title which was given him in consequence of some exploit against the tribe of that name ; probably on account of his having slain an Ietan warrior of distinction.[6]

The countenance of this Indian expresses the qualities which he is known to have possessed in an eminent degree, but which are not common among his race ; he was, when a young man, social, witty, animated, and mercurial in his temperament. Although he never obtained any reputation as an orator, he conversed well, and was an agreeable companion.

When Colonel Long's party were encamped on the Upper Missouri, in 1819, they were visited by a party of Otoes, among whom was Ietan, then a young but a distinguished warrior. A grand dance was performed in honour of the American officers ; in the course of which, the leaders of the greatest repute among the Indians narrated their exploits. Among others, Ietan stepped forward and struck the flagstaff which had been erected, and around which the dancers moved. This ceremony is called *striking the post* ; and such is the respect paid to it, that whatever is spoken by the person who strikes, may be relied upon as strictly true ; and, indeed, it could not well be otherwise, for the speaker is surrounded by rival warriors, who would not fail to detect, and instantly expose, any exaggeration by which he should endeavour to swell his own comparative merits. In recounting his martial deeds, Ietan said he had stolen horses seven or eight times from the Kansas ; he had first struck the bodies of three of that nation, slain in battle.[7] He had stolen horses from the Ietan nation, and had struck one of

their dead.   He had stolen horses from the Pawnees, and
had struck the body of one Pawnee Loup.   He had stolen
horses several times from the Omahas, and once from the
Poncas.   He had struck the bodies of two Sioux.   On a
war party, in company with the Pawnees, he had attacked
the Spaniards, and penetrated into one of their camps; the
Spaniards, excepting a man and a boy, fled, himself being
at a distance before his party, he was shot at and missed,
by the man whom he immediately shot down and struck.
"This," said he, "is the only martial act of my life that I
am ashamed of."

This would be considered by an Indian audience a
highly meritorious catalogue of martial deeds; nor would
the stealing of horses be thought the least honourable of
these daring exploits.   Although the word stealing is used,
and the proceeding itself is attended with the secrecy
of actual theft, yet the act does not involve any idea
of meanness or criminality, but is considered as a lawful capture of the property of an enemy.   They deem it
dishonest to steal from their friends or allies, but their
code of morality justifies any deception or injury towards
an enemy, and affords but slight protection to the person
or property of any who are not bound to them by some
strong bond of interest or friendship.   Many of the wars
of the Indians grow out of these predatory habits, and the
capture of a few horses is repaid by the blood of warriors
and the sacrifice of life.

On the same occasion, alluded to above, we are told:
" In this dance Ietan represented one who was in the act
of stealing horses.   He carried a whip in his hand, as did
a considerable number of the Indians, and around his
neck were thrown several leathern thongs, for bridles and
halters, the ends of which trailed on the ground behind
him; after many preparatory manœuvres he stooped

down, and with his knife represented the act of cutting the hopples of horses; he then rode his tomahawk as children ride their broomsticks, making such use of his whip as to indicate the necessity of rapid movement, lest his foes should overtake him."

The authority already quoted, after remarking that the Indians sometimes indulge in pleasantry in their conversation, adds, that "Shaumonekusse seemed to be eminently witty, a quality strongly indicated by his well-marked features."

The union between the Missouris and Otoes took place about twenty years ago, when the former were conquered and dispersed by the Sauks and Foxes, and their allies, when a few families joined the Osages; a few took refuge among the Kansas, while the chief part of the tribe became amalgamated with the Otoes. Having been previously very nearly assimilated in habits, manners, and language, the union has been cordial, and they may now be considered as one people.

These tribes boast of having faithfully adhered to their professions of friendship towards the American people; not one of whom, they assert, was ever killed by their warriors. Only two white men have been slain by them within the recollection of any living witnesses; one of these was a Frenchman, and the other a Spaniard, was killed by Shaumonekusse, in the manner already alluded to; and although this act was attended by a remarkable display of bravery, which no doubt gained him great credit, he declared publicly that it was the only martial act of his life that he was ashamed of.

This individual is distinguished not only as a warrior, but as a great hunter; and it is evident that he takes no small degree of pride in his exploits in the chase, from the manner in which his head was decorated with the spoils

of the field, when he sat for his portrait.[8] The horns of
the buffalo are worn with a triumph which renders it
probable that a legend of more than ordinary daring is
connected with the identical pair thus ostentatiously
displayed, while the claws of the grisly bear, the fiercest
and most powerful quadruped of our continent, are
suspended round his neck.

When this portrait was taken, Shaumonekusse was a
young and gallant warrior; he has since become the head
man of his tribe, and risen to great influence among his
neighbours.[9] The immediate cause of his rise from a half
to a full chieftain, was the result of a quarrel that
happened between one of his brothers and himself.   In the
fight produced by the quarrel, it was the lot of Shaumonekusse to have his nose bit off, whereupon he shot his
brother. He immediately repaired to the council, and
made known what had happened, when it was decreed
that any man who would bite off his brother's nose
deserves to be shot; and in testimony of the respect
entertained by the chiefs for the promptness of
Shaumonekusse in punishing such an outrage, they elected
him chief.

NOTES

1. The tribal name, spelled *Otto* throughout by McKenney and Hall,
is changed in the present edition to *Oto*, to conform with present official
and popular usage. The name is an adaptation of *Wa-t'o'-ta*, which may
be interpreted as "lechers." This Siouan tribe, which bears closest
relationship with the Iowa and Missouri, are now with the Missouri in
Oklahoma, the two together numbering 390. The name of this chief
contains the term for "prairie wolf," the interpretation twice given in
connection with treaties signed by him, as follows:—Fort Atkinson,
Council Bluffs, Iowa, September 26, 1825 ("Sho-mon-e-ka-sa, the prairie
wolf"); Prairie du Chien, Wis., July 15, 1830 ("I-atan, or Shaumanie-
Cassan, or prairie wolf"); Oto Village, September 21, 1833 ("Jaton,"
i.e., Iatan, or Ietan); Bellevue, Missouri [Omaha, Nebraska], October 15,

1836 (as "Jaton"). The name Ietan or Iatan is the French form of the Siouan name for the Ute, who call themselves Yutawats, or Yuta, and, through misunderstanding, was applied by early plainsmen to any Shoshonean tribe, particularly the Comanche. It is in this last sense that the term is here employed.

2. This tribe call themselves *Osakiwŭgi*, signifying, according to Dr William Jones, "They come forth from beneath," contracted to Saukie, Sauk, and Sac. The name is spelled in many different ways, but the form *Sauk* has come to be the most common designation, and now has official sanction. Information on this tribe is given elsewhere.

3. *Account of an Expedition from Pittsburgh to the Rocky Mountains, performed in the Years* 1819 *and '*20 . . . *under the Command of Major Stephen H. Long.* Compiled by Edwin James. . . . In Two Vols. With an Atlas. Philadelphia, 1823. The proper form of the name Shaumonekusse has not been determined, but it contains the term *man-yi-ka'*, "prairie wolf."

4. He did not sign the first treaty held with his tribe on June 24, 1817. He was fourth among the Indian signers of the treaty of 1825, and the first signer, on behalf of the Oto, of the three subsequent treaties.

5. This would give an aggregate population, for the combined tribes, of 700 to 800, or twice their present number. A reservation was set aside for the Oto and Missouri in Oklahoma in 1881; but their lands have subsequently been allotted to them in severalty, and they are now citizens of the United States. For a summary of the early movements of these two tribes, see McGee, "The Siouan Indians," in *Fifteenth Annual Report of the Bureau of American Ethnology,* pp. 194-195, Washington, 1897.

6. See note 1.

7. This act of "striking" an enemy gave rise to the French-Canadian term *coup.* To "count coup" was to score a personal victory by performing a brave deed—killing an enemy, scalping an enemy, or being the first to strike an enemy, dead or alive. Any one of these entitled a man to be designated a warrior, and to relate his exploits in public. Among some tribes a warrior could count coup by stealing an enemy's horse. Red Cloud, the celebrated Sioux chief, is accredited with having counted coup eighty times, *i.e.,* he had performed as many brave deeds in the face of the enemy.—Mooney in *Handbook of American Indians,* edited by F. W. Hodge, *Bull.* 30, *Bureau of American Ethnology* pt. 1, p. 354, 1907.

8. The portrait was painted by King in 1821, during the visit of Shaumonekusse and his wife to Washington, as noted in the biographical sketch of Hayne Hudjihini, following. See the Rhees list, No. 130, p. lii of the Introduction. A copy, by the same artist, was bequeathed by him to the Redwood Library, Newport, Rhode Island, and bears the

name Chonmonicase (see Introduction, p. liii, No. 10). The only difference between this and the Inman copy herein reproduced is in minor
details. Regarding Shaumonekusse's visit to the East in 1821, the
following extract from *Niles' Register*, December 15, 1821, is of interest :—

"Major O'Fallon, U.S. agent on the Missouri, lately arrived at
Washington city, accompanied by a deputation from the Pawnees,
Omakars, Kansas, Otoes and Missouris. Their object (says the *Intelligencer*) is to visit their Great Father, and learn something of that
civilization of which they have hitherto remained in total ignorance.
They are from the most remote tribes with which we have intercourse,
and they are believed to be the first of those tribes that have ever been
in the midst of our settlements. . . . These red men of the forest
who now visit us are in a complete state of nature. These Indians have
since passed through Baltimore on a trip to the eastward."

9. J. T. Irving, who accompanied Commissioner Ellsworth on his
tour in 1833, for the purpose of negotiating the treaty of that year,
speaks of "The Iotan" as follows :—

"He had evidently brought into service the whole of his wardrobe,
much of which he had received from the whites. His hair was long,
and round it was bound a large piece of skin from the head of the
grisly bear. Round his neck hung a necklace of the claws of the same
animal ; and what was of more importance in his estimation, he was
clothed in a long surtout coat of blue cloth, adorned with red facings
and enormously large brass buttons, and garnished upon each shoulder
with a pair of tarnished, sickly-looking silver epaulettes. From beneath
the skirts of the coat appeared two bare legs ; and he wore a pair of coarse
moccasins of buffalo hide.

"There was a look of comic slyness lurking around the eyes of this
chief, united with an irascible twinkle, which bespoke a character habitually good natured, but prone to occasional gusts of passion. The most
prominent feature of his face, however, had suffered mutilation. The
end of his nose was wanting. I was curious to learn whether this
singular wound had been received in battle or private brawl—and my
inquiries made me acquainted with a curious tale of Indian revenge.
There are a dozen different versions of the story in circulation among
the traders and trappers, but as far as I could ascertain, the following
is the most correct . . ."

Irving then relates how Shaumonekusse lost his nose in a drunken
brawl, it having been bitten off by his brother. He continues :—

"The Iotan was perfectly sobered ; he paused for a moment, looking
intently into the fire without uttering a word, then drawing his blanket
over his head, walked out of the building and hid himself in his own
lodge. On the following morning he sought his brother, and told him
that he had disfigured him for life. 'To-night,' said he, 'I will go to
my lodge and sleep. If I can forgive you when the sun rises, you are
safe ; if not, you die.' He kept his word—he slept upon his purpose ;
but sleep brought not mercy. He sent word to his brother that he had

resolved upon his death, that there was no further hope for him; at the same time he besought him to make no resistance, but to meet his fate as a warrior should.

"His brother received the message, and fled from the village. An Indian is untiring in his pursuit of revenge; and though years may elapse, yet he will obtain it in the end. From the time that it became the fixed purpose of the Iotan to slay his brother, his assiduity never slept; he hunted him for months. He pursued his trail over the prairies; he followed his track from one thicket to another; he traced him through the friendly villages, but without success; for although he was untiring, his brother was watchful, and kept out of his way. The old warrior then changed his plan of action. He lay in wait for him in the forest, crouching like a tiger in the paths which he thought he might frequent in hunting, but he was for a long time unsuccessful. At length one day, while seated on a dead tree, he heard the crackling noise of a twig breaking beneath a cautious footstep. He instantly crouched behind the log, and watched the opposite thicket. Presently an Indian emerged from it, and gazed cautiously around. The Iotan recognised his brother instantly. His careworn face and emaciated form evinced the anxiety and privations that he had suffered. But this was nothing to the Iotan; as yet his revenge was unsated, and the miserable appearance of his brother touched no chord of his heart. He waited until he was within a few feet of him, then sprang from his lurking place and met him face to face. His brother was unarmed, but met his fiery look with calmness and without flinching.

"'Ha! ha! brother,' cried the Iotan, cocking his rifle; 'I have followed you long, in vain—now I have you—you must die.'

"The other made no reply; but, throwing off his blanket, stepped before him and presented his breast. The Iotan raised his rifle, and shot him through the heart.

"His revenge was gratified; but from that hour a change came over him. He became gloomy and morose; shunned the society of his fellow-men, and roamed the woods, where he was nearly driven to suicide by the working of his feelings and the phantasies of his brain. It was not until many years had elapsed that he recovered from the deep anguish caused by this unnatural act of vengeance.

"It was many years after this savage deed that the Iotan was appointed chief of the Oto tribe, and his after conduct fully justified the choice of the nation. To an ingenious skill in devising and planning war parties, he added a desperate daring in carrying them into effect. And though now well stricken in years, there is no warrior more constantly lurking in the path of the enemy; and when it comes to the deadly struggle, no voice is raised in a louder war whoop, and no arm falls heavier upon their foes, than that of the Iotan chief."—J. T. Irving, jr., *Indian Sketches*, Vol. I., pp. 136-147, Philadelphia, 1835. See also p. 175.

HAYNE HUDJIHINI
THE EAGLE OF DELIGHT

HAYNE HUDJIHINI

(OR, THE EAGLE OF DELIGHT)

WE regret that we have but little to say of the original of this pretty picture. Like many handsome women, her face was probably her principal treasure. The countenance does not indicate much character; without the intelligence of the civilised female, it has a softness rarely exhibited by the Indian squaw. There is a Chinese air of childishness and simplicity about it which is rather striking, and which is as foreign to the features of the laborious, weather-beaten female of the prairies as it would be the countenance of a practised belle in one of our cities.[1]

She was the favourite wife of Shaumonekusse; whether the only one, we are unable to say, for the red men are in the habit of multiplying the chances of connubial felicity by marrying as many red ladies as they can support.[2] A great hunter has usually several, while the sluggard, who has gained no reputation by his successes in the chase, is considered as very amply provided with a single helpmeet. We infer from the character of Ietan, as well as from the paraphernalia which decorates his person, that he was entitled by the etiquette and the economy of Indian life to a plurality of wives, and that he was a personage who would probably live up to his privileges.

When he visited the city of Washington, in 1821, Hayne Hudjihini, the Eagle of Delight, was the companion of his journey.   Young, and remarkably handsome, with an interesting appearance of innocence and artlessness, she attracted the attention of the citizens of our metropolis, who loaded her with presents and kindnesses.[3]   Among other things she received many trinkets; and it is said that her lord and master, who probably paid her the flattering compliment of thinking her, when unadorned, adorned the most, very deliberately appropriated them to his own use, and suspended them from his own nose, ears, and neck.   If she was as good-natured as her portrait bespeaks her, she was no doubt better pleased in administering to her husband's vanity, than she would have been in gratifying her own.

Shortly after her return home she died, and the bereaved husband was so sensibly affected by her decease, that he resolved to end his own life by starvation.   With this view he threw himself on her grave, and for several days remained there in an agony of grief, refusing food, and repelling consolation.   His friends, respecting his feelings, suffered him for a time to indulge his sorrow, but at last forced him away, and his immoderate grief became gradually assuaged.

NOTES

1. Her portrait, like that of her husband, was painted at Washington by King in 1821, in which year a deputation of sixteen Indians from the Upper Missouri River tribes visited Washington with agent O'Fallon (see Morse, *Report to the Secretary of War*, Washington, 1822, p. 241). Under No. 131 of the Indian Gallery list (Introduction, p. lii) two portraits are confused, that of Rant-che-wai-me, Female Flying Pigeon, the wife of Ma-ha-ka (Mahaska) being confounded with the picture of the subject of the present sketch.   Like that of her husband, King copied the portrait of Hayne Hudjihini, and this is now in the Redwood Library, Newport, Rhode Island (see the Introduction, p. liv, No. 11).   The

Inman copy, bearing the name Hayne-hud-jikini, and original number 7, is preserved in the Peabody Museum (museum number, 28. 197). It is attributed to King, but bears no date.

2. This is the popular belief, but it is by no means the universal custom among Indians, many tribes being strict monogamists. Where polygyny was practised, the number of wives was usually limited only by the husband's ability to pay the marriage fee to the woman's parents, which was sometimes the equivalent of a considerable sum, and his means of affording his wives proper support. Nor was the wife the common drudge of her lord, as is commonly believed. The labour of the men and the women was divided as justly as the conditions of barbaric life would warrant, and among some Indians the prominence of the women in tribal affairs was notable.

Irving (*Indian Sketches*, I., 175, 1835), speaking of Shaumonekusse and his wives, says:—

" On the first day of our arrival, we were invited to feast with about half the village. The first lodge which we entered was that of the Iotan. We found him sitting cross-legged upon some cushions to receive us. Upon our coming up to him, he presented the commissioner with a seat next himself. Then turning to his wife, he called for the feast, which consisted of dried buffalo flesh, boiled with a large quantity of hard corn. The interior of his abode wore but a dull, dingy look. The rafters were almost invisible for the eddying clouds of smoke lazily seeking the hole in the roof, which served for the chimney.

" This old chief had divided his affections among five wives. They were seated in different parts of the lodge engaged in pounding corn, or chattering over the news of the day. They were evidently under but little subjection. While we were eating with him, the old man took the opportunity to disburthen his heart. He let us into a knowledge of the miseries to which he was subjected from their caprices, and the difficulties which he found in maintaining a proper discipline where there were so many mistresses and but one master."

3. Irving (*Indian Sketches*, II., 68, 1835) thus describes her, but does not mention her by name :—" She was young, tall, and finely formed ; her face, next to that of the wife of the Kioway Indian, was the most beautiful we had met with. Her hair was parted across her forehead, and hung down upon her shoulders. A small jacket of blue cloth was fastened round her shoulders and breast, and a mantle of the same was wrapped around her body.

QUATAWAPEA, OR COLONEL LEWIS

QUATAWAPEA, or *The man on the water who sinks and rises again*, was born at the Pickaway Plains, in Ohio,[1] almost sixty years ago, and was a boy at the great battle of the Kenhawa, in which his tribe acted a conspicuous part.[2] His father and all his ancestors were distinguished for their feats in arms. He was for many years the chief of that band of the Shawanoe[3] tribe which resided at Lewistown, on the sources of the Great Miami of the Ohio.[4] With strangers he passed for a person of much consideration, in consequence of his fine address and appearance. He was a well-formed, handsome man, dressed with much taste and elegance, and was graceful in his deportment. His horse and equipments, rifle, and side-arms, were all of the most costly kind, and few of his race ever appeared so well on public occasions. As a hunter he had no superior; but he was not distinguished in council or in war.

During the late war between the United States and Great Britain, this chief joined the American army with a small band of his braves, and rendered himself extremely useful, on account of his intimate knowledge of the whole country which formed the seat of war on our north-western frontier. Only one martial exploit, however, is recorded to his honour. At a place called Savoirin's Mills, he attacked a small fortification, at the head of his warriors,

168

QUA-TA-WA-PEA, *or* COL. LEWIS
A Shawanoe Chief

with such fury that the British garrison was compelled to evacuate it hastily and seek safety in flight. They were overtaken, and many of them captured; the pursuit was continued for some hours; yet it is a fact highly honourable to this chief and the Shawanoe warriors under his command, that not a scalp was taken nor a prisoner put to death. The British soldiers who were captured were treated with the greatest humanity.

The reader will have observed that it is not uncommon for the Indian warriors and chiefs to have several names, and that many of them are named after eminent persons among their civilised neighbours. Thus the individual before us is better known by those who speak our language only, as *Colonel Lewis*, than by his original Indian designation.

He lived for many years near Waupaghconneta,[5] in Ohio, where he cultivated a large farm, to which he devoted much attention. Unlike most of his race, he had learned the value of property, and exerted himself to increase his possessions. This conduct rendered him unpopular with his tribe, by whom he had never been greatly esteemed; and he was at length deposed by them, under a charge of peculation, in having applied to his own private purposes the money received from the United States for the use of his people.

It is said that his appointment to the station of chief was entirely accidental. Being one of a delegation which visited the seat of Government while General Dearborn was Secretary of War,[6] the superiority of Colonel Lewis in dress and manners probably induced the Secretary to regard him as the most conspicuous person of the party, and he presented him with a medal. On his return the Indians regarding this decoration as an indication of the wishes of the American Government, and desirous to testify their obedience to the hint which they supposed to have been thus given, yielded to him tacitly a precedence which soon grew into a confirmed authority; and such is their rigid notion of discipline, and their habitual respect for their chiefs, that they submitted to him cheerfully while he remained in office. They even retained him for some time after they were satisfied of his unworthiness, at the instance of the agents of our Government, who supported his cause, because they found him inclined to peace and friendly to the whites.[7]

After his deposition from the chieftainship he emigrated with his family and a few followers to the country west of the Mississippi, allotted by the American Government to the Shawanoes, where he died, in 1826.[8]

NOTES

1. The Pickaway Plains are situated $3\frac{1}{2}$ miles south of Circleville, Pickaway County, Ohio. It was here that Logan, the *mingo* chief, made his reputed celebrated speech to Lord Dunmore. See also note 4, p. 98.

2. That is, about the year 1776. At this date, however, young Lewis would have been only two years of age, since the battle of Point Pleasant, at the mouth of the Great Kanawha, in the present West Virginia, was fought October 10, 1774. See note 7, p. 43.

3. That is, the Shawnee.

4. Lewistown was situated in Logan County, Ohio, at the site of the present town of that name, on a tract comprising nearly 40,000 acres, granted to the Seneca and Shawnee by treaties of September 29, 1817, and September 17, 1818. Under the provisions of a treaty held at Lewistown, July 20, 1831, the tract was ceded to the United States, and its occupants agreed to remove west of the Mississippi. "The village of Lewiston derived its name from Captain John Lewis, a noted Shawnee chief. When the county was first settled, there was living with him, to do his drudgery, an aged white woman named Polly Keyser. She was taken prisoner in early life, near Lexington, Ky., and adopted by the Indians. She had an Indian husband and two half-breed daughters."—Howe, *Hist. Coll. Ohio*, II., 102, 1896.

5. Wapakoneta was on the headwaters of the Auglaize, about the present town of the same name, in Auglaize County, Ohio. It was across the watershed, and northwestward from Lewistown. The Wapakoneta tract, comprising 125 square miles, was granted to the Shawnee under the treaties of September 29, 1817, and September 17, 1818, and was ceded to the United States by treaty held at "Wapaghkonnetta," August 8, 1831, in exchange for 100,000 acres west of the Mississippi. The Shawnee of Wapakoneta at the time of the removal numbered about 400.

6. Colonel Henry Dearborn (born 1751; died 1829) distinguished himself in the revolution, and was appointed Secretary of War by President Jefferson, which office he occupied from 1801 till 1809.

7. This is exemplified by the fact that Lewis signed numerous treaties, as follows:—Brownstown, Michigan, November 25, 1808, his name appearing as "Koitawaypie, or Col. Lewis"; Greenville, Ohio, July 22, 1814, as "Quitawepeh, or captain Lewis"; Spring Wells, Michigan, September 8, 1815, as "Quatawwepay, or capt. Lewis"; Rapids of the Miami of Lake Erie, September 29, 1817, as "Quitawepea, or Captain Lewis"; St Mary's, Ohio, September 17, 1818, as "Quitawepa, or Colonel Lewis." He signed, as a witness only, the treaty of St Louis, November 7, 1825, his name appearing as "Quatwapea, or Col. Lewis." The next Shawnee treaty, that of Pleasant Plains, near Lewistown, Ohio, July 20, 1831, was concluded several years after Lewis's death; but one of the signers, "Quashacaugh, or Little Lewis," may have been a son.

8. It would seem that Lewis and his few followers moved west of the Mississippi soon after the treaty of St Louis, November 7, 1825, under the terms of which the Shawnee ceded the lands held by them in south-eastern Missouri, under permit granted to them by the Spanish Government in 1793, in exchange for a tract equal to fifty miles square in eastern Kansas, including the site of the present city of Topeka. See Royce, "Indian Land Cessions," in *Eighteenth Rep. Bur. Amer. Ethnology*, Pt. 2, 1899.

It is not known when Quatawapea's portrait was painted, as there seems to be no record of a visit to Washington subsequently to 1809, when Dearborn was Secretary of War. That King painted his portrait appears from the Inman list in the Peabody Museum, in which it bears number 63 (museum number, 28. 198), but the date is lacking. It has already been shown that the Indian Office did not commence its collection of aboriginal portraits until about 1821. If the picture was painted in Washington between 1801 and 1809, when Quatawapea is known to have visited the capital, it was hardly the work of King, who did not settle in Washington until 1822.

PAYTAKOOTHA

(OR, FLYING CLOUDS)

THE interpretation of the name of this Indian is *Flying Clouds*; but he is better known among the Americans as "Captain Reed." He is a Shawnee of the Chillicothe tribe, but was born in the country of the Creeks. His age, at the time his portrait was taken, is supposed to have been about fifty-five years.[1] Although considered a brave man, he has never gained any distinction as a warrior, but is a very good hunter. He had little popularity or influence in his tribe.[2] In 1833 he was living west of the Mississippi.

Colonel John Johnston,[3] of Ohio, a venerable and highly intelligent gentleman, who was intimately acquainted with the north-western Indians, represents this individual as a wandering, unsettled man, often engaged in embassies between the tribes, and frequently journeying to distant villages. He was considered a peaceable, inoffensive person, without talents, but always disposed to exert himself in reconciling differences between tribes or individuals, and was esteemed by the red people as a benevolent man. However that reputation may have conciliated for him the goodwill of those around him, it gave him not the kind of standing which a daring warrior or a bold intriguing leader would have possessed among the fierce warriors of the forest, and Captain Reed had the common

PAYTA-KOOTHA, *or* FLYING CLOUDS
A Shawnee Warrior

fate of enjoying the respect of his associates, while men of less moral worth directed their councils.

NOTES

1. The portrait was painted by King, according to the Inman copy in the Peabody Museum (original number, 9; museum number, 28. 199), but the date is not given.

2. Nevertheless, he was of sufficient prominence and influence to have signed, on behalf of his tribe, the following treaties:—Greenville, Ohio, August 3, 1795, as " Hah-goosekaw, or Captain Reed" (the same?); Spring Wells, September 8, 1815, as " Mishquathree, or Capt. Reid "; Rapids of the Miami of Lake Erie, Ohio, September 29, 1817, as "Wawathethaka, or Capt. Reed" (under this treaty a grant of land at Wapaghkonetta was made to "Weeasesaka, or Captain Reed"); St Mary's, Ohio, September 17, 1818, as "Red Man, or Capt. Reed"; St Louis, November 7, 1825, as "Capt. Reed, or Pathecoussa." As the Shawnee disposed of their lands in Ohio in the year last named, it is probable that Captain Reed moved to Kansas soon afterward with the remainder of his band. There was a "Read's Town," consisting of a few cabins, in the vicinity of Bellefontaine, Logan County, Ohio, according to Howe, *Historical Collections of Ohio*, II., 102, 1896.

3. Colonel John Johnston, born Ballyshannon, Ireland, 1775; died Washington, D.C., 1861. He went as a lad to Pennsylvania with his father's family; at seventeen he was in the Quartermaster's department in Wayne's army. He later was appointed a clerk in the War Department, and as an officer participated at the funeral services of Washington. He was appointed Indian agent at Upper Piqua, Ohio, by President Madison, which office he held for thirty years.—See Howe, *op. cit.*, 259.

KIONTWOGKY, OR CORNPLANTER [1]

THE Senecas, as we have already stated in another place, were a tribe of the Iroquois, or Five Nations; and, more recently, the Six Nations, when the Tuscaroras were added to the Confederacy,[2] which then consisted of the Mohawks, Oneidas, Onondagoes, Senecas, Cayugas, and Tuscaroras. These Indians were among the earliest who were known to the English, who recognised them as a warlike and powerful people, and took no small pains to conciliate their friendship. In the year 1710, five chiefs of the Iroquois were induced by the British officers to visit England, under the expectation that their savage natures might be softened by kindness, or their fears alarmed by an exhibition of the power and magnificence of the British Sovereign. This event excited much attention in London. Steele mentioned it in his *Tatler* of May 13, 1710, while Addison devoted a number of the *Spectator* to the same subject. Swift, who was ambitious to be a politician, and who suffered no occurrence of a public nature to escape his attention, remarks, in one of his letters to Mrs Johnson: "I intended to have written a book on that subject. I believe he (Addison) has spent it all in one paper, and all the under hints there are mine too." Their portraits were taken, and are still preserved in the British Museum; and Steele says of these illustrious strangers, " They were placed in a handsome apartment, at an upholsterer's in King Street, Covent Garden."

In Oldmixon's *History* we find the following notice : "For the successes in Spain, and for the taking of Doway, Bethune, and Aire, by the Duke of Marlborough, in Flanders, there was a thanksgiving day appointed, which the Queen solemnised at St James's Chapel. To have gone, as usual, to St Paul's, and there to have had *Te Deum* sung, on that occasion, would have shown too much countenance to those brave and victorious English generals who were fighting her battles abroad, while High Church was plotting, and railing, and addressing against them at home. The carrying of five Indian casaques [caciques] about in the Queen's coaches, was all the triumph of the Harleian administration; they were called Kings, and clothed by the playhouse tailor, like other kings of the theatre; they were conducted to audience by Sir Charles Cotterel; there was a speech made for them, and nothing omitted to do honour to these five monarchs, whose presence did so much honour the new ministry."

In a work entitled *The Annals of Queen Anne's Reign, Year the IX, for* 1710, written by Mr Boyer, we find the following remarks: "On the 19th April, Te-ye-neen-ho-ga-prow, and Sa-ga-yean-qua-pra-ton, of the Maquas, Elow-oh-kaom, and Oh-neah-yeath-ton-no-prow, of the river Sachem, and the Genajoh-hore sachem,[3] four kings, or chiefs, of the Six Nations, in the West Indies, which lie between New England and New France, or Canada, who lately came over with the West India fleet, and were clothed and entertained at the queen's expense, had a public audience of Her Majesty, at the palace of St James, being conducted in two of her majesty's coaches, by Sir James Cotterel, master of ceremonies, and introduced by the Duke of Somerset, lord chamberlain." The historian then proceeds to recite a long speech, which these sachems *from the West Indies, between New England and Canada,* are supposed to have made to the British monarch, but which is so evidently of English manufacture, that we refrain from giving it a place. We are further informed, that our chiefs remained in London, after their audience with Her Majesty, about a fortnight, and were entertained by several persons of distinction, particularly the Duke of Ormond, who regaled them likewise with a review of the four troops of Life Guards. In Smith's *History of New York* we are told, "the arrival of these five sachems in England made a great bruit throughout the whole kingdom. The mob followed wherever they went, and small cuts of them were sold among the people."

The visits of Indian chiefs to the more refined and civilised parts of the world are, unhappily, to be regarded only as matter for curiosity, for we do not find that they have produced any beneficial results. The savage gazed with astonishment at the wonders of art and luxury which met his eye at every step, and returned to repeat the marvellous narrative of his travels to hearers who listened without understanding the recital, or being convinced of their own inferior condition. The distance between themselves and the white men was too great to be measured by their reasoning powers. There was no standard of comparison by which they could try the respective merits of beings so different, and modes of life so opposite; and they satisfied themselves with supposing that the two races were created with distinct faculties, and destined for separate spheres of existence. They took little pains to investigate anything which was new or wonderful, but briefly resolved all difficulties by referring them to fatality, or to magic. A few of the more acute obtained distant and misty glimpses of the truth, and were willing to spare the weaker intellects of their people from a knowledge which filled themselves with dread and sorrow; for, in the little which they comprehended of European power, they saw the varied and overwhelming elements of a superiority which threatened their destruction. Hence their wisest and most patriotic chiefs have been prudently jealous of civilisation; while the Indians in general have feared and distrusted that which they could not comprehend. A striking instance, in illustration of these remarks, may be found in the story of an individual belonging to the Iroquois confederacy, upon whom the experiment of a civilised education was fairly tried.[4]

Peter Otsaquette—we give his name as we find it—disguised by an English prefix and a French termination, was an Oneida Indian, of a distinguished family.[5] At the close of the American revolution he attracted the attention of Lafayette, whose benevolent feelings, strongly enlisted, by the intelligence and amiable qualities of the savage boy, induced him to send the young Oneida to France. At the age of twelve, he was placed in the best schools of Paris, and not only became a good scholar, but attained a high degree of proficiency in music, drawing, fencing, and all the accomplishments of a gentleman. His was one of the few native stalks upon which the blossoms of education have been successfully engrafted. Delighted with the French metropolis, and deeply imbued with the spirit of its polite inhabitants, he seems to have forgotten his native propensities, and to have been thoroughly reclaimed from barbarism. He returned to America an altered person, with a commanding figure, an intelligent countenance, the dress of the European, and the grace of a polished man. Proud of his acquirements, and buoyed up with the patriotic hope of becoming the benefactor of his tribe, and the instrument of their moral elevation, he hastened to his native forests. He was welcomed with hospitality; but on his first appearance in public, the Oneidas disrobed him of his foreign apparel, tearing it from his person with indignant violence, and reproaching him with apostasy in throwing off the garb of his ancestors. They forced him to resume the blanket, to grease his limbs with the fat of the bear, and to smear his body with paint. Nor was this enough; he was married to a squaw, and indoctrinated in the connubial felicities of the wigwam. The sequel of his story will be readily anticipated. With no relish for savage life, and without the prospect of happiness or distinction, he sank into intemperance, and so rapid was his degradation, that within three months after his return from Europe, he exchanged the portrait of Lafayette, the gift of his illustrious benefactor, for the means of gratifying the brutal propensity which was now his sole remaining passion.

As our object is to illustrate the Indian character, we may be permitted to extend this digression by relating, before we proceed to the proper subject of the article, another anecdote, which, while it exemplifies the self-possession of the Indian, and the readiness with which he adapts himself to circumstances, shows also how slight are the impressions made upon his mind by the finest incidents, or the most agreeable objects in civilised life. In 1819, an Indian warrior, named Makawitta, happened to be a passenger upon Lake Erie, in the steamboat *Walk-in-the-Water*. On board the same vessel was a sprightly young lady, who, pleased with the fine appearance and manly deportment of the savage, played off upon him some of those fascinating coquetries in which fair ladies are so expert, and which the wisest men are unable to resist and unwilling to avoid. Makawitta was a youth of little over twenty years, neat in his dress, and graceful as well as dignified in his movements; we presume the lady was both witty and handsome, and we are assured that the passengers were highly amused at this encounter between a belle and a beau of such opposite nurture. For some time he sustained his part with admirable tact, but when his fair opponent drew a ring from her finger, and placed it on his, he stood for a moment in respectful silence, at a loss to understand the meaning of the ceremony. A gentleman, who spoke his language, apprised him that the ring was a token of affection; upon which, placing himself in a graceful attitude, he addressed her in an oratorical style, which showed that he entered fully into the spirit of the scene, in the following words :—

"You have conferred the best gift—this ring, emblem of love—of love that lives while the Great Spirit endures. My heart is touched—it is yours for ever.

"I will preserve this ring while I live. I will bear it with me over the mighty waters, to the land of good spirits.

"I am happy to be with you in this wonderful canoe, moved by the Great Spirit, and conducted by the Big Fist of the great deep.

"I wish to be with you until I go to the land where my fathers have gone. Take back the ring, and give me that which I value more—*yourself.*" [6]

On the next day the ring was bartered for a drink of whisky!

Such is the singular race whose history we are endeavouring to exemplify—patient under hardship, subtle in war, inflexible in the stern purpose of revenge, but fickle in every good resolution, and irreclaimable in barbarism. In the multitude, bravery is a common virtue, a prominent and almost a single merit; while here and there a noble character shines like a bright peculiar star among the host of mere warriors, adorned with the highest qualities that dignify and soften the harsher features of manhood.

The name of Cornplanter is very familiar to most of our countrymen, yet we have been unable to obtain the materials for a connected account of his whole career. He was a chief of the Senecas, and the rival of Red Jacket, from whom he differed in character, while he equalled him in influence. Without the commanding genius of Red Jacket, he possessed a large share of the common sense which is more efficient in all the ordinary affairs of life. They were both able men ; both acquired the confidence of their people ; but the patriotism of Red Jacket was exhibited in an unyielding hatred of the whites, between whom and the red men he would have cut off all intercourse, while Cornplanter adopted the opposite policy of conciliation towards his more powerful neighbours. The one was a warrior of unblemished reputation, the other an orator of unrivalled eloquence ; both were shrewd, artful, and expert negotiators, and they prevailed alternately over each other, as opportunities were offered to either for the exertion of his peculiar abilities. The one rose into power when the Senecas were embittered against the whites, and the other acquired consequence when it became desirable to cultivate friendly relations upon the frontier.

The father of Cornplanter was a white man, and is said to have been an Irishman ; but nothing is now known of him, except what may be gathered from a letter of Cornplanter to the Governor of Pennsylvania.[7] This singular production was, of course, dictated to an interpreter who acted as amanuensis, but the sentiments are undoubtedly his own. It was dated in 1822, when the lands reserved for the Indians in the north-western part of Pennsylvania became surrounded by the farms of the whites, and some attempt was made to tax the property of the Seneca chief; in consequence of which he wrote this epistle to the Governor :—

"I feel it my duty to send a speech to the Governor of Pennsylvania at this time, and inform him of the place where I was from—which was at Connewaugus[8] on the Genesee River.

"When I was a child I played with the butterfly, the grasshopper, and the frogs; and as I grew up I began to pay some attention, and play with the Indian boys in the neighbourhood, and they took notice of my skin being of a different colour from theirs, and spoke about it. I inquired of my mother the cause, and she told me that my father was a residenter in Albany. I still eat my victuals out of a bark dish. I grew up to be a young man, and married me a wife, and I had no kettle nor gun. I then knew where my father lived, and went to see him, and found he was a white man, and spoke the English language. He gave me victuals while I was at his house, but when I started home, he gave me no provision to eat on the way. He gave me neither kettle nor gun, neither did he tell me that the United States were about to rebel against the Government of England.

"I will now tell you, brothers, who are in session of the Legislature of Pennsylvania, that the Great Spirit has made known to me that I have been wicked; and the cause thereof has been the revolutionary war in America. The cause of Indians being led into sin at that time, was that many of them were in the practice of drinking and getting intoxicated. Great Britain requested us to join with them in the conflict against the Americans, and promised the Indians land and liquor. I myself was opposed to joining in the conflict, as I had nothing to do with the difficulty that existed between the two parties.

I have now informed you how it happened that the Indians took a part in the revolution, and will relate to you some circumstances that occurred after the close of the war.   General Putnam,[9] who was then at Philadelphia, told me there was to be a council at Fort Stanwix ; and the Indians requested me to attend on behalf of the Six Nations, which I did, and there met with three commissioners who had been appointed to hold the council.[10] They told me that they would inform me of the cause of the revolution, which I requested them to do minutely. They then said that it originated on account of the heavy taxes that had been imposed upon them by the British Government, which had been for fifty years increasing upon them ; that the Americans had grown weary thereof, and refused to pay, which affronted the king.   There had likewise a difficulty taken place about some tea which they wished me not to use, as it had been one of the causes that many people had lost their lives.   And the British Government now being affronted, the war commenced, and the cannons began to roar in our country.

" General Putnam then told me at the council at Fort Stanwix, that by the late war the Americans had gained two objects : they had established themselves an independent nation, and had obtained some land to live upon, the division line of which from Great Britain run through the Lakes.   I then spoke, and said I wanted some land for the Indians to live on, and General Putnam said that it should be granted, and I should have land in the State of New York for the Indians.   He then encouraged me to use my endeavours to pacify the Indians generally ; and as he considered it an arduous task, wished to know what pay I would require.   I replied, that I would use my endeavours to do as he requested with the Indians, and for pay therefor I would take land.   I told him not to pay me money or dry goods, but land. And for having attended thereto I received the tract of land on which I now live, which was presented to me by Governor Mifflin.[11] I told General Putnam that I wished the Indians to have the exclusive privilege of the deer and wild game, to which he assented; I also wished the Indians to have the privilege of hunting in the woods and making fires, which he likewise assented to.

"The treaty that was made at the aforementioned council has been broken by some of the white people, which I now intend acquainting the Governor with. Some white people are not willing that Indians should hunt any more, whilst others are satisfied therewith; and those white people who reside near our reservation tell us that the woods are theirs, and they have obtained them from the Governor. The treaty has also been broken by the white people using their endeavours to destroy all the wolves, which was not spoken about in the council at Fort Stanwix by General Putnam, but has originated lately.

"It has been broken again, which is of recent origin. White people get credit from Indians, and do not pay them honestly according to agreement. In another respect also, it has been broken by white people residing near my dwelling; for when I plant melons and vines in my field, they take them as their own. It has been broken again, by white people using their endeavours to obtain our pine trees from us. We have very few pine trees on our land in the State of New York; and whites and Indians often get into dispute respecting them. There is also a great quantity of whisky brought near our reservation, and the Indians obtain it and become drunken.

"Another circumstance has taken place which is very

trying to me, and I wish for the interference of the Governor. The white people who live at Warren,[12] called upon me some time ago to pay taxes for my land, which I objected to, as I never had been called upon for that purpose before; and having refused to pay, they became irritated, called upon me frequently, and at length brought four guns with them and seized our cattle. I still refused to pay, and was not willing to let the cattle go. After a time of dispute they returned home, and I understood the militia was ordered out to enforce the collection of the tax. I went to Warren, and, to avert the impending difficulty, was obliged to give my note for the tax, the amount of which was forty-three dollars and seventy-nine cents. It is my desire that the Governor will exempt me from paying taxes for my land to white people; and also to cause that the money I am now obliged to pay be refunded to me, as I am very poor. The Governor is the person who attends to the situation of the people, and I wish him to send a person to Alleghany,[13] that I may inform him of the particulars of our situation, and he be authorised to instruct the white people in what manner to conduct themselves towards the Indians.

" The Government has told us that, when difficulties arose between the Indians and the white people, they would attend to having them removed. We are now in a trying situation, and I wish the Governor to send a person authorised to attend thereto, the fore part of next summer, about the time that the grass has grown big enough for pasture.

"The Governor formerly requested me to pay attention to the Indians, and take care of them. We are now arrived at a situation in which I believe the Indians cannot exist unless the Governor should comply with my request, and send a person authorised to treat between us and the

KI-ON-TWOG-KY, *or* CORNPLANTER
A Seneca Chief

white people, the approaching summer. I have now no more to speak."

It is unfortunate that most of the interpreters through whom the productions of the aboriginal intellect have reached us, have been so entirely illiterate as to be equally incapable of appreciating the finer touches of sentiment and eloquence, and of expressing them appropriately in our language. The letter of Cornplanter is distinguished by its simplicity and good sense, and was no doubt dictated in the concise, nervous, and elevated style of the Indian orator, while we have received it in a garbled version of very shabby English. His account of his parentage is simple and touching; his unprotected yet happy infancy, when he *played with the butterfly, the grasshopper, and the frogs*, is sketched with a scriptural felicity of style; there is something very striking in the description of his poverty, when he *grew up to be a young man, and married a wife, and had no kettle nor gun;* while the brief account of his visit to his father is marked by the pathos of genuine feeling. It is to be regretted that he did not pursue the narrative, and inform us by what steps he rose from his low estate to become the head of a tribe. We learn from other sources that he was a successful warrior, and it is probable that the traders and the missionaries, whose interest he espoused, in opposition to Red Jacket, aided in his elevation. In the latter part of the letter he has given a synopsis of the evils which his nation endured in consequence of their alliance with the whites, and which invariably attended the unnatural contact of civilised and savage men.

Cornplanter was one of the parties to the treaty at Fort Stanwix, in 1784, when a large cession of territory was made by the Indians; at the treaty of Fort Harmar, five years afterwards, he took the lead in conveying an immense tract of country to the American Government, and became so unpopular that his life was threatened by his incensed tribe.[14]   But this chief, and those who acted with him, were induced to make these liberal concessions by motives of sound policy; for the Six Nations having fought on the royal side during the war of the revolution, and the British Government having recognised our independence, and signed a peace without stipulating for the protection of her misguided allies, they were wholly at our mercy. In an address sent to the President of the United States, in 1790, by *Cornplanter, Half Town*, and *Big Tree*,[15] we find the following remarks in allusion to these treaties :—

"*Father*,—We will not conceal from you that the Great Spirit, and not men, has preserved Cornplanter from the hands of his own nation, for they ask continually, 'Where is the land upon which our children, and their children after them, are to lie down? You told us that the line drawn from Pennsylvania to Lake Ontario would mark it for ever on the east, and the line running from Beaver Creek to Pennsylvania would mark it on the west, and we see it is not so; for, first one comes, and then another, and takes it away, by order of that people which you tell us promised to secure it to us.' He is silent, for he has nothing to answer. When the sun goes down he opens his heart before the Great Spirit, and earlier than the sun appears again upon the hills, he gives thanks for his protection during the night; for he feels that among men become desperate by the injuries they have sustained, it is God only that can protect him."

In his reply to this address, President Washington remarked : "The merits of Cornplanter and his friendship for the United States are well known to me, and shall not be forgotten; and as a mark of the esteem of the United States, I have directed the Secretary of War to make him a present of two hundred and fifty dollars, either in money or goods, as the Cornplanter shall like best."

It would be tedious to pursue the history of this chief through the various vicissitudes of his life. His reputation as a warrior was gained previous to the American revolution, and during that war. Shortly after that struggle, the lands reserved for the Senecas became surrounded by the settlements of the American people, so as to leave them no occasion nor opportunity for hostilities with other tribes. In his efforts to preserve peace with his powerful neighbours, Cornplanter incurred, alternately, the suspicion of both parties—the whites imputing to him a secret agency in the depredations of lawless individuals of his nation, while the Senecas have sometimes become jealous of his apparent fame with the whites, and regarded him as a pensionary of their oppressors. His course, however, has been prudent and consistent, and his influence very great.

He resided on the banks of the Alleghany River, a few miles below its junction with the Connewango, upon a tract of fine land, within the limits of Pennsylvania, and not far from the line between that state and New York. He owned thirteen hundred acres of land, of which six hundred were comprehended within the village occupied by his people. A considerable portion of the remainder he cultivated as a farm, which was tolerably well stocked with horses, cattle, and hogs. Many of his people cultivated the soil, and evinced signs of industry. The chief favoured the Christian religion, and welcomed those who came to teach it. He lived in simple style, surrounded with plenty, and practising a rude hospitality, while his sway was kind and patriarchal.[16]

In 1815, a missionary society[17] had, at his earnest solicitation, established a school at his village, which at that time promised success.   We are not aware that any permanent results were attained by the effort.

Cornplanter imbibed, in the feebleness of age, the superstition of the less intellectual of his race.   His conscience reproached him for his friendship towards the whites, and in a moment of alarm, fancying that the Great Spirit had commanded him to destroy all evidence of his connection with the enemies of his race, he burned an elegant sword and other articles which he had received as presents.   A favourite son,[18] who had been carefully educated at one of our schools, became a drunkard, adding another to the many discouraging instances in which a similar result has attended the attempt to educate the Indian youth.   When, therefore, the aged chief was urged to send his younger sons to school, he declined, remarking in his broken English, "It entirely spoil Indian."

Cornplanter died on his reservation on the Alleghany River, sometime in the winter of 1836—supposed to have been over ninety years old.[19]   His Indian name was Ki-on-twog-ky.[20]   The likeness we have given of him was taken in New York, about the year 1788, and when the original is supposed to have been in his forty-eighth year.[21]   It was intended for some friend of the Indians, in London, but Captain M'Dougall, who, at that time, commanded a merchant ship, between Philadelphia and Liverpool, and who was to have conveyed it to Liverpool, sailing without it, the portrait fell into the hands of Timothy Matlock, Esq., who cherished it, not only because of its admirable and close resemblance to the original, but because he was indebted to Cornplanter for his life.[22]   At his death the portrait was still cherished by his daughter.   It was from that original the copy before the reader was taken.

NOTES

1. Strictly, the name is *Kaiioñtwaᶜkoⁿ*, signifying "by what one plants," according to Mr J. N. B. Hewitt of the Bureau of American Ethnology, a leading authority on the Iroquoian languages. Cornplanter's name has been written in many ways, some of them hardly recognisable. In previous editions of McKenney and Hall, the name appears as Corn Plant, but it is here changed to the more popular, if not strictly accurate, designation.

2. The Tuscarora tribe was adopted into the Confederacy as the Sixth Nation in 1722.

3. There thus seem to have been four rather than five members of the visiting party.

In " Remarks on the Early American Engravings and the Cambridge Press Imprints (1640-1692)," etc., by Nathaniel Paine, in *Proceedings of the American Antiquarian Society*, Vol. XVII., pt. 3, Worcester, Mass., 1906, the author, speaking of the engravings from these portraits, and of J. Simon, who made them, says :—" There was a John Simon who came to London in the reign of Queen Anne, who was an engraver of some merit, and may have engraved them ; but in the only biographical notice of him that has come to my notice, no mention is made of these prints. It was in 1710 that Major Peter Schuyler took four Indian chiefs to England, where they created quite a sensation. They were received with great ceremonies by the Queen, and the Indians presented her with a set of wampum. The original paintings were said to have been painted for the Queen.

" The engravings were published by subscription in November 1710, and are now quite rare.

" Those owned by the Society are in good condition, and are as follows, all having the imprint : J. Verelst, Pinx. and J. Simon, Fecit. Printed and sold by John King at ye Globe in ye Poultrey, London. (Sizes of plates, $15\frac{1}{2} \times 10\frac{1}{4}$ in.) Tee Yee Neen Ho Ga Ron Emperour of the Six Nations / Sa Ga Yeath Qua Pieth Ton King of the Maquas / Ho Nee Yeath Tan No Ron King of the Generethgarich / Eton Oh Koam King of the River Nation."

See also a letter from M. de Vaudreuil to M. de Ponchartrain, dated Quebec, May 1, 1710, regarding a visit to England by Peter Schuyler, published in the *New York Colonial Documents*, IX., 842-844, 1855; also *The Four Kings of Canada ; Being a Succinct Account of the Four Indian Princes Lately Arriv'd from North America* (etc.), London, 1710. In this rare pamphlet (reprinted, London, 1891), the following appears: "These four Princes, who are Kings of the *Maqua's, Garijhhoore,* and the River *Sachem,* are call'd, the first *Te Ye Neen Ho Ga Prow,* the second *Saga Yean Qua Prab Ton,* the third *Elow Ob Kaom,* the fourth *Oh Nee Yeath Ton No Prow,* with the other two they mention in their Speech to her

Majesty, are the six who possess all the Nations," etc.   The speech " as deliver'd by an Interpreter to her *Britannick* Majesty " is given in full.

4. Compare, for example, in this volume, the references to Mohongo and her companions who visited Europe.   Cornplanter's attitude regarding the wide gulf between the white man and the Indian is well set forth in the following speech delivered by this celebrated Indian, extracted from the *Harrisburg* (Pa.) *Intelligencer*, August 16, 1822 :—

" By an act of the last Legislature, their honours Jesse Moore, and Joseph Hackney, were appointed commissioners to explain the law exonerating Cornplanter from certain taxes.   After the explanation, the following speech was delivered by Cornplanter in the court-house at Warren, on the 4th of July, 1822.

" ' Yesterday was appointed for us all to meet here.   The writing which the Governor sent here pleased us very much.   I think that the Great Spirit is very much pleased that the white people have been so induced to assist the Indians as they have done, and He is pleased also to see the great men of this state, and of the United States, so friendly to us.   We are much pleased with what has been done.

" ' The Great Spirit first made the world, and next the flying animals, and found all things good and prosperous—He is immortal and everlasting.   After finishing the flying animals, He came down on earth, and there stood.   Then He made different kinds of trees and weeds of all sorts, and people of every kind.   He made the spring and other seasons, and the weather suitable for planting.   These He did make, but stills to make whisky to be given to Indians He did not make.   The Great Spirit bids us tell the white people not to give Indians this kind of liquor.   When the Great Spirit had made the earth and its animals, He went into the great lakes, where He breathed as easily as anywhere else, and then made all the different kinds of fish.   The Great Spirit looked back on all that He had made.   The different kinds He made to be separate, and not to mix with and disturb each other ; but the white people have broken His command, by mixing their colour with the Indians ; the Indians have done better by not doing so.   The Great Spirit wishes that all wars and fighting shall cease.

" ' He next told us that there were three things for people to attend to—First, we ought to take care of our wives and children—Secondly, the white people ought to attend to their farms and cattle—Thirdly, the Great Spirit has given the bears and deer to the Indians.   He is the cause of all things that exist, and it is very wicked to go against His will.   The Great Spirit wishes me to inform the people that they should quit drinking intoxicating drink, as being the cause of diseases and death.   He told us not to sell any more of our lands, for He never sold lands to anyone.   Some of us now keep the seventh day ; but I wish to quit it, for the Great Spirit made it for others, but not for the Indians, who ought every day to attend to their business.   He has ordered me to quit drinking any intoxicating drink, and not to lust after any woman but my own, and informed me that by doing so I should live the longer. He made known to me that it is very wicked to lie. Let no one suppose this I have now said is not true.

"'I have now to thank the Governor for what he has done, and have informed him what the Great Spirit has ordered me to cease from, and I wish the Governor to inform others of what I have communicated. This is all I have at present to say.'"

5. This Indian signed the treaty of 1788. He was a well-educated man, and had visited Lafayette in France, but returned to savage life. He was a member of the delegation of chiefs to Philadelphia in 1792, where he died and was buried with military honours. He is also called Peter Otzagert and Peter Jaquette. Peter Otsiequette, perhaps the same Indian, witnessed the Onondaga treaty of 1790.—Information from the Rev. W. M. Beauchamp, Syracuse, N.Y.

6. This entire speech savours more of the interpretation of the white man than of the feeling of the Indian; yet the sequel, which is not unlikely, serves to illustrate the character of the individual.

7. Authorities differ in regard to the name and nationality of Cornplanter's father. It is sometimes spelled O'Bail and O'Beel, and he is said also to have been an Englishman; but Harris (*Publications of the Buffalo Historical Society*, VI., 416, 1893) says he was a Dutchman named Abeel, and Ruttenber (*Tribes of Hudson's River*, 317, 1872) also says he was a Dutch trader. Cornplanter was sometimes known as John O'Bail. See notes 10 and 18.

8. Situated on the west bank of Genesee River, opposite the present Geneseo, Livingston County, New York. By the terms of a contract negotiated between the Seneca tribe and Robert Morris, at Genesee, New York, September 15, 1797, a tract of land, covering two square miles, including the town of "Canawagus," was reserved for the use of the tribe, but it was subsequently sold by them to the State of New York.

9. Evidently Rufus Putnam, son of Israel.

10. The three commissioners referred to were Oliver Wolcott, Richard Butler, and Arthur Lee. The treaty of Fort Stanwix, which post was situated a short distance south-east of the present Rome, Oneida County, New York, was negotiated October 22, 1784, and was the second treaty held between the United States and any of the Indian tribes. The treaty was an important one, for by its provisions the western boundary of the territory of the Six Nations was defined, the country to the west thereof being ceded to the United States, and a tract six miles square was reserved around the "Fort of Oswego" for the use of the Government. The last Indian signer of the treaty was Cornplanter, whose name appears as "Seneka Abeal, Kayenthoghke." Abeal is one of the forms of his father's name. See note 7.

11. See note 16.

12. See notes 4 and 16.

13. That is, Alleghany River.

14. The treaty of Fort Harmar, Ohio, was concluded between General Arthur St Clair and twenty-four representatives of the Six Nations, January 9, 1789, General Joseph Harmar serving as one of the witnesses. Cornplanter's name appears in the treaty as " Gyantwaia, or Cornplanter."

15. Kiandogewa, or Big Tree, and Achiout, or Half Town, were two of the twenty-four signers of the Fort Harmar treaty. For further information regarding this speech, and on Cornplanter generally, see S. G. Drake, *Aboriginal Races of North America*, 15th ed., New York [1880], pp. 607-616.

16. This information is gleaned from S. G. Drake, whose *Book of the Indians* was first published in 1833, and who derived his data respecting Cornplanter's village, also known as Obaletown, from the *Pennsylvania Gazette*, 1792, and *Stansbury's Journal*. About the same locality, prior to the date here referred to (1816), were two Seneca villages, one known as Buckaloon, the other as Yoroonwago, named, apparently, after their respective chiefs. They were destroyed by Colonel Brodhead in 1779. The grant of 640 acres made to Cornplanter by the State of Pennsylvania on March 16, 1796, during the Governorship of the celebrated Thomas Mifflin (1744-1800), was situated on both sides of the Alleghany River, just within the limits of Pennsylvania, but adjoining the New York boundary (see Royce, *Indian Land Cessions*, Pennsylvania map, 1899). At an earlier period Cornplanter lived in a settlement known as Connewango (meaning " at the falls "), also called " Cornplanter's Village," about the site of Warren, Warren County, Pa.; it likewise was destroyed by Colonel Brodhead in 1779. Another Connewango stood on the left bank of the Alleghany, above the site of Tionesta, Forest County, Pa.

17. This was the Western Missionary Society, according to Drake, *op. cit.*, p. 615.

18. Known as Henry Obeal.

19. He died February 18, 1836. A monument erected to his memory on his reservation by the State of Pennsylvania bears the inscription, "aged about 100 years." Cornplanter is said to have been the first temperance lecturer in the United States.

20. See note 1.

21. This portrait was painted in New York City, in the year 1796, by F. Bartoli, and now forms a part of the Bryan collection of the New York Historical Society. See *Catalogue of the Museum and Gallery of*

Art of the New York Historical Society, 1903, Second Part, No. 490, p. 54. The *Catalogue* recognises the portrait as the one reproduced in McKenney and Hall. As the portrait did not belong to the Indian Gallery of the War Department, and was evidently not copied by Inman, it does not appear in the collection of the Peabody Museum.

22. Timothy Matlack (not Matlock), born Haddonfield, New Jersey, in 1730; died near Hornesburg, Pa., April 15, 1829. He was a member of the Society of Friends, but became a " Fighting Quaker " on the outbreak of the revolution, in which he was an active spirit. He was a member of the Committee of Safety in 1776, and a deputy with Franklin and others from Philadelphia to attend the state conference on June 14 of that year. He was a delegate to the Continental Congress in 1780-87, and was long Master of Rolls of the state, with headquarters at Lancaster, but removed to Philadelphia on becoming prothonotary of one of its courts. In 1783 the Committee of Safety presented him with a silver urn. He was one of the contributors, with Franklin, Robert Morris, and others, to the fund for the erection of a free Quaker meeting-house in Philadelphia.

PASHEPAHAW

(OR, THE STABBER)

LITTLE is known of this chief, except that he was of sufficient note among his people to be chosen one of a delegation to visit Washington on business relating to his tribe. He is represented to be vindictive and implacable in his resentments. The Indian agent at Prairie du Chien having offended him, Pashepahaw resolved on revenge, and actually undertook a long journey with the view of killing him. *Taiomah*, whose portrait will appear in the course of this work,[1] hearing of The Stabber's purpose, outsped him, and made known to the agent his bloody design. This timely information, doubtless, saved the agent's life. The untrimmed locks that hang down on The Stabber's shoulders indicate unsatisfied revenge.

It is not probable, if more was known of this ferocious Indian, that his biography would afford any incident of sufficient interest to deserve a large space in our work. There can be no question that the agreeable epithet by which he has chosen to be distinguished is indicative of his character.[2]

The Sauks, as a nation, afford favourable specimens of the Indian race. Among a large number that we have seen, the majority were tall, well-formed, active men, who bestowed much care on the decoration of their persons, and were dignified in their manners. They are a warlike,

194

active, and sprightly people, friendly to the whites, and
hospitable to strangers.   Their principal residence, until
recently, was on the shores of Rock River, in Illinois,
where their hunting grounds comprised the most fertile
and beautiful region of the west.   They have been removed
from those lovely plains to other lands beyond the Mississippi, and their recent haunts are now covered with the
farms of an industrious population.

NOTES

1. See Vol. II.

2. This is a common error, due to misinterpretation of Indian proper
names.   The present subject is properly called *Päshipaho,* meaning " He
who touches lightly in passing," according to Dr William Jones, himself
of Sauk and Fox blood, and the leading authority on their language.

The portrait of Pashepahaw was painted by King, doubtless in 1824,
in which year he was in Washington, and appears as No. 41, " Pa-she-
pah-how, Stabber.   First Chief of the Sankys; a Sac," in the Rhees
list of the Indian Gallery (see the Introduction, p. xlviii).   The Inman
copy in the Peabody Museum bears original number, 56 ; catalogue
number, 28. 200.

Pashepahaw's portrait was again painted in 1834 by George Catlin,
who describes him as " a very venerable old man, who has been for many
years the first civil chief of the Sacs and Foxes."   Catlin calls him " Pash-
ee-pa-hó, the Little Stabbing Chief," and depicts him as " a very old
man, holding his shield, staff and pipe in his hands."   Catlin adds that
he " has long been the head civil chief of this tribe [Sauk]; but, as is
generally the case in very old age, he has resigned the office to those
who are younger and better qualified to do the duties of it " (*Illustrations
of the Manners   .   .   .   of the North American Indians,* 10th ed., Vol. II.,
p. 211, pl. 289, London, 1866 ; *Descriptive Catalogue,* p. 8 [London, 1840]).

Pashepahaw belonged to one of the Fish clans of the Sauk, and was
a signer of the treaties of St Louis, November 3, 1804 (as " Pashepaho,
or the giger "); Fort Armstrong, Rock Island, Illinois, September 3,
1822 (as " Pushee-Paho"); Washington, August 4, 1824 (as " Pah-sha-
pa-ha, or Stubbs "; this treaty was witnessed by McKenney); Fort
Armstrong, September 21, 1832 (as " Pa-she-pa-ho, or the stabber ");
the neighbourhood of Debuque (Dubuque) County, Wisconsin, September
27, 1836 (as " Pa-she-pa-ho"); and on the Mississippi, in Dubuque
County, Wisconsin, opposite Rock Island, September 28, 1836 (as
" Pashapahoo").   *Niles' Register* of July 31, 1824, gives a list, copied

from the *National Journal*, of "six Sankys or Sturgeons" then at the seat of Government, among them being "Pah-she-pah-how (Stabber), 1st chief," and "Kee-o-kuch (Watchful Fox), 1st war chief." "After the transaction of some business [the negotiation of the treaty of August 4], they will proceed through our principal cities as far as New York, and return by way of the lakes."

For additional information regarding this chief and warrior, consult A. R. Fulton, *Red Men of Iowa*, pp. 248-252, 1882. This writer says :— "He became in his old age much given to intemperate habits, and it is quite likely he went down to a drunkard's grave. When very old and feeble he migrated with his people to their new reservation beyond the Missouri, and doubtless for many years his dust has mingled with the soil of Kansas."

PAH-SHE-PAH-AW, *or* THE STABBER
A Sauk Chief

CAATOUSEE

(A CHIPPEWAY)

IT is, perhaps, not to be regretted, that some of the portraits contained in our gallery are those of persons of little repute; for, although many of the biographies may, on this account, be less interesting in themselves, a greater variety of the aspects of the Indian character will, on the whole, be presented to our readers.

The wandering savages who inhabit the sterile and inhospitable shores of the northern lakes are the most miserable and degraded of the native tribes.[1] Exposed to the greatest extremities of climate, and forced by their situation to spend the greater portion of their lives in obtaining a wretched subsistence, they have little ambition, and few ideas, which extend to the supply of their most immediate and pressing wants. The region which they inhabit affords but little game; and when the lakes are frozen, and the land covered with deep snow, there are seasons in which scarcely any living animal can be found, but the wretched tenant of the wigwam, whose habitual improvidence has prevented him from laying up any store for the winter. Lingering at the spot of his temporary residence until the horrors of starvation press him to instant exertion, he must then fly to some distant region, to which the wild animals of the plain, with a truer instinct, have already retreated, or seek a sheltered haunt where he may subsist by fishing. Many

197

perish during these long journeys, or are doomed to disappointment on reaching the place of their destination, and thus they drag out, month after month, their weary existence in the eager search for food.

We know not how the individual before us came to be designated by the name attached to the portrait. The true name is A-qua-o-da, which signifies *Creeping out of the Water*.[2] His usual residence is La Pointe, or Shagoime-koong, upon Lake Superior. He is a person of little repute, either with white or red men. He is too idle to hunt, and has no name as a warrior; nor is his character good in other respects. He is, however, an expert fisherman and canoeman, in which capacity he is occasionally employed by the traders. He has never advanced any pretensions to chieftainship, except to be a chief among the dancers, and in his profuse use of paints and ornaments.[3]

NOTES

1. This can scarcely be regarded as true; indeed, the Chippeway, or Ojibway, tribes may be regarded as among the most vigorous of their race, as witness their numbers (30,000 to 32,000 in the United States and Canada), and the fact that they were powerful enough to drive the Sioux from the country of the Great Lakes to the westward. The statement is probably that of McKenney, who probably saw more of the Chippeway and their neighbours than of any other tribe.

2. The true form of the name is kindly given by Dr William Jones as *Agwā-ō·da*, signifying "He crawls out of the water."

3. The portrait was painted by King, from a drawing by Lewis in 1827 (in August of which year Lewis was with McKenney and Cass at the treaty of Butte des Morts), and appears as No. 115 ("Catoouse") in the Rhees list of the Indian Gallery (see the Introduction, p. li). The Inman copy in the Peabody Museum bears original number, 37; catalogue number, 28. 201.

CAA-TOU-SEE
A Chippeway

CHIPPEWAY SQUAW AND CHILD

The life of the Indian woman, under the most favourable circumstances, is one of continual labour and unmitigated hardship. Trained to servitude from infancy, and condemned to the performance of the most menial offices, they are the servants rather than the companions of man.[1] Upon them, therefore, fall, with peculiar severity, all those vicissitudes and accidents of savage life which impose hardships and privations beyond those that ordinarily attend the state of barbarism. Such is the case with the tribes who inhabit a sterile region, or an inhospitable climate, where the scarcity of food and the rigour of the seasons enhance the difficulty of supporting life, and impose the most distressing burthens on the weaker sex. The Chippeway, or, as they pronounce their own name, the *Ojibway*[2] nation, is scattered along the bleak shores of our north-western lakes, over a region of barren plains, or dreary swamps, which, during the greater part of the year, are covered with snow and ice, and are at all times desolate and uninviting. Here the wretched Indian gleans a precarious subsistence; at one season by gathering the wild rice in the rivers and swamps, at another by fishing, and a third by hunting. Long intervals, however, occur when these resources fail, and when exposed to absolute and hopeless want, the courage of the warrior and the ingenuity of the hunter sink into despair. The woman who, during the season of plenty, was worn down with the

labour of following the hunter to the chase, carrying the
game and dressing the food, now becomes the purveyor of
the family, roaming the forest in search of berries, burrow-
ing in the earth for roots, or ensnaring the lesser animals.
While engaged in these various duties, she discharges also
those of the mother, and travels over the icy plains with
her infant on her back.[3]

NOTES

1. See note 1 under Hayne Hudjihini, p. 166.

2. See note 2, p. 118.

3. This portrait was painted by Lewis at Fond du Lac, Lake Superior,
in August 1826, and is the sixtieth portrait in his *Port-folio*.   The copy
in the Indian Gallery was made by King in the following year (see No.
146 of the Rhees list).   The Inman copy in the Peabody Museum bears
original number, 102 ; and catalogue number, 28. 202, and is ascribed to
King.   The original sketch by Lewis is probably the one titled, " Manner
of carrying a child on a journey," forming the plate facing p. 307 of
McKenney's *Sketches of a Tour to the Lakes*, 1827.

CHIPPEWAY SQUAW AND CHILD

PETALESHARRO[1]

(A PAWNEE BRAVE)

WE have been accustomed from childhood to hear but little of the Indians, except in connection with scenes of blood. The border wars, with their tales of horror, are among the nursery stories that have left the deepest impressions on our memories. This strife between the red and the white man is coeval with the first settlement of the country, and it continues even to this day. The prominent feature in this long period of excitement and of war, and that on which all eyes are more intensely fixed, is the bloodthirsty cruelty of the Indian. This has been so often dwelt upon, and presented to our view under so many shocking forms, as to keep almost constantly before our eyes the war-club, the scalping knife, and the toma-hawk, together with the ferocious red man clad in the skins of beasts, the glare of whose eyes, with his attitude, and his blood-stained limbs, have all combined to fill our minds with terror and our hearts with revenge. Indeed we have been taught to consider the Indian as *necessarily* bloodthirsty, ferocious, and vindictive, until we have viewed him as a being deprived, at the creation of his species, of those faculties whence come the nobler and more generous traits which are the boast and glory of his civilised brother. It is certainly true of the Indian, that his mode of warfare is barbarous. He spares neither age nor sex; and his victim is often subjected to the severest tortures. But it is no less true, that he has never been taught those lessons of humanity which have, under the guidance of civilisation and Christianity, stript war of its more appalling horrors, and without which we should be no less savage than the Indians. Indeed it would be easy to demonstrate, that even when aided by the light of civilisation and professing to be Christians, the white man is no less cruel than the red man; and often, in our conflicts with each other, we come fully up to the savage man in all that is barbarous and revolting.

In our wars with the Indians we have been our own chroniclers. And how rarely has it happened that justice has been done the Indians, not only as to the causes of these wars, but to the conduct of the parties to them? Everything of a palliative nature has been minutely registered, to justify or excuse the white man, whilst the red man has been held up to the view of the world, and consigned over to the judgment of posterity, not only as *the cause* of sanguinary and vindictive conflicts, but as the Moloch of the human race. The Indian has never been able to leave a record of his wrongs; to illustrate his own position, or to justify the desperate means he has resorted to in defence of his inheritance and his life.

However true it is that the Indian mode of warfare is exclusively savage, yet there are exceptions to its barbarities; and we have well-authenticated instances of the most refined humanity, confirming our decided belief, that the Indian is not, by any law of his nature, bereft of the more noble qualities which are the pride and boast of civilised man, or that he is *necessarily* savage. We might enumerate many cases in which the untutored Indian has melted into pity at sight of the perilous condition of the white man, and at the very moment when he was looked upon as an invader and enemy. The most beautiful illustration of the existence of this feeling in the Indian, is in the intervention of Pocahontas, to save the life of Captain Smith. History has recorded that deed, and the civilised world has united in awarding its plaudits to that noble princess.[2] Her memory has been embalmed by a grateful posterity. At the siege of Detroit, the garrison owed its safety to the agency of an Indian woman, who made known to the commanding officer the plans of Pontiac for its destruction and massacre.[3] Indeed the Indian women are remarkable for the exercise of this generous feeling—even among the Indians it is a common occurrence for them, in times of excitement, to secret knives and guns, and all kinds of instruments of death ; and, by so doing, often prevent the shedding of blood.

But this feeling of compassion, this boast of the civilised man and Christian, is not confined to the Indian women. We are not without examples of the same sort among the men. The famous Logan, notwithstanding the wrongs he was made to endure, in his own person and in the persons of his family and kindred, until he exclaimed, in all the bitterness of bereavement, *" There runs not a drop of my blood in the veins of any living creature,"* has left behind him, in honour of his memory, a noble specimen of this humane feeling, in counselling one of his own captives, who was condemned by the council to undergo the severe tortures of the gauntlet, how to escape it ; and when, afterwards, this same captive was condemned to be burned, and Logan, finding that his efforts and his eloquence in his behalf all failed, nobly and bravely advanced, and with his own hands released the prisoner from the stake to which he was bound.[4]

But we hasten to sketch the character of *Petalesharro*, whose portrait is before the reader.

Petalesharro was a brave of the Pawnee tribe. His father, *Letalashaw*, was chief of his band, and a man of renown. Petalesharro early imbibed his father's spirit; often, no doubt, charmed with the songs of the chief, in which he recounted the battles he had fought, and told of the scalps he had taken, his youthful bosom heaved, and his heart resolved to imitate these deeds; and, in his turn, to recount his warlike exploits—tell of his victories, and count the scalps he had taken. Thus impressed, he went early into battle, and soon won the renown and the title of a "*brave*."

We saw him in Washington in 1821, whither he was sent as one of a deputation from his tribe, to transact business with the Government.[5] He was dressed, so far as his half-length discloses it, precisely as he is seen in the portrait. He wore a head-dress of the feathers of the war eagle, which extended, in a double series, down his back to his hips, narrowing as it descended. His robe was thrown carelessly but gracefully over his shoulders, leaving his breast, and often one arm bare. The usual garments decorated his hips and lower limbs; there were the *auzeum*,[6] the leggings, and the moccasins, all ornamented. The youthful and feminine character of his face, and the humanity of its expression, were all remarkable. He did not appear to be older than twenty years, yet he was then believed to be twenty-five.

A fine incident is connected with the history of this Indian. The Pawnee Loups had long practised the savage rite, known to no other of the American tribes, of sacrificing human victims to the *Great Star*, or the planet Venus.[7] This dreadful ceremony annually preceded the preparations for planting corn, and was supposed to be necessary to secure a fruitful season. To prevent a failure of the crop, and a consequent famine, some

individual was expected to offer up a prisoner, of either
sex, who had been captured in war, and some one was
always found who coveted the honour of dedicating the
spoil of his prowess to the national benefit.   The intended
victim, carefully kept in ignorance of the fate that
impended, was dressed in gay apparel, supplied with
the choicest food, and treated with every tenderness,
with the view of promoting obesity, and preparing an
offering the more acceptable to the deities who were
to be propitiated.   When, by the successful employment of these means, the unhappy victim was sufficiently fatted, a day was appointed for the sacrifice,
and the whole nation assembled to witness the solemn
scene.

Some short time before Petalesharro was deputed to
visit Washington, it chanced that an Ietan[8] maid, who
had been taken prisoner, was doomed by her captor
to be offered up to the Great Star, and was prepared
with the usual secrecy and care for the grand occasion.
The grief and alarm incident to a state of captivity
had been allayed by deceptive kindness, and the grateful
prisoner became happy in the society of strangers, who
bestowed upon her a degree of adulation to which she
had probably not been accustomed.   Exempt from
labour, and exalted into an unwonted ease of life,
she soon acquired that serenity of mind and comeliness
of person which rendered her worthy of being offered
to the Great Star as a full equivalent for an abundant
harvest.

The reader will now fancy himself in view of the great
gathering of the Pawnees, and that he is in sight of
the multitude assembled in honour of the sacrifice.   In his
near approach he will hear their orgies.   In the midst
of the circle a stake is brought; its end is sharpened,

when it is driven deep into the ground. Yells and shouts announce that all is ready. In the distance is seen a company of Pawnees; by the side of the leader is a delicate girl. They approach nearer. He who made her captive enters the circle—shouts welcome him. He takes the girl by the hand, and leads her to the fatal spot. Her back is placed against the stake; cords are brought, and she is bound to it. The faggots are now collected, and placed around the victim. A hopeless expression is seen in her eye—perhaps a tear! Her bosom heaves, and her thoughts are of home, when a torch is seen coming from the woods, hard by. At that moment a young brave leaps into the midst of the circle—rushes to the stake—tears the victim from it, and springing on a horse, and throwing her upon another, and putting both to the top of their speed, is soon lost in the distance. Silence prevails—then murmurs are heard—then the loud threats of vengeance, when all retire. The stake and the faggots are all that remain to mark the spot on which, but for this noble deed, ashes and bones would have distinguished. Who was it that intrepidly released the captive maid? It was the young, the brave, the generous *Petalesharro!* Whether it was panic, or the dread of Letalashaw's vengeance that operated, and kept the warriors from using their bows and arrows, and rifles, is not known, but certain it is they did not use them.

Our readers will, perhaps, expect to hear that Petalesharro conducted the maiden to her own people, and received the reward which valour deserves from beauty. But mere gallantry formed no part of this adventure. It was not induced, not rewarded, by love. The Indian is very scriptural in his belief, that man is the head of the woman; but he is equally strong in the faith, that the female, if she has fair play, is quite as able to take care of herself as a man. Having escorted her into the broad plains, beyond the precincts of the Pawnee village, and supplied her with provisions, he admonished her to make the best of her way to her own nation, which was distant about four hundred miles, and left her to her fate and her reflections. She lost no time in obeying such salutary counsel, and had the good fortune, the next day, to fall in with a war party of her own people, by whom she was safely carried home.

Can the records of chivalry furnish a parallel to this generous act? Can the civilised world bring forward a case demonstrating a higher order of humanity, united with greater bravery? Whence did the youthful Petalesharro learn this lesson of refined pity? Not of civilised man. Great as have been the efforts of the good and the merciful, from the days of Eliot and Brainerd[9] to our own times, to enlighten the Indians, none had ever yet reached the *Pawnees*, to instruct them, or to enrapture their thoughts by such beautiful illustrations of the merciful. It was the impulse of nature—nature cast in a more refined mould; and, probably, as the sequel will show, nurtured by the blood and spirit of a noble though untaught father.

The tidings of this deed accompanied Petalesharro to Washington. He and his deed soon became the theme of the city. The ladies especially, as is their nature, hastened to do him honour.[10] A medal was prepared. A time was appointed for conferring upon him this merited gift. An assembly had collected to witness the ceremony. He was told, in substance, that the medal was given him in token of the high opinion which was entertained of his act in the rescue of the Ietan maid. He was asked by the ladies who presented it to accept and wear it for their sake; and told, when he had another occasion to save a captive woman from torture and from the stake, to look upon the medal, think of those who gave it, and save her, as he had saved the Ietan girl. The reply of Petalesharro was prompt and excellent, but the interpretation of it was shocking! He was made to say, "I did it (rescued the girl), in *ignorance. I did not know that I did good!* I now know that I did good, by your giving me this medal." We understood him to mean this; and so, we have no doubt, he spoke, in substance, though not in our words:—"He did not know, till now, that the act he had performed was meritorious; but, as his white brothers and sisters considered it a good act, and put upon it so high a value, he was *glad they had heard of it.*" We would almost venture to represent the words of the brave in reply to the compliment. We saw the medal put on his neck, and saw him take it in his hand, and look at it. Holding it before him, he said: "This brings rest to my heart. I feel like the leaf after a storm, and when the wind is still. I listen to you. I am glad. I love the pale faces more than I ever did, and will open my ears wider when they speak. I am glad you heard of what I did. I did not know the act was so good. It came from my heart. I was ignorant of its value. I now know how good it was. You make me know this by giving me this medal."

The rescue of the Ietan girl might, if a solitary act, be looked upon as the result of impulse, and not as proceeding from a generous nature. It happens, however, not to stand alone, as the only incident of the sort in the life of Petalesharro. One of his brother warriors had brought in a captive boy. He was a Spaniard. The captor resolved to offer him in sacrifice to the Great Star. The chief, Letalashaw, had been for some time opposed to these barbarous rites. He sent for the warrior, and told him he did not wish him to make the sacrifice. The warrior claimed his right, under the immemorial usages of the tribe. They parted. Letalashaw sent for his son, and asked what was to be done to divert the captor from his purpose. Petalesharro promptly replied : " I will take the boy, like a brave, by force." The father thought, no doubt, that danger would attend upon the act, and resolved on a more pacific mode. It was to buy the boy. He accordingly gave out his intention, and those who had goods of any kind, brought them to his lodge, and laid them down as an offering on the pile which the chief had supplied from his own stores.[11] The collection having been made, the captor was again sent for, and, in the authoritative tone of a chief, thus addressed : " Take these goods, and give me the boy." He refused, when the chief seized his war-club and flourished it over the head of the captor. At the moment, Petalesharro sprang forward, and said : " Strike ! and let the wrath of his friends fall on me." The captor, making a merit of necessity, agreed if a few more articles were added, to give up the boy to the chief. They were added, and thus the captive was saved. The merchandise was sacrificed instead of the boy. The cloth was cut into shreds, and suspended upon poles, at the spot upon which the blood of the victim had been proposed to be shed, and the remainder of the articles burned. No subsequent attempt to immolate a victim was made.

Petalesharro succeeded his father in the chieftainship of his tribe, and became highly distinguished in that station.[12]

We conclude this sketch with the following stanzas,

published some years ago in the *New York Commercial Advertiser*, on the rescue of the Ietan maid :—

THE PAWNEE BRAVE.

The summer had fled, but there linger'd still
   A warmth in the clear blue skies ;
The flowers were gone, and the night wind's chill
Had robed the forest and the woody hill
   In richest of Autumn dyes.

The battle was fought, and the deadly strife
   Had ceased on the Prairie plains ;
Each tomahawk—spear—and keen-edged knife
Was red with the current of many a life,
   It bore from the severed veins.

The Pawnee followed his victor band
   That sped to their home afar—
The river * is passed, and again they stand,
A trophied throng, on their own broad land,
   Recounting the deeds of war.

A beautiful captive maid was there,
   Bedeck'd as a warrior's bride—
The glossy braids of her ebon hair,
Interwoven with gems, and adorned with care,
   With the jet of the raven vied.

Her beaded robes were skilfully wrought,
   With shells from the river isles,
The fairest that wash from the ocean, brought
From the sands by a brave young Chief, who sought
   The meed of her sweetest smiles.

Beneath the boughs of an ancient oak—
   They came to the council ground ;
No eloquent tongue for the maiden spoke,
She was quickly doomed, and their shouts awoke
   The woods to the piercing sound.

---

* The battle alluded to was fought with a trans-Mississippian tribe.

And when on her olive cheek, a tear
  Stole out from her lustrous eye,
A youth from th' exulting crowd drew near,
And whispered words in her startled ear,
  That told her she was *not* to die.

They hurried away to the fatal spot,
  Deep hid in the forest shade ;
And bound her fast, but she murmured not—
They bared her breast for the rifle shot,
  And brow for the scalping blade.

Then forth to the work of death they came,
  While the loud death song was heard—
A hunter skilled in the chase, whose aim
Ne'er missed the heart of his mountain game—
  He waited the signal word !

One instant more, ere the maid should bleed,
  A moment and all were done—
The Pawnee sprang from his noble steed,
Unloosed her hands, and the captive freed—
  A moment—and they were gone !

Then swift as the speed of the wind, away
  To her distant home they hied—
And just at the sunset hour of day,
Ere the evening dew on the meadow lay,
  She stood at her father's side.

                                        H.

NOTES

1. The name of this celebrated chief is given by John B. Dunbar (*Magazine of American History*, IV., No. 4, 261, 270, April 1880) as Pit'-ă-le-shar-u, meaning "Chief of Men." His son bore the same name. According to the same authority, Pitalesharu the elder died in 1841, and the son in 1874. Grinnell (*Pawnee Hero Stories*, 396, 1893) says the son, Pi'-ta Le-shar, was shot and died of his wounds shortly before the removal of the Pawnee from Nebraska to Indian Territory in 1874.

2. Although we hesitate to shatter this pretty romance, the evidence that this celebrated Indian woman saved the life of Captain Smith is by no means convincing.

3. See Francis Parkman, *The Conspiracy of Pontiac*.

4. Consult Brantz Mayer, *Tah-gah-jute or Logan*, 1867. Logan's father is said to have been a white man, probably a Frenchman, born in Canada. His mother was an Iroquois, probably a Cayuga.

5. For a reference to the visit of this Pawnee deputation to Washington late in 1821, see *Shaumonekusse*, note 8, p. 162. From the fact that Petalesharro was in Washington in this year, it may be assumed that this was one of the first Indian portraits painted by King after his removal to the capital. The original is not known to exist; and from the fact that it does not appear in the Rhees list, it is possible that it was not painted for the Indian Gallery at the War Department. However, a "coppy from Charles King, September 19, 1822," of a painting bearing the inscription, "Loup Pawnee, Generous Chief" (which on comparison shows identity with the accompanying engraving of Petalesharro), is preserved in the United States National Museum (see the Introduction, p. liv, No. 5). An engraving by S. S. Jocelyn, from the King painting, appears as a frontispiece of Jedidiah Morse's *Report to the Secretary of War . . . on Indian Affairs* (Washington, 1822), with the title, "A Pawnee Brave / Son of Old Knife." In the Appendix to Morse's *Report* (pp. 247-249) occurs an "Anecdote of a Pawnee Brave," which, with the narrative of Petalesharro's rescue of the captive "Ietan" woman appearing in S. H. Long's *Account of an Expedition from Pittsburgh to the Rocky Mountains* (Vol. I., pp. 357-359, Philadelphia, 1823), no doubt forms the basis of McKenney and Hall's present account of this noteworthy Indian. Compare also, Wetmore, *Gazetteer of the State of Missouri*, p. 333, 1837.

6. The Chippeway term for breech or loin cloth, evidently a misprint of Schoolcraft's *âuzeaun*, rendered *ansiân* by Baraga, *Dictionary of the Otchipwe Language*, Montreal, 1878.

7. John B. Dunbar (*Magazine of American History*, Vol. VIII., 1882, pp. 738-741) gives a very interesting account of this ceremony, and also of the rescue by Pitalesharu:—

"One form of sacrifice formerly practised in the tribe, or rather in one band, for the other bands emphatically disclaimed any share in the barbarous rite, stood apart in unhappy prominence. This was the offering of human sacrifices (captives); not burning them as an expression of embittered revenge, but sacrificing them as a religious ordinance. What the origin of this terrible practice was the Pawnees could never explain, and I am inclined to regard it as a fortuitous element in their system. The rite was confined to the Ski'-di band [Pawnee Loups], and was no doubt of long standing; yet the Arikaras, who are nearly related to the Ski'-di, and have always maintained intercourse with them, never have admitted the practice, and to all appearance the denial of the other bands was supported by fact. The sacrifice was made to the morning star, *o-pir'-i-kut*, which, with the Ski'-di especially, was an object of superstitious veneration. It was offered about corn-planting time, and the design of the bloody ordeal was to conciliate that being, and secure a good crop. Hence, it has been supposed that the morning star was regarded by them as presiding over agriculture, but this was a mistake. They sacrificed to that star simply because they feared it, imagining that it exerted malign influence if not well disposed. It has also been stated that the sacrifice was made annually. This, too, was an error. It was made only when special occurrences were interpreted as calling for it. The victim was usually a girl or young woman taken from their enemies. The more beautiful the unfortunate was, the more acceptable the offering. When it had been determined in a council of the band to make the sacrifice, the person was selected, if possible, some months beforehand and placed in charge of the doctors, who treated her with the utmost kindness. She was fed plentifully that she might become fleshy, and kept in entire ignorance of her impending doom. During this time she was made to eat alone, lest having by chance eaten with any one of the band, she would, by the law of hospitality, become that person's guest, and he be bound to protect her. On the morning of the day finally fixed for the ordeal, she was led from lodge to lodge throughout the village, begging wood and paint, not knowing that these articles were for her own immolation. Whenever a stick of wood or portion of red or black paint was given her, it was taken by the doctors attending, and sent to the spot for the final rite. A sufficient quantity of these materials having been collected, the ceremony was begun by a solemn conclave of all the doctors. Smoking the great medicine pipe, displaying the contents of the medicine bundle, dancing, praying, etc., were all had and repeated at different stages of the proceeding. A framework of two posts, about four and a half feet apart, was set in the ground, and to them two horizontal cross-pieces, at a height of two and seven feet, were firmly fastened. Between the post a slow fire was built. At nightfall the victim was disrobed, one half of her person painted black, the other red, and fastened with thongs, her right wrist and ankle to one upright, her left ankle and wrist to the other. A throng of boys crowding round, each provided with a small bow and a bundle of halms of the tall joint-grass (*Tripsacum dactyloides*), began shooting these joints as arrows at the breast and body of the unfortunate sufferer. The sharpened points of the shafts penetrated the skin and fatty substance beneath and there remained, the oily matter oozing out and trickling from the numerous exposed extremities into the fire below. These exposed ends sometimes took fire, and burned like tiny torches from the body of the writhing victim. After this sickening sight had continued sufficiently long, an old man, previously appointed, discharged an arrow at the heart of the unfortunate, and freed her from further torture. The doctors forthwith cut open the chest, took out the heart and burned it. The smoke rising from the fire in which it was burning was supposed to possess wonderful virtues, and implements of war, hunting, and agriculture were passed through it to insure success in their use. The flesh was hacked from the body, buried in the corn patches, thrown to the dogs, or disposed of in any way that caprice might direct. The skeleton was allowed to remain in position till, loosened by decay, it fell to the ground. . . .

"The last known instance of this sacrifice was in April 1838. It is probable that it has been repeated once or twice since, but this is not positively known. The winter previous to the date given, the Ski'-di, soon after starting on their hunt, had a successful fight with a band of Oglala Dakotas; killed several men, and took over twenty women and children. Fearing that the Dakotas, according to their tactics, would retaliate by coming upon them in overwhelming force, they returned to their village before taking a sufficient number of buffalo. With little to eat, they lived miserably, lost many of their ponies from scarcity of forage, and worst of all, one of the captives proved to have the small-pox, which rapidly spread through the band, and in the spring was communicated to the rest of the tribe. All these accumulated misfortunes the Ski'-di attributed to the anger of the morning star; and accordingly they resolved to propitiate its favour by a repetition of the sacrifice, though in direct violation of a stipulation made two years before that the sacrifice should not occur again.

"In connection with its abolition, the oft-told story of Pit'-a-le-shar-u is recalled. Sa'-re-cĕr-ish (Angry Chief), second chief of the Cau'-i band, was a man of unusually humane disposition, and had strenuously endeavoured to secure the suppression of the practice. In the spring of 1817 the Ski'di arranged to sacrifice a Comanche girl. After Sa'-re-cĕr-ish had essayed in vain to dissuade them, Pit'-a-le-shar-u, a young man, about twenty years of age, of almost gigantic stature, and already famed as a great brave, conceived the bold design of rescuing her. On the day set for the rite he actually cut the girl loose, after she had been tied to the stakes, placed her upon a horse that he had in readiness, and hurried her away across the prairies till they were come within a day's journey of her people's village. There, after giving necessary directions as to her course, he dismissed her, himself returning to the Pawnees. The suddenness and intrepidity of his movements, and his known prowess, were no doubt all that saved him from death at the moment of the rescue and after his return. Twice afterward he presumed to interfere. In one instance, soon after the foregoing, he assisted in securing by purchase the ransom of a Spanish boy who had been set apart for sacrifice. Several years later also (*circa* 1831) he aided in the attempted rescue of a girl. The resistance on this occasion was so determined that even after the girl had been bought and was mounted upon a horse behind Major Dougherty, at that time general agent at Bellevue, to be taken from the Ski'-di village, she was shot by one of the doctors. The magnanimous conduct of Sa'-re-cĕr-ish and Pit'-a-le-shar-u in this matter stands almost unexampled in Indian annals."

J. T. Irving (*Indian Sketches*, II., 146-153, 1835) says the second rescue occurred in May 1833, and relates that on the attempt of Major Dougherty to prevent the sacrifice of the girl, who was a Cheyenne, she was shot with an arrow, torn limb from limb, and her blood smeared on the bodies of the assembled Pawnee. See also Schoolcraft, *Western Scenes and Reminiscences*, Auburn, 1853, pp. 402-403.

8. Printed "Itean" in previous editions, and here corrected. The maid was a Comanche. Bell's account in Morse's *Report* (see note 10) refers to the woman as a Paduca, which is the Sioux name for the Comanche. See Dunbar's account in the preceding note, and compare *Shaumonekusse*, note 1, p. 162.

9. John Eliot, "the Indian Apostle," born Widford, Hertfordshire, England, in 1604; died Roxbury, Mass., May 21, 1690; laboured among the Indians of Massachusetts, translating many works into their language, including the entire Bible. Consult Pilling, *Bibliography of the Algonquian Languages*, Washington, 1891.

David Brainerd, born Haddam, Conn., April 20, 1718; died Northampton, Mass., October 9, 1747. His missionary labours were among the Stockbridge and Delaware Indians. See his journals, published under the titles, *Mirabilia Dei apud Indicos* and *Divine Grace Displayed*, published in 1746, and biographies by Jonathan Edwards (1749), second edition edited by Sereno E. Dwight (1822), third edition by J. M. Sherwood (1884).

10. The episode is of sufficient interest to warrant repetition here from Morse's *Report*, above cited (pp. 247-248):—

" ANECDOTE OF A PAWNEE BRAVE.—The facts in the following anecdote of a Pawnee Brave, son of Old Knife, one of the delegation who visited Washington the last winter, highly creditable to his courage, his generosity, and his humanity, were taken by permission from a very interesting MS. Journal of Capt. Bell, of his expedition with Major Long, to the foot of the Rocky Mountains, in 1821, and are sanctioned by Major O'Fallon, Indian Agent, near the scene of the transaction here related, and also by the Interpreter who witnessed this scene.

" This Brave, of fine size, figure, and countenance, is now about twenty-five years old. At the age of twenty-one, his heroic deed had acquired for him in his nation the rank of "the bravest of the brave."* The savage practice of torturing and burning to death their prisoners existed in this nation.† An unfortunate female taken in war, of the Paduca nation, was destined to this horrid death. The fatal hour had arrived : the trembling victim, far from her home and her friends, was fastened to the stake ; the whole tribe was assembled on the surrounding plain, to witness the awful scene. [Then follows an account of the rescue.]

"The publication of this anecdote at Washington led the young

---

* The Braves are warriors who have distinguished themselves in battle, and stand highest in the estimation of the tribe.

† This custom does not now exist in the surrounding tribes.

ladies of Miss White's Seminary in that city, in a manner highly credit-able to their good sense and good feeling, to present this brave and humane Indian with a handsome silver medal, with appropriate inscrip-tions, as a token of their sincere commendation of the noble act of rescuing one of their sex, an innocent victim, from a cruel death. Their address delivered on this occasion is sensible and pertinent, closing as follows :—

"'Brother—Accept this token of our esteem—always wear it for our sakes, and when again you have the power to save a poor woman from death and torture, think of this and of us, and fly to her relief and her rescue.'

"THE PAWNEE's REPLY.—'Brothers and sisters—This will give me ease more than I ever had, and I will listen more than I ever did to white men.

"'I am glad that my brothers and sisters have heard of the good act that I have done. My brothers and sisters think that I did it in ignorance, but I now know what I have done.

"'I did it in ignorance, and did not know that I did good; but by giving me this medal I know it.'"

11. "For this purpose [the Knife Chief] repaired to Mr Pappan [A. L. Papin, a trader], who happened to be in the village for the purposes of trade, and communicated to him his intentions. Mr Pappan generously contributed a considerable quantity of merchandise, and much was added by himself, by Petalesharoo, and other Indians."—Long, *op. cit.*, p. 359. It is from this source that McKenney and Hall no doubt obtained their information of this episode.

12. It is somewhat difficult to determine the treaties of which Petaleshorro was a signer, by reason of the number of prominent Pawnee who were so called. Sâ-ní-toă-rish (see *Sharitarish* in Vol. II.) informed Murray in 1835 that several chiefs bore the name (Murray, *Travels in North America*, I., London, 1839). The subject of the present sketch was a member of the Chaui division, but his name is not attached to any treaty in behalf of the Loups, unless it be "Scar-lar-la-shar, the Man Chief," appended to the general treaty with the Pawnee at Fort Atkinson, Council Bluffs, Iowa, September 30, 1825, which treaty was signed also by Petalesharro's father, "La-ta-le-shar, the knife chief." The treaty of St Louis, June 20, 1818, was signed on the part of the Pawnee Republics, *i.e.*, the Kitkehahki, by "Rarnleshare, the Chief Man." The treaty of October 9, 1833, at Grand Pawnee village, was signed by Pe-tah-lay-shah-rho, on behalf of the Grand Pawnees, as the Chaui division was commonly called; that of August 6, 1848 (seven years after Petalesharro's death), at Fort Childs, on the south side of the Platte, Nebraska, is signed on behalf of the Pawnee Loups by French Chief and Big Chief, neither of whom is identifiable with Petalesharro's son. It would therefore seem that there were at least three prominent Pawnee Chiefs bearing the same name within

PETALESHARRO
A Pawnee Brave

a comparatively few years, which has the appearance of an hereditary tribal title.

Dunbar, speaking of the son of this famous chief, who bore the name of his father, and whose portrait he gives, says: "The family of Pitalesharu has long been eminent in the Cau'-i band of the Pawnee tribe. As nearly as can be ascertained, Pitalesharu, the subject of this sketch, was born in 1823, and throughout his entire life he was a fine example of the true Indian. His father, of the same name, gained a wide notoriety in his day for the heroism and energy he displayed in endeavouring to suppress the custom of human sacrifices in the Ski'-di band of the tribe. From him the son inherited a character marked by great earnestness and honesty, and singularly devoid of aught that savoured of pretension. In early life he was naturally ambitious of position and influence, but sought them by the only legitimate means, personal prowess. Frequent stories have been rife in the tribe illustrative of his youthful intrepidity. The exact truth of many of these is now unattainable, and some are no doubt apocryphal. The reality of the following, however, is reasonably certain, as it is current among the Ski'-di themselves. After the resolute measures of Pitalesharu's father, the offering of human sacrifices by this band to the morning star (*ho-pir'-i-kuts*), as a public ceremonial, was discontinued; but on a few occasions the inhuman rite was repeated unbeknown to the remainder of the tribe. Being informed of this, Pitalesharu immediately headed a movement for its entire abolition, and persisted in his effort till successful, though thereby he incurred the violent resentment of the whole Ski'-di band. Once he thwarted a contemplated immolation after the preliminaries were already begun, by direct personal interference. Amid an angry throng of Ski'-di braves, whose bows were drawn and guns actually raised, he commanded a cessation of further proceedings, and secured it. . . . His name, which had been assumed when quite young, he wished should be understood as indicating somewhat of the position he aimed to occupy among them, i.e., *pit'-ă-le-shar-u*, a chief of men. (It will be observed that philologically this name is the exact equivalent of the choice Homeric epithet, αναξ ανδρων)."—John B. Dunbar in *Magazine of American History*, November 1880.

Petalesharro the elder became well known to Murray, who camped with the Ski'-di on Loup River in 1835. This writer does not give either this Indian or his father, the Knife Chief, a fair reputation; but judging from a statement by Dunbar, Murray's behaviour among the Pawnee was not such as to gain the friendship of these important chiefs. Murray admired Pa⁶-ta⁶-la°-cha'rò's physique (Vol. I., p. 444), and regarded him as "the strongest and most formidable Indian in the camp."

CHONCAPE

(OR, BIG KANSAS)

CHONCAPE, although of the Ottos tribe (Ottoe, as it is commonly spelled, and *always* pronounced),[1] of which he is second chief, is called *Big Kansas*, a name borrowed from another tribe.[2] We know but little of the history of this chief. The Ottos, or Ottoes, own and occupy a country on the Missouri, east and south of the boundary line dividing the Sauks and Foxes, and Ioways, from the Sioux. They were troublesome during the war of 1812 with Great Britain, and frequently harassed and interrupted the trade between Missouri and New Mexico.

The first treaty between the United States and the Ottos tribe was made in 1817. It is entitled, " A Treaty of Peace and Friendship." The preamble restores the parties to the same relations which they occupied towards each other previous to the war with Great Britain. The first article declares that all injuries or acts of hostility shall be mutually forgiven and forgotten. The second establishes perpetual peace, and provides that all the friendly relations that existed between the parties before the war shall be restored. In the third and last, the chiefs and warriors acknowledge themselves and their tribe to be under the protection of the United States of America, and of no other nation, power, or sovereign whatever.[3]

A second treaty was concluded between the United States and the Ottos and Missouries, at the Council Bluffs, in 1825. In this treaty those tribes admit that they reside within the territorial limits of the United States; acknowledge the supremacy of the United States, and claim their protection; they also admit the right of the United States to regulate all trade and intercourse with them. Other conditions are included in this treaty; among these, the mode of proceeding, in case injury is done to either party, is settled, as is a condition in relation to stolen property; and especially it is agreed that the Ottos will not supply by sale, exchange, or presents, any nation or tribe, or band of Indians, not in amity with the United States, with guns, ammunition, or other implements of war.

Among the names of the eighteen signers to this treaty, we find *Shunk-co-pee*. This is our Choncape. The scribe who wrote his name Shunk-co-pee, wrote it as it sounded to his ears. *Chon*, sounded to him as *Shunk*— and this may be regarded as one of the thousand instances serving to illustrate the difficulty of handing down the name of an Indian. The ear of the writer of it governs, and the pen obeys. Another scribe, of some other country, would probably, in following the sound of this Indian's name, have written it *Tshon-co-pee*; and thus we might have had three Indians manufactured out of one.[4]

The rapidly increasing trade between Missouri and the Mexican dominions, and the frequent interruptions which it had experienced from the Ottos and other Indian tribes, the ground of whose more distant excursions lay in the route of its prosecution, suggested the importance of this treaty. But the conditions of a treaty with distant and roving bands of Indians, who are as wild and untamed as their buffalo, were not relied upon as of sufficient strength out of which to erect barriers for the protection of the trade which the treaty of 1825 was mainly intended to secure. There was one other resort on which greater reliance was placed; and that was, to select and bring to Washington, and through our populous cities, some of the leading chiefs of those bands whose pacific dispositions it had become of such moment to secure. Among those who were selected for this object was Choncape.[5] We are to infer from this that he was a man of influence at home; and that he had the confidence of his tribe. It is to the reports of such a one only that the Indians will listen; and it was the design that he and his comrades should not only witness our numbers and our power, but that the reports that should be made of both, on their return, should operate upon the fears of their tribes, and thus render more secure our trade with the Mexican frontier.

That Choncape had won trophies in war is no more to be doubted than that he had been in contact with the grizzly bear whose claws he wears as an ornament around his neck, in token of his victory over that animal. But, while he was at Washington, he was peaceful in his looks and orderly in his conduct. Nothing occurred while on his visit to that city to mark him as a chief of any extraordinary talents. The impression he left on our mind was, that he was entitled to the distinction which his tribe had conferred upon him in making him a chief, and to be chosen as one of a party to come among us, behold our strength, and report upon it to his people. He said nothing which we heard that is worth recording, and did nothing of which he or his tribe should be ashamed.

CHON-CA-PE, *or* BIG KANSAS
An Oto Chief

NOTES

1. See *Shaumonekusse*, note 1, page 161.

2. Referring to the Kansa tribe, from which the state of Kansas derives its name. It would therefore properly be "Big Kansa."

3. This was the treaty concluded between William Clark and Auguste Chouteau, June 24, 1817, the place not being given. Choncape's name does not seem to appear as a signer, the first signature on the part of the Oto tribe being that of Chongatonga, Big Horse.

4. In this treaty of Fort Atkinson (Council Bluffs, Iowa), concluded by Henry Atkinson and Benjamin O'Fallon, September 26, 1825, the name appears as "Shunk-co-pe," in *Treaties between the United States of America and the Several Indian Tribes*, Washington, 1837. McKenney and Hall seem to have fallen into their own pit, for they overlook the name "Kansa-tauga" (intended for Kansa-tonga) signed to the treaty of Prairie du Chien, July 15, 1830, as well as the name Big Kaw (Kaw being a traders' form of Kansa) appended to the treaties of Otto Village, Platte River, Nebraska, September 21, 1833, and Bellevue, Upper Missouri (Omaha, Nebraska), October 15, 1836, although it should be said that the last-mentioned treaty may have been too late for consideration in the book. For an account of the council held at the time of the 1833 treaty, see J. T. Irving, *Indian Sketches*, I., 1835. Regarding Choncape, this writer says :—

"The Big Kaw is a short, thick Indian, rather good natured, but gifted with a large supply of mulish obstinacy, and a temper like gunpowder. Oppose him—flash!—he is in a blaze; the children scamper; the squaws scatter; the rabble vanish. None stay to listen to the outpourings of his wrath, unless it may be one or two old fellows, who are too decrepit to get out of his way, or are blessed with so happy a hardness of hearing as to render it agreeable to them to be conversed with, even though by a man in a passion.

"The family of this chief consists of several wives, and a son, who is one of the most intelligent young men in the village. He, however, is the very counterpart of the old man in disposition; and when the two get fairly excited, the village is in an uproar. If the quarrel is commenced in a lodge, the building is instantly vacated by the rest of its occupants, until the silence which reigns within gives notice that the storm has blown over. Upon these occasions, it is said that those who return generally find the old man looking very foolish and the son very angry. From that it is suspected that the former is held in subjection by his graceless offspring. Be that as it may, the young warrior still retains a strong affection for his fond old father. Although in his anger he sometimes oversteps the bounds of propriety, and conducts himself in an indecorous manner towards him, yet upon the whole he is looked upon as a pattern of filial piety, particularly as he permits nobody to bully his father but himself."—Irving, *ibid.*, 173.

5. Choncape was a member of the deputation that visited Washington in 1821 with Major O'Fallon, the Indian agent. Shaumonekusse and Petalesharro were noted members of this party. The portrait was painted by King, and in the Rhees list (No. 94), evidently through a misprint, the name appears as "Chou-cape-otos, Half Chief," for *Chou-cape, Otos Half Chief.* The Inman copy in the Peabody Museum bears original number 92, and museum number 28. 203, and is labelled "Chon-ca-pe Big Kansas." While in Philadelphia in the same year the portraits of "Caussetongua, or Big Kanzas of the Ottoe Tribe," and "Sharitourishe, Chief of the Grand Pawnees," were sketched from life on a single canvas, 17 × 23 inches, by the celebrated John Neagle (1796-1865), and in 1861 were presented to the Historical Society of Pennsylvania. Neither of the portraits bears sufficient likeness to those reproduced in these volumes to enable recognition, but the ear ornaments and necklaces are the same.

WANATA

(OR, THE CHARGER)

THIS is a fine picture, and represents a very distinguished personage. Although the Sioux are divided into several tribes, governed by different leaders, this individual, in consideration of his paramount influence, is called the grand chief. His dress exhibits an air of state and dignity which is often assumed by the aboriginal chiefs, but is seldom so successfully displayed. It consists of a long robe of the skin of the buffalo, skilfully prepared by the Indian women by a laborious process, which renders it at once soft and white. Figures are traced upon this material with paint, or worked into it with splinters of the quills of the porcupine, dyed with the most gaudy colours. The plumage of the bird is tastefully interwoven; and the whole is so disposed as to form a rude but appropriate dress for the powerful ruler of a savage people.

Mr Keating, in his narrative of *The Expedition to the Source of the St Peter's*,[1] describes an interview with this chief, and gives an account of his person and apparel which nearly conforms with the portrait in this number. "He was dressed in the full habit of an Indian chief; we have never seen a more dignified-looking person, or a more becoming dress. The most prominent part of his apparel was a splendid cloak or mantle of buffalo skins, dressed so as to be of a fine white colour; it was decorated with small

223

tufts of owl's feathers, and others of various hues, probably
a remnant of a fabric once in general use among the
aborigines of our territory, and still worn in the north-east
and north-west parts of this continent, as well as in the
South Sea Islands; it is what was called by the first European visitors of North America the feather mantles and
feather blankets, which were by them much admired. A
splendid necklace, formed of about sixty claws of the grizzly
bear, imparted a manly character to his whole appearance.
His leggings, jacket, and moccasins, were in the real Dakota
fashion, being made of white skins, profusely decorated
with human hair; his moccasins were variegated with the
plumage of several birds. In his hair he wore nine sticks,
neatly cut and smoothed, and painted with vermilion; these
designated the number of gunshot wounds which he had
received; they were secured by a strip of red cloth; two
plaited tresses of his hair were allowed to hang forward;
his face was tastefully painted with vermilion; in his hand
he wore [bore] a large fan of the feathers of the turkey;
this he frequently used.

"We have never seen a nobler face, or a more impressive character, than that of the Dakota chief, as he stood
that afternoon, in this manly and characteristic dress, con-
templating a dance performed by the men of his own
nation. . . . It would require the utmost talent of the artist
to convey a fair idea of this chief; to display his manly
and regular features, strongly stamped, it is true, with the
Indian character, but admirably blended with an expression of mildness and modesty; and it would require no
less talent to represent the graceful and unstudied folds of
his mantle."

Another interview with this chief is thus described :—
"As we appeared upon the brow of the hill which commands the Company's fort,² a salute was fired from a

number of Indian tents, which were pitched in the vicinity, from the largest of which the American colours were flying. And as soon as we had dismounted from our horses, we received an invitation to a feast which Wanata had prepared for us. The gentlemen of the company informed us that as soon as the Indians had heard of our contemplated visit, they had commenced their preparations for a festival, and that they had killed three of their dogs. We repaired to a sort of pavilion which they had erected, by the union of several large skin lodges. Fine buffalo robes were spread all around, and the air was perfumed by the odour of sweet scenting grass which had been burned in it. On entering the lodge we saw the chief seated near the further end of it, and one of his principal men pointed out to us the place which was destined for our accommodation ; it was at the upper end of the lodge ; the Indians who were in it taking no further notice of us. These consisted of the chief, his son, a lad about eight years old, and eight or ten of the principal warriors. The chief's dress presented a mixture of the European and aboriginal costume ; he wore moccasins and leggings of splendid scarlet cloth, a fine shirt of printed muslin, over this a frock coat of fine blue cloth, with scarlet facings, somewhat similar to the undress uniform coat of a Prussian officer ; this was buttoned and secured round the waist by a belt. Upon his head he wore a blue cloth cap, made like a German fatigue cap. A very handsome Mackinaw blanket, slightly ornamented with paint, was thrown over his person."

The writer describes the countenance of Wanata as prepossessing. The portrait before us indicates a thoughtful and resolute, if not a generous, disposition.[3] He is, however, a very magnificent savage, and has an air of command which is sufficiently regal.

The Dakotas are the Arabs of Western America.

Inhabiting the vast prairies which lie between the
Mississippi and the Missouri, they wander extensively
over those beautiful plains in search of game, or in pursuit
of their enemies, roaming often beyond their proper limits,
to the shores of the northern lakes, and to the banks of
the Arkansas and Red Rivers.   The topography of their
country makes them horsemen, the vast extent and even
surface of the prairies rendering the service of the horse
particularly desirable.   Upon this noble animal they perform their long journeys, charge their enemies in battle, or
chase the buffalo.   They are expert and fearless riders,
managing their horses with a surprising degree of dexterity,
and using them with equal success in the chase or in war.

Wanata is chief of the Yanktonas, a tribe of the Sioux,
or Dakota Indians, whose proper residence is on the waters
of the River St Peter, which empties into the Mississippi
a short distance below the Falls of St Anthony.   They are
divided into six bands, and have altogether about four
hundred and fifty lodges, which contain a population of
between five and six thousand, of whom thirteen hundred
are warriors.   Few chiefs can lead so many followers to
battle.   The whole Dakota nation is estimated to comprise
sixty thousand souls.   The Yanktona, or, as it is otherwise written, Yanktoanan, is one of the most important of
the tribes, and may now be ranked as the first, in conse-
sequence of the influence of Wanata.   The word Yanktona
signifies *fern leaf.* They do not dwell in permanent
houses, but in fine skin lodges, made of the hide of the
buffalo, neatly dressed and decorated, and which they
move with facility from place to place.[4]

At the early age of eighteen Wanata was distinguished
as a warrior, and fought against the Americans under the
command of his father, who was then chief of the tribe,
and who cherished a mortal hatred against the American

people.[5] During the last war between Great Britain and the United States, he joined the former, and was one of a murderous band of savages collected by Colonel Dixon, under whom he fought at Sandusky, where he was wounded. He has since professed friendship towards the United States, but he is well known to be a crafty leader, who would favour or plunder any party, as his interest might dictate. His position, however, is now such as to place him in our power, and offers him little inducement to incur the displeasure of our Government. On the other hand, he continues to cultivate a good understanding with his former friends. Ranging through all the country, from the tributary streams of the St Peter's to Lake Winnipeg, he often comes in contact with the inhabitants of the British colony in that isolated region, who have endeavoured to conciliate this powerful and wily savage by valuable presents, which he receives as the tribute due to his high reputation. He has had the sagacity to render this intercourse a source of regular profit, by practising successfully on the fears of those colonists.

There is an incident in the life of this chief which is highly illustrative of the superstition as well as the fortitude of the Indian character. On the eve of a journey which he made in 1822, in which he was likely to be exposed to great danger from the Chippeways, he made a vow to the sun, that if he should return safe, he would abstain from food and drink for four days and nights, and would distribute among his people all his property of every description. Returning, without accident, his first care was to celebrate the "Dance of the Sun"—a ceremony so shockingly painful and revolting, that we can scarcely imagine a sufficiently strong inducement for its voluntary performance. Deep incisions were made in the breast and arms, so as to separate the skin from the flesh, in the form of loops, through which a rope was passed, and the ends fastened to a tall vertical pole, erected for the purpose in front of his lodge. He began the horrid exercise at the commencement of his fast, and continued it throughout the four days, sometimes dancing, and frequently throwing his whole weight upon the cord which was passed through his skin, and swinging to and fro in this painful position. At the conclusion he sunk exhausted, and was relieved by his friends. After the ceremony was over, he distributed among his people all his property, consisting of his lodges, dogs, guns, trinkets, robes, and several fine horses; and he and his two wives, abandoning their tent, with its furniture, took up their lodging in the open air.[6]

When the Rickara[7] villages, on the Missouri, were burned in 1823, by the troops under Colonel Leavenworth, in retaliation for some acts of depredation committed by them, that tribe retired from the place, but returned in 1824. Wanata seized this occasion to strengthen his power; and, encouraged by traders who had been ill-treated by the Rickaras, he made war upon that tribe, which, weakened and dispirited by the chastisement recently inflicted on them, made but a feeble resistance. He burned their villages again, and drove them from the country. Here he established himself, between the Rickaras and Mandans; and he has ever since retained his conquest.

Wanata was only twenty-eight years old when visited by the party under Colonel Long, whose description of him we have copied. Our portrait was taken some years later.[8] He is a tall and finely-formed man, more than six feet in height. His manners are dignified and reserved, and his attitudes, though studied, are graceful. He is now about forty-five years of age, and commands more

WA-NA-TA, *or* THE CHARGER
Grand Chief of the Sioux

influence than any other Indian chief on the continent. His rule over his own tribe is absolute. He has no rival or compeer. He resorts neither to presents nor to persuasion to secure obedience, but issues his peremptory mandates, which are never disputed.

The traders speak of him as one who may be trusted, because it is policy to be at peace with the whites; but they place no confidence in his friendship, and have little faith in his integrity. Brave, skilful, and sagacious, he is grasping, artful, and overbearing; it is safer to secure his interest than to trust to his generosity or mercy.[9]

NOTES

1. *Narrative of an Expedition to the Source of St Peter's River, Lake Winnepeek, Lake of the Woods, &c., &c.* . . . *Under the Command of Stephen H. Long, Major U.S.T.E.* Compiled from the Notes of Major Long, Messrs Say, Keating, and Colhoun, by William H. Keating, A.M., &c. In Two Volumes. Philadelphia, 1824. The following description of Wanotan, as he is here called, occurs on pp. 429-437 of Vol. I. A portrait of "Wanotan and his son" forms the frontispiece.

2. At Lake Traverse, Minnesota, where the interview occurred.

3. His proper name is Wa-a'-na-taɲ (the ɲ is nasalised), signifying, "One who makes an attack." The portrait was painted by King in 1826, as noted in the Rhees *Catalogue* (see the Introduction, p. li), No. 119: "Waa-na-taa. Grand Chief of the Sioux." It does not appear by name among the Inman copies in the Peabody Museum. At the treaty of Prairie du Chien, Wis., August 19, 1825, Wanata (whose name is signed in the form, "Wan-na-ta x Yancton, or he that charges on his enemies") addressed Commissioners Clark and Cass as follows :—
"My Fathers,—There are many Chiefs of the Sioux among us. One will speak for the upper bands and one for the lower bands. We are glad to hear what you have said. We smoke the pipe with pleasure. Although I am a young man, I wanted a bounty from my father—I got it yesterday. You also have spoken to us of our land. As our red brethren have delayed replying until to-morrow, we will do likewise."— *National Journal*, Nov. 12, 1825.

4. The proper name of this tribe of the Dakota confederacy is I-hank'-toɲ-waɲ-na, Gallicised "Yanktonais," and signifying "Little

End Village," not "fern leaf," as McKenney and Hall record it from Keating's *Long's Expedition.* The Upper Yanktonai are now on the Standing Rock reservation, North Dakota, with the Pabaksa, or "Cuthead" division, on the Devil's Lake reservation, in the same State; the Lower Yanktonai, or Hunkpatina, are mostly on Crow Creek reservation, South Dakota, with some on Standing Rock reservation, North Dakota. The total Yanktonai population is about 4500. The population of the tribes of the entire Dakota confederacy is about 26,000.

5. Wanata's father was Red Thunder, known to the Chippeway as Shappa, "The Beaver," a member of the Pabaksa, or Cut-head, band of Yanktonai. Wanata was seventeen years of age at the beginning of the war of 1812.

6. For information respecting this Sun Dance of the Plains tribes, consult the writings of George A. Dorsey on the Arapaho, Cheyenne, and Ponca ceremonies, in *Field Columbian Museum Publications*, Nos. 75, 102, 103, Chicago, 1903-1905; J. O. Dorsey in *Eleventh Annual Report of the Bureau of Ethnology*, Washington, 1894; Miss Alice C. Fletcher, "The Sun Dance of the Ogallala Sioux," in *Proc. Am. Assn. Adv. Science*, XXXI., 1882; Grinnell, *The Indians of To-day*, Chicago, 1900; Grinnell in *Jour. Amer. Folk-Lore*, IV., 307, 1891; Long, *Expedition to the Rocky Mountains*, I., 276, 1823; and, for an allied ceremony, Catlin, *O-kee-pa: A Religious Ceremony; and Other Customs of the Mandans*, Philadelphia and London, 1867. The ceremony is still practised, but without the revolting ordeal of self-torture.

7. The Arikara, a Caddoan tribe now under the Fort Berthold agency, North Dakota, and numbering 387 in 1906.

8. Wanata was born about 1795, was visited by Long in July 1823, and, as we have seen, his portrait was painted by King in 1826. He was therefore forty-one years of age when Volume I. of McKenney and Hall first appeared in 1836. Wanata died in 1848. A Sisseton chief who bore the same name was painted by Catlin in 1835 (*Descriptive Catalogue* [London, 1840], p. 13) and was killed in 1839 (S. R. Riggs, *Grammar and Dictionary of the Dakota Language*, 207, 1851).

9. For further information respecting this celebrated chief, consult, in addition to the authorities already noted, Doane Robinson's excellent "History of the Dakota or Sioux Indians," in *South Dakota Historical Collections*, compiled by the State Historical Society, Vol. II., Aberdeen, S. D., 1904, 508 pages; also, S. G. Drake, *Aboriginal Races of North America*, 15th edition, New York [1880]; the *Collections of the Minnesota Historical Society*; Neill, *History of Minnesota*, 1858.

PEAHMUSKA

(A FOX CHIEF)

THIS person was the principal chief of the Fox, or Musquakee tribe, and was considered a peaceable, well-disposed man.[1] An Indian of such a character has little history; if not signalised by exploits of war, revenge, or depredation, his slothful life is expended in pursuits which afford no incident worthy of record. His summers are spent in the chase, and his winters in sleep.

The Musquakees, as is remarked in another place, are the remnant of a tribe once powerful, but now incorporated with the Sauks, and the chief has but a narrow sphere of duty or influence.

Although Peahmuska lived an inoffensive, reputable life, we are sorry to record that he died by violence. He was proceeding, a few years ago, to Prairie du Chien, with a small party, consisting of eight or ten warriors of his tribe, and had encamped for the night within a day's journey of that place, when a party of Menominies, who had secretly pursued them, surprised the sleeping band and murdered them all, except one, who had the good fortune to escape. In revenge for this massacre, a war party of Sauks and Foxes afterwards stole upon a number of Menominies at Prairie du Chien, and slew them all, within sight of the American fort. The commanding officer, considering his authority insulted, and desiring to put a stop to these retaliatory measures, demanded of the Sauks the delivery of the murderers, but Keokuk, the head chief, replied, that they were so numerous that it was impossible for him to take them. The offenders, in the meanwhile, expecting that some attempt would be made by the agents of the American Government to punish their audacity, had banded themselves under Black Hawk, and were preparing for war. It was during the existence of this state of excitement that some other collisions took place which led to the war in which Black Hawk figured as the principal leader.

The Sauks and Foxes are considered to be a hospitable people, and friendly to the whites; but, in the prosecution of their wars, or schemes of revenge, are regarded, even by the Indians, as remarkably cunning and treacherous. They relate of themselves, with great exultation, an exploit which they deem highly creditable to their character as warriors. A party of them, while on a hunting expedition, fell in with an equal number of Ioways, with whom they were then at peace, but against whom they cherished a secret hatred, arising out of some ancient feud. Professing to be delighted at the meeting, they invited the Ioways to a feast; and when their unsuspecting guests were seated round the banquet, consisting of a roasted dog, each warrior of the Sauk and Fox party selecting his victim, the whole of the Ioways were shot at the same instant; after which the murderers devoured the feast in triumph. Such is the daring and the chivalry of the red man; such the deeds of gratuitous extermination which often characterise them, and which, in connection with other destroying influences, are operating in passing these people away from among the nations of the earth.

PEAH-MUS-KA
A Fox Chief

NOTE

1. Dr William Jones informs us that the name is properly *Pyämaskiwᵃ*, signifying "Twister." This Indian was a member of the Celestial Chief clan of the Foxes. The accompanying portrait is by King, and was No. 104 of the Indian Gallery collection, according to the Rhees list (see the Introduction, p. li), in which the name is recorded as "Pee-mash-ka. Fox winding in his course." A copy by King is in the Redwood Library of Newport, Rhode Island (see the Introduction, p. liv, No. 12). The portrait is not mentioned by name in the list of Inman copies in the Peabody Museum. Of the seven members of the Fox tribe who visited Washington in 1824, as mentioned by *Niles' Register* for July 31, copied from the *National Journal*, one was "Pee-mash-ka (the Fox winding his course), chief"; and of the four who signed the treaty concluded at Washington, August 4 (with McKenney as one of the witnesses), the name of "Pea-mash-ka, or the Fox winding his horn" [*sic*] appears. Other treaties signed by this chief are : Portage des Sioux, September 14, 1815 (as "Pierremaskkin, the fox who walks crooked"), and Prairie des Chiens, August 19, 1825 (as "Pee-ar-maski, the jumping sturgeon"). In these names we have to contend with both the meanings given by incompetent interpreters and the careless misprints occurring in the published treaties. The Prairie du Chien treaty of July 15, 1830, is signed by "Pasha-sakay, son of Piemanschie," indicating that the latter was no longer chief at this time, and giving a clue to the date of the killing of the party of Foxes by the Menomini near Prairie du Chien, as later mentioned by McKenney and Hall. Definite information on what appears to be this massacre is afforded by James H. Lockwood, in "Early Times and Events in Wisconsin," *Collections of the State Historical Society of Wisconsin*, II., 170-171, 1856, as follows :—

"In 1830, a party of Sauks and Foxes killed some Sioux on or about the headwaters of Red Cedar River, in the now State of Iowa; and the same season a band of Fox Indians, who resided about where Dubuque now is, had occasion to visit Prairie du Chien on business with the Agent, whom they had previously informed that they would arrive on a certain day. An Indian called the Kettle was their chief. It was generally believed that John Marsh gave the Sioux information of the coming of the Foxes, and of the time they were expected; and on the morning of the day appointed for the arrival of the Foxes at Prairie du Chien, a small war party of young Sioux made their appearance here, and joined by a few of the Menomonee young men, proceeded down the Mississippi to the lower end of the Prairie du Pierreaux, some twelve or fifteen miles below Prairie du Chien, where a narrow channel of the Mississippi runs close to that end of the prairie, fringed with small trees, bushes, and grass. They knew the custom of the Indians in going up stream to avail themselves of all such wide channels, as there was less current in them than in the broad river; and secreting themselves among the bushes, trees, and grass, awaited their unsuspecting victims. When the Foxes came within point-blank shot, they all fired upon them, killing their chief Kettle and several others. The Foxes finding their chief killed, returned down the river to carry the news of their misfortune to the tribe, while the Sioux and Menomonees returned home with the tidings of their victory, and to dance over it. They passed through Prairie du Chien, and remained a short time here, but for some accountable reason, no notice whatever was taken of it.

"The signs of several war parties of the Foxes were reported to have been seen on the opposite side of the river during the year; but they effected nothing until sometime, I think, in June 1831, when a considerable number of Menomonees had collected at Prairie du Chien, and encamped on an island near the eastern shore of the Mississippi, about one-fourth of a mile from the old Fort Crawford. They had obtained whisky enough for all to get socially drunk upon, and it is rare to find a Menomonee who will not get drunk when he has the chance; and they had carried their revels far into the night, until men, women, and children were beastly drunk. About two hours before day, a Fox war party, that had been watching their movements, fell upon them in that helpless state, and killed about thirty of them. By this time, some of the more sober of them were aroused, and commenced firing upon the Foxes, who fled down the river, pursued a short distance by the Menomonees."

For additional information, consult A. R. Fulton, *Red Men of Iowa*, 275-277, Des Moines, 1882.

CATAHECASSA

(OR, BLACK HOOF)

THE Shawanoe [1] nation was one of the most warlike of the North American tribes. Little is known of their history previous to the middle of the last century, about which time they emigrated from Florida, under circumstances which lead to the belief that their numbers had recently been much reduced by war. They seem to have been always a restless and enterprising people; for although their former residence was unquestionably upon the sea-coast, they had often penetrated to Tennessee and Kentucky in their wars or hunting expeditions. On their removal to the west a portion of them settled in Ohio, and the remainder ascended to Western Virginia and Pennsylvania. Immediately after the peace of 1763, the whole nation, consisting of four tribes, and numbering several thousand warriors, collected upon the Miami, at Piqua, where they remained until they were driven away by the Kentuckians, at the close of the revolutionary war. Their next residence was on the waters of the Maumee of Lake Erie, whence they removed, after the treaty of Greenville, to Wapakonetta, in Ohio; and, finally, a remnant of about eighty souls, to which this once fierce and powerful nation had dwindled, removed in 1833 to the western shore of the Mississippi.

These extensive wanderings are to be attributed, in part, to the erratic propensities of the Indians; but in many cases they are the result of force, either of tribe against tribe, or of the more operative power of the white man.   The Indian nations, when first visited by Europeans, appeared, in many instances, not to have resided long upon the spots where they were found.   Since we have had the opportunity of observing their habits, we have seen them continually changing place ; but in many cases it has been in pursuit of the game, which had receded into the interior ; in others, these migrations were caused by conflicts among themselves, but of later years especially, by the wrongs, the injustice, and the power of the white man.

We are not informed as to the cause which drove the Shawanese from Florida [2] ; or why, passing over the prolific borders of the Ohio, which are known to have abounded in game at that time, a portion of them should wander to a more northern and less fertile region.   Judging, however, from their subsequent history, we may suppose that they were induced by the rumour of wars between the English and French, to approach the scene of action, in search of plunder.   We hear of them first at the memorable defeat of Braddock, in 1755.   That battle holds a melancholy pre-eminence in the annals of border warfare.   It was one of the earliest occasions on which the savages dared to attack a regular force ; and the entire annihilation of a numerous and well-appointed army of European troops gave them a confidence which led to a long series of disasters. In the hostilities which succeeded, and continued with little intermission for forty years, the Shawanese were among the most daring, audacious, and persevering of our foes.   They were conspicuous actors in the sanguinary battle at Point Pleasant, where General Lewis, at the head of a gallant band of Virginians, defended his position successfully against a vigorous and obstinate attack made by a numerous body of savages.[3]   In the campaigns of

CA-TA-HE-CAS-SA, *or* BLACK HOOF
Principal Chief of the Shawanese

Harmar, St Clair, and Wayne, they were foremost in every battle ; while the early settlers of Western Virginia, Kentucky and Ohio found them ever the inveterate and uncompromising foes of the white man. They were considered as not only warlike, but treacherous and intriguing ; and some of the other tribes accused them of being the instigators of those destructive wars which for many years disturbed our borders, and were not less disastrous to the Indians than to the civilised settlers of the wilderness. They asserted, that after peace had been made, and when the other tribes were disposed to observe their treaties in good faith, the Shawanese would secretly provoke the whites by committing a murder, or by some other act of hostility, in such a manner as to leave it doubtful who was the real offender. The whites, in retaliation, would attack the nearest village, or the first party of Indians who might fall in their way, and all the tribes in the vicinity would become entangled in the war. There might be some exaggeration and some truth in these statements, but there is little question that this nation was daring, restless, and treacherous. They retained this character to the last. During a period of several years preceding 1811, the famous Tecumthe, and his brother the Prophet, kept the frontier in a state of continual alarm by their intrigues and depredations. In the last-mentioned year they made an audacious and well-concerted attack on the American army, commanded by General Harrison, and were severely chastised by that intrepid officer ; and during the war between Great Britain and the United States, which immediately succeeded, this tribe engaged with alacrity in the British cause, and were continually in the field, until, by the death of Tecumthe and the loss of many of their warriors, the spirit of the nation was broken down.[4]

Engaged continually in war, the leading men of the

Shawanoe nation, ever since that people has been known by the whites, were persons of ability and courage. The most conspicuous of those who lived in our own times were Catahecassa, or Black Hoof—Shemenetoo, or the Snake, and Tecumthe.

Black Hoof [5] was one of the greatest warriors of his race, and it is supposed that few individuals have ever been engaged in so many battles. He was present at the defeat of Braddock in 1755, and fought through all the subsequent wars until the treaty of Greenville in 1795. Among the Indians none are compelled to go to battle; public opinion is the only law by which any individual is bound to perform military service; and the war chiefs have no authority but such as is derived from the voluntary obedience of their followers. When a warrior conceives himself capable of leading an enterprise he forms his plan, announces his intention, and publicly appoints a time and place at which he may be met by those who may be disposed to join him. When the party is assembled, properly equipped, painted, and prepared in all respects, the leader explains his whole plan, which is usually assented to; if any warrior, however, chooses to make a suggestion, it is listened to with respect, and duly weighed; but after the whole plan has been concerted, the leader assumes the responsibility of its execution, and his followers render him the most implicit obedience throughout the enterprise. The number, therefore, and the character of the party are determined by the reputation of him who proposes to take the direction. If the invitation is given by a person of little repute, few accept it, and those few are warriors of inferior note, or youths who are willing to embrace any occasion to go to war; while, on the other hand, the bravest warriors will enlist eagerly under one who has already gained distinction. In other cases, where the leader is respectable, but not eminent, he is followed by his personal friends, or by a small band who may be gained by solicitations, or induced by the prospect of plunder. An ambitious young warrior, who is desirous to become a war chief, but has not yet established any claims to popular favour, will sometimes induce two or three of his friends to accompany him on a hostile expedition ; and, if successful, will on the next occasion be able to enlist a larger train. The practical effect of this system is obvious : the warrior who, in leading a small party at the commencement of his career, discovers sagacity, coolness, cunning, and patience, gains the confidence of his tribe, and if fortune continues to smile, rises gradually into a partisan of established reputation, while another, equally brave, who betrays a want of talent, sinks into the ranks, and ceases to be regarded as a suitable person to command in war.

The success of Black Hoof, both in planning and in execution, was so great that he gained the entire confidence of his nation, and could always command the services of any number of volunteers. He was known far and wide as the great Shawanoe warrior, whose cunning, sagacity, and experience were equalled only by the fierce and desperate bravery with which he carried into operation his military plans. Like the other Shawanoe chiefs, he was the inveterate foe of the white man, and held that no peace should be made, nor any negotiation attempted, except on the condition that the whites should repass the mountains, and leave the great plains of the West to the sole occupancy of the native tribes.

He was the orator of his tribe during the greater part of his long life, and was an excellent speaker. The venerable Colonel Johnston,[6] of Piqua, to whom we are indebted for much valuable information, describes him as the most

graceful Indian he had ever seen, and as possessing the
most natural and happy faculty of expressing his ideas.
He was well versed in the traditions of his people; no
one understood better their peculiar relations to the
whites, whose settlements were gradually encroaching on
them, or could detail with more minuteness the wrongs
with which his nation was afflicted.   But although a stern
and uncompromising opposition to the whites had formed
his policy through a series of forty years, and nerved his
arm in a hundred battles, he became at length convinced
of the madness of an ineffectual struggle against a vastly
superior and hourly increasing foe.   No sooner had he
satisfied himself of this truth, than he acted upon it with
the decision which formed a prominent trait in his character.   The temporary success of the Indians in several
engagements previous to the campaign of General Wayne,
had kept alive their expiring hopes; but their signal defeat
by that gallant officer convinced the more reflecting of
their leaders of the desperate character of the conflict.
Black Hoof was among those who decided upon making
terms with the victorious American commander; and
having signed the treaty of 1795, at Greenville, he
remained faithful to his stipulations during the remainder
of his life.[7]   From that day he ceased to be the enemy of
the white man; and as he was not one who could act a
negative part, he became the firm ally and friend of those
against whom his tomahawk had been so long raised in
vindictive animosity.   He was their friend, not from
sympathy or conviction, but in obedience to a necessity
which left no middle course, and under a belief that submission alone could save his tribe from destruction; and
having adopted this policy, his sagacity and sense of
honour alike forbade a recurrence either to open war or
secret hostility.

Catahecassa was the principal chief of the Shawanoe
nation, and possessed all the influence and authority
which are usually attached to that office, at the period
when Tecumthe, and his brother the Prophet, commenced
their hostile operations against the United States.
Tecumthe had never been reconciled to the whites. As
sagacious and as brave as Black Hoof, and resembling
him in the possession of all the better traits of the savage
character, he differed widely from that respectable chief
in his political opinions. They were both patriotic, in the
proper sense of the word, and earnestly desired to preserve the remnant of their tribe from the destruction that
threatened the whole Indian race. Black Hoof, whose
long and victorious career as a warrior placed his courage
far above suspicion, submitted to what he believed inevitable, and endeavoured to evade the effects of the storm
by bending beneath its fury; while Tecumthe, a younger
man, an influential warrior, but not a chief, with motives
equally public spirited, was no doubt biased, uncon-
sciously to himself, by personal ambition, and suffered his
hatred to the white man to overmaster every other feeling
and consideration. The one was a leader of ripe fame,
who had reached the highest place in his nation, and could
afford to retire from the active scenes of warfare; the
other was a candidate for higher honours than he had yet
achieved; and both might have been actuated by a
common impulse of rivalry, which induced them to espouse
different opinions in opposition to each other.

During several years immediately preceding 1811, the
British Cabinet prosecuted with renewed vigour their
favourite policy of exciting the western savages into active
hostilities against the United States. The agents of that
Government traversed the frontier, holding councils with
the Indians, and seeking to inflame them by artful

harangues, or to bribe them by liberal presents. The success of these intrigues is too well known. The tomahawk and firebrand were again busied in the fearful work of desolation, and a merciless war waged, not against the forts and armies of the American Government, but upon the property and lives of individuals, upon the fields and firesides of a scattered population of enterprising farmers.

Tecumthe engaged eagerly in these scenes, and devoted all the energies of his bold genius to his darling scheme of fomenting the discord which should bring about a general war between the Americans on one side and the united Indian tribes on the other. Aided by his brother the Prophet [4]—a deceitful, treacherous, but cunning man—he endeavoured to enlist his own nation in the great conspiracy, but found an insurmountable obstacle in the determined opposition of Black Hoof, who, having made a treaty of peace with the United States, resolved to maintain his plighted faith. In vain did Tecumthe intrigue, harangue, and threaten ; in vain did the pretended Prophet practise his incantations—equally in vain did the British agent spread out his alluring cargo of trinkets and munitions. Black Hoof preserved his integrity ; the older and more reputable part of the tribe adhered to him ; while the young and thoughtless, the worthless and dissolute, joined by a similar class from other tribes, followed the Prophet to his new town, and commenced a system of robbery and murder which, doubtless, formed the extreme point to which either he or they had extended their views—while the more politic Tecumthe regarded them as a mere banditti, pushed forward to embroil the English with the Americans, and to force the savage tribes into a general war. The firmness with which Black Hoof stood aloof on this occasion, and his success in restraining the majority of his nation, showed alike his prudence, his foresight, and his popularity. His course was honourable to his judgment and his integrity.

Another trait in the character of this Indian is highly creditable, and indicates a perception of the social virtues not usually found in savage life. He lived forty years in harmony with one wife, and reared a numerous family, whom he treated with kindness, and by whom he was greatly beloved. The policy of the Indians in this respect is not fully understood. They permit, but do not in general encourage, polygamy. There is no law nor custom among them which forbids a plurality of wives[8]; but they do not consider it creditable for any man to marry more women than he can support; and it is even considered a proof of weakness for a warrior to encumber himself with too large a family. The capacity to support a family differs among them, as with us, though not to the same extent. Their chief dependence for food being on the chase, the most expert hunter is best able to provide a subsistence; and the evils of poverty are most severely felt by those who are lazy, physically weak, or destitute of sagacity in finding game. Those who have established a reputation in war or in hunting, have each a small train of friends and defenders, composed of their sons and nephews—of youths who attach themselves to an experienced man for the benefit of his counsel or protection, or of the improvident who need a leader. When a distinguished warrior, therefore, speaks of *his young men*, he alludes to this train of relatives or pupils, who support him in his quarrels, and follow him to the chase; while a chief employs the same form of expression in a more enlarged sense, as applicable to the young warriors of his nation. This explanation affords a key to one of the sources of the slight distinction in rank which exists among the Indians. Distinction in war or hunting draws around its possessor a band of two or three, or sometimes more, devoted followers, who, in a society where force is often the only law, increase the power of their leader, while they add to his wealth by attending him in the chase, and thus increasing his means of procuring food.   A warrior of this rank may, with propriety, grace his wigwam with several wives, and may even require the services of more than one to carry home his game and perform the drudgery of his numerous family; while the improvident or unsuccessful hunter, or a youth who must rely entirely upon himself, may not venture to indulge himself with the same liberality.   These distinctions are closely observed by the Indians in every tribe with which we are acquainted, and nothing more certainly provokes their contempt than the marrying an unreasonable number of wives. Black Hoof, as we have seen, was satisfied with one; Tecumthe had but one at a time, while the hypocritical Prophet, who from laziness or incapacity was not an active hunter, maintained a number of wives, who were supported by the contributions which he artfully levied upon his credulous followers.   The two former were respected as men even by their enemies, while the latter, as soon as he ceased to be sustained in his imposture by his politic and manly brother, sunk into disrepute.   He died recently in Missouri.

An intelligent gentleman who spent many years among the Shawanese in the discharge of public duties, and was often accompanied in long journeys through the wilderness by Black Hoof, describes him as a lively, agreeable, and instructive companion.   On one of these occasions he shot a deer when he was more than ninety years of age.   He preserved his eyesight to the last, and never used or needed glasses, nor was known to be sick.   He was a small man, about five feet eight inches in height, well-proportioned and active, and had a remarkably intelligent countenance.

He died at Wapakonnetta in 1831, at the age of from one hundred and five to one hundred and twelve years.[9]

There was a peculiarity in the eloquence of this chief which distinguished him from the speakers of his race, who are usually grave and monotonous. He generally commenced his public harangues with some pleasant, facetious, or striking remark, thrown out to please his audience and gain their attention. He would play awhile round his subject, until he saw the rigid features of the stern warriors around him beginning to relax, and then dive into it, becoming more earnest as he proceeded, until at last the whole energy of his vigorous mind was concentrated into a powerful and well-digested effort.

It would be unjust to omit a feature in the character of Catahecassa which reflects upon him the highest credit. The practice of burning prisoners at the stake was not only prevalent among the western tribes, but was, we think, resorted to with the greatest frequency, and attended with the most brutal circumstances, during the wars in which the Shawanese bore a conspicuous part, and in which Black Hoof was a prominent leader. They did not sacrifice them to the Great Star, or any other favourite deity, as among the Pawnees, but generally in revenge for their losses or their wrongs. Notwithstanding the determined hostility of this chief against the whites, he invariably opposed that atrocious custom, and has often declared that he never witnessed such occurrences but twice, on both which occasions he was present accidentally. We are happy to record that the more intelligent of the principal men of the Shawanese coincided in condemning these shocking cruelties. Tecumthe was never known to insult a prisoner; and on several occasions during the last war, he upbraided the British officers for their cruel treatment of captive Americans.

Another Shawanoe chief, the aged Biaseka, or The Wolf, once returned home after an absence of several months, and finding the village nearly deserted, was informed that the people were engaged in burning a prisoner beyond the precincts of the town. Without communicating his intentions, he loaded a pistol and proceeded to the spot. The wretched captive was bound to the stake, the torch ready to be applied, and a ferocious multitude eagerly waiting to glut their savage appetite with the miseries of the victim. The chief passed through the crowd without speaking to anyone, and, approaching the prisoner, placed the pistol to his head, and blew out his brains—coolly remarking, that he disapproved of the torture of a defence-less person, and had prevented it by despatching the captive.[10]

NOTES

1. See note 2, page 42. The form *Shawano* is more nearly correct, but *Shawnee* is now the common form of the tribal name and has long been in official use.

2. The Shawnee are not known ever to have lived within the limits of the present Florida peninsula, so that the statement is correct only so far as it refers to Florida in early historic time, when it comprised the entire Atlantic seaboard from the peninsula northward indefinitely. See Cyrus Thomas, "The Shawnees in Precolumbian Times," *American Anthropologist*, IV., 109, 237, Washington, 1891.

3. See note 7, p. 43.

4. See *Tenskwautawaw* in this volume, p. 75.

5. Dr William Jones informs us that the common form of the native name of this warrior, Catahecassa, is Maʻkatähŭshkashᵃ, signifying "One with black hoof."

6. See note 3, p. 173.

7. The treaties signed by Black Hoof are as follows :—Greenville, Ohio, August 3, 1795 (as "Cutthewekasaw, or Black Hoof"); Fort Wayne, Indiana, June 7, 1803 (as "Cuthewekasaw, or Black Hoof"); Fort Industry, Ohio, July 4, 1805 (as "Cutheaweasaw, or Black Hoff");

Brownstown, Michigan, November 25, 1808 (as " Makatewekasha, or Black Hoof"); Greenville, Ohio, July 22, 1814 (as "Cutewecusa, or Black Hoof"); Spring Wells, September 8, 1815 (as "Cutaweskeshah, or black hoof"); Rapids of the Miami of Lake Erie, Ohio, September 29, 1817 (as "Cateweekesa, or Black Hoof"); and St Mary's, September 17, 1818 (as "Cuttewekasa, or Black Hoof"). He did not sign the St Louis treaty of 1825, in which year he was about eighty-five years of age. He died six years later, at Wapakoneta, Ohio.

8. See note 1, p. 166.

9. For Wapakoneta, see *Quatawapea,* note 5, p. 171. The estimate of Black Hoof's age is here doubtless exaggerated. A more conservative figure would be ninety years, as he was born about 1740. B. Drake (*Life of Tecumseh,* Cincinnati, 1856, p. 45) gives his age at the time of his death as 110 years.

10. The painter of the accompanying portrait and the date are not known. It formed No. 40 of the Indian Gallery, according to the Rhees list, but it is not recorded by name in the catalogue of the Inman collection in the Peabody Museum. None of the Shawnee treaties concluded prior to Black Hoof's death was negotiated at Washington, and no record of a visit of this celebrated chief to the seat of Government is available.

A CHIPPEWAY MOTHER AND HER CHILD

In a preceding number we have exhibited a sketch of an Indian mother on a journey, with her child on her back. We present, now, a mother in the act of suckling her infant.[1] The reader will suppose the cradle before him to have been only a moment before leaning against a tree, or a part of the wigwam. The mother, having seated herself on the ground, and disengaged her breast from its covering, has taken the cradle at the top, and is drawing it towards her; while the child, anxious for its nourishment, sends its eyes and lips in the direction of the breast. This is one mode of suckling infants among the Indians. When the child has attained sufficient strength to sit alone, or to walk about, the cradle is dispensed with. Then it is taken by the mother and placed on her lap, she being in a sitting posture; or, if she have occasion to make a journey on foot, a blanket, or part of a blanket, is provided—two corners of which she passes round her middle. Holding these with one hand, she takes the child by the arm and shoulder with the other, and slings it upon her back. The child clasps with its arms its mother's neck, presses its feet and toes inward, against, and (as far as the length of its legs will permit) around her waist. The blanket is then drawn over the child by the remaining two corners, which are now brought over the

CHIPPEWAY MOTHER AND CHILD

mother's shoulder, who, grasping all four of these in her hand, before her, pursues her way. If the child require nourishment, and the mother have time, the blanket is thrown off, and the child is taken by the arm and shoulder, most adroitly replaced upon the ground, received upon the lap of the mother, and nourished. Otherwise, the breast is pressed upward, in the direction of the child's mouth, till it is able to reach the source of its nourishment, while the mother pursues her journey. This is the cause of the elongation of the breasts of Indian mothers. They lose almost entirely their natural form.

The cradle, in which the reader will see the little prisoner, is a simple contrivance. A board, shaven thin, is its basis. On this the infant is placed, with its back to the board. At a proper distance, near the lower end, is a projecting piece of wood. This is covered with the softest moss, and when the cradle is perpendicular the heels of the infant rest upon it. Before the head of the child there is a hoop, projecting four or five inches from its face. Two holes are bored on either side of the upper end of the board, for the passage of a deer skin, or other cord. This is intended to extend round the forehead of the mother, as is seen in a previous number, to support the cradle when on her back.[2] Around the board and the child, bandages are wrapped, beginning at the feet, and winding around till they reach the breast and shoulders, binding the arms and hands to the child's sides. There is great security in this contrivance. The Indian woman, a slave to the duties of the lodge, with all the fondness of a mother, cannot devote that constant attention to her child which her heart constantly prompts her to bestow. She must often leave it to chop wood, build fires, cook, erect the wigwam, or take it down, make a canoe, or bring home the game which her lord has killed, but which he disdains to shoulder. While thus employed her infant charge is safe in its rude cradle. If she place it against a tree, or a corner of her lodge, it may be knocked down in her absence. If it fall backwards, then all is safe. If it fall sideways, the arms and hands being confined, no injury is sustained; if, on the front, the projecting hoop guards the face and head. The Indian mother would find it difficult to contrive anything better calculated for her purpose. To this early discipline in the cradle, the Indian owes his erect form; and to the practice, when old enough to be released from the bandages, of bracing himself against his mother's waist, with his toes inward, may be traced the origin of his straightforward gait, and the position of his foot in walking; which latter is confirmed afterwards by treading in the trails scarcely wider than his foot, cut many inches deep by the travel of centuries.

It is but justice, in this place, to bear our testimony to the maternal affection of the Indian women, in which they fall nothing behind their more civilised and polished sisters. We have often marked the anxiety of an Indian mother bending over her sick child; her prompt obedience to its calls, her untiring watchfulness, her tender, and so far as a mother's love could make it so, refined attentions to its claims upon her tenderness. In times of danger we have witnessed her anxiety for its security, and her fearless exposure of her own person for its protection. We have looked upon the rough-clad warrior in the solitude of his native forests, attired in the skins of beasts, or wrapped round with his blanket, and realised all our preconceived impressions of his ferocity, and savage-like appearance— but when we have entered the lodge and beheld, in the untutored mother, and amid the rude circumstances of her condition, the same parental love and tender devotion to her children, we had known in other lands, and in earlier years—we have almost forgotten that we stood beside the threshold of the ruthless savage, whose pursuits and feelings we had supposed to have nothing in common with ours, and have felt that, as the children of one Father, we were brothers of the same blood—heirs of the same infirmities—victims of the same passions; and, though in different degrees, bound down in obedience to the same common feelings of our nature. Persecuted and wronged as he has been, the Indian has experienced the same feelings; and, on more than one occasion, in the rude eloquence of his native tongue, has given them vent, in words not far different from those of Cowper, with which we will conclude this sketch :—

> " I was born of woman, and drew milk
> As sweet as charity from human breasts.
> I think, articulate, I laugh, and weep,
> And exercise all functions of a man.
> ————————————Pierce my vein,
> Take of the crimson stream meand'ring there,
> Search it, and prove now, if it be not blood,
> Congenial with thine own; and if it be,
> What edge of subtlety canst thou suppose,
> Keen enough, wise and skilful as thou art,
> To cut the link of brotherhood, by which
> One common Maker bound me to the kind."

NOTES

1. This formed the central figure of a painting made by Lewis at the treaty of Fond du Lac in 1826, and is the fifty-seventh illustration in his *Port-folio.* It was probably No. 145 of the Indian Gallery, and is perhaps No. 102 (catalogue No. 28. 202) of the list of Inman copies in the Peabody Museum, bearing the title "Squaw and Child," without date, rather than Inman's No. 113, "Mother and Child," which was painted in 1825. The Inman copy reproduced in McKenney and Hall is a much more attractive picture than Lewis's reproduction. Inman did

not follow Lewis closely, having altered somewhat the woman's posture, her necklace, and other lesser details. The Lewis drawing forms a plate facing page 290 of McKenney's *Tour to the Lakes,* but here it is little less than a caricature.

2. The authors here refer to the illustration of the "Chippeway Squaw and Child" in this volume. For an interesting paper on "Cradles of the North American Aborigines," see O. T. Mason in *Report of the U.S. National Museum for* 1887, Washington, 1889.

OKEE-MAKEE-QUID
A Chippeway Chief

OKEEMAKEEQUID

(A CHIPPEWAY CHIEF)

OUR acquaintance with Okeemakeequid began and ended in 1826, at La Fond du Lac Superior.[1] On arriving there, among the multitude of Indians, collected for the purpose of attending a treaty, our interest was at once excited in relation to Okeemakeequid. His countenance was intellectual, and wore an unusually civilised expression. After having been at La Fond du Lac for some days, we determined to have built a first-rate canoe of bark, which is the only kind of canoe used in these lake regions. On inquiring for an experienced hand among the Indians for that purpose, we were referred to Okeemakeequid. He appeared directly, and the bargain was soon made. On expressing our apprehensions that the structure of the canoe might consume more time than we could spare, we were told to name our own time. We did so, and the answer was, "*It shall be done!*" In a moment afterwards we saw Okeemakeequid and his assistant striding in the direction of a piece of level ground bordering the water, and about two hundred yards from our encampment, followed by a train of women and children. Then the squaws reappeared, bearing on their backs rolls of birch bark, followed by the little children with rolls of wattap (the root of the red cedar, or fir), which is used to confine the bark of a canoe to its frame. Mr Schoolcraft, in an

253

admirably drawn poetic description of the birch canoe, says [2]—

> "The bright leafy bark of the betula tree,
> A flexible sheathing provides;
> And the fir's thready roots drew the parts to agree,
> And bound down its high swelling sides."

All the materials being ready, the work was commenced with great spirit. As it has not fallen to the lot of many persons, into whose hands this work may fall, to witness the building of a birchen canoe, we will avail ourselves of an extract from our work—*Tour to the Lakes*, to describe the process. The ground being laid off, in length and breadth, answering to the size of the canoe (this was thirty-six feet long, and five feet wide in its widest part), stakes are driven at the two extremes, and thence on either side, answering, in their position, to the form of the canoe. Pieces of bark are then sewn together with wattap, and placed between those stakes, from one end to the other, and made fast to them. The bark thus arranged hangs loose and in folds, resembling in general appearance, though without their regularity, the covers of a book with its back downwards, the edges being up, and the leaves out. Cross pieces are then put in. These press out the rim, and give the upper edges the form of the canoe. Next, the ribs are forced in—thin sheathing being laid between these and the bark. The ribs press out the bark, giving form and figure to the bottom and sides of the canoe. Upon these ribs, and along their whole extent, large stones are placed. The ribs having been previously well soaked, they bear the pressure of these stones, till they become dry. Passing round the bottom, and up the sides of the canoe to the rim, they resemble hoops cut in two, or half circles. The upper parts furnish mortising places for the rim; around and over which, and through the bark, the wattap is wrapped. The stakes are then removed, the seams gummed, and the fabric is lifted into the water, where it floats like a feather.[8]

We soon learned that Okeemakeequid was one of ten children of the most remarkable old squaw in those parts. Her name was Oshegwun. From childhood this woman had been the subject of affliction. When about fourteen years old she accompanied her father, with five lodges of his band, amounting to forty persons, on a hunting expedition. They had killed a deer, and were in the act of cooking it, when they were attacked by about one hundred Sioux. Fifteen of the Chippeways were killed; three only surviving the first assault. Oshegwun ran off—was overtaken and tied. A contention arose between two Sioux for the captive. One of them struck his war-club into her back, and otherwise wounded her. She fell, crying, "They are killing me." At this moment she heard the crack of a rifle, when she became unconscious. Towards evening she was aroused by the pressure of a hand upon her arm. It was her father's. He saw the struggle between the two Sioux for his child, when, levelling his rifle, he killed them both. He was too much engaged in the fight to go to the spot, but sought it afterwards. On arriving at it he found his daughter gone, she having crawled a quarter of a mile. He tracked her by her blood on the snow. She was scalped in two places, on the right and left of her crown—the knife passing round her throat, cut a deep gash, driving in pieces of wampum, which remained there. She survived, however, and lived to marry three husbands, all of whom treated her unkindly, and to be the mother of nine sons and one daughter. She was subsequently cured of a disease in the forefinger, by Okeemakeequid, after the Indian fashion, by placing it on a block, laying a knife across it, and with a single blow upon the knife with the eye of a hatchet, cutting it off.

We were shown all these wounds; and also witnessed a scalping scene, by her two sons, Okeemakeequid and his brother, who went through the blank motions over the head of the mother, to show how the Sioux performed that ceremony. At this time, 1826, Oshegwun was about sixty years of age.[4]

The dress in which Okeemakeequid appears is not a Chippeway, but a Sioux dress. The Indians would often jibe him about the circumstances under which he got it. At the treaty of Prairie du Chien, in 1825, peace was concluded, which terminated a war of nearly two hundred years' duration, between the Sioux and Chippeways. In memorial of this occurrence a Sioux warrior proposed to exchange dresses with Okeemakeequid. The latter acceded to the proposition. After the exchange had been made, the Sioux, looking Okeemakeequid archly in the face, and pointing to the head-dress, said, "*Brother*, when you put that dress on, feel up there—there are five feathers; I have put one in for each scalp I took from your people —remember that!"

NOTES

1. This, of course, refers to McKenney's journey to Lake Superior in 1826, on August 5th of which year he and Lewis Cass negotiated the treaty with the Chippeway, as noted in our Introduction. This treaty was signed by "Ogeemaugeegid," with eight others, on behalf of the Vermilion Lake band, and a Maw-gaw-gid, seemingly the same individual although confessedly not a chief, formally addressed the commissioners in treaty council two days before its conclusion (*Tour*, p. 466). There is little doubt that the original portrait was painted by Lewis, who was present at the treaty, although it does not appear in his *Portfolio;* his name is not mentioned in connection with it in the Indian Gallery list (No. 117, "O-kee-ma-kee-guid, The Chief that speaks," probably for *Ŏgimȃgigit*), and it is accredited to King in the list of Inman

copies in the Peabody Museum. "Ogemaunkeketo" signed the treaty of Saginaw, Michigan, September 24, 1819.

2. In his *Tour to the Lakes* (pp. 317-318), McKenney, addressing Secretary of War James Barbour, says: "I am now happily relieved from all further necessity of referring, in the way of description, to these singular conveyances, which you will bear in mind are *wholly of Indian invention, and which the white man has never been able to improve,* by having had addressed to me by my friend Mr Schoolcraft, the following beautiful description of the one in which we voyaged to this place; and in which I shall return, taking Mr Lewis with me to sketch the pictured rocks, etc." Then follows "The Birchen Canoe," in ten verses, of which the one here quoted is quite sufficient.

3. The original description is in McKenney's *Tour,* pp. 319-320.

4. These details are extracted from the *Tour,* pp. 290-291, 295-296. The author adds: "Two of her sons are here, and are two of the best-looking men I have seen; and she has with her also one daughter. She promised to come over this morning and sit for her likeness." This she evidently did, as a lithographic portrait of O-shee-gwun, wearing a hood, faces p. 291. This unquestionably was drawn by Lewis, although it does not appear in his *Port-folio.* The woman, accompanied by the two sons, visited McKenney the evening of the same day and exhibited the scars of the wounds she had received as a girl at the hands of the Sioux. McKenney also remarks that the likeness of one of the scalped woman's husbands was in his office at Washington, but his name is not given.

WAEMBOESHKAA

(A CHIPPEWAY CHIEF)

AMONG the most remarkable chiefs we met with at the treaty of La Fond du Lac Superior, in 1826, was Waemboeshkaa, a Chippeway chief. Our attention was attracted more by his style of dress than by any particular part that he bore in the ceremonies of that occasion. He was the only Indian present who seemed to have a right conception of the kingly crown, and to have succeeded in constructing a very successful imitation of that appendage of royalty. It is true, the materials were far from costly; they were a mixture of feathers, glossy and very beautiful, from the drake's breast, and of the bills and feathers from the head of the woodpecker. In place of bracelets of metal, his wrists were similarly ornamented, whilst his neck was encircled with horsehair, coloured with vermilion. His pipe was made gay with the same materials, and his pouch had been the object of his special attentions. His blanket was sound and large, and clean. He was one of the representatives of the Sandy Lake band. He arrived late at the treaty ground; and, on joining the assemblage, appeared conscious that whatever he might lack in other accomplishments, he was the superior of all present in the ornaments of his person. There did not, however, appear to be anything deficient in him in other respects;

258

he was thoughtful, respectful, and conducted himself throughout with great propriety.

We might not, perhaps, have singled him out on account of his dress, if the seven hundred Indians of both sexes and of all ages by whom he was surrounded had not formed so disadvantageous a contrast. They were among the worst clad and most wretched body of Indians we ever met with. Our remarks made at the time are now before us; we give the following extract:—"Never before had we witnessed such a display, nor such an exhibition of nakedness and wretchedness; nor such varieties of both. From the infant, tied to its cradle and to the back of its mother, to the Big Buffalo; from the little fellow with a dress made of raccoon skins, himself not much above the size of that animal, and looking, except his face, for all the world like one of them on its hinder feet, to Waemboeshkaa, one of the Sandy Lake chiefs, dressed like king Saul." So we denominated this chief at the time; and he bore a very remarkable likeness to that personage, crown and all, as we have seen him sketched by those who have indulged their fancy in presenting to the world their imaginings of this renowned personage.

Whatever of humiliation might have been produced by those who were lowest in the scale of want was relieved by suitable presents before we left the treaty ground. Waemboeshkaa, it is true, received his due proportion, and maintained, therefore, his superiority in personal wealth and endowments.

We parted from this chief at the conclusion of the treaty and have heard nothing of him since; nor did we learn at the time that he had ever particularly distinguished himself, (not even by much smoking, for all Indians are inveterate smokers,) but inferred that, either by descent, or exploits in war, he was high in the confidence of his band, otherwise he would not have been deputed to attend the treaty in the capacity of chief.

NOTE

The portrait was painted by Lewis at Fond du Lac in 1826, and is the seventy-first plate in his *Port-folio*. Evidently the same individual, seated beneath two trees and represented as smoking his calumet, faces page 331 of McKenney's *Tour*, on which page is the information extracted for the present description. This illustration bears the title, "Chippeway Chief with his calumet & pouch." The Lewis portrait, reversed, with the pipe-wrappings altered and the bowl of the pipe coloured blue, whereas in Lewis's drawing it is red, to represent catlinite, appears in Volume I. of the folio edition of McKenney and Hall, accredited to C. B. King, who was actually only the copyist. The changes noted were made probably by Inman. In the Indian Gallery collection the original bore No. 132 ("Wa-em-boush-haa"). The Inman copy ("Wa-em-boesh-ka") in the Peabody Museum bears original number, 16; catalogue number, 28. 207. The costume of this Indian can hardly be regarded as representing rank, as he was not of sufficient importance, it seems, to have been one of the six members of the Sandy Lake band who signed the treaty—at least his name is not recognisable.

WA-EM-BOESH-KAA
A Chippeway Chief

McINTOSH

(A CREEK CHIEF)

McIntosh, whose admirable likeness is before the reader, was a half breed, of the Muscogee or Creek nation. His father was a Scotsman; his mother a native of unmixed blood. McIntosh was intelligent and brave. In person he was tall, finely formed, and of graceful and commanding manners. To these qualities he probably owed his elevations to the chieftainship of the Coweta tribe.[1]

We know little of the early history of this chief. The first notice we have of him is after his junction with the American forces in 1812. General Floyd[2] mentions him in his report of the battle, or, as it may with more propriety be termed, the *massacre* of Autossee; on which occasion two hundred Creeks were slain. The Indians were surprised in their lodges, and killed before they could rally in their defence. McIntosh and his Indian forces are reported by General Floyd to have "fought with an intrepidity worthy of any troops."

Autossee was a favourite spot, and had been selected by the chiefs of eight of the Creek towns for a last and desperate stand against the invading army; but the sudden and unexpected attack of General Floyd terminated the contest. The chiefs of Autossee and Tallassee were among the slain.

261

McIntosh is again spoken of by the Commanding General, Jackson,[3] as Major McIntosh, and is said by that officer, in his report of the famous battle of the Horseshoe, to have "greatly distinguished himself."[4]   He also signalised himself in the Florida campaign by various acts of gallantry.

We shall leave our warrior chief for awhile, and glance at a subject of great public interest, in relation to which he was destined to act a conspicuous part, and which finally brought about his death.

In 1802, a compact was entered into between the United States and the State of Georgia; the fourth article of which stipulates, "that the United States shall, at their own expense, extinguish, for the use of Georgia, as early as the same can be *peaceably* effected, on *reasonable* terms, the Indian title to the lands within the forks of the Oconnee and Oakmulgee Rivers, etc. etc.; and that the United States shall, in the same manner, also extinguish the Indian title to *all* the other lands within the State of Georgia."

The United States, in pursuance of this compact, proceeded from time to time, by treaties, to extinguish the Indian title to lands within the limits of Georgia. The first treaty of cession, after the formation of the compact, was concluded on the Oconnee River, near Fort Wilkinson, in the month of June following; a second was negotiated in the City of Washington, in June, 1806; a third was the treaty of conquest, of August, 1814; a fourth treaty was negotiated in January, 1818; a fifth in January, 1821.[5]   Under these several treaties, the Indian title to about fifteen millions of acres of land was extinguished; and the United States paid Georgia, in money, one million two hundred and fifty thousand dollars in lieu of lands which had been ceded to the Indians.

These various and successful efforts to fulfil the intention of the compact of 1802, so early as 1811, alarmed the Creeks. In order to arrest this inroad upon their domain, they enacted a law in that year, at Broken Arrow,[6] forbidding, under the penalty of death, the sale of any more lands, except by the chiefs of the nation, ratified in general council. This law was formally re-enacted in 1824, at the Polecat Springs. McIntosh is said to have proposed this law.

After the treaty of 1821, various unsuccessful efforts were made to consummate the stipulations of the compact of 1802; but the Creeks refused to listen to any overtures. Meanwhile, the Executive of Georgia became impatient of the delay, and opened a highly excited and painful correspondence with the Government at Washington, in which the President was charged with bad faith; and, among other things, with attempting to defeat the objects of the treaty by the introduction of schools and other plans of civilisation and improvement among the Indians. If you enlighten the Indians as to the value of their possessions, it was argued, you increase the difficulty of obtaining their consent to part with them. It was answered by the Federal Executive, that everything on the part of the United States had been done in good faith; and the improvement of the Indians, which was complained of, was only a continuation of the policy adopted by Washington, and continued throughout the successive administrations to the present time. This policy, which one would think needed no defence before a civilised and Christian people, was maintained by unanswerable arguments. No efforts, consistent with principle, were spared by the Executive at Washington to gratify the desires of Georgia, nor did Congress ever refuse the means to effect a purchase of all the lands held by the Creeks within her limits.

During the latter part of the administration of President Monroe, Messrs Campbell and Meriwether were appointed commissioners to make another attempt to treat with the Creek Indians. Letters were received at Washington from the commissioners, inquiring whether the Executive would recognise a treaty entered into with McIntosh? They were answered by the Secretary of War, Mr Calhoun, that no treaty would be respected unless made with the chiefs of the nation. Meanwhile the commissioners called a meeting of the Indians at the Indian Springs, a reservation occupied by McIntosh. Among those who attended was the Chief of Tuckhabatchee. When the proposition was made by the commissioners to purchase their country, that chief rose and said: "You asked us to sell more lands at Broken Arrow; we told you we had none to spare. I told McIntosh then, that *he knew* no land could be sold except in full council, and by consent of the nation." The chief then added: "We have met here at a very short notice —only a few chiefs are present from the upper towns; and many are absent from the lower towns." He concluded by saying : "That's all the talk I have to make, and I shall go home." Whereupon he left the ground, and returned to Tuckhabatchee. Though McIntosh had attended the meeting to sell the country, he is said at this point to have wavered. He looked round among the Indians, but saw no chief of influence, except Etomie Tustennuggee, whose consent he had procured to his scheme. The commissioners, however, intent upon the treaty, calmed the fears of McIntosh by a promise of protection from the United States. The treaty which had been prepared was read and signed by the commissioners, by " *William McIntosh, head chief of the Cowetas* " —*Etomie Tustennuggee*, by his X, and by thirteen others,

McINTOSH
A Creek Chief

who, though chiefs, were of inferior rank; and, lastly, by about fifty men of no rank or power whatever, many of them being of the lowest and most degraded of their countrymen.[7]

This treaty was executed at the Indian Springs, on the 12th of February, 1825, and on the 2nd of March following reached Washington. The very speed by which it had been transmitted indicated the fears entertained by the commissioners, and by Georgia, that the nation would protest against it, and cause its rejection. The Creek agent, Colonel Crowell,[8] sent with it to Washington a protest against its validity. This confirmed the apprehensions of the Secretary of War, who, as it was generally understood, preferred delaying its submission to the Senate until further information could be received from the Indians, or to reopen the negotiation with a view to obtain the ratification of the treaty by the acknowledged chiefs of the nation. It was feared, that, if the treaty should prove, so far as the Creek nation was concerned, invalid, its ratification by the Senate would create intense excitement, and be the signal for bloodshed among the Indians. President Monroe, however, thought proper to lay the treaty before the Senate, together with the agent's protest, and leave it to that body to decide, as in its wisdom it might think best. He was led to this course by the consideration that the term of his office was about to close. The treaty was accordingly sent to the Senate, and was ratified on the 7th of March, 1825. Meanwhile Mr Adams had succeeded to the presidency—the treaty was returned to him from the Senate, and *approved*.

The Creek nation had now become greatly excited; and McIntosh, fearing the result, claimed protection from Georgia. We believe it was promised. The Creeks, however, had resolved on revenge. Menawa, whose likeness will appear in this work,[9] and who is called the "Great Warrior," was commissioned by the chiefs to raise a party, to march to the Indian Springs, and execute the judgment of their law upon McIntosh, on his own hearth-stone. They were also directed to slay Etomie Tustennuggee, and any other chiefs who had acceded to the treaty. With the usual promptitude of the Indians in the prosecution of bloody business, Menawa was soon at the head of one hundred of his Oakfuskee braves, and after a rapid march arrived before the house of the fated McIntosh, before day, on the morning of the first of May, just seventy-seven days after the signing of the treaty. The house having been surrounded, Menawa spoke :—"Let the white people who are in this house come out, and so will the women and children. We come not to injure them. McIntosh has broken the law made by himself, and we have come to kill him for it." This summons was obeyed by all to whom it was addressed. McIntosh's son, Chilly, who, having signed the treaty, was in the list of meditated victims, was enabled, by his light complexion, to pass out with the whites, and escaped. Only two remained, and these were McIntosh and Etomie Tustennuggee. The house was fired; the two victims, forced by the flames, appeared at the door, where they were received by a shower of bullets, and instantly killed. A half-breed, named Sam Hawkins,[10] was taken the same day and hanged; and Ben, his brother, also a half-breed, was fired upon and severely wounded, but escaped. Menawa was careful to give out that the white people should not be molested; that the Creek nation meant only to punish those who had violated their law.

This bloody tragedy greatly excited the people of Georgia. Governor Troup threatened vengeance. It was feared that the State of Georgia might make it necessary for the General Government to interfere, and that these two powers might come in collision. President Adams, however, met the crisis with coolness and resolution, and at length the fever abated, and Georgia, though still demanding the possession of *all* the Indian lands within her limits, subsided into comparative quiet. Upon minute inquiry into the circumstances of the treaty of the Indian Springs, it was abandoned, and a new treaty was made at Washington on the 4th of January, 1826. The first article of the treaty of Washington declared the treaty of the Indian Springs "to be null and void to every intent and purpose whatever; and any right or claim arising from the same is declared to be cancelled or surrendered."

It is not difficult to imagine the inducements which led McIntosh to enter upon this treaty in defiance of the law of his nation, and its bloody penalty. He probably foresaw that his people would have no rest within the limits of Georgia, and perhaps acted with an honest view to their interests. The intercourse he had enjoyed with the army of the United States, and the triumph of their arms over the desperate valour of the Indians, which he had witnessed at Autossee, the Horseshoe, and in Florida, induced him to believe he would be safe under the shadow of their protection, even from the vengeance of his tribe. But there were, besides, strong appeals to his cupidity, in the provisions of the treaty of the Indian Springs, and in its supplements. By one of these, the Indian Spring reservation was secured to him; and by another it was agreed to pay him for it twenty-five thousand dollars. Moreover, the second article of the treaty provided for the payment to the Creek nation of four hundred thousand dollars. Of this sum he would of course have received his share. Such inducements might have been sufficiently powerful to shake a virtue based upon a surer foundation than the education of a heathen Indian could afford. Besides this, he was flattered and caressed by the commissioners, who were extremely eager to complete the treaty, and taught to believe that he was consulting the ultimate advantage of the nation. These considerations, in some measure, remove the odium from his memory. But it must still bear the stain which Indian justice affixes to the reputation of the chief who sells, under such circumstances, the graves of his fathers.

Out of this occurrence arose two parties among the Creek Indians. One was composed of the bulk of the nation, the other of the followers of McIntosh, headed by his son, Chilly. The latter were intent on immediate removal. To aid them in this, the treaty of Washington, of January 24, 1826, provided for an examination of the country west of the Mississippi, and for the distribution of one hundred thousand dollars among the friends and followers of the late General McIntosh, if their party should number three thousand persons; fifteen thousand to be paid immediately after the ratification of the treaty, and the residue on their arrival west of the Mississippi. Provision was also made to ascertain the damages sustained by the friends and followers of General McIntosh, in consequence of the treaty of the Indian Springs, and contrary to the laws of the Creek nation.

Every disposition was manifested by the General Government to heal those breaches, and quiet those animosities which had been produced by that unfortunate treaty. No subsequent collisions happened between the parties.

The Creek nation were not long permitted to retain an inch of ground in Georgia. The treaty of Washington provided for a cession of the whole of it, except a small strip on the Chattahoochee. This, Georgia insisted on having. In 1827, a special commission was made out, directing Colonel McKenney, after he should have executed certain trusts confided to him, as joint commissioner with Governor Cass, in the Lake Country, to pass over to the Mississippi, descend the river, and thence proceed into the country occupied by the four southern tribes, to negotiate with the Creeks for the remnant of their inheritance in Georgia. This duty was performed. A treaty was concluded on the 15th of November, 1827, and ratified on the 4th of March following, which quieted for ever the controversy between Georgia and the United States, so far as it related to the Creek Indians.[11]

The Creeks retired to their possessions in Alabama. But they were not long left in peace even there. That State demanded their removal from her limits, and was soon gratified by the General Government. A final treaty was made with this wretched people.[12] Subdued in spirit, and impoverished, they at length yielded to the power more than the persuasion of the whites, and crossed the Mississippi. Their present condition is said to be deplorable.[13]

McIntosh died as he had lived, bravely. He knew the fate that awaited him, and met it like an Indian warrior. Having been thrown into the society of the more polished of our people, and having been the associate of our officers in the wars on our southern borders, he had acquired all the manners and much of the polish of a gentleman. He lived in great comfort; possessed slaves, whom he treated kindly, and at his death was about forty years of age.

We do not know enough of his family to furnish a sketch of its members. Chilly McIntosh is an intelligent young man of good manners, and has considerable influence with his people, who emigrated with him to the West. One of the daughters, we believe, married a Mr Hawkins, a sub-agent of the Government.[14]

NOTES

1. His name appears also as MacIntosh, but he usually signed his name "Wm. McIntosh." Coweta, or Kawita, is the name of two former Lower Creek towns on Chattahoochee River, in Russell County, Alabama, situated two and a half miles apart, and commonly distinguished as Upper Kawita and Kawita Talahasi, or "Kawita old town," in various forms of spelling. The latter was the "public establishment" of the Lower Creeks and the headquarters of the agent. In 1799 it could muster 66 warriors, and about the year 1833 the town contained 289 families. From the fact that Kawita was regarded as the assembly place of the Lower Creeks, the name was frequently used synonymously with Lower Creeks, as Kusa, or Coosa, the name of the capital of the Upper Creeks, was sometimes used to designate that part of the tribe. In 1775, Bartram (*Travels*, p. 387, 1792) spoke of Kawita Talahasi as the "bloody town, where the micos, chiefs, and warriors assemble when a general war is proposed; and here captives and State malefactors are put to death." Consult Gatschet in *Handbook of American Indians*, edited by F. W. Hodge, I., 669, 1907, and his *Migration Legend of the Creek Indians*, I., 1884.

2. General John Floyd, born at Beauford, South Carolina, October 3, 1769; died in Camden County, Georgia, June 24, 1839. In 1813 he was elected brigadier-general of the Georgia militia, and commanded at the battle of Atasi (or Autossee as it is here called, apparently after Drake) against the Creeks, November 29, 1813, in which he was severely wounded. On January 27, 1814, he commanded at Camp Defiance in battle with the same Indians. After serving in the Georgia Legislature from 1820 until 1827, he was elected to Congress for one term, and was later a major-general of militia. Atasi (from the Creek *ă'tăssa*, "war-club") was an Upper Creek town on Tallapoosa River, in Macon County, Alabama. In 1756 it contained forty-three warriors, and when seen by Benjamin Hawkins in 1799 it was a poor, miserable-looking place. When the Creeks were removed to Indian Territory the name was applied to a new settlement in the Creek Nation.

3. General Andrew Jackson, afterward President of the United States.

4. The battle of the Horseshoe Bend of Tallapoosa River, in the present Tallapoosa County, Alabama, the final blow to the Creek hostilities, was fought March 27, 1814. In this battle nearly a thousand Creek warriors were killed.

5. The first of the treaties herein mentioned was signed by the United States commissioners and the Creeks near Fort Wilkinson on

June 16, 1802, and was ratified by Congress, January 11, 1803; the second treaty was negotiated at Washington, November 14, 1805; and was confirmed June 2, 1806 (this treaty was signed by McIntosh); the third treaty, or "treaty of conquest," was concluded by General Jackson at Fort Jackson, Alabama, August 9, 1814, and ratified February 15, 1816 (this treaty is signed by "William McIntosh, jr., major of Cowetau"); the fourth treaty was concluded at the Creek Agency, January 22, 1818, and confirmed March 28 following, William McIntosh being one of the signers; the treaty of Indian Springs (on the headwaters of Ocmulgee River, in the present Butts County, Georgia), January 8, 1821, was ratified by Congress on March 2. McIntosh was the first of the twenty-five Indian signers of this fifth treaty.

6. A translation of the Creek name *Hlekatchka*. It was situated on a trail ford crossing Chattahoochee River (for which reason it was also called Horse-path Town), probably in Russell County, Alabama. It was destroyed in 1814, but subsequently was re-established, and in 1832 had 331 families.

7. The commissioners who negotiated the treaty were Duncan G. Campbell and James Meriwether, whose signatures are followed by those of "William McIntosh, head chief of Cowetaus," "Etommee Tustunnuggee, of Cowetau," and forty-nine others. Attached to the treaty, and made a part thereof, is a quitclaim by the tribe to William McIntosh of a reservation including Indian Springs, "upon which there are very extensive buildings and improvements," and an agreement on the part of the commissioners to purchase McIntosh's holdings for $25,000. The entire transaction was little short of highway robbery of the tribe.

8. John Crowell, Agent for Indian Affairs, witnessed the treaty.

9. See Volume II.

10. Sl. Hawkins was one of the two interpreters who signed the treaty of January 8, 1821.

11. See the Introduction, p. xvi.

12. This treaty was concluded at Washington, March 24, 1832, and was ratified April 4 following. Lewis Cass was the commissioner for the United States in this negotiation.

13. The Creek Indians are now one of the Five Civilized Tribes of Oklahoma, and are all citizens of the United States. For many years they maintained their own form of government, patterned after that of the United States, and until recently held a reservation of 626,044 acres. In 1906 there were 11,081 Creeks "by blood," and 6265 freedmen— negroes who, or whose parents, had been held in bondage by members of the tribe. In the same year the United States held in trust for the Creeks the sum of $2,472,930, yielding an annuity of $123,646, and in addition the tribe received, through leases of tribal lands, etc., nearly

$200,000, all in addition to individual earnings.   When, in 1907, Indian Territory was consolidated with Oklahoma and was admitted to the Union as a State, the Creek national government was abolished and the former tribal lands are now held in severalty.   The great Creek Nation, therefore, is now a thing of the past.

14. The portrait of Chilly was painted by J. M. Stanley in June 1843, but was burned in the Smithsonian fire of 1865.   Stanley says of him (*Portraits of North American Indians*, Washington, 1852, page 14): " He speaks English fluently, and has seen much of civilized life, having spent much time at Washington transacting business with heads of Departments in behalf of his people.   He is among the first men of his nation."

ONGPATONGA

(OR, BIG ELK)

THERE are few aboriginal chiefs whose character may be contemplated with so much complacency as that of the individual before us, who is not only an able but a highly estimable man. He is the principal chief of his nation, and the most considerable man among them in point of talent and influence. He uses his power with moderation, and the white men who have visited his country all bear testimony to his uniform fair dealing, hospitality, and friendship. He is a good warrior, and has never failed to effect the objects which he has attempted; being distinguished rather by the common sense and sagacity which secure success, than by the brilliancy of his achievements.[1]

While quite a young man, he performed an exploit which gained him great credit. The Omahas had sent a messenger of some distinction upon an embassy to the Pawnee Loups,[2] who, instead of receiving him with the respect due to his character, as the representative of his nation, treated him with contempt. Ongpatonga, though young, was a chief of some distinction, and immediately took upon himself to revenge the insult. He determined to do this promptly, before the aggressors could be aware of his intention, and while the sense of injury was glowing in the bosoms of his people. Placing himself at the head of the whole population of his village, men, women, and children, he proceeded to the Pawnee town, and attacked it so suddenly, and with such a show of numbers, that the inhabitants deserted it without attempting a defence.   He then destroyed the village and retired, taking with him a valuable booty, consisting chiefly of horses.

The Omahas inhabit the shores of the Missouri River, about eight hundred miles above its confluence with the Mississippi.   They of course hunt over those beautiful and boundless prairies which afford pasturage to the buffalo, and are expert in the capture of that animal, and the management of the horse.   They have but one permanent village, which consists of huts formed of poles, and plastered with mud.   A fertile plain, which spreads out in front of their town, affords ground for their rude horticulture, which extends to the planting of corn, beans, pumpkins, and water-melons.   This occupation, with the dressing of the buffalo skins procured in the previous winter's hunt, employs the spring months of the year ; and in June they make their arrangements for a grand hunting expedition.   A solemn council is held in advance of this important undertaking, at which the chiefs, the great warriors, and the most experienced hunters deliberately express their opinions in relation to the route proposed to be pursued ; the necessary preparations, and all other matters connected with the subject.   A feast is then given by an individual selected for the purpose, to which all the chief men are invited, and several of the fattest dogs are roasted for their entertainment.   Here the principal chief introduces again the great subject of debate, in a set speech, in which he thanks each person present for the honour of his company on an occasion so important to the nation, and calls upon them to determine whether the state of their stock of provisions will justify their remaining longer, to allow the women time to weed their corn, or whether they shall proceed at once to the pastures of the game. If the latter be the decision of the company, he invites them to determine whether it would be advisable to ascend the running water or seek the shores of the Platte, or extend their journey to the black hills of the south-west, in pursuit of wild horses. He is usually followed by some old chief, who compliments the head-man for his knowledge and bravery, and congratulates the tribe on their good fortune in having so wise a leader. Thus an Omaha feast very much resembles a political dinner among ourselves, and is improved as a fit occasion for great men to display their eloquence to the public, and their talent in paying compliments to each other. These consultations are conducted with great decorum, yet are characterised by the utmost freedom of debate; every individual, whose age and standing is such as to allow him, with propriety, to speak in public, giving his opinion. A sagacious head-man, however, is careful to preserve his popularity by respecting the opinion of the tribe at large, or, as we should term it, *the people;* and for that purpose, ascertains beforehand, the wishes of the mass of his followers. Ongpatonga was a model chief in this respect; he always carefully ascertained the public sentiment before he went into council, and knew the wishes of the majority in advance of a decision; and this is, probably, the most valuable talent for a public speaker, who may not only lead, by echoing the sentiments of those he addresses, but, on important points, insinuate with effect the dictates of his own more mature judgment.

After such a feast as we have described, others succeed; and the days of preparation for the grand hunt are filled with games and rejoicings; the women employing themselves in packing up their movables, and taking great care to make themselves important by retarding or accelerating the moment of departure.   At length the whole tribe moves off in grand cavalcade, with their skin lodges, dogs, and horses, leaving not a living thing in their deserted village, and proceed to the far distant plains, where the herds of buffalo "most do congregate."   About five months in the year are spent by this nation at their village, during which they are occupied in eating, sleeping, smoking, making speeches, waging war, or stealing horses ; the other seven are actively employed in chasing the buffalo or the wild horse.

The Omahas have one peculiarity in their customs which we have never noticed in the history of any other people.   Neither the father-in-law nor mother-in-law is permitted to hold any direct conversation with their son-in-law ; it is esteemed indelicate in these parties to look in each other's faces, or to mention the names of each other, or to have any intercourse, except through the medium of a third person.   If an Omaha enters a tent in which the husband of his daughter is seated, the latter conceals his head with his robe, and takes the earliest opportunity to withdraw, while the ordinary offices of kindness and hospitality are performed through the female, who passes the pipe or the message between her father and husband.[3]

Ongpatonga married the daughter of Mechapa, or the Horsehead.[4]   On a visit to his wife one day, he entered the tent of her father, unobserved by the latter, who was engaged in playing with a favourite dog, named Arrecat-tawaho,[5] which, in the Pawnee language, signifies Big Elk —being synonymous with Ongpatonga in the Omaha. This name the father-in-law was unluckily repeating, without being aware of the breach of good manners he was committing, until his wife, after many ineffectual winks and signs, struck him on the back with her fist, and in that tone of conjugal remonstrance which ladies can use when necessary, exclaimed : "You old fool! have you no eyes to see who is present ? You had better jump on his back, and ride him about like a dog!" The old man, in surprise, ejaculated "Wah!" and ran out of the tent in confusion.[6] We know scarcely anything so odd as this singular custom, which seems to be as inconvenient as it is unmeaning.

The Big Elk has been a very distinguished orator; few uneducated men have ever cultivated this art with more success. We have before us a specimen of his oratory, which is very creditable to his abilities. ―In 1811, a council was held at the Portage des Sioux, between Governor Edwards and Colonel Miller, on the part of the American Government, and a number of Indian chiefs of different nations. One of the latter, the Black Buffalo, a highly respected Sioux chief, of the Teton tribe, died suddenly during the conference, and was buried with the honours of war. At the conclusion of the ceremony Ongpatonga made the following unpremeditated address to those assembled :—"Do not grieve. Misfortunes will happen to the wisest and best of men. Death will come, and always comes out of season. It is the command of the Great Spirit, and all nations and people must obey. What is past, and cannot be prevented, should not be grieved for. Be not discouraged nor displeased, that in visiting your father here, you have lost your chief. A misfortune of this kind, under such afflicting circumstances, may never again befall you; but this loss would have occurred to you perhaps at your own village. Five times have I visited this land, and never returned with sorrow or pain. Misfortunes do not flourish particularly in one path; they grow everywhere. How unhappy am I that I could not have died this day, instead of the chief that lies before us. The trifling loss my nation would have sustained in my death, would have been doubly repaid by the honours of such a burial. They would have wiped off everything like regret. Instead of being covered with a cloud of sorrow, my warriors would have felt the sunshine of joy in their hearts. To me it would have been a most glorious occurrence. Hereafter, when I die at home, instead of a noble grave, and a grand procession, the rolling music, and the thundering cannon, with a flag waving over my head, I shall be wrapped in a robe, and hoisted on a slender scaffold, exposed to the whistling winds, soon to be blown down to the earth—my flesh to be devoured by the wolves, and my bones trodden on the plain by wild beasts. Chief of the soldiers! (addressing Colonel Miller,) your care has not been bestowed in vain. Your attentions shall not be forgotten. My nation shall know the respect that our white friends pay to the dead. When I return I will echo the sound of your guns."[7] Had this speech been uttered by a Grecian or a Roman orator, it would have been often quoted as a choice effusion of classic eloquence. It is not often that we meet with a funeral eulogium so unstudied, yet so pointed and ingenious.

This chief delivered a speech to the military and scientific gentlemen who accompanied Colonel Long in his expedition to the Rocky Mountains, in 1819-20, in which he asserted that not one of his nation had ever stained his hands with the blood of a white man.[8]

The character of Ongpatonga is strongly contrasted with that of Washinggusaba, or the Black Bird, one of his predecessors. The latter was also an able man, and a great warrior, but was a monster in cruelty and despotism. Having learned the deadly quality of arsenic from the traders, he procured a quantity of that drug, which he secretly used to effect his dreadful purposes. He caused it to be believed among his people, that if he prophesied the death of an individual, the person so doomed would immediately die; and he artfully removed by poison everyone who offended him, or thwarted his measures. The Omahas were entirely ignorant of the means by which this horrible result was produced; but they saw the effect, and knew from mournful experience that the displeasure of the chief was the certain forerunner of death; and their superstitious minds easily adopted the belief that he possessed a power which enabled him to will the destruction of his enemies. He acquired a despotic sway over the minds of his people, which he exercised in the most tyrannical manner; and so great was their fear of him, that even when he became superannuated, and so corpulent as to be unable to walk, they carried him about, watched over him when he slept, and awoke him, when necessary, by tickling his nose with a straw, for fear of disturbing him too abruptly. One chief, the Little Bow, whom he attempted ineffectually to poison, had the sagacity to discover the deception, and the independence to resist the influence of the impostor; but being unable to cope with so powerful an oppressor, he withdrew with a small band of warriors, and remained separated from the nation until the decease of the Black Bird, which occurred in the year 1800.[9] It is creditable to Ongpatonga, who shortly after succeeded to the post of principal chief, that he made no attempt to perpetuate the absolute authority to which the Omahas had been accustomed, but ruled over them with a mild and patriarchal sway.

In a conversation which this chief held, in 1821, with some gentlemen at Washington, he is represented as saying—"The same Being who made the white people made the red people; but the white are better than the red people"; and this remark has been called a degrading one, and not in accordance with the independent spirit of a native chief. We think the comment is unjust. Having travelled through the whole breadth of the United States, and witnessed the effects of civilisation in the industry of a great people, he might readily infer the superiority of the whites, and make the observation with the candour which always formed a part of his character. But it is equally probable that the expression was merely complimentary, and was uttered in the same spirit of courtesy with the wish which he announced at the grave of the Teton,[10] that he had fallen instead of the deceased.[11]

This chief is a person of highly respectable character. His policy has always been pacific; he has endeavoured to live at peace with his neighbours, and used his influence to keep them upon good terms with each other. He has always been friendly to the whites, and kindly disposed towards the American Government and people; has listened to their counsels, and taken pains to disseminate the admonitions which have been given for the preservation and happiness of the Indian race. He is a man of good sense and sound judgment, and is said to be unsurpassed as a public speaker. He bears an excellent reputation for probity; and is spoken of by those who know him well, as one of the best men of the native tribes. He is one of the few Indians who can tell his own age with accuracy. He is sixty-six years old.[12]

NOTES

1. Miss Alice C. Fletcher, whose studies of the Omaha tribe in association with Mr Francis La Flesche, a member of the tribe, are so well known, informs us that the name is derived from ŏɲpŏɲ, "elk," and tŏɲga, "big." The nasalized *n*, here written ɲ, being rather elusive, has not always caught the ear of the white frontiersman, hence the elision before the *t*.

ONG-PA-TON-GA, *or* THE BIG ELK
Chief of the Omahas

2. That is, the Skidi division of the Pawnee. See *Petalesharro*, note 12, p. 216. This division lived on the Loup fork of Platte River, Nebraska. Their village was always west of the other Pawnee.

3. The same custom prevails among the Navaho tribe of Arizona and New Mexico, but only so far as the woman and her son-in-law are concerned in the taboo.

4. We are informed by Miss Fletcher that this is the Dakota, or Sioux, name *Michapa*, meaning "Little Star," borrowed by a man in the Kansa gens of the Omaha. The episode here related by McKenney and Hall is extracted from Long's *Expedition to the Rocky Mountains*, Vol. I., p. 253, 1823.

5. This seems to be an error. The Pawnee word for elk is "nah" (pronounced nearly *nagh*). The term probably signifies "big horn," from *ariki*, horn; *tirihu*, big.

6. The impression is here given that the Omaha lived habitually in tents, or tipis, whereas the typical Omaha dwelling was the earth-lodge, a permanent structure. Tipis were used while on the hunt, or when travelling.

7. See John Bradbury, *Travels in the Interior of North America in the years 1809, 1810, and 1811*, Liverpool, 1817, for the "Oration delivered by the Big Elk, the chief of the Maha nation, over the grave of the Black Buffaloe, chief of the Tetons, a tribe of the Sioux, at the Portage des Sioux, 14th July, 1813." Compare also Donaldson in *Report of the National Museum for 1885*, Washington, 1886, p. 73. The proper date seems to have been 1815, on July 18, 19, and 20 of which year, at Portage des Sioux, several treaties were negotiated by William Clark, Ninian Edwards, and Auguste Chouteau; R. Wash serving as secretary to the Commissioners, and Colonel John Miller signing as a witness.

8. See Long, Vol. I., pp. 175, 194; Morse, *Report to the Secretary of War*, 246, 1822.

9. Long, *ibid.*, pp. 223-228.

10. In both references to this Sioux the name of his tribe is erroneously given in previous editions as "Ietan."

11. For Ongpatonga's conversation, see Morse, *op. cit.*, p. 249; and for the criticism to which McKenney and Hall refer, consult S. G. Drake, *Aboriginal Races*, 15th edition, 1880, p. 633 (1st edition, 1832).

12. Long gives much additional detail regarding Ongpatonga. He was much pitted with smallpox, and his nose was "like that of a European, the opposite to the Roman curve" (Vol. I., pp. 193-194). Dougherty, the agent, once heard another Indian refer to Ongpatonga's nose as being like that of a mule (*ibid.*, p. 234). These characteristics are not apparent in the accompanying portrait, painted by King, evidently while Ongpatonga was in Washington in 1821, as mentioned in the text. It is No. 90 of the Indian Gallery list (see the Introduction, p. 1), and bore the title "Au-pantan-ga, Big Elk. Mohas Chief; a great orator." In confirmation of this, Long says: "He speaks with great emphasis, and remarkably distinct" (I., p. 193). The Inman copy in the Peabody Museum bears original number, 45; catalogue number, 28. 208. Ongpatonga posed in 1833 for George Catlin, who illustrates the portrait, showing "his tomahawk in his hand and his face painted black, for war," in plate 146 of his *Illustrations of the Manners, etc.,* Vol. II. He visited Washington again early in December 1837, as a member of a deputation under agent Dougherty.

Ongpatonga signed, on behalf of the Omaha tribe, the treaties of Prairie du Chien, Wisconsin, July 15, 1830 (his name appearing as "Opau-tauga, or the big elk"), and Bellevue (Omaha), Nebraska, October 15, 1836 (in which his name is signed "Big Elk"). In each instance his name appears as the first signer.

MAHASKAH

(OR, WHITE CLOUD, AN IOWA CHIEF)

MAHASKAH, or White Cloud, the elder, was the son of Mauhawgaw, or the Wounding Arrow, who was principal chief of the Pauhoochee, or pierced-nose nation of Indians.[1] Mauhawgaw emigrated, some hundred and fifty years ago, from Michilimackinac[2] to the west bank of the Iowa River, and selected a position near its mouth, where his band kindled their fires and smoked their pipes to the Great Spirit. The name given to this river by Mauhawgaw was *Neohoney*, or "The Master of Rivers." Having built his village, he was greeted with a salutation from the Sioux. A pipe was sent to him by that tribe, with an invitation to a dog feast, made in honour of the Great Spirit. He accepted the invitation, and joined in the ceremony. Whilst at the feast, and, no doubt, reposing in the most perfect security, he was suddenly attacked; but, though surprised, he succeeded in killing one man and three women, before he was slain. This outrage upon the national honour has never been forgiven.

The portrait before the reader is that of the son of Mauhawgaw, who was thus treacherously slain. The Iowas, indignant at the conduct of the Sioux, resolved immediately on revenge. They raised a war party. Of this party, the son, Mahaskah, was the legitimate chief; but being young, and having never distinguished himself in battle, he declined taking the command, but by virtue of his right he conferred upon a distinguished and tried warrior the authority to lead his warriors against the Sioux—stating, at the time, that he would accompany the expedition as a common soldier, and fight till he should acquire experience, and gain trophies enough to secure to him the confidence of his people. Arrangements being made, the party marched into the Sioux country, and gained a great victory, taking ten of the enemy's scalps. The young Mahaskah brought home, in his own hand, the scalp of the Sioux chief in whose lodge the life of his father had been so treacherously taken.

Having thus shown himself a brave, he assumed the command of his warriors and of his tribe. His war adventures were numerous and daring. He was in eighteen battles against various bands, and was never defeated. In one of his expeditions against the Osages, with whom his conflicts were many, he arrived on the north bank of the Missouri, and while there, and engaged in trying to stop an effusion of blood from his nose, he espied a canoe descending the river, in which were three Frenchmen. Wishing to cross over with his party, he called upon the Frenchmen to land and assist him. The Frenchmen not only refused, but fired upon the Indians, wounding one of White Cloud's braves. The fire was instantly returned, which killed one of the Frenchmen. White Cloud had, so far, taken no part in this little affair, but on seeing one of his braves wounded, he called for his gun, saying, "You have killed one of the rascals, I'll try if I cannot send another along with him to keep him company to the *Chee*."—Chee means the house of the Black Spirit.

As usual, the whites raised a great clamour against the Iowas, giving out, all along the borders, that they were killing the settlers. A party was raised and armed, and marched forthwith against Mahaskah and his warriors. They were overtaken. White Cloud, not suspecting their designs, and being conscious of having committed no violence, was captured, and thrust into prison, where he remained many months. He finally made his escape, and succeeded in reaching his own country in safety. He then married four wives. It is the custom of the tribe, when husbands or brothers fall in battle, for a brave to adopt their wives or sisters. White Cloud found, on his return, four sisters who had been thus deprived of their protector, all of whom he married. Of these, Rant-chewaime, or the Female Flying Pigeon, was one, and the youngest. Her fine likeness, with a sketch of her character, will succeed this narrative.

Often, after White Cloud had thus settled himself, was he known to express his regret at having permitted his warriors to fire upon the Frenchmen. On these occasions he has been seen to look upon his hand, and heard to mutter to himself, "There is blood on it." He rejoiced, however, in the reflection that he had never shed the blood of an American. And yet his father's death, and the manner of it, made him restless, and rendered him implacable against the perpetrators of that outrage and their allies. Not long after his escape from prison and return to his home, and soon after his marriage, he planned an expedition against the Osages. He resolved to march with a select party of ten braves to the Little Osage plains, which lie south of the Missouri River, and about two hundred and fifty miles above St Louis. Arriving at the plains, a favourable opportunity soon offered, which was seized by Mahaskah, and the battle commenced. It was his misfortune, early in the conflict, to receive a rifle ball in his leg, just above the ankle. He had succeeded,

however, before he was wounded, in taking three of the
enemy's scalps, when he sought a retreat, and found one
under a large log that lay across a watercourse.   The
Osages followed close upon him—being guided by the
blood that flowed from his wound; but they lost the trail
on arriving at the watercourse, for Mahaskah had taken
the precaution to step into the water some distance below
the log, by which stratagem he misled his pursuers, for
they supposed he had crossed over at the place where
they last saw blood.   He remained under the log, which
lay on the water, with just so much of his nose out as to
enable him to breathe.

In the night, when all was silence save the tinkling
of the bells of the Indian horses in the plains below,
Mahaskah left his place of concealment, and coming up
with one of the horses, mounted him and made off in the
direction of his home, which was on the river Des Moines.
Arriving at the Missouri, he resorted to the Indian mode
of crossing, which is, to tie one end of the halter around
the head or neck of the horse, and, taking the other end
between his teeth, he drives the animal into the water,
and unites his own exertions as a swimmer to those of
the horse, and is by this means carried over in safety.   In
all these difficulties he took care not to part with either
his gun or his scalps.   On arriving at home he paraded
his trophies, and ordered the scalp dance to be danced.
Not being able, on account of his wound, to lead the dance
himself, he placed the scalps in the hand of Inthehone, or
the Big Axe,[3] who, being the first brave of his band,
was entitled to the distinction.   Mahaskah accompanied
the presentation of the scalps to Big Axe with these
words: "I have now revenged the death of my father.
My heart is at rest.   I will go to war no more.   I told
Maushuchees, or Red Head (meaning General Clark),[4]

when I was last at St Louis, that I would take his peace talk. My word is out. I will fight no more."

In the year 1824, Mahaskah left home, being one of a party on an embassy to Washington, leaving his wives behind him, their number having increased to seven. When about one hundred miles from home, and near the mouth of the river Des Moines, having killed a deer, he stopped to cook a piece of it. He was seated, and had just commenced his meal, when he felt himself suddenly struck on the back. Turning round, he was astonished to see Rantchewaime standing before him with an uplifted tomahawk in her hand! She thus accosted him: "Am I your wife? Are you my husband? If so, I will go with you to the Mawhehunneche, (or the American big house,) and see and shake the hand of Incohonee" (which means "great father"). Mahaskah answered: "Yes, you are my wife; I am your husband; I have been a long time from you; I am glad to see you; you are my pretty wife, and a brave man always loves to see a pretty woman."

The party arrived at Washington. "A talk" was held with President Monroe; the present of a medal was made to Mahaskah, and a treaty was concluded between the United States and the Iowas. It is a treaty of cession, of limits, etc., and of considerations therefor. These considerations include a payment, in that year, of five hundred dollars, and the same sum annually, for ten years thereafter. Provision is made for blankets, farming utensils, and cattle; and assistance is promised them in their agricultural pursuits, under such forms as the President might deem expedient.[5]

The following occurrence happened at Washington during that visit. Mahaskah would occasionally indulge in a too free use of ardent spirits. On one of these occasions he was exercising one of an Indian husband's privileges on the Flying Pigeon. The agent,[6] hearing the scuffle, hastened

to their room.   Mahaskah, hearing him coming, lifted up
the window sash and stepped out, forgetting that he was
two storeys from the ground.   In the fall he broke his arm ;
yet so accustomed had he been to fractures and wounds,
that he insisted on riding the next day, over rough roads
and pavements, a distance of at least two miles, to see a
cannon cast.   A few days after, he sat to King, of Washington, for his portrait.[7]   The reader will remark a com-
pression of his eyebrows.   This was caused by the pain he
was enduring whilst the artist was sketching his likeness.

On his return to his country and home, Mahaskah began
in earnest to cultivate his land—he built for himself a double
log-house, and lived in great comfort.   This, he said, was
in obedience to the advice of his "great father."

Soon after his return to his home, it was his misfortune
to lose his favourite wife, and under very painful circumstances.   They were crossing a tract of country.   Mahaskah,
having reason to apprehend that hostile bands might be
met with, kept in advance.   Each was on horseback; the
Flying Pigeon carrying her child, Mahaskah the younger,
then about four years old.   Turning, at a certain point, to
look back to see what distance his wife was from him, he
was surprised (his position being a high one, enabling him
to overlook a considerable extent of country) not to see her.
He rode back, and, sad to relate, after retracing his steps
some five or six miles, he saw her horse grazing near the
trail, and presently the body of his wife near the edge of a
small precipice, with her child resting its head upon her
body.   The horror-stricken chief, alighting near to the spot,
was soon assured of her death !   Standing over her corpse,
he exclaimed, in his mother tongue : " *Wau-cunda-menia-
bratuskunnee, shungau-menia-nauga-nappo !* "—which, being interpreted, means—"God Almighty ! I am a bad man.
You are angry with me.   The horse has killed my wife ! "

MA-HAS-KAH, *or* WHITE CLOUD
An Iowa Chief

At the moment, the child lifted its head from the dead body of its mother, and said: "Father, my mother is asleep!"

The inference was, that the horse had stumbled and thrown her. The occurrence took place about four days' journey from his home. Mahaskah, within that time, was seen returning to his lodge, bearing the dead body of Rantchewaime, with his child in his arms. He proceeded at once to dispose of the corpse. His first business was to gather together all the presents that had been made to her at Washington; also whatever else belonged to her, and to place them, with the body, in a rude box; and then, according to the custom of the Indians of that region, the box was placed upon a high scaffold. This mode of disposing of the dead has a twofold object—one is, to elevate the body as high as possible in the direction of the home of the Great Spirit; that home being, according to their belief, in the sky; the other is, to protect the corpse from the wolves, whose ravages would disfigure it, and render it unsightly in the eyes of the Great Spirit. This much of the ceremony over, the chief killed a dog, made a feast, and called his braves together. A second dog, and then a horse were killed. The dog was fastened, with his head upwards, to the scaffold, while the tail of the horse had a position assigned to it on that part of the scaffold nearest the head of the deceased. On the head of the dog was placed a twist of tobacco.

These ceremonies have their origin in a superstition of the nation, which attributes every death to the anger of the Great Spirit, who is supposed to be always in motion, searching for the spirits of those who have recently died, with the calumet, or pipe of peace in his mouth. As the scaffold is approached by this mysterious Being, the watchful dog is expected to see and address him—inform him of the locality of the body, and invite him to take the tobacco, and smoke. This offer the Indian believes is always accepted. The Great Spirit then proceeds to reanimate and remodel the dead body; to restore the trinkets and property of the deceased; impart vitality to the dog and the horse, and commission them forthwith, the one to bear the deceased to the land of game and of plenty—the other, to hunt the deer in the regions of the blessed.

In 1833, the son of an Iowa chief of distinction, named Crane, was killed by the Omahas. A party of Iowas applied to Mahaskah to head them in the pursuit of the enemy. He replied : "I have buried the tomahawk ; I am now a man of peace." He added : "The treaty made with our great father provides for the punishment of such outrages." The party, however, resolved that they would punish the aggressors. They made an incursion into the enemy's country, and returned, bringing with them six scalps. The customary feast was prepared, and all was made ready for the scalp dance ; but Mahaskah refused to partake of the one, or participate in the other.

The murders on both sides having been reported to the Government, General Clark was directed to cause the Iowas to be arrested. This duty was assigned to their agent, General Hughes, who called on the chief, Mahaskah, to whom he made known the order. Mahaskah answered : "It is right; I will go with you." The offenders were arrested and conveyed to Fort Leavenworth. While confined there, one of the prisoners called Mahaskah to the window of his dungeon, and looking him full in the face, said : "Inca (father), if ever I get out of this place alive, I will kill you. A brave man should never be deprived of his liberty, and confined as I am. You should have shot me at the village."

Unfortunately for Mahaskah, that Indian succeeded in making his escape from prison. He forthwith went in pursuit of the object of his revenge. Mahaskah was found encamped on the Naudaway,[9] about sixty miles from his village. His pursuer and party attacked him with guns, tomahawks, and clubs, and slew him. After he was dead, one of the party remarked, that "he was the hardest man to kill he ever knew." This was in 1834, Mahaskah being then about fifty years old.

The tidings of Mahaskah's death soon reached his village. One of the murderers escaped and sought refuge among the Otoes; but, on learning the cause of his visit to them, they shot him in their camp. The other, with the utmost indifference, returned to the village of the murdered chief. Young Mahaskah,[10] now the successor of his father, and principal chief of the nation, on hearing the news of his father's death, and that one of the murderers had returned to the village, went immediately to his lodge, killed his dogs and horses, and with his knife cut and ripped his lodge in every possible direction. This last act especially, is an insult to which no brave man will submit. Having hurled this defiance at one of the murderers of his father, and expressed his contempt for him under every possible form, he turned to the assassin, who had observed in silence the destruction of his property, and, looking him sternly in the face, said: "You have killed the greatest man who ever made a moccasin track on the Naudaway; you must, therefore, be yourself a great man, since the Great Spirit has given you the victory. To call you a dog would make my father less than a dog." The squaw of the murderer exclaimed to her husband, "Why don't you kill the boy?" He replied, "He is going to be a great brave, I cannot kill him." So saying, he handed the young chief a pipe, which he refused, saying, "I will leave you in the hands of the braves of my nation." To which the inflexible murderer replied, "I am

not going to run away; I'll meet your braves to-morrow."
The Indian knew full well the fate that awaited him. He
felt that his life was forfeited, and meant to assure the
young chief that he was ready to pay the penalty.

The next day a general council was convened. The
case was submitted to it. The unanimous voice was,
"He shall die." It was further decreed that young
Mahaskah should kill him; but he declined, saying, "I
cannot kill so brave a man"; whereupon he was shot by
one of the principal braves. His body was left on the
ground, to be devoured by wolves, as a mark of the disgust
of the tribe, and of their abhorrence of the assassin of their
chief.

It is customary among the Iowas, and the neighbouring tribes, for the wives and children of the deceased to
give away everything which had belonged to him and his
family. This custom was rigidly adhered to on the
occasion of Mahaskah's death. His surviving squaws
went into mourning and poverty. The mourning is kept
up for six moons, and consists, in addition to the blacking
of the face, in much wailing, and in the utterance of long
and melancholy howls. At its expiration, the tribe
present the mourners with food and clothing, and other
necessaries of savage life. One of Mahaskah's widows,
however, named Missorahtarrahaw, which means, "The
Female Deer that Bounds over the Plains," refuses to this
day to be comforted, saying, her husband "was a great
brave and was killed by dogs"—meaning, low, vulgar
fellows.

The subject of this memoir was six feet two inches in
height, possessed great bodily strength and activity, and
was a man of perfect symmetry of person, and of uncommon
beauty.

The Iowas were once the most numerous and powerful, next to the Sioux, of all the tribes that hunt between the Mississippi and Missouri Rivers. They have been reduced by wars, the smallpox, and by whisky, to about thirteen hundred souls.[11]

NOTES

1. Miss Alice C. Fletcher informs us that Mahaskah, "White Cloud," is properly "Moɲhashka," while Mauhaugaw is strictly "Moɲhaga," signifying "bristling with arrows," as a wounded buffalo with many arrows sticking in him. The "Pauhoochee" are the Iowa Indians, *Pahoja, Pahodje, Pahocha*, being translated by Long (*Exped. Rocky Mountains*, I., 339, 1823) as "gray snow," by Hamilton (*Trans. Nebraska Historical Society*, I., 47, 1885) as "dusty men," and by Maximilian, Prince of Wied Neu-Wied (*Travels*, 507, 1843) as "dust noses." The name appears in the form *Pah8tet*, on Marquette's map of 1673.

2. The name is usually applied to a village near the site of the present Mackinaw, Michigan, but in this instance it is more probably used to designate an extensive tract of territory in the northern part of the lower peninsula of Michigan. The Iowa lived in the neighbourhood of the mouth of Blue Earth River, Minnesota, just prior to the arrival there of Le Sueur in 1701, whence they removed and "established themselves toward the Missouri River." The period of one hundred and fifty years here given seems to have been a rather long span for the lifetime of the father and his son Mahaskah. The latter was born about the year 1784, thus making it impossible for his father to have removed from the Michigan country to Iowa River about 1690. It would seem more likely that this Mahaskah was a grandson of Mauhawgaw, and that two persons, father and son, bearing the name Mahaskah, are confused.

3. This Indian signed the treaty with the Iowa tribe held at Portage des Sioux, September 16, 1815, his name appearing as "Eniswahanee, the big axe."

4. General William Clark, brother of George Rogers Clark, the celebrated Indian fighter, and the companion of Meriwether Lewis on the "Lewis and Clark expedition." Resigning from the army in 1807, he served as Indian agent until appointed by Congress brigadier-general for Upper Louisiana. In 1813 President Madison appointed him Governor of Missouri Territory, which office he held until Missouri was erected into a State in 1821. In the following year President Monroe appointed him Superintendent of Indian Affairs at St Louis, which office he held until his death in that city, September 1, 1838.

5. For this treaty of Washington, concluded August 4, 1824, and ratified January 18, 1825, see *Treaties between the United States and the Several Indian Tribes*, Washington, 1837, pp. 317-318. McKenney was a witness to this treaty.

6. G. W. Kennerly, who signed the treaty as a witness.

7. See Nos. 97 and 131 of the Rhees list of the Indian Gallery collection, in the Introduction, pp. li, lii. Under No. 131, Rant-che-wai-me, Mahaka (Mahaska), and Hayne Hudjihini the favourite wife of Shaumonekusse, are confused.

When George Catlin was among the Iowa tribe in 1832, he painted the portrait of "Notch-ee-ning-a, No Heart, called 'White Cloud,' Chief of the Tribe; necklace of grizzly bear's claws, and shield, bow and arrows in his hand." (*Descriptive Catalogue* [London, 1840], p. 26.) In his *Illustrations of the Manners, etc.* (10th ed., II., London, 1866, p. 22), Catlin says: "The present chief of this tribe is Notch-ee-ning-a (the White Cloud, plate 129), the son of a very distinguished chief of the same name, who died recently, after gaining the love of his tribe, and the respect of all the civilised world who knew him. . . . The son of White Cloud, who is now chief, and whose portrait I have just named, was tastefully dressed with a buffalo robe, wrapped around him, with a necklace of grizzly bear's claws on his neck; with shield, bow and quiver on, and a profusion of wampum strings on his back." The date above given (1832) would seem to indicate that the statement by McKenney and Hall to the effect that Mahaskah was killed in 1834 is an error. But there is great confusion here. In Vol. II. of the present work appears the biography of Notchimine, who is no other than Notch-ee-ning-a, as is shown by the fact that the accompanying portrait is identical with the original, still preserved in the United States National Museum. In this latter biography, as well as in the account of Young Mahaskah, following, the statement is made that "Notchimine" was a brother of White Cloud, meaning White Cloud I. The fact of the case is that Catlin confused the two, perhaps for the reason that Notchininga, or Notchimine, was the village or peace chief, while his nephew, Mahaskah II., was the hereditary tribal chief. See the biography of Young Mahaskah, following, and compare, for further information, Fulton, *Red Men of Iowa*, pp. 109-124, Des Moines, 1882. Fulton says that Mahaskah II. was known also as Wi-e-wa-ha, thus indicating that the name Mahaskah was an hereditary chieftainship title rather than a personal designation, and explaining the appearance of "Wyingwaha, or hard heart," as the first signer of the treaty with the Iowa tribe at Portage des Sioux, December 26, 1815. This chief was doubtless no other than Mahaskah I. The treaty of Washington, August 4, 1824, as signed by "Ma-hos-kah (White Cloud)"; that of Prairie du Chien, August 19, 1825, by "Ma-hos-ka, the white cloud"; that of Prairie du Chien, July 15, 1830, by "Mauhoos Kan, white cloud." The next Iowa treaty was concluded in 1836, after the death of Mahaskah I. The names "Mah-hos-ka (White Cloud), chief"; "Mah-ne-hah-nah (Great Walker), chief"; and "Rant-che-che-wai-me (Female Flying Pigeon, Mah-has-kah's wife—Iowa squaw)" appear in a list of Indians "now at the seat of Government," in the *National Journal,* reprinted in *Niles Register* of July 31, 1824.

8. Andrew S. Hughes, a sub-agent.

9. The Nodaway River, a tributary of the Missouri, in north-western Missouri.

10. See his biography following.

11. The population of the tribe in 1906 was 334, of whom 246 were in Kansas and 88 in Oklahoma.

RANTCHEWAIME

(OR, FEMALE FLYING PIGEON)

THIS portrait is a perfect likeness of the wife of Mahas-kah, a sketch of whose life precedes this. Rantchewaime means "Female Flying Pigeon." She has been also called "The Beautiful Female Eagle that Flies in the Air." This name was given to her by the chiefs and braves of the nation, on account of her great personal beauty.[1]

We have already, in the sketch of her husband's life, made the reader acquainted with the tragic end of this interesting woman. It remains for us to speak of her character. General Hughes, the agent of the tribe, who was well acquainted with her, speaks of her in terms of unmixed approbation. She was chaste, mild, gentle in her disposition, kind, generous, and devoted to her husband. A harsh word was never known to proceed from her mouth; nor was she ever known to be in a passion. Mahaskah used to say of her, after her death, that her hand was shut, when those who did not want came into her presence; but, when the poor came, it was like a strainer, full of holes, letting all she held in it pass through. In the exercise of this generous feeling she was uniform. It was not indebted for its exercise to whim, or caprice, or partiality. No matter of what nation the applicant for her bounty was, or whether at war or peace with her tribe, if he were hungry, she fed him; if naked, she clothed him;

and if houseless, she gave him shelter. The continual exercise of this generous feeling kept her poor. She has been known to give away her last blanket—all the honey that was in the lodge, the last bladder of bear's oil,* and the last piece of dried meat.

Rantchewaime was scrupulously exact in the observance of all the religious rites which her faith imposed upon her. Her conscience is represented to have been extremely tender. She often feared that her acts were displeasing to the Great Spirit, when she would blacken her face and retire to some lone place, and fast and pray. The Iowas, like all other Indians, believe in a Great Spirit,[2] and in future rewards and punishments; and their priests make frequent sacrifices of dogs and horses, to appease the anger of their God. For their virtue, which, with these Indians, means courage, kindness, honesty, chastity, and generosity, they believe most sincerely they will be rewarded; and, for bad actions, they as fully believe they will be punished. Among these they enumerate dishonesty, laziness, the sacrifice of chastity, etc. But they do not view the stealing of a horse in the light of a dishonest act—they class this among their virtues.

Rantchewaime has been known, after her return from Washington, to assemble hundreds of the females of her tribe, and discourse to them on the subject of those vicious courses which she witnessed during that journey, among the whites, and to warn them against like practices. The good effect of such a nice sense of propriety has been singularly illustrated among the Iowas. It is reported, on unquestionable authority, that an illegitimate child has never been known to be born among them. It is true, uncles (parents do not interfere, the right being

* Bear's oil is kept in bladders, and used by the Indians in cooking, for the same purposes for which we use lard or butter.

in the uncle, or the nearest relative) sometimes sell their
nieces for money or merchandise, to traders and engagees.
Marriages thus contracted frequently produce a state of
great connubial happiness; but, if the purchaser abandon
his purchase, she is discarded, and is never taken for a
wife by a brave, but is left to perform all the drudgery of
the lodge and the field, and is treated as an outcast.

An affecting incident occurred in 1828, on the Missouri.
A connection, by purchase, had been formed between a
trader and an Iowa maid. They lived together for some
time, and had issue, one child. The trader, as is often the
case, abandoned his wife and child. The wife, agitated
with contending emotions of love and bereavement, and
knowing how hard would be her fate, strapped her child
to the cradle, and throwing it on her back, pursued her
faithless husband. She came within sight of him, but he
eluded her. Arriving at the top of a high bluff that overlooked the country, and after straining her eyes by looking
in every direction to catch a glimpse of him, or to see the
way he was travelling, in vain, she stepped hastily to a
part of the bluff that overhung the Missouri, and exclaim-
ing, "O God! all that I loved in this world has passed
from my sight; my hopes are all at an end; I give myself
and child to thee!" sprang into the river, and with her
child was drowned.

We have spoken of the firm belief of the Iowas in a
future state. What that state is, in their view of it, we
will now briefly state. They believe, that after death, and
after they are found by the Great Spirit—who, as we have
said in a preceding sketch, is constantly going about with
a pipe of peace in his mouth, seeking the bodies of the
dead—they are guided by him to a rapid stream, over
which always lies a log that is exceedingly slippery.
Those who are destined to be happy are sustained by

the Good Spirit in crossing upon this slippery log. The moment they reach the opposite shore, they are transported to a land filled with buffalo and elk, the antelope and beaver; with otters, and raccoons, and muskrats. Over this beautiful land the sun always shines; the streams that irrigate it never dry up, whilst the air is filled with fragrance, and is of the most delightful temperature. The kettles are always slung, and the choicest cuts from the buffalo, the elk, etc., are always in a state of readiness to be eaten, whilst the smoke of these viands ascends for ever and ever. In this beautiful and happy country the departed good meet, and mingle with their ancestors of all previous time, and all the friends that preceded them, all recognising and saluting each other.

But when the wicked die, they are guided to this slippery log, and then abandoned, when they fall into the stream, and, after being whirled about in many directions, they awake and find themselves upon firm ground, but in the midst of sterility, of poverty, and of desolation. All around them are snakes, lizards, frogs, and grasshoppers; and there is no fuel to kindle a fire. This barren land is in full view of the beautiful country and of all its delights, whilst over it constantly pass the odours of the viands; but from a participation in anything there, they are forever debarred.

In this belief Rantchewaime grew up. It was to gain admission into this heaven, and to avoid this place of punishment, she so often went into retirement to pray; and all her virtues and good works, she believed, were put down as so many titles to this beautiful heaven. There can be little doubt that a mind thus formed, and a conscience thus tender, would, under the guidance of the Christian faith, and the enlightening influence of our most holy religion, have carried their possessor to the highest attainments, and made her a bright and a shining light.   It is impossible to contemplate a child of Nature so gifted in all that is excellent, without feeling a regret that the principles of a more rational religion had not reached Rantchewaime, and that she had not participated in its enjoyments.   But He to whom she has gone will know how to judge her.   Certain it is, of those to whom little has been given but little will be required; and although Rantchewaime may not have found the heaven she aspired to reach, she has found one far more delightful, and as eternal.

NOTES

1. For the portrait in the Indian Gallery of the War Department, see *Mahaskah*, note 7, p. 294.   A copy of this portrait of Rantchewaime by King was made by the same artist, and was bequeathed by him to the Redwood Library of Newport, Rhode Island (see the Introduction, p. liv, No. 14).   This copy exhibits even greater refinement of features than the reproduction in McKenney and Hall.   The Inman copy in the Peabody Museum bears museum number 57. 30.

2. For the Indian concept of a Great Spirit, see note 13, p. 102.

RANT-CHE-WAI-ME, *or* FEMALE
FLYING PIGEON

YOUNG MAHASKAH

(CHIEF OF THE IOWAS)

THIS is the son of Mahaskah the elder, and Rantchewaime. On the death of his father, young Mahaskah took charge of his family. Inheriting by birth the title and pre-rogatives of chief, it was supposed he would assume the authority of one; but this he refused to do, saying, he would not occupy the place of his father unless called to that station by a majority of his people. This decision being made known to the nation, a general council was called, by which he was elected chief without a dissenting voice. He was then in the twenty-fourth year of his age. The decision of the council being announced to him, he thus addressed it :—"One of my sisters, and other young women, have been taught to spin and weave. My father approved this and encouraged it. He also taught the lessons of peace, and counselled me not to go to war, except in my own defence. I have made up my mind to listen always to that talk. I have never shed blood; have never taken a scalp, and never will, unless compelled by bad men, in my own defence, and for the protection of my people. I believe the Great Spirit is always angry with men who shed innocent blood. I will live in peace."

This talk clearly indicated the policy he had resolved to pursue; and, that the force of example might be added to his precept, he immediately engaged in agricultural pursuits. He has now under cultivation about sixteen acres of land, on which he raises corn, pumpkins, beans, squashes, potatoes, etc., all which are well attended, and cultivated with great neatness—the plough being the principal instrument; and this he holds in his own hand. The surplus produce he distributes with great liberality among his people. This, and his father's example, have had a most beneficial effect upon his tribe. Mahaskah not only follows, thus practically, the example set by his father, but he also counsels his people, on all suitable occasions, to abandon war and the chase, and look to the ground for their support. He is, literally, the monarch of his tribe. Naucheninga, or No Heart,[1] his father's brother, acts in concert with, and sustains him nobly, in these lessons of industry and peace.

Young Mahaskah considered that great injustice had been done by the United States Government to his people, in failing, by a total disregard of the stipulations of the treaty of 1825,[2] to keep off intruders from his lands, and in overlooking the obligations of that treaty in regard to the conduct of the Sauks and Foxes of the Mississippi, who had not only made large sales of the mineral regions about what are called Du Buque's mines,[3] without consulting the Iowas—who, by the treaty, are entitled to an equal portion of that country—but who also threatened in their talks to advance within the limits of the Grand and Des Moines Rivers, and take possession of the country. In view of these things, young Mahaskah called on the United States agent, and made known his grievances. The agent replied, that his will was good to see justice done to the Iowas, but that he had no power to enforce it. Mahaskah resolved to proceed immediately to Washington, and appeal in person to his "great father," and ask for redress. This intention of the chief was made known to the Government. The answer was, in substance, "There is no appropriation to pay his expenses." He then determined to make the visit at his own cost, which he did in the winter of 1836-37, selecting for his companion a notable brave, called the Sioux Killer,[4] whose portrait will follow this, and of whose life and actions we have something to say. The Iowas engaged the services of Major Joseph V. Hamilton and Major Morgan, and invested them with full power to adjust their difficulties with the Government. Major Morgan declined, Major Hamilton consented; when, in company with their long tried and faithful agent, General Andrew H. Hughes, the party started for Washington.[5]

Mahaskah had indulged the hope that these difficulties might be adjusted at St Louis, and thereby save the trouble and expense of pursuing their journey to Washington. With this view, he visited the old and constant friend of his people, General William Clark,[6] who received the chief and his party with all the kindness which has so long characterised his intercourse with the Indians of the far West. But he was unable to redress the grievances complained of, and therefore declined to interfere in the adjustment of their claims. He, however, gave Mahaskah a letter, which was addressed to Major Hamilton, to be laid before the President, together with a very able petition which had been prepared. The petition was addressed to Andrew Jackson, President of the United States, or his successor; and also to the Congress of the United States; the object being that, if the President had no authority to interfere, Congress might confer it.

The young chief and his party were received with great kindness by the authorities at Washington. He told, in his own simple but eloquent style, the story of his wrongs, and claimed the interposition of the Government. He was promised, in reply, that his business should be attended to, and his grievances redressed. Reposing entire confidence in these promises, he was satisfied. A medal was presented to him, and other testimonials of respect shown him. After remaining about ten days, he returned in February, 1837, to his own country. The portrait before the reader was taken during that visit, by that celebrated artist, King, the same who had taken, previously, a large portion of those which embellish this work.[7]

In person, young Mahaskah is about five feet ten inches high, and so finely proportioned as to be a model, in all respects, of a perfect man. The reader will see, on turning to his portrait, how striking is its resemblance to his father's, and how clearly it indicates the character of the man. Around his neck are seen the same bear's claws which his father had long worn before him.

It happened when Mahaskah was at Washington, that the agent for this work was there also. He waited on the party, and exhibited the specimen number. As he turned over the leaves bearing the likenesses of many of those Indians of the far West who were known to the party, Mahaskah would pronounce their names with the same promptness as if the originals had been alive and before him. Among these was the likeness of his father. He looked at it with a composure bordering on indifference. On being asked if he did not know his father, he answered, pointing to the portrait, "That is my father." He was asked if he was not glad to see him. He replied: "It is enough for me to know that my father was a brave man, and had a big heart, and died an honourable death, in doing the will of my great father"—referring to the duty he was engaged in, as stated in his father's life, which resulted in his death.

Another leaf being turned over, he said: "That is Shaumonekusse, the Oto chief"; and added, "he is a brave and sensible man, and I am glad to see him." They had long been friends; in fact, ever since Mahaskah was a boy, they had smoked the calumet together. The portrait of the Eagle of Delight, wife of Shaumonekusse, was then shown to him. "That," said he, "is my mother." The agent assured him he was mistaken. He became indignant, and seemed mortified that his mother, as he believed her to be, should be arranged in the work as the wife of another, and especially of a chief over whom his father had held and exercised authority. The colloquy became interesting, until at last some excitement on the part of Mahaskah grew out of it. On hearing it repeated by the agent, that he must be mistaken, Mahaskah turned and looked him in the face, saying, "Did you ever know the child that loved its mother, and had seen her, that forgot the board on which he was strapped, and the back on which he had been carried, or the knee on which he had been nursed, or the breast that had given him life?" So firmly convinced was he that this was the picture of his mother, and so resolved that she should not remain by the side of Shaumonekusse, that he said: "I will not leave this room until my mother's name, Rantchewaime, is marked over the name of Eagle of Delight."[8] The agent for the work complied with this demand, when his agitation, which had become great, subsided, and he appeared contented. Looking once more at the painting, he turned from it, saying, "If it had not been for Waucondamony," the name he gave the agent for the work, which means, "Walking God," so called, because he attributed the taking of these likenesses to him, "I would have kissed her, but Waucondamony made me ashamed."

Soon after this interview the party went to King's

gallery, where are copies of many of these likenesses, and among them are both the Eagle of Delight and the Female Flying Pigeon.[9] The moment Mahaskah's eye caught the portrait of the Female Flying Pigeon, he exclaimed, " *That* is my mother; that is her fan; I know her now. I am ashamed again." He immediately asked to have a copy of it, as also of the Eagle of Delight, wife of Shaumone-kusse, saying of this last, " The Oto chief will be so glad to see his squaw, that he will give me one hundred horses for it."

It was most natural that Mahaskah should have mis-taken the Eagle of Delight for his mother, and no less so, when they were seen together, that he should become convinced of his error. His mother, it will be recollected, was killed when he was only four years old. She and the Eagle of Delight were neighbours and friends, and much together; and were particular in braiding their hair alike, and dressing always after the same fashion, and, generally, in the same kind of material. He knew, moreover, that the Eagle of Delight was of royal birth, and, though a child, he recollected she had a blue spot on her forehead, which is the ensign of royalty. In the portrait before him, the colourer had omitted the spot; not seeing this, and seeing the braided hair and the dress, and the strong resemblance to the features of his mother as they remained impressed upon his memory, he was easily deceived. The moment, however, he came into the presence of his mother's likeness, and had both before him, he knew her on whose back he had been carried, the knee on which he had been nursed, and the breast that had given him life; and even the fan in her hand served to recall the mother he had loved, and painfully to remind him of her melan-choly death—for he said that she had that same fan in her hand when the horse fell with her. In the other painting before him, he saw the blue spot. He was no longer mistaken, and rejoiced in once more beholding so good a mother. It is scarcely necessary to add, that copies of both were sent to him, and that both he and Shaumone-kusse, the husband of the Eagle of Delight, were made happy, the one in receiving back, as from the dead, a mother so beloved; the other, a wife whose loss he deeply deplores.

NOTES

1. See *Mahaskah,* note 7, p. 294. This Indian, under the form Notchimine, is treated in Vol. II. His name is interpreted more strictly "No Heart of Fear," which has a very different meaning.

2. This was the treaty concluded at Prairie du Chien, Wisconsin, August 19, 1825, between William Clark and Lewis Cass on behalf of the United States, and various representatives of the Sioux, Winnebago, Menominee, Chippewa, Ottawa, Potawatomi, Sauk, Fox, and Iowa tribes. The treaty, which was ratified February 6, 1826, was negotiated for the purpose of promoting peace among these tribes, and of establishing boundaries among them and the other tribes who lived in their vicinity; but the boundaries agreed on under its provisions seem never to have been established. The joint interest of the Iowa and the Sauk and Foxes is provided for by Article 3. On September 15, 1832, the affiliated Sauk and Fox tribes ceded to the United States a vast tract of land in eastern Iowa, covering almost the entire area of the State immediately bordering on the Mississippi, this cession having been required as an indemnity for the expenses of the Black Hawk war. A reservation in south-eastern Iowa was set apart for the Sauk and Foxes under the treaty last mentioned, but this was ceded to the United States by treaty of September 28, 1836.

3. Referring to the mines of Julian Dubuque, on the Mississippi, where the city in Iowa that bears his name now stands. Dubuque was a French trader, who with ten others settled there in 1788 to mine lead, thus forming the first settlement by whites within the State. The place was abandoned on Dubuque's death in 1810, and was not reoccupied until 1833.

On the Dubuque lead mines, John Bradbury (*Travels in the Interior of America,* Liverpool, 1817, pp. 255-256) says:

"Formerly, these Indians gave permission to a person of the name of Dubuque to dig lead: he resided at their village, being much respected by them, and acquired some property, the management of which, after his death, fell into the hands of Augustus Choutou, of St Louis, who, in 1810, advertised for sale Dubuque's property in the mines, or his right of digging lead. It was bought by Colonel Smith, the proprietor of Mine Belle Fontaine, and Mr Moorhead of St Louis, for about 3000 dollars. They ascended the Mississippi with an armed party, to take possession, but were very roughly handled by the Indians, and happy in having escaped with their lives. The Indians immediately afterwards called a council, and being fearful of giving offence to the American Government, they sent deputies to St Louis, to plead their cause before Governor Howard and General Clarke, who performed their mission with great ability; first disclaiming any intention to continue the grant beyond the life of Dubuque, and, secondly, any wish to offend the Government of the United States, by driving away Smith and Moorhead. They next stated, that when the Great Spirit gave the land to the Red Men, their ancestors, he foresaw that the White Men would come into the country, and that the game would be destroyed; therefore, out of his great goodness, he put lead into the ground, that they, their wives and children, might continue to exist: They lastly appealed to the justice of their Great Father, the President of the United States. Governor Howard and General Clarke approved of their conduct, and assured them of the protection of the Government." Thus temporarily ended a chapter in the history of the Sauk and Fox tribe, which, but for the interposition of two honest officials, might have ended disastrously for the Indians as early as 1810. Consult also, Schoolcraft, *Summary Narrative*, 169 *et seq.*, 1855, and his *View of the Lead Mines of Missouri*, New York, 1819; McKenney, *Memoirs*, 131, 1846.

4. See *Shauhaunapotinia*, p. 326.

5. Andrew S. Hughes, sub-agent, and Joseph V. Hamilton, " Sutler Dragoons," were witnesses to the treaty with the Iowa and the Sauk and Foxes concluded at Fort Leavenworth, September 17, 1836. This treaty bears the name of " Mo-hos-ca, or white cloud."

6. See *Mahaskah*, note 4, p. 293. The portrait is not listed by name in the Rhees *Catalogue*, but the portraits of Neomoune and Nauchewingga, evidently members of the same deputation, are included, and bear numbers 101 and 103. Shauhaunapotinia likewise does not appear in the list; but see Nos. 1 and 134, both Iowa Indians.

7. While Catlin was in London exhibiting his collection of Indian paintings in 1844, a party of fourteen Iowa Indians, accompanied by G. H. C. Melody and by Jeffrey Doraway, a mulatto interpreter who had been reared in the tribe, arrived in that city, permission for the journey having been given by J. M. Porter, Secretary of War, in 1843. These Indians were shown in London as a part of Catlin's exhibit, under joint agreement with Melody, and were afterward taken to other cities in England, Scotland, Ireland, and France, until 1846. A performance was given at the Music Hall, George Street, Edinburgh, February 3-6, 1845, the admission fee being one shilling, "children half-price." Ten

YOUNG MA-HAS-KAH
Chief of the Iowas

dances, two songs, and one " Farewell song and dance," were among the numbers on the programme, the whole of which is characteristic of the professional showman. After announcing that "the Ioway Indians were visited by nearly 3000 persons one evening, in the Town Hall, Birmingham," Catlin announces "a little handbook, describing all their games, dances, etc., by Geo. Catlin, for sale at the door." The title-page of this interesting production of twenty-eight pages reads :—

Unparalleled exhibition. / The fourteen / Ioway Indians / and their / interpreter, / just arrived from the upper Missouri, near / the Rocky mountains, North America. / "White Cloud," / the head chief of the tribe, is with this interesting / party, giving them that peculiar interest, which / no other party of American Indians have had in a / foreign country; and they are under the immediate / charge of / G. H. C. Melody, / who accompanied them from their country, / with their favorite interpreter, / Jeffrey Doraway. / Price sixpence.
London : / W. S. Johnson, "Nassau steam press," Nassau-street / Soho. / MDCCCXLIV.

The fourteen Indians forming the party were as follows :—*Chiefs :* (1) Mew-hu-she-kaw (White Cloud), first chief of the nation, in whom we recognise Mahaskah II.; (2) Neu-mon-ya (Walking Rain), third chief ; (3) Se-non-ty-yah (Blister Feet), great medicine man. *Warriors and Braves :* (4) Wash-ka-mon-ya (Fast Dancer); (5) Shon-ta-gi-ya (Little Wolf); (6) No-ho-mun-ya (One who gives no attention); (7) Wa-tan-ye (One always foremost); (8) Wa-ta-we-bu-ka-na (Commanding General), the son of Walking Rain, 10 years old. *Squaws :* (9) Ruton-ye-we-ma (Strutting Pigeon), White Cloud's wife ; (10) Ruton-we-me (Pigeon on the Wing); (11) Oke-we-me (Female Bear that walks on the back of another); (12) Koon-za-ya-me (Female War Eagle sailing); (13) Ta-pa-ta-me (Sophia), Wisdom, White Cloud's daughter ; (14) Corsair (a pappoose). See the accompanying figure from Catlin's drawing (p. 310).

In his sketch of the Iowa tribe, Catlin says : "This tribe lost two-thirds of its numbers a few years since, by the ravages of the smallpox ; and the remainder of them are now living under the authority of Mew-hu-she-kaw [Mahaskah], the White Cloud, the hereditary chief, and son of a famous chief of that name who died a few years since. This young man, only 32 [?] years of age, has by several humane and noble acts since he inherited the office, proved himself well worthy of it, and has thereby gained the love of all his tribe, and also the admiration of the President of the United States, who has granted him the unusual permission to make the journey to Europe, and to select such a party as he chose to bring with him ; and he, having chosen them according to merit, as warriors, has brought the aristocracy of the tribe. The stature of this man is about five feet ten inches, and he may generally be recognised in the group by his beautiful head-dress of war—eagles quills—necklace of grizzly bears' claws, and the skin of a white wolf hanging down over his back. [See No. 1 in accompanying figure, from Catlin's drawing.] His features are roman, with a benignant expression, but rather embarrassed, from a defect in one of his eyes."—(Pp. 5-6.)

Regarding the portrait of Mahaskah, Catlin speaks as follows in his *Notes of Eight Years' Travel and Residence in Europe* (Vol. II., pp. 2-3, 1848) : " White Cloud, the head chief of the tribe, was of the party [of ' fourteen Ioway Indians,'] and also the war-chief, Neu-mon-ya (the Walking Rain). These two chiefs, whose portraits were then hanging in my collection, had stood before me for their pictures several years previous in their own village, and also one of the warriors now present, whose name was Wash-ka-mon-ya (the Fast Dancer)."

Of the fourteen members of the party three never again saw their native land. The first to die was the infant Corsair, the son of Little Wolf, or Roman Nose, and Rutonyeweema. This baby, who was named

3   5   14   11   7   12   4   10   2   8   1   9   6

from an Ohio River boat on which the party had travelled, died just after the arrival of the Indians in Dundee, and was buried at Newcastle-on-Tyne. Little Wolf succumbed to an attack of pulmonary tuber-culosis in a Liverpool hospital; his wife died of the same disease in the Salle Valentino, Paris, and was buried in the cemetery of Montmartre (Catlin's *Notes*, II., pp. 170, 272).

While in Paris, Catlin was commissioned by Louis Philippe to copy several of his Indian portraits, including that of Mahaskah. On their completion they were presented to the King at an audience at the Tuileries. The portrait of Mahaskah from which this copy was made is not mentioned by Catlin in his *Illustrations of the Manners, etc.*, nor in his *Descriptive Catalogue* of 1840. We find it noted, however, in the *Catalogue Descriptive and Instructive of Catlin's Cartoons* (New York, 1871, p. 5), as " Mu-hú-she-kaw (The White Cloud); oldest son of the Chief, and heir apparent." In this case, as before, Notch-e-níng-a is given as the Chief, thus making Mahaskah his son; but this, as we have seen, is an error.

Respecting Mahaskah's defective eye, mentioned by Catlin, Fulton (*Red Men of Iowa*, p. 124, 1882) says:

" The second Ma-has-kah, who has been mentioned as the son of the beautiful but unfortunate Rant-che-wai-me, was at the time of the removal of the Iowas from their Iowa home [in 1836] the head chief of the tribe, holding that position by hereditary right. He seems to have inherited but few of the virtues of his great father or of his amiable mother. The son, whose name is sometimes given as Wi-e-wa-ha (defined also as meaning White Cloud), became dissipated and sottish, not remarkable for anything except his thirst for liquor. One of the results of his debaucheries was the loss of one of his eyes. At the age of thirty-six he was the husband of three wives."

8. See *Mahaskah*, note 7, p. 294, regarding the confusion of portraits in the Indian Gallery list.

9. As mentioned in the Introduction, King's studio and gallery were situated for many years on the east side of Twelfth Street, North-west, between E and F streets. As previously noted, King made a copy of each of these portraits for his own collection, and bequeathed them to the Redwood Library, Newport, Rhode Island. (See the Introduction, p. liv, Nos. 11 and 14.)

NESOUAQUOIT

(OR, THE BEAR IN THE FORKS OF A TREE)

NESOUAQUOIT, being interpreted, means, *The Bear in the forks of a tree*.[1] The portrait before the reader was taken at the city of Washington, in the winter of 1837, Nesouaquoit being, at that time, about forty years of age.[2] He is full six feet high, and in his proportions is a model of manly symmetry. He is a Fox Indian, and the son of the famous chief Chemakasee, or the Lance.[3] This chief is yet living, but being old and superannuated, has retired from the chieftainship of his band, having conferred upon his son, Nesouaquoit, all his authority and dignity.

In 1812, soon after the United States had declared war against Great Britain, the agents of that kingdom, then among us, sought to draw the band, of which Chemakasee was chief, into an alliance with them. A council was held, at which a proposal to this effect was formally made. Chemakasee answered, by saying, "We will not fight *for* the red coats, but we will fight *against* them." This laconic response being final, a strong excitement was produced, which threatened not only the peace, but the lives of Chemakasee's band. To relieve them from this perilous situation the United States Government directed that they should be removed to a place of security, and protected against both the British and their Indian allies. General Clark, being charged with this order, caused them to be removed to Fort Edwards, where they were kept, and fed, and clothed at the expense of the United States, till the termination of the war.[4] The band numbered then about four hundred souls.

After the war, Chemakasee, instead of returning to his former position, and renewing his relations with the Sauks and Foxes of the Mississippi, determined to avoid the one and decline the other—so he sought a country by ascending the Missouri, until, arriving at La Platte, he settled on that river, near the Black Snake Hills, where he continues to reside.[5]

In 1815, a treaty was concluded between this band and the United States, the third Article of which stipulates that a just proportion of the annuities, which a previous treaty had provided to be paid to the Sauk and Fox Indians, should be paid to the Foxes of La Platte.[6] By some strange oversight this provision of the treaty had been overlooked—unintentionally, no doubt, by the Government, whilst the age and infirmities of Chemakasee, it is presumed, caused him to forget it. An arrearage of twenty years had accumulated, when Nesouaquoit, having succeeded to the chieftainship of his band, resolved to ascertain why the Government had so long delayed to fulfil this stipulation. He first held a conference with the agent; but this officer had no power over the case. He then resolved to visit Washington, and plead the cause of his people before his "great father"; and, if he should fail there, to present it to Congress. But he had one great difficulty to overcome, and that was to raise the money to pay his expenses to Washington. To accomplish this he opened a negotiation with a Mr Risque, of St Louis, who agreed to pay his expenses to Washington and home again, for "*three boxes and a half of silver*"— equivalent to three thousand five hundred dollars. That he might be punctual in paying the loan, he ordered his hunters to collect furs and peltries of sufficient value, and have them ready for the St Louis market in time to redeem his pledge for the return of the money. This being done, he started upon his mission. Arriving at Washington, he explained the object of his visit. This he did in a firm and decided manner. The authorities recognised his claim, and he was assured that the provisions of the treaty in favour of his people, though so long overlooked, should be scrupulously fulfilled, and respected in future. Having attained the object of his mission he returned home, highly pleased with its result.

This chief is, perhaps, the only Indian of whom it can be said—*he never tasted a drop of spirituous liquor or smoked a pipe!* Of many thousands, and perhaps hundreds of thousands, it might be truly affirmed, that they never tasted a drop of spirituous liquor, but that was before this bane of the Indians had found its way into their country; but, with this single exception, we believe it can be said of no Indian—*he never smoked a pipe!*⁷ It is certainly remarkable that, in the present abundance of these aboriginal luxuries, Nesouaquoit should have the firmness to abstain from both.

His antipathy to whisky extends to those who sell it. He will not permit a whisky dealer to enter his country. Indeed, whenever a trader, not informed of the determined purpose of this chief to keep his people free from the ruinous effects of whisky, has strolled within his borders, he has been known to knock in the heads of his casks, and with the staves beat him out of his country. Though thus temperate, and free from the exciting influence of whisky and tobacco, Nesouaquoit is known to be as brave an Indian as ever made a moccasin track between the Missouri and Mississippi Rivers.

This chief has seven wives, who live as Indian wives generally do, in the most perfect harmony with each other. He is remarkable for his generosity, giving freely of what he has to all who need assistance.   To those who visit his lodge he is represented as being most courteous; and this exterior polish he carefully preserves in his intercourse with his people.   But his aversion to traders is perfect. He has long since formally interdicted marriage between them and the women of his band.   So stern is his resolution on this point, that no union of the kind has been known since he succeeded to the rank of chief.   In his deportment towards the whites he is most friendly, but he maintains his own rights with firmness and dignity.

NOTES

1. The name is interpreted by Dr William Jones, the leading authority on the Sauk and Fox Indians, to be strictly *Näsāwaʻkwatwᵃ*, meaning " He of the forked tree." This Indian belonged to the Bear gens of the Fox tribe.

2. The occasion of the visit was in furtherance of a project, initiated by Young Mahaskah earlier in 1827, having in view the adjustment of the relative claims of the Iowa, the Sauk and Fox, and other tribes, under the treaty of 1825 (see *Young Mahaskah*, note 2).   The various delegations to Washington at this time—the autumn of 1837—consisted of seventy-four Indians of various tribes, which met in council during several days, and on October 5th were heard by the Secretary of War. The Sauk and Fox party alone numbered twenty-six males, four females, and four children, who reached Washington, October 1, under the charge of Agent Joseph M. Street.   In addition there were four Sauk and Foxes under Major Pilcher, agent for the Upper Missouri tribes, who reached Washington earlier.   The celebrated Keokuk and Black Hawk were members of the party.   It is probably because there were more famous Indians in Washington at this time than one artist could paint, that Cooke's services were brought into requisition, as several portraits were made by him in 1837.   It was evidently believed at first that the Indians would not submit to sitting for their portraits.   Says the *National Intelligencer* for September 29, 1837 :

" We are sorry to learn that the Indian Chiefs in the city have, under some superstitious impression, declined to sit for their portraits.   Thus it is to be feared that an excellent opportunity will be lost of adding to the valuable stock of Indian portraits now in possession of the Department."

On completing their business at the seat of Government, which resulted in the treaty of October 21, 1837, the Sauk and Foxes made a tour of the northern cities, receiving especial attention in Boston.

Although painted by King, the portrait of Nesouaquoit does not appear in the Rhees list of the Indian Gallery collection. The original, however, still exists, and recently at least (in 1907), was in possession of Mr George D. Smith, a bookseller of 50 New Street, New York City, who listed it at $600.00. Mr Smith catalogues it as "the original portrait of the chieftain of the Fox tribe, framed, and numbered 'No. 51,' 30 by 25 inches, painted in oil colors by Charles Bird King for the folio edition of McKenney and Hall's *History of the Indian Tribes of North America*. . . . This is the famous original of one of the first portraits in McKenney and Hall's invaluable work. . . . The present portrait has been considered his masterpiece. It has been preserved with the utmost care through all the years which have passed since 'NE-SOU-A-QUOIT' sat for it in Washington in the winter of 1837, and is to-day in the original frame and in unusually fine condition. The reproduction in the *History of the Indian Tribes of North America*, although an excellent piece of work, inadequately represents this notable painting, which has always been regarded as the most remarkable example of Indian portraiture now extant."

Mr Smith's statement that the portrait was painted by King expressly for McKenney and Hall's work would seem to have some foundation in fact, inasmuch as it does not appear in the Rhees list, nor is it noted in the list of Inman copies in the Peabody Museum. Another portrait of this chief, by King, is in the Redwood Library, Newport, Rhode Island, representing the subject seated, with a metal tomahawk in his left hand, blade uppermost, his right hand resting on his knee; medal, beaded necklace, earrings, and belt; leggings and moccasins, but without the fur cape and feathers shown in the accompanying portrait. The face and arms are striped with paint, and the head-dress is much the same in both portraits, but the scalp feather in the Redwood Library picture points to the Indian's left instead of the right.

Nesouaquoit signed the following treaties:—St Louis, May 13, 1816 (as "Nasawarku, or the Forks"); Fort Armstrong, February 3, 1822 (as "Nasowakee" ?); Prairie du Chien, August 19, 1825 (as "Nausa-wa-quot, the bear that sleeps on the forks"); Prairie du Chien, July 15, 1830 (as "Mussaw-wawquott"); Fort Armstrong, September 21, 1832 (as "Me-shee-wau-quaw, or the dried tree"); Fort Leavenworth, September 17, 1836 (as "Ne-sa-au-qua, bear"); near Dubuque, September 27, 1836 (as "Au-sa-wa-kuk"); near Dubuque, September 28, 1836 (as "A-sho-wa-huk"). It is interesting to note that he did not sign either of the Washington treaties with the two bands of Sauk and Foxes, concluded October 21, 1837, although a member of the delegation. The treaty of Washington, May 18, 1854, is signed by

NE-SOU-A-QUOIT
A Fox Chief

"Ne-son-quoit, or Bear," and that of Great Nemaha agency, Nebraska, March 6, 1861, by "Ne-sour-quoit." By provision of this last treaty, Nesouaquoit was granted in fee-simple a tract of 160 acres.

3. His name is properly *Shĕmakasi*ᵃ, "He of the little lance," according to Dr Jones.

4. Fort Edwards "was on the east side of the Mississippi, three miles below the foot of the rapids, and directly opposite the two islands which divided the outlet of the Des Moines into three channels. Half a mile south-west of the fort was Cantonment Davis, its precursor, abandoned when the works were completed. The locality is practically Warsaw, in Hancock County, Illinois. A full description of this establishment as it was at the time of Long's visit in August 1817 is given in his report, as given in *Minn. Hist. Coll.*, II., part 1, 1860, 2nd ed., 1890, pp. 77-80. It had been building since June 1816, and was not quite finished in 1817" (Coues, *Exped. Zebulon Montgomery Pike*, I., 14. New York, 1895). It occupied a bluff some 80 or 100 feet above the level of the river (McKenney, *Memoirs*, I., 1846; see also letter of Hooper Warren, dated Galena, August 16, 1829, in "The Edwards Papers," *Chicago Historical Society's Collections*, III., p. 425, Chicago, 1884). The fort was named in honour of Ninian Edwards, first Governor of Illinois, after whom Edwardsville and Edwards County also were named.

5. This was the treaty negotiated at Portage des Sioux, Missouri, September 13, 1815, with the "Sacs of the Missouri." The third Article provided that "the United States on their part promise to allow the said Sacs of the Missouri River, all the rights and privileges secured to them by the treaty of St Louis before mentioned, and also, as soon as practicable, to furnish them with a just proportion of the annuities stipulated to be paid by that treaty, provided they shall continue to comply with this and their former treaty." The previous treaty referred to was that concluded at St Louis, November 3, 1804, General William Henry Harrison being the treaty commissioner. Under this treaty the United States agreed to pay an annuity of $1000 in goods, $600 of which was for the Sauk and $400 for the Foxes, the value to be based on the first cost of the goods. The former treaty was signed by Chemakasee, under the form "Shamaga, the lance."

6. The Black Snake Hills country is the immediate neighbourhood of the present St Joseph, Missouri, on the east side of the Missouri River. Here was situated Joseph Robidoux's trading post, established in 1826, which became the centre of the Iowa Indian trade, and formed the nucleus of the town of St Joseph, incorporated in 1845, the name being adapted from the Christian name of Robidoux. This north-western corner of Missouri was ceded to the United States by treaty of Prairie du Chien, Wisconsin, July 15, 1830.

7. This, of course, does not apply to the Indians of the South-West, who smoked cigarettes instead of pipes, and, like Indians generally, usually for ceremonial purposes rather than for pleasure.

MOANAHONGA

(OR, GREAT WALKER)

MOANAHONGA, which signifies *Great Walker*, was an Iowa brave. This name was conferred upon him, not for his having performed any great feat as a walker against time, as in the case of the Sioux Killer, but on account of his great muscular strength, which enabled him to endure the toils of the chase, and to lead war parties over a vast extent of country, without appearing to be fatigued. This brave, like the Sioux Killer, was called by another name, by which he was more generally known, viz., *Big Neck*; and he was also known by the name of Winaugusconey, or *The man who is not afraid to travel*; the meaning of which is, that he would traverse large tracts of country alone, utterly reckless of danger, relying for protection and defence upon his courage and great physical strength, both of which he possessed in an extraordinary degree.

Moanahonga was of a morose and sour disposition; the result, doubtless, of his having been the descendant of obscure parents, which circumstance much impeded his advancement to the higher honours to which his bravery, skill, and talents entitled him. He was emulous of glory, but found himself always held in check by the lowness of his origin. There was nothing which he valued so highly as the honours and dignity of a chieftain, and to this elevation he constantly aspired; seeking ardently, by daring

318

exploits, to challenge the admiration of his nation, and in the midst of some blaze of glory, to extinguish all recollection of the meanness of his descent. As was natural, under such circumstances, he was envious of distinction in others; and the more exalted the incumbent the more he disliked him. He even avoided those who were in command, because of his aversion to being the subordinate of any; and acting under the influence of this feeling, he would separate himself from his band and people, build a lodge of his own, and, taking with him as many as had been won over to him by his bravery, exercise the authority of their chief.

This brave was one of a party led by General Clark to Washington, in 1824, at which time he united with Mahaskah in concluding a treaty, by which they ceded all their lands lying within the State of Missouri, amounting to some millions of acres, for the remuneration of five hundred dollars per annum, for ten years, in connection with some other paltry considerations.[1] It appears he did not comprehend the import of the treaty; and, on his return to his country, finding it over-run with the whites, who had taken possession of the ground that covered the bones of his ancestors, he is said to have become greatly affected. He sought relief, but was told the treaty was made, and that he and Mahaskah had sold the country. He continued to endure this state of things until 1829, when, unable to sustain it any longer, he determined to go to St Louis, and state his grievances to General Clark. On his way thither, he encamped on the borders of the river Chariton, his party consisting of about sixty persons. While there, resting his comrades from the fatigues of their march, a party of whites came up, having with them some kegs of whisky. It was not long before the Indians were completely besotted, when the whites plundered them of their blankets and horses, and whatever else was of value, and retired.   Recovering from their debauch, the Indians felt how dearly they had paid for the whisky with which the whites had regaled them, and being hungry, one of the young men shot a hog.   Big Neck rebuked him, saying, "That is wrong; it is true, we are poor, and have been robbed, but the hog was not ours, and you ought not to have shot it."

It was soon rumoured along the borders that the Indians were destroying the property of the settlers, and the dead hog was brought in evidence to prove the charge; whereupon a company of about sixty white men was raised, and marched to the Indian camp.   They ordered Big Neck to leave the country instantly, adding, if he delayed they would drive him out of it with their guns. Big Neck thought it prudent to retire, and leaving his encampment he went fifteen miles higher up into the country, to a point which he believed was beyond the boundary of the State.   While there, this same party, having pursued them, arrived.   Seeing them coming, and not suspecting that there was now any cause of quarrel, Big Neck stepped from his lodge unarmed, with his pipe in his mouth, and his hand extended towards the leader of the party, in token of friendship.   The pipe is a sacred thing; and is, among most of the Indian tribes, the emblem of peace; nor have they ever been known to permit any outrage to be committed upon a man who advances towards another with this symbol of peace in his mouth. While in the act of reaching his hand to the leader of the party, and as the Indians came out of their lodges to see the cavalcade of white men, they were fired upon.   One child was killed, as was also the brother of Big Neck, who fell at his side.   Enraged by this assault, the Indians flew to their arms, their number of fighting men being about thirty; and against such fearful odds, Big Neck, supported by Maushemone, or the Big Flying Cloud, resolved to contend. The white man who had shot the child was killed on the spot. Big Neck shot James Myers, the leader of the party, in the thigh; at about the same moment, a white man, named Win, shot a squaw, sister of Big Neck; as she fell, she exclaimed, "Brother! I am going to die innocent—avenge my blood!" She had scarcely spoken, when an Indian, sometimes called Ioway Jim, and at others, Major Ketcher, levelled his rifle and discharged its contents into Win's thigh, fracturing the bone. A furious fight ensued, in which the whites were defeated, and driven from the ground.

Win, being unable to escape, was found on the battle ground by his exasperated enemies, who immediately prepared to burn their victim. A pile was raised around him and fired. As the flames began to encircle him, Big Neck, pointing to the dead and wounded, thus addressed the murderer of his people :—

"See there! look! You have killed all that was dear to me—my brother, my brother's wife, and her child. See the blood—it flows before you. Look at that woman; her arm was never raised against an American; the child never wronged you—it was innocent; they have gone to the Great Spirit. I came to meet you with the pipe of peace in my mouth. I did you no wrong; you fired upon me, and see what you have done—see my own wife with her head bleeding; though not dead, she is wounded. Now listen— you are not a *brave*, you are a *dog*. If you were a *brave*, I would treat you as a *brave*, but as you are a *dog*, I will treat you as a *dog!* "

Here Big Neck paused, listened to the crackling of the faggots, and with his knife drawn, eyed his victim for a moment, when, as the flames burst forth, and were approaching the body, he sprang over them, scalped the fated Win, and, while yet alive, cut open his breast, tore out his heart, bit off a piece of it, then throwing it back into the flames, it was consumed with the body.

The tidings of this affair soon reached the settlements; everywhere it was proclaimed, "The Indians are killing the whites!" Most of the border settlers abandoned their homes. An order was issued from Jefferson Barracks, to the officer in command at Fort Leavenworth, to march forthwith against the Indians. A large detachment of United States infantry was sent from Missouri in a steamboat, whilst the Governor ordered out the militia. The agent of the Iowas, General Hughes,[2] was required to co-operate. The militia were marched direct to the battle ground, and thence back again, having accomplished nothing. The first step taken by the agent was to deliver eleven of the principal men of the Iowa nation as hostages for the good conduct of that people. With these, General Leavenworth returned with his command to St Louis. The agent then proceeded with four men to the battle ground; taking the trail from thence, he pursued Big Neck and his party to the Upper Mississippi, and to the waters of the lower Iowa River, a distance but little, if any, short of four hundred miles. Here he fell in with Taimah, or The Bear Whose Screams Make the Rocks Tremble,[3] and his son, Apanuse,[4] who were on the Polecat River, near Fort Madison.[5] From Taimah and his son he learned where Big Neck was encamped, and was accompanied to the spot by a party of Sauks and Foxes. Caution became necessary; and as they approached Big Neck's party, they lay concealed in the day, and advanced upon it only in the night. Just before day, having had the camp in view the previous evening, when all was still, the agent approached, and stepped quickly into Big Neck's lodge. Here he was safe; for, in accordance with the Indian practice, no outrage is ever permitted upon any person, though an enemy, who takes refuge within a lodge; no blood is allowed to stain the ground within its precincts. Big Neck was just in the act of raising himself from his buffalo skin, as the agent entered his lodge. The object of the visit was explained. But few words were spoken, when Big Neck said : " I'll go with you; a brave man dies but once—cowards are always dying." Whereupon he surrendered himself and his party. They were marched to the Rapide Des Moines.[6] On arriving there, Big Neck ordered his squaws to return. The agent at once interpreted the object, and turning to his four men, said : " Get your guns ready, for Big Neck means to kill us." The squaws ascended the hill that rises from the margin of the river at that place, and were clustering about its summit; and just as they were turning to witness the murder of the agent and his four men, a point which makes out into the river was suddenly turned by the advance of a little fleet of five boats, filled with United States troops, under the command of Lieutenant Morris. The squaws, seeing this, rushed suddenly down the hill, with howls and cries, and throwing themselves at the agent's feet, begged for their lives. The inference was, that they supposed the plot for the destruction of the agent and his companions had been discovered, and that the Indians would be made to atone for it with their lives. A moment longer, and the agent and his men would have been slain. This was one of those rare and timely interpositions that can be resolved into nothing short of the agency of Providence.

Eleven of the principal Indians, including Big Neck, were transferred to these boats and conveyed to St Louis, whilst the residue, in charge of one of General Hughes's men, were sent across the country in the direction of their homes. Arriving at St Louis, arrangements were made for the trial of the prisoners on a charge of murder, which it was alleged had been committed in Randolph County.[7] The trial was then ordered to take place in that County, whither the prisoners were conveyed. The jury, without leaving their box, brought in a verdict of *Not guilty.*

Big Neck, being now on friendly terms with the agent, agreed to accompany him to his village. He was in deep distress, and went into mourning, by blacking his face, nor did he ever remove this symbol of grief to the day of his death. He was asked his reason for this. He answered, "I am ashamed to look upon the sun. I have insulted the Great Spirit by selling the bones of my fathers—it is right that I should mourn."

About five years after his trial, Big Neck lead a war party of about fifty men in pursuit of a party of Sioux, who had penetrated the country to his village and stolen nine of his horses. He took with him in this expedition a famous brave, called Pekeinga, or the Little Star.[8] The party soon came within sight of the Sioux, who fled, throwing behind them their leggings and moccasins, and dried buffalo meat, which indicated their defeat. Big Neck, however, was resolved on punishing them, and ordered his men to charge. The Sioux had taken refuge in a large hazel thicket, above which towered trees thick set with foliage, into two of which two Sioux, one a chief, had climbed. Each of these Sioux selected his man, one of them Big Neck, the other the Little Star, and as the party rushed into the thicket they both fired—Big Neck was shot through the breast; the Little Star fell dead from his horse. Seeing them fall, the two Sioux sprang from the trees to take their scalps. The Sioux chief, who had shot Big Neck, hastened to his body, and while in the act of taking his scalp, the dying savage drew his knife with one hand, and with the other grasped the Sioux, brought him in contact with him, threw

MOA-NA-HON-GA, *or* **GREAT WALKER**
An Iowa Chief

him, and then, with his remaining strength, fell upon the body of the Sioux, and stabbed and scalped him. When they were found, that was their position—the Sioux on the ground, and Big Neck lying across his dead body, with his scalp dripping with blood in one hand, and his knife firmly grasped in the other.

On witnessing this spectacle, both parties retired from the fight, each deeply deploring the death of their favourite chief; and interpreting so great a calamity unto the anger of the Great Spirit, they made peace, and remain friends to this day.

NOTES

1. This treaty of August 4, 1824, purported to cede lands that had already passed into the possession of the Government by treaty with the Osage tribe, November 10, 1808.

It was during the visit to Washington in 1824 that Moanahonga's portrait was painted by King. See the Rhees list in the Introduction, p. 1, No. 88, where the name appears as "Man-ne-hah-na, Great Walker." This was one of the portraits copied by King and bequeathed by him to the Redwood Library (Introduction, p. liii, No. 5). It does not appear by name in the list of Inman copies in the Peabody Museum.

Moanahonga signed the treaties of Portage des Sioux, Missouri, September 16, 1815 (as "Manuhanu, the great walker"), and Washington, August 4, 1824 (as "Mah-ne-hah-nah, Great Walker"). McKenney was a witness to this treaty, and Mahaskah was the only other signer in behalf of the tribe. Neither the next treaty, concluded at Prairie du Chien, August 19, 1825, nor the treaty made at the same place, July 15, 1830, was signed by Moanahonga, whose death occurred about 1834.

2. See *Young Mahaskah,* note 5, p. 308.

3. See *Taiomah* in Vol. II.

4. See *Appanoose* in Vol. II.

5. Now Skunk River, which enters the Mississippi between Fort Madison and Burlington, south-eastern Iowa.

6. That is, to the vicinity of the present Keokuk, Iowa.

7. In central Missouri. Chariton River now forms the boundary of its north-western corner.

8. He signed as "Pie-kan-ha-igne, the little star," the treaty of Prairie du Chien, July 15, 1830. The circumstance here narrated occurred about 1834.

SHAUHAUNAPOTINIA

(OR, THE MAN WHO KILLED THREE SIOUX)

THE import of the name is, *The man who killed three Sioux*. Why he is so called will appear in the sequel. He is also called Moanahonga, which means *Great Walker*. Shauhaunapotinia is an Iowa, and was, when his likeness was taken in 1837, twenty-one years of age.[1]

It is customary among the Iowas for boys, when they arrive at the age of eight or ten years, to select companions of about the same age. A companionship thus formed ripens into a union which nothing but death is ever permitted to dissolve. The parties become inseparable; are seen together in their sports, and in riper years in the chase; and, when in battle, they are side by side. Their most confidential secrets are told without reserve to each other, and are afterwards treated as if confined but to one breast.[2] Shauhaunapotinia had formed a fellowship of this abiding sort with an Iowa boy, which lasted till his companion had reached his nineteenth, and himself his eighteenth year, when the Sioux destroyed this endearing relationship by killing Shauhaunapotinia's companion. This occurrence took place about one hundred miles from the nearest Sioux village. The moment the tidings of his friend's death reached Shauhaunapotinia, he resolved on revenge. He went into mourning by blacking his face, and secretly left his village and sought the enemy. Coming upon the Sioux in their encampment, of about four hundred lodges, he rushed in among them like a maniac, and with his knife stabbed a brave, whom he instantly scalped; then rushing from the encampment in the direction of his village, he fell in with, and killed and scalped two squaws, bringing to his home three scalps; and all this was the work of twenty-four hours, the distance travelled in that time being one hundred miles! Hence his name—the Sioux Killer, because of his success in killing and scalping three Sioux—and the Great Walker, because of his having travelled over such an extent of country in so short a time.

On reaching his village he made known where he had been, and what was his object, and showed the scalps in testimony of his triumph. On hearing the statement, and seeing his trophies, the chiefs and braves of his nation immediately bound round his legs, just below his knees, skins of the polecat, these being the insignia of bravery. Young Mahaskah immediately adopted him as his friend, companion, and counsellor; hence his presence with him recently at Washington City.[3] To his bravery Shauhaunapotinia added the qualities of a wit, and is represented as having no equal in the nation. His waggeries are so numerous, and so diversified, as to leave him master of all the circles of fun and frolic in which he mingles.

Shauhaunapotinia, when he joined Mahaskah, was destined, for the first time in his life, to see and be among white people. On arriving at Liberty, Clay County, Missouri, he gave signs of great uneasiness. On one occasion he came running to the agent in great trepidation, without his blanket, saying, "Father, these white people are fools." "Why do you call them fools?" asked the agent. "Why," replied the Sioux Killer, "they make their fires in the wrong part of their wigwams ; why don't they make them as we do, in the middle ? I am almost frozen. And that," he continued, " is not all; the white people look at me; maybe they want to kill me. I want to go home." The agent explained to him that the fire was built where all white people build it, at one end of their wigwam; and assuring him that the whites were only curious, and had no unkind intentions towards him, he became reconciled, and agreed to proceed. He gave signs, however, of affliction, by blacking his face, and sitting quietly by himself in some lone place for two days.

We have in this anecdote an illustration of the truth, that before the mind can bring itself to stand unappalled before danger, it must become accustomed to it; and not only to danger in the abstract, but to its variety, and under all its forms. Now, here was an Indian who, to revenge the death of his friend, could travel alone and undismayed, a hundred miles into the enemy's country, rush into an encampment of four hundred lodges, strike down a brave and scalp him, and return, killing two other Indians by the way; and yet, when placed in a new country, amidst other than his forest scenes, and among a people of another colour, of whom he knew nothing, he was made to tremble and be afraid at a look! The same knowledge of the white man, the same acquaintance with his habits and mode of warfare, and especially the opportunity of measuring arms with him in a fight or two, would have elevated this Indian's courage to an equal height to which it proved itself capable of rising when he made that desperate attack upon the Sioux in their own encampment. Some writer, we remember, in speaking of the fearless character of the British seamen,

SHAU-HAU-NAPO-TINIA
An Iowa Chief

says, "Brave, because bred amidst dangers—great, because accustomed to the dimensions of the world." It is highly probable, that were a seaman taken from the bravest of the brave, and conveyed away from the ship, with whose strength and power he had become familiar, and placed in a wilderness among savages, he would shrink from their scrutiny, and realise a depression in the scale of his courage as did the Sioux Killer when removed from the theatre of his victories, and conveyed among a people who were new to him, and of whom he knew nothing.

NOTES

1. His portrait does not appear by name in the Rhees *Catalogue* of the Indian Gallery collection, but that it was painted by King is known from the list of Inman copies in the Peabody Museum, in which the name is recorded as "Shau-hau-napo-tinia, Great Walker" (original number, 82; catalogue number, 28. 209). See *Mahaskah*, note 4, p. 293, and *Young Mahaskah*, note 6, p. 308.

2. Such friendship, which calls to mind the fidelity of the Pythagorean Damon and Pythias, are not uncommon among the Siouan tribes, of which the Iowa are one. Riggs (*Dakota Grammar, Texts, and Ethnography*, 196, 1893) thus speaks of it: "One of the customs of the olden time, which was potent both for good and for evil, and which is going into desuetude, was that of fellowhood. Scarcely a Dakota young man could be found who had not some special friend or *koda*. This was an arrangement of giving themselves to each other, of the David and Jonathan kind. They exchanged bows, or guns, or blankets—sometimes the entire equipment. In rare cases they exchanged wives. What one asked of the other he gave him; nothing could be denied. This arrangement was often a real affection, sometimes fading out as the years pass by, but often lasting to old age."

3. That is, in the winter of 1836-37.

TAHCHEE

(OR, DUTCH)

TAHCHEE is the Cherokee word for *Dutch*. How the
individual before us acquired this name we are not informed, except that he obtained it in his infancy from his
own people. In process of time, as its import became
known, it was translated into the word *Dutch*, by which
he is most usually called.[1] He was born about the year
1790, at Turkey Town,[2] on the Coosa River, in a district of
country then composed of the wild lands of the United
States, but now included in the State of Alabama, and
was forty-seven years of age when his portrait was taken.
The picture is an admirable likeness.[3] Tahchee is five
feet eleven inches high, of admirable proportions, flexible
and graceful in his movements, and possesses great
muscular power and activity; while his countenance expresses a coolness, courage, and decision, which accord
well with his distinguished reputation as a warrior.

He is the third of the four sons of Skyugo, a famous
Cherokee chief, and had thus, by inheritance, a claim to
rank which is always respected among the Indians, when
supported by merit. At an early age, in company with
his mother, and an uncle who was called Thomas Taylor,
he emigrated to the St Francis River in Arkansas; but as
his family was among the first of those who were induced,
by the encroachment of the whites, to remove to the west

of the Mississippi, and his own age not more than five years, he retains but a faint recollection of the exodus.[4] The country in which they sought a refuge was a wilderness into which the white man had not intruded—a broad and fertile land, where extensive prairies alternating with luxuriant forests, afforded shelter and pasturage to vast numbers of the animals most eagerly sought by the hunter. The young Tahchee was early initiated in the arts and perils of the chase. He remembers when he first went forth, a slender but ardent boy, in search of game, that his uncle prepared a gun, by cutting off part of the barrel, so as to render it portable and easily managed in the hands of the young hunter. Thus early is the native of the forest trained to these arts of woodcraft, and taught to face the dangers of the wild, and the extremities of the weather; and it is through the means of such culture that he becomes so expert in all that relates to hunting and border warfare, and so indifferent to every other occupation or amusement.

For the first three years his exertions were confined to the immediate neighbourhood of his residence; but at the end of that period he was permitted to accompany a regular hunting party upon one of those long expeditions so common among the American tribes, and which indeed occupy the greater portion of the lives of those among them who are active and ambitious. He was absent a year, following the game from place to place, roaming over an immense region of wilderness, and enduring all the vicissitudes attendant upon long journeys, the succession of the seasons, and the ever-varying incidents of the chase. Those who have hunted only for sport, can form but a faint conception of the almost incredible dangers and fatigues endured by the Indians in these protracted wanderings, during which they travel to distant regions, often meet, and more often cunningly elude their enemies, and suffer the most wonderful privations. Their lives are a continuous succession of feasting and starvation, of exertion and sleep, of excitement, intense anxiety, and despondency, through all which they pass without becoming weary of the savage life, or learning in the hard school of experience the wisdom which would teach them to imitate the examples of the ant and the bee, by making provision for the winter during the season of harvest.

On the return of Tahchee, after this long absence, he reached home late at night, and knocked at the door of his mother's cabin, who, supposing it to be some drunken Indian, called out to him angrily to go away, as she had no whisky to give him. Dutch, who, like a true Indian, would rather effect his object by indirection, than by any open procedure, went round the maternal mansion, which was but a flimsy fabric of logs, whose weak points were well known to him, and attempted to enter at a window, but was met by his amiable parent, who stood prepared to defend her castle against the unknown intruder, armed with a tough and well-seasoned stick, with which she was wont to stir her hominy. He was, of course, compelled to retreat, but soon after succeeded in effecting, at some other point, a practicable breach, by which he entered, and was immediately recognised and cordially welcomed by his mother.

After remaining at home but three months, he accompanied another party composed of about fifteen hunters, to the Red River, who, being unsuccessful, soon returned. During their absence, another party of Cherokees were attacked upon White River by the Osages, who killed several, and took one prisoner—a cousin of Tahchee being among the slain. The tidings of this insult incited the Cherokees to immediate measures of retaliation, and a

TAH-CHEE, *or* DUTCH
A Cherokee Chief

war party was raised, consisting of thirty-two individuals,
headed by Cahtateeskee, or the Dirt Seller. Though but
a mere boy, Dutch was permitted to join the expedition,
probably in virtue of his consanguinity to one of the slain;
but, as is customary on such occasions, the burthen of
carrying the kettles and other baggage fell to his lot, for
the Indian warrior never condescends to perform any
labour that can be shifted off upon the less dignified
shoulders of a youthful or feminine companion. At their
first encampment, the Dirt Seller, who was his uncle,
raised him to the station of a warrior, by a ceremony,
which, however simple, was doubtless as highly prized by
the young Cherokee as was the honour of knighthood by
our scarcely less barbarous ancestors. The leader of the
hostile band, having cut a stick, and fashioned it with his
knife into the form of a war-club, presented it to his
promising relative with these words: "I present this
to you; if you are *a Brave*, and can use it in battle, keep
it; if you fail in making it, as a warrior should, effective
upon the living, then, as a boy, strike with it the bodies of
the dead!" Tahchee received this interesting token of his
uncle's regard with becoming reverence, and used it on
subsequent occasions in a manner which reflected no disgrace upon his worthy family. They shortly after came upon
an encampment of the enemy, in the night, which they
surprised, and attacked just before daybreak. Tahchee,
fired with zeal and incited by the recent admonition of his
uncle to prove his manhood, slew two of the enemy with
his war-club, and secured the customary evidence of savage
prowess by taking their scalps. The Osages were defeated
with the loss of sixteen of their warriors, who were killed
and scalped, while not a man was killed on the side of the
Cherokees. The only blood drawn from our young hero
was by a wound from his own knife while in the act of

performing, for the first time, the operation of scalping a
fallen enemy.   His daring and successful conduct gained
him great renown, and when, on the return of the party,
the scalp dance was celebrated, with the usual ceremonies,
the honour of being recognised as a warrior was unanimously
conceded to the youthful Tahchee.   His subsequent career
has amply fulfilled the promise thus early indicated, and
a long series of warlike exploits has conclusively proved
that both his skill and courage are of the highest order.

An active war between the Osages and Cherokees
succeeded the events which we have noticed : excursions
and inroads were made on both sides during two or three
years, and many hard battles were fought in which both
were alternately victorious ; but although Tahchee served
actively throughout the whole war, no party to which he
was attached was ever defeated or lost a man, nor was he
wounded.

After a vindictive and harassing war, a peace was at
length concluded, which was happily so well cemented
that Tahchee and a friend, being on a hunting expedition,
wandered into the Osage country, and were so well
received that they remained among their former enemies
for fourteen months, during which time Tahchee learned
to speak the Osage language, and, by conforming with the
habits of that tribe, gained their esteem, and became
identified with them in manners and feeling.   He joined
one of their war parties in an expedition against the
Pawnees, but returned without having met with an
enemy.

During his residence among the Osages, he, of course,
engaged with them in hunting as well as in war.   On one
occasion, being on a hunt with a large party, their provisions became scarce, and a few of the most active young
men were selected to go out and kill buffaloes.   He was

asked if he could shoot the buffalo with an arrow; for, as the Cherokees inhabit a wooded country, where these animals are not so abundant as upon the prairies over which the Osages roam, and where the practice of chasing them on horseback is not common, he was not supposed to be expert in this species of hunting. He, however, replied confidently that he thought he could do anything that could be done by their own young men, and was accordingly joined to the number. Each of the hunters was furnished, at his departure, with a certain number of arrows, and was expected, on his return, to account for the whole, and especially to assign a sufficient excuse for the loss of any that might be missing. They set out on horseback, completely equipped for the hardy and exciting sport, and succeeded in finding a herd grazing upon the plain. Having cautiously approached, without alarming the game, until they were sufficiently near for the onset, the finest animals were selected, and the hunters dashed in among them. The affrighted herd fled, and the hunters, each marking out his victim and pursuing at full speed, pressed forward until the superior fleetness of the horse brought him abreast of the buffalo, when the hunter, who had previously dropped the reins, and guided his steed by a well-understood pressure of the heel in either flank, discharged his arrow with an aim which seldom erred, and with a force so great as to bury the missile in the body of the huge creature. Several of the herd were killed, but our friend Dutch was unsuccessful, in consequence of the provoking interference of a large bull, which several times, as he was on the point of discharging an arrow, prevented him from doing so by crossing his path, or interposing his unwieldy body between the hunter and his prey. Incensed at having his object thus frustrated, he discharged an arrow at the bull, which penetrated the shoulder of the animal, but without inflicting a wound severe enough to prevent the latter from escaping with the shaft. On the return of the party, Tahchee was reprimanded for having lost an arrow, and threatened with corporal punishment, it being customary in that nation to whip the young men when they lose or throw away their arrows. He excused himself by saying that he was ignorant of their customs and unaware of the impropriety of throwing an arrow at random. Upon this, Claymore, a distinguished chief, interfered, and by his own authority forbade the punishment.

He returned again to his people, and in the succeeding autumn set out upon a long hunt with no other companion than three dogs. He ascended the Arkansas River in a canoe to the mouth of the Neosho,[5] and then pushed his little bark up the latter as far as there was sufficient water for this kind of navigation, and, being unable to proceed further by water, he abandoned his canoe and travelled on foot across a region of prairies, several hundred miles, to the Missouri River. Here he employed himself in hunting and trapping until he secured ninety beaver skins, with which he returned to the spot at which he had left his canoe. On his return home he stopped at an Osage village on the margin of the Neosho, where he learned that a celebrated Cherokee chief and warrior named Chata, who had made the former peace with the Osages, had been killed by them while hunting in company with Bowles, who afterwards led a party of Cherokees into Texas and formed a settlement.[6] Three other Cherokees of another party had been killed, and as retaliation was expected to ensue, as a matter of course, a war between the tribes was inevitable. Dutch was therefore admonished that his life was in danger, and having been kindly supplied with moccasins and parched corn, was requested to depart.

In this little history we see a curious, though a common picture, of savage life. An individual betakes himself alone to the forest to spend months in wandering and hunting. Day after day he pushes his little canoe against the current of a long river until he has traced its meanders nearly to the fountain-head, leaving the ordinary hunting grounds of his people hundreds of miles in the rear, touching warily at the villages of tribes known to be friendly, and passing by stealth those at which he might encounter an enemy. When the stream affords him no longer a practicable highway, he hides his canoe in the grass or bushes, and bends his solitary way, across immense plains, in search of some secluded spot, where, undisturbed by any intruder, he may pursue the occupation of the hunter. Returning, loaded with the spoils of the chase, he must again trace his long, and weary, and solitary route through the haunts of open foes and faithless friends, uncertain who to trust, or what changes the revolution of several months may have effected in the relations of his tribe. And he reaches his home at last, after a series of almost incredible dangers and hardships, with the acquisition of a few skins, which are exchanged for a bottle of whisky, and a supply of gunpowder, and, having enjoyed a brief revel, and a long rest, is driven forth again by necessity, or the love of a vagrant life, to encounter a repetition of the same savage vicissitudes.

Soon after the return of Tahchee, a Cherokee woman was killed by the Osages, and being the daughter of an aged female who had no male relatives to revenge the murder, the bereaved mother came to him in deep distress, and, with tears in her eyes, besought him to become the avenger of the injury. He complied with the request, and, having raised a war party, led them against the enemy, nor did he return without bringing with him a sufficient number of bloody trophies to satisfy the mourning relatives of the deceased.

After a brief but active war, peace was again established between the belligerent parties—if that can be called a peace which may be interrupted by the bad passions of any individual who may choose to gratify his propensity for stealing horses, or shedding human blood, regardless of the vengeance which is sure to follow, and of the war into which his misconduct is certain to plunge his tribe.

The treaty made by the United States with the Cherokees, in the year 1828,[7] gave great dissatisfaction to many of that tribe, and was so offensive to Tahchee that he determined to abandon the country.

On this occasion, our friend Dutch removed to Red River, where he resided three years, when he emigrated to Bowles's settlement in Texas. A year afterwards he went with a war party against the Tawakanaks, of whom fifty-five were killed and their village destroyed, while but five of Tahchee's party were slain.[8] He next returned to Red River, on whose banks, near the junction of the Kiamiska,[9] he lived three years, continuing to make war upon the Osages. The Government of the United States having, in various treaties with the Indian tribes, stipulated that they should live in peace, and having undertaken to interpose their authority, if necessary, for the preservation of harmony, had forbidden this war between the Cherokees and Osages, and as Tahchee was now an active partisan leader, he was admonished to discontinue his predatory career. Persevering in a course of inveterate hostility, when most of the leaders of his tribe had consented to a peace, the commanding officer of the American army for that district offered a reward of five hundred dollars for his capture.

Intelligence of this offer was conveyed to Tahchee by some of his friends, who sought to prevail on him to fly; but it served only to make him more desperate. To show his utter contempt of this mode of securing his capture, he started in the direction of the fort, and, approaching a trading-house near the mouth of the Neosho[10] at which were some Osages, he sprang in among them, and, within hearing of the drums of the fort, killed and scalped one. With his rifle in one hand, and the bleeding trophy in the other, he made for a precipice near by, and, as he sprang from it, a rifle ball grazed his cheek—but he made his escape in safety to Red River, where he received a message from the Indian agent of the United States, and Colonel Arbuckle, the commanding officer, inviting him to return; he at first declined, but on being informed that it was the wish of his Great Father, and assured that the offer of a reward was recalled, he buried the tomahawk and came back. In one of the late expeditions of a portion of our army, Dutch was chosen by the commanding officer to accompany it. To his accurate knowledge of the country to be traversed, he added the skill of the hunter. He went, therefore, in the twofold capacity of guide and hunter. His services on this occasion were of incalculable value. He literally fed the troops. No man knew better than he where to find the buffalo, how to capture him, and from what part of his body to cut the choicest pieces. To the question we put to him, "How many buffaloes have you killed?" he answered, "So many I cannot number them." And to another, "What parts of the animal are considered the best?" he replied, "The shoulder, including the hump, and the tongue."

The cheerfulness with which he bore his toils and his exposures, in the twofold capacity referred to, in connection with the great fidelity with which he executed the trust, gained him great applause, and made him a general favourite. He demonstrated his character to be sound, and that he was a man to be relied on.

He had now abandoned his warlike life, and, having built a house on the Canadian River, turned his attention to peaceable pursuits. He has persisted ever since in this mode of life, cultivated the soil, and lives in comfort. His stock of cattle and ponies is the largest in that region, and he has evidently discovered that it is to his interest to live at peace with his neighbours. His deportment is mild and inoffensive, and he enjoys the respect of those around him. The family of Tahchee consists of his second wife, a son, and a niece whom he adopted in her infancy, and has reared with the tenderness of a parent.

This distinguished warrior has been engaged in more than thirty battles with the Osages and other tribes, and has killed with his own hand, twenty-six of the enemy; but, with the exception of a slight scratch on the cheek, has never been wounded.

NOTES

1. The name as given by Mooney ("Myths of the Cherokee," *Nineteenth Report of the Bureau of American Ethnology,* pt. 1, p. 534, Washington, 1900) is strictly *Tătsǐ'*.

2. A translation of *Gŭn'-dǐ'gaduhŭñyǐ,* "Turkey settlement," from Turkey, or Little Turkey, its chief. The town was situated on the west bank of the river, opposite the present Center, in Cherokee County, Alabama.—Mooney, *op. cit.,* p. 521. See note 8, p. 397.

3. There is no record of the painting either in the Rhees *Catalogue* or in the list of Inman copies, nor is it known when the portrait was made. The only Cherokee treaty held at Washington from the time the

collection in the Indian Gallery had its inception, in 1821, and the publication of Vol. I. of the folio edition of McKenney and Hall in 1836, was that of May 6, 1828; but Tahchee did not sign this treaty, which proved so offensive to him. Numerous deputations of the Cherokee, however, visited Washington prior to this time, notably in October 1821, February 1823, and March 1824, when members of the Arkansas band were at the seat of Government (Royce in *Fifth Annual Report of the Bureau of Ethnology,* pp. 243-246). Possibly Tahchee was a member of one or more of these parties. The Camp Holmes treaty of August 4, 1835, was signed by "Dutch," the name appearing as the first of the two signers; the Washington treaty of August 6, 1846, was signed by "Wm. Dutch," referred to in the treaty also as Captain Dutch. His father, here called Skyugo, signed the treaties of the Holston, July 2, 1791 (as Skyuka); Philadelphia, June 26, 1794 (as Skyuka); and Washington, January 7, 1806 (as Skeuha).

The portrait of Tahchee in Mooney's "Myths of the Cherokee" (*op. cit.*), is accredited to Catlin, 1834; but this is a mistake, as the accompanying picture (Plate VI.) is from McKenney and Hall. Catlin's sketch is quite different, representing the subject with a very light beard. Moreover it was painted in 1836.

Regarding this Indian, whom he calls Tuch-ee, Catlin (*Illustrations of the Manners, etc.*, II., 121-122, London, 1866) says:

"Besides the Cherokees in Georgia, and those that I have spoken of in the neighbourhood of Fort Gibson, there is another band or family of the same tribe, of several hundreds, living on the banks of the Canadian River, an hundred or more miles south-west of Fort Gibson, under the government of a distinguished chief by the name of *Tuch-ee* (familiarly called by the white people, 'Dutch,' plate 218). This is one of the most extraordinary men that lives on the frontiers at the present day, both for his remarkable history, and for his fine and manly figure, and character of face.

"This man was in the employment of the Government as a guide and hunter for the regiment of dragoons, on their expedition to the Camanchees, where I had him for a constant companion for several months, and opportunities in abundance, for studying his true character, and of witnessing his wonderful exploits in the different varieties of the chase. The history of this man's life has been very curious and surprising; and I sincerely hope that someone, with more leisure and more talent than myself, will take it up, and do it justice. I promise that the life of this man furnishes the best materials for a popular tale, that are now to be procured on the Western frontier.

"He is familiarly known, and much of his life, to all the officers who have been stationed at Fort Gibson, or at any of the posts in that region of country.

"Some twenty years or more since, becoming fatigued and incensed with civilized encroachments, that were continually making on the borders of the Cherokee country in Georgia, where he then resided, and probably foreseeing the disastrous results they were to lead to, he beat up for volunteers to emigrate to the West, where he had designed to go, and colonize in a wild country beyond the reach and contamination of civilized innovations; and succeeded in getting several hundred men, women, and children, whom he led over the banks of the Mississippi, and settled upon the headwaters of White River, where they lived until the appearance of white faces, which began to peep through the forests at them, when they made another move of 600 miles to the banks of the Canadian, where they now reside; and where, by the system of desperate warfare, which he has carried on against the Osages and the Camanchees, he has successfully cleared away from a large tract of fine country, all the enemies that could contend for it, and now holds it, with his little band of myrmidons, as their own undisputed soil, where they are living comfortably by raising from the soil fine crops of corn and potatoes, and other necessaries of life; whilst they indulge whenever they please, in the pleasures of the chase amongst the herds of buffaloes, or in the natural propensity for ornamenting their dresses and their war-clubs with the scalp-locks of their enemies."

Donaldson (*National Museum Report for 1885*, p. 207) says he was engaged in more than thirty battles with the Osage and other Indians, and killed with his own hands twenty-six of his adversaries. He died about 1843.

4. In 1809 a delegation visited and inspected the lands on Arkansas and White Rivers, whither it was proposed to remove the conservative element of the Cherokee then in Georgia and Alabama. The report was favourable, and a large number of the Indians signified their intention to remove at once. " As no funds were then available for their removal, the matter was held in abeyance for several years, during which period families and individuals removed to the western country at their own expense until, before the year 1817, they numbered in all two or three thousand souls. They became known as the Arkansas, or Western Cherokee."—(Mooney, *Myths of the Cherokee, op. cit.*, p. 102.) It was evidently during one of these earlier movements that Tahchee's family went to the Arkansas country.

5. The Grand or Neosho River enters the Arkansas at the present Fort Gibson, Cherokee Nation, Oklahoma.

6. This prominent chief of the Western Cherokee, also called "The Bowl" by the whites (a translation of his native name *Diwá'li*), was killed by the Texans in 1839 (Mooney, *Myths, op. cit.*, p. 516).

7. See note 3.

8. The Tawákoni, a Caddoan tribe which in 1719 lived in what is now the Creek Nation, Oklahoma, but later they shifted to the Brazos and Trinity Rivers in Texas, and in 1822 were said to number 1200, but by 1840 they had become reduced to fewer than half that number, and resided on a branch of the Colorado River of Texas. They steadily declined in population; in 1850 they were reported to number 140, on the Upper Brazos. They are now with the Wichita, in Oklahoma, of whom they are a sub-tribe, and although they are no longer officially recognised, they number perhaps about 100.

9. The Kiamichi, in the present Choctaw Nation, Oklahoma.

10. See note 5, and consult Mooney, *Myths, op. cit.*, p. 141.

ANACAMEGISHCA

(OR, FOOT PRINTS)

HERE is a forest chieftain with a name sufficiently long to gratify the most aristocratic veneration for high-sounding titles, but which, we regret to inform such of our readers as may not happen to be versed in the Ojibway tongue, dwindles, when interpreted, into the humble appellation of *Foot Prints*.[1] How he acquired it, we are unable to say, but that it is an honourable designation, we are prepared to believe from the character of the wearer, who is a person of no small note. He is descended from a line of hyperborean chiefs who, like himself, have held undisputed sway over a clan of the Chippewas inhabiting the borders of Rainy Lake. His great grandfather, Nittum,[2] was an Ottawa, who emigrated from Lake Michigan to the Grand Portage and Rainy Lake, at the time when the great North-West Company, whose doings have been so admirably described by our countryman Irving,[3] began to prosecute their traffic in parts North-westward from the Grand Portage.

Nittum was an uncommon man. So great was his sagacity and conduct, that, although not a native of the region or tribe into which he had boldly cast his lot, he soon came to be regarded as the head chief of the Kenisteno nation.[4] He attained a reputation for bravery, activity, and prudence in council, as well as for the decision of character evinced in all the vicissitudes of a busy and perilous career,

344

A-NA-CAM-E-GISH-CA, *or* FOOT PRINTS
A Chippeway Chief

which extended beyond the region of Rainy Lake,[5] and elevated him above the surrounding warriors and politicians. So great was the veneration in which he was held by the Indians, that the agents of the North-West Company took especial pains to conciliate his favour while living, and to honour his remains after death. The scaffold upon which, according to the custom of the Chippewas, his body was deposited, was conspicuously elevated, near the trading house at the Grand Portage, and the savages saw, with admiration, a British flag floating in the breeze over the respected relics of their deceased chief. When these politic traffickers in peltry removed their establishment from Kamenistaquoia to Fort William,[6] they carried with them the bones of Nittum, which were again honoured with distinguished marks of respect; and the living continued to be cajoled by a pretended reverence for the memory of the dead. This is the same "*Nitum*" mentioned in the "History of the Fur Trade" prefixed to *Mackenzie's Voyages*.

Nittum was succeeded in the chieftainship by his son Kagakummig, the *Everlasting*,[7] who was also much respected in the high latitude of Rainy Lake and the Lake of the Woods. After his death, his son Kabeendushquameh, a person of feeble mind and little repute, swayed the destinies of this remote tribe, until, in the fullness of time, he also was gathered to his fathers. He left several sons, of whom the subject of this notice is within one of the youngest, but is nevertheless the successor to the hereditary authority of chief. He is a good hunter, and well qualified to sustain the reputation of his family. Of a disposition naturally inclining to be stern and ferocious, but with sufficient capacity to appreciate his own situation and that of his people, as well as the conduct of those who visit his country for the purpose of traffic, he conducts himself with propriety, and is considered a man of good sense and prudence. He is the first of his family who has acknowledged fealty to the American Government. This chief takes a lively interest in the condition and prospects of his band, and, in the year 1826, evinced a desire to cultivate amicable relations with the American people, by performing a long and painful journey to attend the council held at Fond du Lac by Governor Cass and Colonel McKenney.[8] He is six feet three inches in stature, and well made. Of his feats in war or hunting no particular accounts have reached us. There are no newspapers at Rainy Lake, and it is altogether possible for a person to attain an eminent station without having his frailties or his good deeds heralded by the trump of fame.

NOTES

1. The name is given to the writer by a Minnesota Chippewa, visiting Washington in February 1908, as *Ĭnakŭmĭgishkŭng*, signifying "He who makes impressions in the earth," but not necessarily with the foot. Baraga gives "*inakamiga*, the ground, soil, or country, is such . . . ," and "*nin mangishkam* [or] *nin mamăngishkam*, I leave small tracks behind me."

2. Evidently cognate with Chippewa *nitam*, "the first." Alexander Mackenzie (*Voyage from Montreal . . . to the Frozen and Pacific Oceans*, London, 1801, p. lvi) says: "This [the Chaudière of Rainy River, in northern Minnesota] is also the residence of the first chief, or Sachem, of all the Algonquin tribes, inhabiting the different parts of this country. He is by distinction called Nectam, which implies personal preeminence." In his vocabulary (p. cxiv) Mackenzie gives *nicam* (Cree) and *nitam* (Algonquin) for "first." See note 12, p. 61.

3. See Washington Irving, *Astoria*.

4. From *Kinishtino*, or *Kenistenoag*, the Chippewa name for the Cree.

5. The Chippewa of this region were the Kuchĭchĭwĭnĭnĭwŭg, or Kojejewininiwug, popularly called by the whites "Rainy Lake Chippewa," from their habitat.

6. Kamenistaquoia, Kamanitiquia, Kamanitiguia, Kaministigoya,

Kaministiquia, Caministiquia, Gamenestigoua, etc., is correctly *Kahma-natigwayah*, meaning " Pigeon River," from a stream of that name in the north-eastern corner of Minnesota, near the mouth of which the Grand Portage was situated, according to Warren in *Minn. Hist. Soc. Coll.*, V., 137, 1885. The Grand Portage was originally so called (Chippewa *Kecheonegumeng*, according to Warren) " from the fact that a portage of ten [nine] miles is here made to Pigeon River, to avoid the rapids which preclude navigation even for canoes." In 1803 the trading post at the Grand Portage was abandoned and a new one built near the mouth of Kaministiqua River, some miles northward, near the north-west Lake Superior shore; this in 1807 was named Fort William, in honour of William Macgillivray, an attaché of the North-West Fur Company. The present town still bears the name. Coues (*Henry-Thompson Journals*, I., 7, 217, 219-220 *seq.*) invariably makes Fort William and Kaministiquia one and the same, and indeed the name may have been transferred to the new post on the abandonment of that at the Grand Portage.

7. *Kágige*, perpetual, everlasting, eternal. The word is never used alone, but is always connected with a noun or a verb, as *Kagigékamig*, perpetually, eternally, for ever and ever.—Baraga, *Otchipwe Dict.*, 179, 1880.

8. He was the only representative of the Rainy Lake band of Chippewa to sign this treaty of August 5, 1826, his name appearing as Aanubkumigishkunk. It was on this occasion, no doubt, that his portrait was painted by J. O. Lewis. It was copied by King in the following year, as noted in the Rhees *Catalogue*, No. 56 : " A-na-cam-o-gush-ia. Chippeway Chief from Rainy Lake." In the list of Inman copies in the Peabody Museum it bears catalogue number 28. 210, and the name " A-na-cam-e-gisk-ca, Foot Prints." This portrait does not appear in the Lewis *Port-folio*.

WABISHKEEPENAS

(OR, THE WHITE PIGEON)

THIS portrait is not embraced in the gallery at Washington, but, being authentic, is added to our collection in consideration of the interesting illustration which it affords, of a remarkable, though not unusual feature, in the Indian character.

During the visit of Governor Cass and Colonel McKenney, at Fond du Lac Superior, in 1826, they met with this individual, who was pining in wretchedness and despondency under the influence of a superstition which had rendered him an object of contempt in the eyes of his tribe.[1] "An Indian opened the door of my room to-day," says Colonel McKenney in his journal, "and came in, under circumstances so peculiar, with a countenance so pensive, and a manner so flurried, as to lead me to call the interpreter. Before the interpreter came in, he went out with a quick but feeble step, looking as if he had been deserted by every friend he ever had. I directed the interpreter to follow him, and ascertain what he wanted, and the cause of his distressed appearance. I could not get the countenance of this Indian out of my mind, nor his impoverished and forlorn looks."

It seems that in 1820, when Governor Cass and Mr Schoolcraft made a tour of the Upper Lakes, they were desirous of visiting the celebrated copper rock, a mass

WA-BISH-KEE-PE-NAS, *or* THE WHITE
PIGEON
A Chippeway

of pure copper of several tons weight, which was said to exist in that region, but found some difficulty in procuring a guide, in consequence of the unwillingness of the Indians to conduct strangers to a spot which they considered sacred. The copper rock was one of their *manitos*—it was a spirit, a holy thing, or a something which in some way controlled their destiny—for their superstitions are so indistinct, that it is in most cases impossible to understand or describe them.[2] The White Pigeon was prevailed upon to become their guide, but lost his way, to the great disappointment of the travellers, who were anxious to inspect a natural curiosity the character of which was supposed to have been mistaken, if, indeed, its existence was not wholly fabulous. How it happened that an Indian of that region failed to find a spot so well known to his tribe, is not explained. The way might have been difficult, or the guide confused by the consciousness that he had undertaken an office that his people disapproved. The band, however, attributed his failure to the agency of the *manito* who, according to their belief, guards the rock, and who, to protect it from the profanation of the white man's presence, had interposed and shut the path. Under the impression that he had offended the Great Spirit, he was cast off by the tribe, but would probably have soon been restored to favour, had not further indications of the displeasure of the Deity rendered it too certain that the crime of this unhappy man was one of the deepest dye. A series of bad luck attended his labours in the chase. The game of the forest avoided him ; his weapons failed to perform their fatal office ; and the conviction became settled that he was a doomed man. Deserted by his tribe, and satisfied in his own mind that his "good spirit" had forsaken him, he wandered about the forest a disconsolate wretch, deriving a miserable subsistence from the

roots and wild fruit of that sterile region. Bereft of his
usual activity and courage, destitute of confidence and
self-respect, he seemed to have scarcely retained the
desire or ability to provide himself with food from day
to day.[3]

The American commissioners, on hearing the story of
the White Pigeon's fault and misfortunes, became interested in his fate. They determined to restore him to the
standing from which he had fallen, and having loaded him
with presents, convinced both himself and his tribe that his
offence was forgiven, and his luck changed. Governor
Cass, afterwards, procured a better guide, and succeeded
in finding the copper rock, which is really a curiosity, as
will be seen on reference to our life of Shingaba W'Ossin.

Another incident, which occurred at Fond du Lac,
may be mentioned, as exemplifying the superstitions of
this race. An Indian having killed a moose deer, brought
it to the trading-post for sale. It was remarkably large,
and Mr A. Morrison, one of the agents, was desirous to preserve the skin as a specimen. For this purpose a frame was
prepared, and the skin, properly stuffed, was stretched and
supported so as to represent the living deer in a standing
posture. About this time the Indians were unsuccessful
in taking moose, but were wholly ignorant of the cause
of their ill-fortune, until one of them, happening to visit the
post, espied the stuffed deer, and reported what he had
seen to his companions. The band agreed at once that
their want of success was attributable to the indignity
which had been offered to the deceased deer, whose spirit
had evinced its displeasure by prevailing on its living
kindred not to be taken by men who would impiously
stuff their hides. Their first business was to appease the
anger of this sensitive spirit. They assembled at the post,
and with respectful gravity marched into the presence of

the stuffed moose. They seated themselves around it, lighted their pipes, and began to smoke. The spirit of the deer was addressed by an orator, who assured it that the tribe was innocent of the liberty which had been taken with its carcass, and begged forgiveness. In token of their sincerity, the pipes were placed in the deer's mouth, that it might smoke too; and they separated at last, satisfied that they had done all that a reasonable spirit of a moose deer could ask, and fully assured that its anger was appeased. But they were not willing that the exhibition should be continued. Mr Morrison, to pacify them, took down the effigy, and when they saw the horns unshipped, the straw withdrawn, the frame broken, and the hide hung on a peg, as hides are wont to be hung, they were satisfied that all was right.

NOTES

1. This Indian was the first signer of this treaty of August 5, 1826, on behalf of the Ontonagon band of Chippewa, his name appearing as Waubishkeepeenaas, intended for Wabĭshkĭpĭnäs, meaning "white bird," not pigeon, according to Dr William Jones. Baraga gives "I am (it is) white," *wábishkis;* "small bird," *bineshi;* "large bird," *binéshi.* Schoolcraft spells his name Wabiskipinais, and analyses it as from *wabiska,* white (transitive animate), and *penasee,* a bird (*Summary Narrative of an Exploratory Expedition to the Sources of the Mississippi River in 1820,* Philadelphia, 1855, p. 96).

There is no doubt that the painting was made by Lewis, who was present at Fond du Lac during the treaty negotiations, although it does not appear in his *Port-folio.* It is, however, reproduced as a plate facing page 281 of McKenney's *Tour to the Lakes,* with the title, "Wad-bis-kil-e-nais." Of him McKenney says, in addition to the information regarding his superstition and his trip with Cass and Schoolcraft (pp. 280-281): "His name is Wa-bish-kee-pe-nas, or the White Pigeon. I shall have his likeness sketched."

McKenney and Hall, it will be noted, were not especially anxious to advertise their rival Lewis, even to the extent of giving him credit for his paintings.   The portrait of Wabishkeepenas is not listed by name in the Inman collection of the Peabody Museum.

2. See *Shingaba W'Ossin*, note 10, p. 61.

3. See Schoolcraft's *Summary Narrative, op. cit.*, and his *Personal Memoirs*, p. 111 (Philadelphia, 1851), for an account of this episode. The silver medal shown in the portrait of Wabishkeepenas is doubtless the one presented by Governor Cass during this trip, as mentioned by Schoolcraft (*Summary Narrative*, p. 99).

TSHUSICK

(A CHIPPEWA WOMAN)

A PORTION only of the history of this extraordinary woman has reached us. Of her early life we know nothing; but the fragment which we are enabled to present is sufficiently indicative of her strongly marked character, while it illustrates with singular felicity the energy of the race to which it belongs. In tracing the peculiar traits of the Indian character, as developed in many of the wild adventures related of them, we are most forcibly struck with the boldness, the subtlety, the singleness of purpose, with which individuals of that race plan and execute any design in which they may be deeply interested.

The youth of ancient Persia were taught to speak the truth. The lesson of infancy, inculcated with equal care upon the American savage, is, to keep his own council, and he learns with the earliest dawnings of reason the caution which teaches him alike to deceive his foe and to guard against the imprudence of his friend. The story of Tshusick shows that she possessed those savage qualities quickened and adorned by a refinement seldom found in any of her race; and we give it as it was communicated to the writer by the gentleman who was best acquainted with all the facts.

In the winter of 1826-27, on a cold night, when the snow was lying on the ground, a wretched, ill-clad, way-worn female knocked at the door of our colleague, Colonel McKenney, then Commissioner of Indian Affairs, at the City of Washington. She was attended by a boy, who explained the manner in which she had been directed to the residence of Colonel McKenney. It seems that, while wandering through the streets of Georgetown in search of a shelter from the inclemency of the weather, she was allured by the blaze of a furnace in the shop of Mr Haller, a tin worker. She entered, and eagerly approached the fire. On being asked who she was, she replied, that she was an Indian, that she was cold and starving, and knew not where to go. Mr Haller, supposing that Colonel McKenney, as Commissioner for Indian Affairs, was bound to provide for all of that race who came to the seat of Government, directed her to him, and sent his boy to conduct her. On this representation the Colonel invited her into his house, led her to a fire, and saw before him a young woman, with a ragged blanket around her shoulders, a pair of men's boots on her feet, a pack on her back, and the whole of her meagre and filthy attire announcing the extreme of want. She described herself to be what her complexion and features sufficiently indicated, an Indian, and stated that she had travelled alone, and on foot, from Detroit. In reply to questions which were put to her, for the purpose of testing the truth of her story, she named several gentlemen who resided at that place, described their houses, and mentioned circumstances in reference to their families which were known to be correct. She then proceeded, with a self-possession of manner, and an ease and fluency of language that surprised those who heard her, to narrate the cause of her solitary journey. She said she had recently lost her husband, to whom she was much attached, and that she attributed his death to the anger of the Great Spirit, whom she had always venerated, but who was no doubt offended with her, for having neglected to worship Him in the manner which she knew to be right. She knew that the red people did not worship the Great Spirit in an acceptable mode, and that the only true religion was that of the white men. Upon the decease of her husband, therefore, she had knelt down and vowed that she would immediately proceed to Washington, to the sister of Mrs Boyd, who, being the wife of the Great Father of the white people, would, she hoped, protect her until she should be properly instructed and baptized.

In conformity with this pious resolution, she had immediately set out, and had travelled after the Indian fashion, not by any road, but directly across the country, pursuing the course which she supposed would lead her to the capital. She had begged her food at the farmhouses she chanced to pass, and had slept in the woods. On being asked if she had not been afraid when passing the night alone in the forest, she replied that she had never been alarmed, for that she knew the Great Spirit would protect her.

This simple, though remarkable recital, confirmed as it was by its apparent consistency, and the correctness of the references to well-known individuals, both at Detroit and Mackinaw, carried conviction to the minds of all who heard it. The Mrs Boyd alluded to was the wife of a highly respectable gentleman, the agent of the United States for Indian Affairs, residing at Mackinaw, and she was the sister of the lady of Mr Adams, then President of the United States. It seemed natural that a native female, capable of acting as this courageous individual had acted, should seek the protection of a lady who held the highest rank in her nation, and whose near relative she knew and respected. There was something of dignity, and much of romance, in the idea of a savage convert seeking at the mansion of the chief magistrate the pure fountain of the religion which she proposed to espouse, as if unwilling to receive it from any source meaner than the most elevated.

Colonel McKenney recognised in the stranger a person entitled alike to the sympathies of the liberal and the protection of the Government, and, in the exercise of his official duty towards one of a race over whom he had been constituted a sort of guardian, immediately received his visitor under his protection, conducted her to a neighbouring hotel, secured her a comfortable apartment, and placed her under the especial care of the hostess, a kind and excellent woman, who promised to pay her every requisite attention.

On the following morning, the first care of the commissioner was to provide suitable attire for the stranger, and, having purchased a quantity of blue and scarlet clothes, feathers, beads and other finery, he presented them to her; and Tshusick, declining all assistance, set to work with alacrity, and continued to labour without ceasing, until she had completed the entire costume in which she appears arrayed in the portrait accompanying this notice—except the moccasins and hat, which were purchased. There she sits, an Indian belle, decorated by her own hands, according to her own taste, and smiling in the consciousness that a person to which Nature had not been niggard, had received the most splendid embellishments of which art was capable.[1]

Tshusick was now introduced in due form at the presidential mansion, where she was received with great kindness; the families of the Secretary of War, and of other gentlemen, invited and caressed her as an interesting and deserving stranger. No other Indian female,

TSHUSICK
A Chippewa Woman

except the Eagle of Delight,[2] was ever so great a favourite
at Washington, nor has any lady of that race ever presented
higher claims to admiration. She was, as the faithful
pencil of King has portrayed her, a beautiful woman.
Her manners had the unstudied grace, and her conversation the easy fluency of high refinement. There was
nothing about her that was coarse or commonplace.
Sprightly, intelligent, and quick, there was also a womanly
decorum in all her actions, a purity and delicacy in her
whole air and conduct, that pleased and attracted all who
saw her. So agreeable a savage has seldom, if ever,
adorned the fashionable circles of civilised life.

The success of this lady at her first appearance on a
scene entirely new to her, is not surprising. Youth and
beauty are in themselves always attractive, and she was
just then in the full bloom of womanhood. Her age
might have been twenty-eight, but she seemed much
younger. Her dress, though somewhat gaudy, was
picturesque, and well calculated to excite attention by its
singularity, while its adaptation to her own style of beauty,
and to the aboriginal character, rendered it appropriate.
Neat in her person, she arranged her costume with taste,
and, accustomed from infancy to active exercise, her limbs
had a freedom and grace of action too seldom seen among
ladies who are differently educated. Like all handsome
women, be their colour or nation what it may, she knew
her power, and used it to the greatest advantage.

But that part of Tshusick's story which is yet to be
related is, to our mind, the most remarkable. Having
attended to her personal comforts, and introduced her to
those whose patronage might be most serviceable, Colonel
McKenney's next care was to secure for her the means of
gratifying her wish to embrace the Christian religion.
She professed her readiness to act immediately on the

subject, and proposed that the Colonel should administer the rite of baptism—he being a great chief, the father of the Indians, and the most proper person to perform this parental and sacerdotal office. He of course declined, and addressed a note to the Reverend Mr Gray, Rector of Christ Church, in Georgetown, who immediately called to see Tshusick. On being introduced to him, she inquired whether he spoke French, and desired that their conversation might be held in that language, in order that the other persons who were present might not understand it, alleging as her reason for the request, the sacredness of the subject, and the delicacy she felt in speaking of her religious sentiments. A long and interesting conversation ensued, at the conclusion of which Mr Gray expressed his astonishment at the extent of her knowledge, and the clearness of her views, in relation to the whole Christian scheme. He was surprised to hear a savage, reared among her own wild race, in the distant regions of the northern lakes, who could neither read nor write, speak with fluency and precision in a foreign tongue, on the great doctrines of sin, repentance, and the atonement. He pronounced her a fit subject for baptism; and accordingly that rite was administered, a few days afterwards, agreeably to the form of the Episcopalian Church, in the presence of a large company. When the name to be given to the new convert was asked by Mr Gray, it appeared that none had been agreed on; those of the wife and daughter of the then Secretary of War were suggested on the emergency, and were used.[3] Throughout this trying ceremony she conducted herself with great propriety. Her deportment was calm and self-possessed, yet characterised by a sensibility which seemed to be the result of genuine feeling.

Another anecdote shows the remarkable tact and

talent of this singular woman. On an occasion when
Colonel McKenney introduced her to a large party of his
friends, there was present a son of the celebrated Theobald
Wolfe Tone, a young Frenchman of uncommon genius and
attainment.[4] This gentleman no sooner heard Tshusick
converse in his native tongue, than he laughed heartily,
insisted that the whole affair was a deception, that Colonel
McKenney had dressed up a smart youth of the Engineer
Corps, and had gotten up an ingenious scenic representation for the amusement of his guests—because he considered it utterly impossible that an Indian could speak
the French language with such purity and elegance. He
declared that her dialect was that of a well-educated
Parisian. We do not think it surprising that a purer
French should be spoken on our frontier than in the
province of France. The language was introduced among
the Indians by the priests and military officers, who were
educated at Paris, and were persons of refinement, and it
has remained there without change. The same state of
facts may exist there which we know to be true with
regard to the United States. The first emigrants to our
country were educated persons, who introduced a pure
tongue ; and the English language is spoken by Americans
with greater correctness than in any of the provincial
parts of Great Britain.

We shall only add to this part of our strange eventful
history, that all who saw Tshusick at Washington were
alike impressed with the invariable propriety of her
deportment ; her hostess especially, who had the opportunity of noticing her behaviour more closely than others,
expressed the most unqualified approbation of her conduct.
She was neat, methodical, and pure in all her habits and
conversation. She spoke with fluency on a variety of
subjects, and was, in short, a most graceful and interesting

woman. Yet she was a savage, who had strolled on foot from the borders of Lake Superior to the American capital.

When the time arrived for Tshusick to take her departure, she was not allowed to go empty-handed. Her kind friends at Washington loaded her with presents. Mrs Adams, the lady of the President, besides the valuable gifts which she gave her, entrusted to her care a variety of articles for her young relatives, the children of Mr Boyd, of Mackinaw. It being arranged that she should travel by the stage-coaches as far as practicable, her baggage was carefully packed in a large trunk; but as part of her journey would be through the wilderness, where she must ride on horseback, she was supplied with the means of buying a horse; and a large sack, contrived by herself, and to be hung like panniers across the horse, was made, into which all her property was to be stowed. Her money was placed in a belt to be worn round her waist; and a distinguished officer of the army, of high rank, with the gallantry which forms so conspicuous a part of his character, fastened with his own hand this rich cestus upon the person of the lovely tourist.[5]

Thus pleasantly did the days of Tshusick pass at the capital of the United States, and she departed burthened with the favours and good wishes of those who were highest in station and most worthy in character. On her arrival at Barnum's hotel in Baltimore, a favourable reception was secured for her by a letter of introduction. Mrs Barnum took her into her private apartments, detained her several days as her guest, and showed her the curiosities of that beautiful city. She then departed in the western stage for Frederick, Maryland; the proprietors of the stages declined receiving any pay from her, either for her journey to Baltimore or thence west, so far as she was heard of.

Having thus with the fidelity of an impartial historian described the halcyon days of Tshusick, as the story was told us by those who saw her dandled on the knee of hospitality, or fluttering with childlike joy upon the wing of pleasure, it is with pain that we are obliged to reverse the picture. But beauties, like other conquerors, have their hours of glory and of gloom. The brilliant career of Tshusick was destined to close as suddenly as that of the conqueror of Europe at the field of Waterloo.

On the arrival of the fair Chippewa at Washington Colonel McKenney had written to Governor Cass, at Detroit, describing in glowing language the bright stranger who was the delight of the higher circles at the metropolis, and desiring to know of the Governor of Michigan her character and history. The reply to this prudent inquiry was received a few days after the departure of the subject of it. The Governor, highly amused at the success of the lady's adventure, congratulated his numerous friends at Washington on the acquisition which had been gained to their social circle, and in compliance with the request of his friend, stated what he knew of her. She was the wife of a short, squat Frenchman, who officiated as a scullion in the household of Mr Boyd, the Indian agent at Mackinaw, and who, so far from having been spirited away from his afflicted wife, was supporting her absence without leave with the utmost resignation. It was not the first liberty of this kind which she had taken. Her love of adventure had more than once induced her to separate for a season the conjugal tie, and to throw herself upon the cold charity of a world that has been heartless, but which had not proved so to her. She was a sort of female swindler, who practised upon the unsophisticated natures of her fellow-men, by an aboriginal method of her own invention. Whenever stern necessity, or her own pleasure, rendered it expedient to replenish her exhausted coffers, her custom had been to wander off into the settlements of the whites, and, under a disguise of extreme wretchedness, to recite some tale of distress; that she had been crossed in love; or was the sole survivor of a dreadful massacre; or was disposed to embrace the Christian religion; and such was the effect of her beauty and address, that she seldom failed to return with a rich booty. She had wandered through the whole length of the Canadas to Montreal and Quebec, had traced the dreary solitudes of the northern lakes, to the most remote trading stations; had ascended the Mississippi to the Falls of St Anthony, and had followed the meanders of that river down to St Louis, comprising within the range of her travels the whole vast extent of the northern and north-western frontier, and many places in the interior. Her last and boldest attempt was a masterpiece of daring and successful enterprise, and will compare well with the most finished efforts of the ablest impostors of modern times.

It will be seen that Tshusick had ample opportunities for obtaining the information which she used so dexterously, and for beholding the manners of refined life, which she imitated with such success. She had been a servant in the families of gentlemen holding official rank on the frontier, and in her wanderings been entertained at the dwellings of English, French, and Americans of every grade. Her religious knowledge was picked up at the missionary stations at Mackinaw, and from the priests at Montreal, and her excellent French resulted partly from hearing that language well spoken by genteel persons, and partly from an admirable perception and fluency of speech that is natural to a gifted few, and more frequently found in women than in men. Although an impostor and vagrant she was a remarkable person, possessing beauty, tact, spirit, and address which the highest born and loveliest might envy, and the perversion of which to purposes of deception and vice affords the most melancholy evidences of the depravity of our nature.

Tshusick left Washington in February, 1827,[6] and in the month of June following Colonel McKenney's official duties required him to visit the north-western frontier. On his arrival at Detroit, he naturally felt some curiosity to see the singular being who had practised so adroitly on the credulity of himself and his friends, and the more especially, as he learned that the presents with which she had been charged by the latter had not been delivered. On inquiry, he was told she had just gone to Mackinaw. Proceeding on his tour, he learned at Mackinaw that she had left for Green Bay ; from the latter place she preceded him to Prairie du Chien ; and when he arrived at Prairie du Chien, she had just departed for St Peter's. It was evident that she had heard of his coming, and was unwilling to meet him ; she had fled before him from place to place, probably alone, and certainly with but slender means of subsistence, for more than a thousand miles, giving thus a new proof of the vigilance and fearlessness that marked her character.

In reciting this singular adventure, we have not been able to avoid entirely the mention of names connected with it, but we have confined ourselves to those of persons in public life, whose stations subject them without impropriety to this kind of notice. The whole affair affords a remarkable instance of the benignant character of our Government, and of the facility with which the highest functionaries may be approached by any who have even a shadow of claim on their protection. Power does not assume, with us, the repulsive shape which keeps the humble at a distance, nor are the doors of our rulers guarded by tedious official forms, that delay the petitions of those who claim either mercy or justice.

The beautiful story of Elizabeth, by Madame Cottin, and of Jeannie Deans, by Scott, are both founded on real events, which are considered as affording delightful illustrations of the heroic self-devotion of the female heart ; of the courage and enthusiasm with which a woman will encounter danger for a beloved object. Had the journey of Tshusick been undertaken, like those alluded to, to save a parent or a sister, or even been induced by the circumstances which she alleged, it would have formed a touching incident in the history of woman, little inferior to any which have ever been related. She came far, and endured much ; emerging from the lowest rank in society, she found favour in the highest, and achieved, for the base purpose of plunder, the success which would have immortalised her name, had it been obtained in a virtuous cause.[7]

This remarkable woman is still living, and, though broken by years, exhibits the same active and intriguing spirit which distinguished her youth. She is well known on the frontier ; but, when we last heard of her, passed under a different name from that which we have recorded.

NOTES

1. The portrait, as later mentioned, was painted by King in 1827. See the Rhees list (Introduction, p. liii, No. 147). The Inman copy in the Peabody Museum bears catalogue number 57.031. The meaning of the name could not be given by either of two members of the Mille Lac Chippewa of Minnesota visiting Washington in 1908, nor by the niece of W. W. Warren, the historian of the tribe.

2. Hayne Hudjihini, whose biography and portrait appear in this volume, p. 165.

3. As appears in note 7, the name given her was Lucy Cornelia Barbour, the Honourable James Barbour of Virginia, to whom McKenney owed so much, and to whom he addressed his letters during the tour to the Lakes, being then Secretary of War.

4. William Theobald Wolfe Tone, the son, was born in Dublin, Ireland, April 29, 1791; died in New York, October 10, 1828. After the death of his father, the Irish patriot and French general, he was adopted as a child of the French Republic, by the Directorate. Serving with distinction in the French army, he came to the United States in 1816, studied law, and wrote papers on military tactics. He was appointed a second lieutenant in the United States army in 1820, but resigned in 1826. He was the author of several works, including the *School of Cavalry* (Georgetown, D.C., 1824). See Appleton's *Cyclopædia of American Biography*.

5. This was General Alexander Macomb (born Detroit, Michigan, April 3, 1782; died Washington, D.C., June 25, 1841), who became Major-General and General-in-Chief of the army in 1828.

6. This date varies in the different editions, the first folio edition having 1837, and later editions 1829. This is evidently an error, as Tshusick appeared in Washington in the winter of 1826-27, and in the following summer McKenney made his second and last trip to the Lake country.

7. "A Letter from Thomas L. McKenney, Esq., Superintendent of Indian Affairs, to his friend in Baltimore, dated Georgetown, May 15, 1828," and published in the *National Intelligencer* of Washington, sheds some interesting information respecting this woman. It reads in part :—

"And so you have seen the *squibs* respecting the 'Princess,' and the charge of my circulating, throughout my tour last year, the pamphlet on the subject of the 'Six Militiamen,' and also the charge made against me by Mr Wickliffe, of Kentucky, in the House of Representatives, of having expended $5000 of the Government money in a single bill, in some tavern, somewhere on the Lakes; and want to know my views of politics ? etc. . . .

"It is true, I have seen now and then the notice which the newspapers take of these things—but aware that these matters (except one) are merely things of the moment, and meant to amuse the frivolous, and feed the appetite of the vulgar, and that they are held in contempt by the virtuous—I have smiled at them, and let them pass. But as you have asked me 'to write you all about them,' I will do so.

"And first, in regard to the 'Princess.' This woman was brought to my door last winter by a boy who lives with Mr Haller, a tinner in this town, one very cold night about 8 o'clock. He said she had gone into their shop to warm herself, and being an Indian, Mr Haller had directed

him to show her the way to my house.   That was the first time I had
ever seen the woman, or knew that such an one existed.   I asked her to
come in, and if she was hungry?   She answered, she was hungry, and
came in.   I shall never forget her miserable appearance—ragged—
shivering—dirty—with a pair of men's shoes on, three-fourths worn—a
blanket worn to the threads—not quite a full petticoat—a garden or
pasteboard bonnet covered with coarse cotton, and tumbled and dirty—
and a pack of miserable offall clothing at her back, even worse than that
she had on—fingers frost-bitten, and half mittens on—altogether, like
Otway's old hag, her appearance 'Bespoke variety of wretchedness.'

"While she was eating, I asked her where she was from?   She
answered, Mackinaw.   Who do you know there?   Mother and Father
Boyd (the Indian Agent and lady) Mr and Mrs Stuart, Mr Ferry, and
others—all of whom were known to me.   Who else do you know?   Mr
Johns[t]on's family at the Sault de St Marie.   Who do you know at
Detroit?   Father Cass and his family.   She then described the Governor's
house, and where certain paintings hung, etc., so as to satisfy me she
was not an impostor.   I provided accommodation for her at Mr Holtzman's, and the next day, in pursuance of the usage of the Department,
ever since it has been known to me, and the provision of Congress for
such objects, I bought and sent her some coarse scarlet and blue cloth,
some thread, needles, and beads, out of which she made a suit of clothing after the fashion of her People.

"Having lived in Mr Boyd's, Mr Stuart's, and Gov. Cass's families,
as she told me, and, as I have since ascertained, was true, she had contracted a fine address—her manners were remarkable for their propriety,
and before leaving Mr Holtzman's and the city, she had acquired the
respect and good will of a great many persons, who had been led by
curiosity to see her, and these she took with her.

"She one day told me she 'wanted to be made Christian,' as she
expressed it.   I ascertained her meaning was to be baptized.   She said
she had promised the Great Spirit, if ever she came among Christian
People, she would be baptized.   I informed the Rev. Mr Gray, of
Georgetown, of her wish, and he went to see her.   He told me, after
his interview, that she had surprised him by the intelligence with which
she discoursed, in French, on those subjects ; and that he had concluded
to administer to her that sacrament.   It was done, and I gave her the
name of Lucy Cornelia Barbour.   This practice is customary.   We have
five hundred Indian youths, of both sexes, now bearing the names of
our most distinguished families, and they are pleased to bear them.
There is nothing now, therefore, in this ; and certainly no one will
suppose that this name was given in derision.   It was more to please the
Indian than to honor or dishonor any one.

"On questioning her as to her object in coming here, I learned that,
having lived with Mrs Boyd (Mrs Adams's sister), and having heard Mrs
B. often speak of her, and having come on a visit to the Oneida Indians
in New York, she thought, being that near, she would continue on and

see Mrs Adams. This was all reasonable and praiseworthy. She did visit Mrs Adams, and gave her information of her sister's family, as I learned, and by her good conduct procured for herself a friendly reception there and elsewhere.

"It is true her likeness was taken; it hangs in the office of Indian Affairs with the rest, and preserving the female costume of the North West, and is, withal, a fine portrait. She never attempted to put herself off as a 'princess.' I never heard of this until the imaginative Noah, a good humored kind of person, as we all think, in one of his squibs, conferred upon her this title, when others, not perhaps as good natured as he, have bandied it about.

"She left Washington, after having collected the bounty of many, and after about ten days' tarrying (since which time I have never seen her); and left a name for propriety of conduct in all respects (whatever her real character may be) highly creditable to her. The first sight I ever had of her, was at my door, a poor, shivering, miserable object; and the last, when in presence of Gen. Macomb, I gave her means to assist her in getting home.

"This is the history of the 'Princess,' about whom so many silly things have been squibbed off, through certain newspapers."

MAJOR RIDGE

(A CHEROKEE CHIEF)

THE subject of this biography received from his parents, in infancy, the name of Nung-noh-hut-tar-hee, or *He who slays the enemy in the path*. After arriving at the age of a hunter, on being asked, "Which way did you come into camp?" he would reply, "I came along the top of the mountain." This answer being frequently repeated, it was seized upon as indicating a characteristic habit in the young hunter, who was thenceforward called Kah-nung-da-tla-geh, or *The man who walks on the mountain's top*. The name by which he has been subsequently known may have been derived from the Cherokee words which signify the summit or ridge of a mountain.[1]

The date of the birth of this individual is not known, as the Cherokees, previous to the recent invention of an alphabet of their tongue,[2] possessed no means by which they could record the ages of their children. It is believed that he is about sixty-six years old, which would fix the date of his nativity at about the year 1771. He was born at a Cherokee town called Highwassie, situated upon the river of the same name, and on the edge of a beautiful prairie encircled by forest.[3] It is just at this point that the Highwassie breaks through a range of lofty mountains with great velocity and power. The scenery affords a fine combination of the grand and beautiful; and those who imagine that the germs of poetry and eloquence may be planted in the young mind by the habitual contemplation of bold and attractive landscape, would readily select this as a spot calculated to be richly fraught with such benign influences. The father of Ridge was a full-blood Cherokee, who, though not distinguished in the council of the nation, was a famous hunter, and had once taken the scalp of an Indian warrior on the Kaskaskia River. The subject of this notice was the fourth son of his parents, but the first who reached the years of maturity; and of two brothers and a sister younger than himself, but one survives, who is the father of Elias Boudinot.[4] His mother was a respectable Cherokee woman of the half blood, her father being a white man, of whose origin or history we have not been able to collect any information.

The most prominent feature in the early reminiscences of Ridge refers to the distressed situation to which the Cherokees were reduced by the invasions of the white people, who burned their villages and killed their people. When his father, wearied of these hostile incursions, resolved on flight, he took his family in canoes down the Highwassie to the Tennessee River, and ascended the smaller branches of that stream to the Sequochee [4a] mountains, in whose deep glens and rock-bound fastnesses they were secure from pursuit. Here the game abounded, and the young hunter received his first lessons. His father taught him to steal with noiseless tread upon the grazing animal—to deceive the timid doe by mimicking the cry of the fawn—or to entice the wary buck within the reach of his missile by decorating his own head with antlers. He was inured to patience, fatigue, self-denial, and exposure, and acquired the sagacity which enabled him to chase with success the wild cat, the bear, and the panther. He watched the haunts, and studied the habits of wild animals, and became expert in the arts which enable the Indian hunter at all seasons to procure food from the stream or the forest.

Having continued in this primary and parental school until he reached the age of twelve, the young Indian was considered as having made a proficiency which entitled him to be advanced to a higher grade of studies; and a superstitious rite [5] was required to be performed to give due solemnity to the occasion. The usages of the nation made it requisite that his martial training should be preceded by a formal dedication to the life and business of a warrior, and an invocation to the Great Spirit to endue him with courage and good fortune. For this purpose his parents solicited the assistance of an aged warrior, whose numerous achievements in battle had established for him a high reputation; and whose sagacity and valour gave him, in the estimation of his tribe, the envied rank of an Ulysses. The assent of the war chief was conveyed in the brief avowal that *he would make him dreadful.* The ceremony took place immediately. The hoary brave, standing upon the brink of a mountain stream, called upon the Great Spirit to fill the mind of the young warrior with warlike inclinations and his heart with courage. He then, with the bone of a wolf, the end of which terminated in several sharp points, scratched the naked boy from the palm of one hand along the front of the arm, across the breast, and along the other arm to the hand—and in like manner lines were drawn from the heels upward to the shoulders, and from the shoulders over the breast downward to the feet—and from the back of one hand along the arm, across the back, and to the back of the other hand. The lines thus made each covered a space of two inches in width, and consisted of parallel incisions which penetrated through the skin, and caused an effusion of blood along their entire

extent.[6] He was then required to plunge into the stream
and bathe, after which the war chief washed his whole
body with a decoction of medicinal herbs; and, in conclusion, he was commanded not to associate with the female
children, nor to sit near a woman, nor, in short, to suffer
the touch of one of that sex during the space of seven
days. At the end of this term the war chief came to him,
and after delivering an address to the Great Spirit, placed
before the young candidate food, consisting of partridges
and mush. The partridge was used on this occasion
because, in its flight, this bird makes a noise with its wings
resembling thunder, while in sitting or walking it is
remarkably silent and difficult to discover—and thus were
indicated the clamour of the onset, and the cautious stealth
which should govern the movements of the warrior at all
other times. It is thus that the Indian is made in early
life the subject of superstition, is taught to believe himself
supernaturally endued with courage, and is artificially
supplied with qualities which might otherwise never have
been developed in his mind.

When Ridge was fourteen years of age, a war party was
made up at Cheestooyee,[7] where his parents then resided;
the warriors danced the war dance, and sung war songs
to induce the young men to join in the expedition. These
martial exercises had such an effect upon young Ridge,
that he volunteered against his father's wishes and in
despite of the tears of his mother, and went, with two
hundred of the tribe, against a fort of the Americans in
Tennessee, which was assaulted without success. In this
expedition he endured, without a murmur, great hardship
and dangers.

In the same year the whites made an irruption at a
place called the Cherokee Orchard, and retired after
killing one Indian. The Cherokees, expecting that their

enemies would return, arranged a force of about two hundred men in an ambuscade, near the Orchard, and had spies posted to watch the fords of the river Tennessee, where it was expected the white people would cross. It was soon reported that thirty horsemen and six men on foot were approaching. The Cherokees were divided into two parties, one of which was to attack the whites in front, while the other was to throw itself across their rear, to intercept their retreat. The whites being taken by surprise, were beaten, and sought safety in flight. Those on foot were taken and killed, while the horsemen plunged into the river, where they continued to maintain the unequal conflict with great obstinacy. A few who rode strong and fleet horses, escaped by clambering up a steep bank and the rest were slain. One of the Cherokees having overtaken a white man who was ascending the bank after recrossing the river, grappled with him in deadly fight. The white man being the stronger, threw the Indian, when a second came to the assistance of the latter, and while the gallant Tennessean was combating with two foes, Ridge, who was armed with only a spear, came up and despatched the unfortunate white man, by plunging his weapon into him. This affair was considered highly creditable to Ridge, the Indians regarding not courage only, but success, as indicative of merit, and appreciating highly the good fortune which enables one of their number to shed the blood of an enemy, in however accidental or stealthy a manner.

Soon after this affair, he conducted his father, who was sick, to a place more distant from the probable scene of war, and then joined a large army composed of the combined forces of the Creeks and Cherokees; the latter led by the chiefs Little Turkey [8] and White Dog, and the former by Chinnubbee. [9] The object of this enterprise was to take Knoxville, then the chief place in Tennessee; but it was not successful. In consequence of a disagreement among the chiefs, they returned without attacking the headquarters of the white settlements, after capturing a small garrison near Maryville.[10]

In another affair Ridge was scarcely more fortunate. He joined a company of hunters, and passed the Cumberland mountain into Kentucky, to chase the buffalo and the bear. While thus engaged, their leader, who was called Tah-cung-stee-skee, or The Remover, proposed to kill some white men for the purpose of supplying the party with tobacco, their whole store of which had been consumed. Ridge was left with an old man to guard the camp; the remainder of the party set out upon this righteous war, and after a brief absence returned with several scalps and some tobacco, which had been taken out of the pockets of the slain. This incident affords an example of the slight cause which is considered among savages a sufficient inducement for the shedding of blood. We know not who were the unhappy victims; they might have been hunters, but were as probably the members of some emigrant family which had settled in the wilderness, whose slumbers were broken at midnight by the war whoop, and who saw each other butchered in cold blood by a party of marauders who sought to renew their exhausted store of tobacco! We are told that Ridge was so greatly mortified at having been obliged to remain inactive, far from the scene of danger, that he actually wept over the loss of honour he had sustained, and that his grief was with difficulty appeased.

He returned home after an absence of seven months, and found that both his parents had died during that period, leaving him, still a youth, with two younger brothers and a sister, to provide for themselves, or to depend upon the cold charity of relatives, whose scanty subsistence was derived from the chase. Under these depressing circumstances he spent several years in obscurity, but always actively engaged either upon the war-path in predatory excursions against the whites, or in hunting expeditions to remote places where the game abounded. On one occasion, when he was about seventeen years of age, he with four others killed some white men upon the waters of Holston, during one of those brief seasons of peace which sometimes beamed on the frontier, like sunny days in the depth of winter—a peace having been declared during the absence of this party. That unfortunate act was the cause of a new war. The enraged whites collected a force, invaded the Cherokees who were holding a council at Tellico,[11] and killed a large number of their warriors. This event affords another illustration of the brittle nature of compacts between the inhabitants of the frontier, accustomed to mutual aggression, and ever on the watch to revenge an insult, or to injure a hated foe ; while it shows also that the beginnings of these wars are often the result of the most fortuitous causes—growing more frequently out of the mistakes or lawless acts of individuals than from any deliberate national decision.

Ridge and his companions, having been detained by the sickness of one of their number, did not arrive at the encampment of the tribe, at the Pine Log,[12] until after the consequences of their rash act had been realised in the slaughter of some of the principal men of the nation by the white people. They were coldly received : the relatives of the slain were incensed, and disposed to take revenge for their loss upon the young men who had occasioned the misfortune, nor were there wanting accusers to upbraid them openly as the authors of a great public

calamity.   Having no excuse to offer, Ridge, with a
becoming spirit, proposed to repair his error as far as
possible, by warding off its effects from his countrymen.
He raised the war whoop, entered the village as is
customary with those who return victorious, and called
for volunteers to march against the enemy—but there was
no response; the village was still, no veteran warrior
greeted the party as victors, and those who mourned over
deceased relatives scowled at them as they passed.   The
usual triumph was not allowed, and the young aggressors,
so far from being joined by others in a new expedition, fell
back abashed by the chilling and contemptuous reception
which they met.   One old man alone, a conjurer, who
had prophesied that when these young men should return,
the war pole would be ornamented with the scalps of their
enemies, felt disposed to verify his own prediction by
having those bloody trophies paraded upon the war post,
and he exerted himself to effect a change in the public
mind.   At length the voice of one chief declared that
fallen relatives would be poorly revenged by shedding the
blood of friends, and that if satisfaction was required it
should be taken from the pale faces.   He then commenced
the war song, at the sound of which the habitual thirst of
the Indian for vengeance began to be excited; the young
men responded, and volunteers offered themselves to go
against the common enemy, among whom Ridge was the
first.   The party proceeded immediately against a small
fort on the frontier, which they took, and murdered all the
inmates—men, women, and children.   Ridge has since
frequently related the fact, that the women and children
were at first made prisoners, but were hewn down by the
ferocious leader Doublehead, who afterwards became a
conspicuous man, and a tyrant in the nation; he spoke of
this foul deed with abhorrence, and declared that he turned

aside, and looked another way, unwilling to witness that which he could not prevent.[13]

We pass over the events of the border wars which succeeded, and continued for two years to harass this unhappy reign, embracing a vast number of skirmishes and petty massacres, which gave scope to individual address and boldness, but produced no military movements upon any extended scale, nor any general battle. The last invasion by the whites was conducted by General Sevier, who penetrated to the head of Coosa, and then returned to Tennessee.[14] Two years afterwards a general peace was concluded with President Washington by a Cherokee delegation, sent to the American capital, at the head of which was the celebrated Doublehead. They returned, bringing a treaty of peace, and accompanied by an agent of the American Government, Colonel Silas Dinsmore, who took up his residence in the Cherokee country, and commenced instructing the Indians in the use of the plough, the spinning-wheel, and the loom.[15]

The government of the Cherokee nation was, at that time, vested in a council, composed of the principal chief, the second principal chief, and the leading men of the several villages, who made treaties and laws, filled the vacancies in their own body, increased its number at will, and in short, exercised all the functions of sovereignty. The executive and more active duties were performed chiefly by the junior members, a requisite number of whom were admitted for that purpose. At the age of twenty-one Ridge was selected, we are not told at whose instance, as a member of this body, from the town of which Pine Log[16] was the head man. He had no property but the clothes he wore, a few silver ornaments, and a white pony, stinted, old, and ugly, which he rode to the council. The Indians are fond of show, and pay great respect to personal

appearance and exterior decoration. On public occasions
they appear well mounted, and are ostentatious in the
display of their wealth, which consists in horses, weapons,
trinkets, and the trophies of war and hunting ; and this
pride is the more natural as the property thus exhibited
consists of the spoils won by the wearer. A mean
appearance is, therefore, in some degree an evidence of
demerit ; and when Ridge presented himself before the
assembled nation, wretchedly mounted and in meagre
attire, he was held in such contempt that it was proposed
to exclude him from the council. But the old men
invited him to a seat near them, and shook him by the
hand, and the younger members one by one reluctantly
extended to him the same sign of fellowship. During the
first council he did no more than listen to the speeches of
the orators, seldom indicating any opinion of his own.
The powers of the mind are but little exercised in an Indian
council, especially in a season of peace, when there is
nothing to provoke discussion, and these assemblages are
convened rather in obedience to custom than for the
actual discharge of business. But the time was approaching when the public concerns of the Cherokees were to
become more complicated and important, and its councils
to assume a higher dignity and interest.

It would be difficult to point out with accuracy the
primary causes, or to detect the first germs, of the partial
civilisation which has been introduced among the
Cherokees. In the memoir of Sequoyah we briefly
suggested several incidents which, as we suppose, exerted
a combined influence in the production of this benign
effect. Referring the reader to that paragraph, we shall
only remark here that Ridge entered upon public life just
at the period when a portion of his nation began to turn
their attention to agriculture, and of course to acquire

property, and to need the protection of law.   New regula-
tions and restraints were requisite to suit the novel
exigencies of a forming state of society; while the less
intelligent part of the people withheld from war, and not
yet initiated in the arts of peace, remained in a state of
restless and discontented idleness but little in unison with
the enterprising spirit of their leaders, and as little con-
genial with the growth of civilisation.   It was necessary,
therefore, that those who executed the laws should be firm
and vigorous men; and among this class Ridge was soon
distinguished as one possessing the energy of character so
important in a ruler.   At the second council in which he
sat, one of the ancient laws of the Cherokees was abrogated
at his suggestion.   According to immemorial usage, the
life of a murderer was at the disposal of the relatives of the
deceased, who might put him to death, or accept a price
for the injury.   Blood for blood was the rule, and if the
guilty party fled, his nearest relative might be sacrificed in
his place.   The nation was divided into seven tribes, each
preserving a distinct genealogy, traced through the female
line of descent : and these tribes were held sacredly bound
to administer this law, each within its own jurisdiction,
and to afford facilities for its execution when the aggressor
fled from one tribe to another.[17]   And we may remark here
as a curious illustration of the principle of Indian justice,
that the object of this law was not to punish guilt, to
preserve life, or to prevent crime ; neither the protection
of the weaker, nor the conservation of the peace of society
was its object; it was the *lex talionis* administered simply
to appease individual passion—its sole purpose was revenge.
For if anyone killed another by accident, his life was as
much forfeited as if he committed a wilful homicide, and
if he could not be readily found, the blood of his innocent
relative might be shed : the most inoffensive and respect-

able person might be sacrificed to atone for the crime or the carelessness of a vagabond kinsman. Ridge, in an able speech, exposed the injustice of that part of this law which substituted a relative for a fugitive murderer, and successfully advocated its repeal. The more difficult task remained, of enforcing obedience to the repealing statute—a task which involved the breaking up of an ancient usage, and the curbing into subjection one of the wildest impulses of the human bosom, the master passion of the savage—revenge; and this was to be effected in a community newly reorganised, still barbarous, and unused to the metes and bounds of a settled government. But Ridge, having proposed the measure, was required to carry it into effect, and readily assumed upon himself that responsibility; taking the precaution, however, to exact from every chief a promise that he would advocate the principle of the new law, and stand prepared to punish its infringement. It was not long before an opportunity occurred to test the sincerity of these pledges. A man who had killed another, fled. The relations of the deceased were numerous, fearless, and vindictive, prompt to take offence, and eager to imbue their hands in blood upon the slightest provocation. They determined to resent the injury by killing the brother of the offender. The friends of the latter despatched a messenger to Ridge, to advise him of the intended violation of the new law, and implore his protection; and he, with a creditable promptitude, sent word to the persons who proposed to revenge themselves, that he would take upon himself the office of killing the individual who should put such a purpose into execution. This threat had the desired effect, not only in that instance, but in causing the practice of substituting a relative in the place of an escaped homicide, to be abandoned.

About this time the subject of this memoir was married

to a Cherokee girl, who is represented as having been handsome and sensible—who possessed a fine person, and an
engaging countenance, and sustained through life an
excellent character.

The Cherokees lived at that time in villages, having corn
fields, cultivated by the squaws, and enclosed in a common
fence, which, by excluding the idea of separate property,
cut off the strongest inducement to industry.   Their
dwellings were rude cabins, with earthen floors, and
without chimneys.   Ridge determined, after his marriage,
to build a house, and cultivate a farm ; and accordingly he
removed into the wilderness, and reared a mansion of logs,
which had the luxury of a door and the extravagant
addition of a chimney.   Nor was this all : a roof was
added, of long boards, split from logs, and confined in
their places by *weight poles*—and thus was completed the
usual log cabin of the frontier settler, an edifice which ranks
in architecture next above the lodge or wigwam.   And here
did the Indian warrior and his bride, forsaking the habits
of their race, betake themselves to ploughing and chopping,
knitting and weaving, and other Christian employments,
while insensibly they dropped also the unpronounceable
heathen names in which they had hitherto rejoiced, and
became known as Major Ridge and Susannah.   It is hardly
necessary to remark, that one of the first things which the
Indian learns from his civilised neighbour is his love of
titles, and finding that every gentleman of standing on the
frontier had one, and that neither a commission nor a
military employment are necessarily inferred from the
assumption of a martial designation, he usually, on taking
an English name, prefixes to it the title of Captain or
Major.[18]

The residence of Major Ridge was in the Ookellogee
valley, where he lived more than eighteen years, employed

in rural pursuits, and gathering about him herds and other property.[19] He seems to have entirely abandoned the savage life, and settled quietly down in the enjoyment of the comforts of civilisation. His family consisted of five children, one of whom died in infancy, another was deficient in mind, and the other three were well educated. His son John,[20] after attending the mission school at Brainerd, was sent to Cornwall in Connecticut, where he spent four years under the instruction of the Reverend Herman Daggett. He here fell in love with a beautiful and excellent young lady, Miss Northrop, who reciprocated his affection, and after an engagement of two years they were married—she leaving for him, her parents, brothers, sisters, and friends, and identifying herself with the Cherokees, among whom she has ever since resided. This couple have six children. The influence of this lady has already been most benignantly exerted over the rude people with whom her lot has been cast; but the extent of her usefulness will not be fully known nor appreciated until it shall be seen in the exertions of her children, whom she is carefully training up in the precepts of the Bible. The daughters of Major Ridge were also educated. One of them married and died early; the other is an accomplished young lady, of superior mind, who has travelled through most of the States of the Union, and who devotes herself with a Christian and patriotic ardour to the improvement of her countrywomen. The whole family are professors of religion, and are exemplary in their lives.

The interesting domestic avocations in which Major Ridge was now busily engaged did not withdraw him from his public duties. He continued to be an active member of the council, in which he gradually rose to be an influential leader, and he was the orator usually chosen to announce and explain to the people the decrees of that body. He was also engaged in riding what was termed the judicial circuit. To enforce the laws among a barbarous people required a vigorous administration, and this office was assigned to twelve horsemen, persons of courage and intelligence, who were the judges, jurors, and executors of justice. Major Ridge was placed at the head of this corps, whose duty it was to ride through the nation, to take cognisance of all crimes and breaches of law, and to decide all controversies between individuals. In the unsettled state of the community, the want of forms, and the absence of precedent, much was left to their discretion; and after all, these decisions were enforced rather by the number, energy, and physical power of the judges, than through any respect paid to the law itself.

In addition to these arduous duties as a magistrate, Ridge was active and useful in his example as a private man. He encouraged the opening of roads, and caused some to be made at his own expense. He advocated all public improvements, and endeavoured to inculcate a taste for the refinements of civilisation. He built a house, planted an orchard, and went forward in the march of improvement, until his farm was in a higher state of cultivation and his buildings better than those of any other person in that region, the whites not excepted.

About the close of the administration of President Jefferson, the question as to emigrating to the west of the Mississippi began to be agitated among the Cherokees. Enolee, or Black Fox,[21] the successor of Little Turkey, was head chief of the nation. He, with Tah-lon-tus-kee,[22] Too-chay-lor, The Glass,[23] The Turtle at Home, and others, began to advocate the removal; the public mind became greatly excited, and those who possessed oratorical talents employed them in popular harangues. While the people were discussing the subject, the chiefs had matured their plan, and were proceeding to carry it into effect without the public consent which the usages of the nation required, but for which they intended to substitute a hasty vote of the council. Accordingly, at a council held at a post within the limits of Tennessee, Black Fox, and a few other leaders, acting in concert with Colonel R. J. Meigs, the agent of the United States, brought forward a project for sending a delegation to Washington, to exchange their country for lands farther west. The deputies were already nominated by the head chief; his *talk* to the President of the United States was delivered to Tah-lon-tus-kee, the leader of the deputation; and a vote of the council only was wanting to sanction what had been done, and to authorise the making of a treaty under which the nation should be removed to a far distant wilderness. That *talk* was in substance as follows :—" Tell our Great Father, the President, that our game has disappeared, and we wish to follow it to the West. We are his friends, and we hope he will grant our petition, which is to remove our people towards the setting sun. But we shall give up a fine country, fertile in soil, abounding in watercourses, and well adapted for the residence of white people. For all this we must have a good price." This bold and artful movement had the desired effect : the people, who had discussed the subject without reference to a decision so sudden and conclusive, were not ready for the question : they were taken by surprise, and as it was not expected that anyone would have the moral courage to rise in opposition under such circumstances, it only remained to take a vote, which would so far commit the nation as to preclude any future debate. A dead silence ensued—the assembly was apparently awed, or cajoled into compliance, when Ridge, who had a spirit equal to the occasion, and who saw with indignation that the old men kept their seats, rose from the midst of the younger chiefs, and with a manner and tone evincing great excitement, addressed the people. "My friends," said he, "you have heard the talk of the principal chief. He points to the region of the setting sun as the future habitation of this people. As a man he has a right to give his opinion; but the opinion he has given as the chief of this nation is not binding; it was not formed in council in the light of day, but was made up in a corner— to drag this people, without their consent, from their own country, to the dark land of the setting sun. I resist it here in my place as a man, as a chief, as a Cherokee, having the right to be consulted in a matter of such importance. What are your heads placed on your bodies for, but to think, and if to think, why should you not be consulted? I scorn this movement of a few men to unsettle the nation, and trifle with our attachment to the land of our forefathers! Look abroad over the face of this country —along the rivers, the creeks, and their branches, and you behold the dwellings of the people who repose in content and security. Why is this grand scheme projected to lead away to another country the people who are happy here? I, for one, abandon my respect for the will of a chief, and regard only the will of thousands of our people. Do I speak without the response of any heart in this assembly, or do I speak as a free man to men who are free and know their rights? I pause to hear." He sat down in the midst of acclamations. The people declared that his talk was good, that the talk of the head chief was bad; the latter was deposed upon the spot, and another appointed in his place. The delegation was changed, so that a majority of it were opposed to emigration, and Ridge was added to the number.[24]

The advantage of travelling through the United States was not thrown away upon this intelligent and liberal-minded Indian. He visited the capital of a great nation, passing through many populous towns and a great extent of cultivated country—was introduced to President Jefferson, and became acquainted with many refined persons. He returned with a mind enlarged by travel, and with a renewed ardour in the cause of civilisation.

The authority which we follow, having supplied us with few dates, we are not able to state at what time the ferocious Doublehead rose into power among the Cherokees, nor is it very important.[25] He was bold, ambitious, and possessed of uncommon sagacity and talent. He had strong friends, and, by prudently amassing such property as the condition of the country rendered attainable, was considered wealthy. With these advantages he became a prominent man; and when the Cherokees began to establish something like a civil government, and to create offices, he succeeded in placing himself in the most lucrative posts. But as he sought office with selfish views, he very naturally abused it, and made himself odious by his arbitrary conduct. He not only executed the laws according to his own pleasure, but caused innocent men to be put to death who thwarted his views. The chiefs and the people began alike to fear him, and a decree was privately made that he should be put to death. Ridge was chosen to perform the office of executioner, which he boldly discharged, by going with a few followers to Doublehead's house and killing him in the midst of his family; after which, he addressed the crowd who were drawn together by this act of violence, and explained his authority and his reasons. It is impossible for us to decide how far such an act may have been justified by the demerits of the victim, and the patriotic motives of him who assumed the office of avenger. To settle the relative merits of the Brutus and the Cæsar, is seldom an easy task; and it is rendered the more difficult in this instance, in consequence of the absence of all evidence but that of the friends of the parties.   There seems, however, to be sufficient reason to believe that Ridge sincerely desired to promote the civilisation of his race, that Doublehead, his equal in talent and influence, but a savage at heart, entertained less liberal views, and that the removal of the latter was necessary to the fair operation of the great experiment to which Ridge was now devoting all his energies.

Shortly after the return of Ridge from Washington, a great excitement occurred among the Cherokees, on the subject of civilisation.   Heretofore the improvement of this nation had been gradual and almost imperceptible. A variety of causes acting together, led to a chain of natural consequences which, by easy degrees, had produced important changes in the habits of the people. The insulated position of the nation, the intermixture of a half-breed race, the vicinity of the white settlements, the visits of the missionaries, and the almost miraculous invention of Sequoyah, had all contributed to infuse the spirit of civilisation.   But though many were converted, the great majority remained wrapped in the impenetrable mantle of barbarism, unaffected by these beneficent efforts, or regarding them with sullen apathy or stupid suspicion. A mass of ignorance, prejudice, and vice excluded the rays of civilisation, as the clouds of unwholesome vapour exhaled from the earth shade her bosom from the genial warmth of the sun.   But what, previous to the period at which we have arrived, had been merely doubt or disinclination, now began to assume the form of opposition. Some of the Cherokees dreamed dreams, and others received, in various ways, communications from the Great Spirit all tending to discredit the scheme of civilisation. A large collection of these deluded creatures met at

Oostanalee town,[26] where they held a grand savage feast, and celebrated a great medicine dance, which was performed exclusively by women, wearing terrapin shells, filled with pebbles, on their limbs, to rattle in concert with their wild uncouth songs. An old man chanted a song of ancient times. No conversation was allowed during the ceremony; the fierce visage of the Indian was bent in mute attention upon the exciting scene, and the congregated mass of mind was doubtless pervaded by the solemnising conviction that the Great Spirit was among them. At this opportune crisis, a deputation from Coosa Wathla[27] introduced a half-breed Cherokee from the mountains, who professed to be the bearer of a message from heaven. His name was Charles.[28] He was received with marked respect, and seated close to Ridge, the principal person present, and who, though he deplored the superstition that induced the meeting, had thought proper to attend, and ostensibly to join in the ceremonies. The savage missionary did not keep them long in suspense; he rose and announced that the Great Spirit had sent him to deliver a message to his people; he said he had already delivered it to some of the Cherokees in the mountains, but they disbelieved, and had beaten him. But he would not desist; he would declare the will of the Great Spirit at all hazards. The Great Spirit said that the Cherokees were adopting the customs of the white people. They had mills, clothes, feather beds, and tables—worse still, they had books, and domestic cats! This was not good— therefore the buffaloes and other game were disappearing. The Great Spirit was angry, and had withdrawn his protection. The nation must return to the customs of their fathers. They must kill their cats, cut short their frocks, and dress as became Indians and warriors. They must discard all the fashions of the whites, abandon the use of any communication with each other except by word of mouth, and give up their mills, their houses, and all the arts learned from the white people. He promised, that if they believed and obeyed, then would game again abound, the white man would disappear, and God would love his people. He urged them to paint themselves, to hold feasts, and to dance—to listen to his words, and to the words the Great Spirit would whisper in their dreams. He concluded by saying, if anyone says that he does not believe, the Great Spirit will cut him off from the living.

This speech, artfully framed to suit the prejudices of the Indians, and to inflame the latent discontent of such as were not fully enlisted in the work of reform, caused a great excitement among them. They cried out that the talk was good. Major Ridge perceived at once the evil effect that would be produced by such harangues, and, with his usual decision, determined not to tamper with the popular feeling, but to oppose and correct it. He rose in his place, and addressing the tumultuous assemblage with his wonted energy, said : "My friends, the talk you have heard is not good. It would lead us to war with the United States, and we should suffer. It is false ; it is not a talk from the Great Spirit. I stand here and defy the threat that he who disbelieves shall die. Let the death come upon me. I offer to test this scheme of impostors !" The people, mad with superstition, rushed upon the orator who dared thus to brave their fury, and rebuke their folly, and would probably have put him to death, had he not defended himself. Being an athletic man, he struck down several of the assailants, but was at last thrown to the ground, and his friend, John Harris, stabbed at his side. Jesse Vaun[29] and others rallied round him, and beating back the crowd, enabled him to rise ; and at length an old chief had sufficient influence over the infuriated savages to quell the tumult. As the tempest of passion subsided, the fanaticism which had caused it died away. The threat of the pretended messenger of heaven had proved false. His challenge had been accepted, and the daring individual who had defied him, lived, an evidence of his imposition.

The storm of fanaticism passed on to the Creek nation, among whom dreams were dreamed, and prophets arose who professed to have talked with the Great Spirit. The daring and restless Tecumthe, who had traversed the wilderness, for several hundred miles, for the purpose of stirring the savages to war against the Americans, appeared among the Creeks at this juncture, and artfully availed himself of a state of things so well suited to his purpose. Besides bringing tidings from the Great Spirit, he brought assurances from the British king, and greetings from the Shawanoe nation. The Creeks rose against their chiefs, broke out into war against the United States, and having surprised the frontier post of Fort Mimms, massacred the whole garrison, without distinction of age or sex.[30]

These events occurred at a period the most gloomy in the history of our frontier settlements, the most hapless in the melancholy record of the destiny of the red man. The jealousies between Great Britain and America were rapidly approaching to a crisis, and the prospect of a war between these nations opened a wide field for the turbulence of savage passion and the craft of savage intrigue. The extensive frontier of the United States, from the Lakes to the Gulf of Mexico, became agitated. Emissaries, prophets, and mercenary traders were at work in every direction, having various interests and purposes, but alike bent upon setting all the elements of discord in motion.

General William McIntosh,[31] a half-breed Creek, and
one of their head men from Coweta, was on a visit to the
Cherokee nation, when the faithless and tragic outrage was
perpetrated at Fort Mimms[32]; and, by order of the chiefs,
he was escorted back to his own country by a chosen
band of Cherokees, at the head of whom was Ridge.   On
their arrival at Coweta, they found the council of the
Creek nation assembled.   The head chief, Big Warrior,[33]
of Tuckabachee,[34] was there, endeavouring to devise
measures to secure his people from the impending danger
of a civil war and a war with the United States.   The
chiefs were in favour of a pacific policy, but they were
overruled by a large majority, who, under the malign
influence of the prophets, breathed only vengeance against
the whites, and uncompromising hostility against every
measure and every advocate of Christianity or civilisation.
The Big Warrior, having drawn a band of faithful friends
about him for his present protection, applied to the
United States authorities for assistance to put down this
rebellion; and sent to the Cherokee nation a *talk*, together
with a piece of tobacco, tied with a string of various
coloured beads, to be smoked in their council.   Ridge was
the bearer of the tobacco and the *talk* of the Creek chief,
and in his name demanded aid to put down the *Red Sticks*,
as the insurgent party were called[35]; and, in an animated
speech, he urged the object of his mission before the
council at Oostanalee.   He maintained that the hostile
portion of the Creeks, in making war against the whites,
had placed the Cherokees in a condition which obliged
them to take one side or the other.   That in the unsettled
state of the country, no distinction would be known but
that of Indians and white men, and a hostile movement
by any tribe would involve the whole in war.   He insisted
further, that if the Creeks were permitted to put down

their chiefs, and be ruled by the prophets, the work of civilisation would be subverted, and the Red Sticks, in their efforts to re-establish a state of barbarism, would destroy all the southern tribes. The council listened with attention, and having considered the arguments of Ridge, declared that they would not interfere in the affairs of their neighbours, but would look on, and be at peace. "Then," said Ridge, "I will act with volunteers. I call upon my friends to join me." A number of brave men, the most conspicuous persons in the nation, came forward; the people imbibed the spirit, until at last the chiefs were constrained to reverse their recent decision in council, and declare war.

The Government of the United States had, by this time, taken steps to punish the massacre at Fort Mimms, and to protect the border settlements. General White,[36] of Tennessee, with a body of the militia of that State, accompanied by Major Ridge and a number of Cherokee warriors, marched into the Creek nation, and returned with many prisoners.

On his arrival at home, Major Ridge sent runners through the nation to collect volunteers for another expedition, and, with the assistance of the other chiefs, raised eight hundred warriors, whom he led to the headquarters of General Jackson,[37] at the Ten Islands, in Alabama. Under this commander, destined to become eminently successful in his military exploits, the army moved towards the position of the Creeks, who occupied a fortified camp in a bend of the Talapoosa River, which from its shape was called the Horseshoe.[38] This little peninsula was connected with the mainland by a narrow isthmus, across which the Creeks had thrown a strong breastwork of logs, pierced with loopholes, while the remainder of the circumference was surrounded and protected by the deep

river.   Within the area was a town and camp, in the midst
of which was a high post painted red, and at the top of
this were suspended the scalps of the white people who
had been slain in the war.   The Creek warriors, naked,
and painted red, danced round this pole, and assembled
about it, to narrate their exploits in battle, for the purpose
of exciting in each other the principle of emulation, and
the desire of vengeance.   General Jackson, with his usual
energy of purpose, resolved to attack the enemy without
delay.   The main body of his army advanced upon the
breastwork, while General Coffee,[39] with a detachment of
the militia and the Cherokee allies, forded the Talapoosa
below, and surrounded the bend of the river.   It was not
intended that this division should cross into the camp, nor
were they provided with boats; but the Cherokees becoming anxious to join in the assault, two of them swam over
the river, and returned with two canoes.   A third canoe
was secured by the activity of a Cherokee, who brought it
from the middle of the river, after the Creeks who occupied
it had been shot by the Tennessee riflemen.   Major Ridge
was the first to embark; and in these three boats the
Cherokees crossed, a few at a time, until the whole body
had penetrated to the enemy's camp.   A spirited attack
was made upon the rear of the enemy, by which their
attention was diverted from the breastwork, and material
aid given to a daring charge then making upon it, by
the regulars and militia.   The breastwork was carried; the
troops poured into the camp, the Indians pressed upon its
rear, and the Creeks sought shelter behind numerous logs
and limbs of forest trees, which had been strewn about to
impede the advance of the assailants, and afford protection
to themselves in the last resort.   Here they fought with
desperation.   Thinned by the sharpshooters, and hemmed
in on all sides, they scorned to ask for quarter—or, perhaps,

MAJOR RIDGE
A Cherokee Chief

unaccustomed to that courtesy of civilised warfare which allows the vanquished to claim his life, they knew not how to make the demand. They continued to fight, and to shout the war whoop, selling their blood dearly to the last drop. Driven at last from their lurking places, they plunged into the thicket of reeds that margined the river, but the sword and the tomahawk found them here, and their last dismal refuge was in the deep current of the Talapoosa. Here too the rifle-ball overtook them, and the vindictive Cherokees rushed into the water in the fury of the pursuit. Few escaped to report the tragic story of that eventful day.

Ridge was a distinguished actor in this bloody drama; and we are told that he was the first to leap into the river in pursuit of the fugitives. Six Creek warriors, some of whom had been previously wounded, fell by his hand. As he attempted to plunge his sword in one of these, the Creek closed with him, and a severe contest ensued. Two of the most athletic of their race were struggling in the water for life or death, each endeavouring to drown the other. Ridge, forgetting his own knife, seized one which his antagonist wore and stabbed him; but the wound was not fatal, and the Creek still fought with an equal chance of success, when he was stabbed with a spear by one of Ridge's friends, and thus fell a hero who deserved a nobler fate.[40]

Thus ended the massacre of the Horseshoe, the recital of which we have made as brief as was consistent with fidelity to our task. We take no pleasure in recording these deeds of extermination; but they form a portion of history, and, unhappily, the story of border warfare is always the same; for it is always war embittered by party feud, personal injury, and individual hatred—a national quarrel aggravated by private griefs and inflamed by bad passions.

After the Creek war, Major Ridge visited Washington as a delegate from his nation, to President Madison, to adjust the northern boundary of their country; and he again represented his people on a similar mission during the administration of Mr Monroe.[41]   He had now become a prominent man, and when Alexander Saunders, an influential Cherokee, and the personal friend of Ridge, proposed to divide the nation and organise a new council, it was chiefly through his exertions that the scheme was defeated.

After the death of Charles R. Hicks, the Cherokees were governed by John Ross, who, being a person of some education, led them to adopt a constitution and laws in imitation of those of the United States.[42]   We pass over the controversy that ensued between the Cherokees and the State of Georgia, and between the latter and the United States, with the single remark that Georgia objected to the organisation of a government by Indians within her limits; and insisted that the American Government should extinguish the title of the Cherokees, and remove them to other lands.[43]   Major Ridge had been among those who were opposed to the emigration of his people; he had favoured the plan of establishing a regular government, and the introduction of education and Christianity, and had believed that these improvements could be more successfully cultivated by remaining in their own country than in a region of wilderness where all the temptations to a relapse into savage habits would be presented.   But when, after a bitter and fruitless contest, it was found that Georgia adhered inflexibly to her determination, and the Government of the United States would not interfere,[44] he saw that sooner or later the weaker party must submit or be crushed, and he now used his influence to induce the Indians to remove to the new home pointed out to them.

His views were supported by the members of a delegation that visited Washington in 1832, and who, after appealing to the Government and conversing with many eminent public men and intelligent citizens, whose sympathies were strongly enlisted in their cause, came to the conclusion that it would be best to do at once that to which they would be finally compelled. John Ross with a majority of the Cherokees maintained a different policy, and an unhappy spirit of party was engendered by this diversity of opinion. Major Ridge was accused of entertaining opinions hostile to the interest and happiness of the people —was regularly impeached, and cited to appear before a council to be held in the autumn of 1833, to answer a charge of treason. But when the time arrived his accusers endeavoured to put off the trial; betraying evidently their own convictions of his innocence, and their willingness to hold over him an accusation which, while neither established nor refuted, might neutralise his influence. This attempt, however, failed, and the charge was dismissed.

Major Ridge is one of the very few individuals who, after being reared in the habits of the savage, have embraced the employments and comforts of civilised life. In youth we have seen him pursuing the chase for a livelihood, and seeking the war-path with all the Indian avidity for bloodshed and plunder. Gradually withdrawing from these occupations, he became a cultivator of the soil, a legislator, and a civil magistrate; exhibiting in each capacity a discretion and dignity of character worthy of a better education. His house resembled in no respect the wigwam of the Indian—it was the home of the patriarch, the scene of plenty and hospitality.

He showed the sincerity of his own conversion from barbarism by giving to his children the advantages of education, and rearing them in habits of morality and temperance. All of them have professed the Christian religion and sustained fair reputations; while Major Ridge, surrounded by his descendants, enjoys in his old age the respect and confidence earned by a long life of active industry and energetic public service.[45]

NOTES

1. Regarding Ridge's names, Mooney ("Myths of the Cherokee," *Nineteenth Report of the Bureau of American Ethnology*, Washington, 1900, p. 528) gives the following in his glossary:
"*Nûñnä'hi-dihĭ'* (abbreviated *Nûñ'nä-dihĭ'*)—'Path-killer,' literally, 'he kills (habitually) in the path,' from *nûn'nâhi*, 'path,' and *ahihĭ'*, 'he kills' (habitually); 'I am killing,' *tsi'ihŭ'*. A principal chief, about the year 1813. Major John Ridge was usually known by the same name, but afterward took the name *Gûnûñ'da'légĭ*, 'one who follows the ridge,' which the Whites made simply Ridge."

2. See *Sequoyah*, p. 130 of this volume.

3. Hiwassee, the English form of *Ayuhwási*, signifying "meadow," "savannah," was the name of several former Cherokee settlements, the most important of which, distinguished by the Cherokee as *Ayuhwási Egwä'hĭ*, or Great Hiwassee, was on the north bank of Hiwassee River, at the present Savannah ford, above Columbus, Polk County, Tennessee. Another was farther up the river at the junction of Peachtree creek, above Murphy, Cherokee County, North Carolina (Mooney, *op. cit.*, p. 512).

4. Boudinot's Cherokee name is *Gălăgína*, signifying either "male deer" or "turkey." He was educated in the mission school at Cornwall, Connecticut, which he entered in 1818 at the instance of the philanthropist whose name he adopted. By resolution of the Cherokee council in 1827 a national paper was authorized, and in 1828 the *Cherokee Phœnix* appeared under Boudinot's editorship. It existed for six years, when publication ceased, and was not resumed until after the removal of the tribe from the south to Indian Territory, when its place was finally taken in 1844 by the *Cherokee Advocate*. From 1823 until he was murdered, June 22, 1839, on account of his support of the "Ridge treaty" by the terms of which the Cherokee were removed to the West (see note 43), Boudinot was joint translator with Rev. S. A. Worcester of a number of the Gospels. In 1833 he wrote *Poor Sarah; or, the Indian Woman*, in the syllabic characters invented by Sequoyah, a new edition of which was issued from the Park Hill Press, Indian Territory, in 1843.

See Pilling, *Bibliography of the Iroquoian Languages,* 1888 ; and Mooney, *op. cit.*

4a. The Sequatchie River flows into the Tennessee below Chattanooga, in Marion County, following in its course the Walden range—the "Sequochee mountains" here referred to. The name, according to Mooney, is from *Si'gwetsi'*, the meaning of which has been lost.

5. Whether "superstitious" or not depends entirely on the point of view. The term "religious" is more appropriate for these Indian rites and ceremonies, since it places them in their proper category. They were solemn in every degree, and are at least as deeply rooted as are the religious rites of people of the highest enlightenment.

6. For further information regarding "scratching" as a feature of certain Cherokee ceremonies, see Mooney, *op. cit.,* pp. 230, 476, and the same author's "Cherokee Ball Play" (*Am. Anthropologist,* April 1890), and "Sacred Formulas of the Cherokee" (*Seventh Rep. Bureau of Ethnology,* 1891); also Adair, *History of the American Indians,* 1775, pp. 46, 120.

7. Cheestooyee is *Tsistúyi,* "Rabbit place," a former Cherokee settlement on the north bank of Hiwassee River, at the entrance of Chestua Creek, in Polk County, Tennessee. The name of Choastea Creek of Tugaloo River, in Oconee County, South Carolina, is also probably a corruption of the same word. Tsistúyi is likewise the name of Gregory Bald, a high peak of the Great Smoky range, eastward from Little Tennessee River, on the boundary between Swain County, North Carolina, and Blount County, Tennessee (Mooney, *Myths of the Cherokee,* 538).

8. Little Turkey was chief of the settlement of Gûn'-dǐ'gaduhûñyǐ, "Turkey settlement," commonly called Turkey Town. See *Tahchee,* note 2, p. 340.

9. Chinnubbee, also known as Chinnaby. At the time of the Creek rebellion in 1813 he had a "fort" at Ten Islands on Coosa River, Alabama. He signed several Creek treaties.

10. This was probably the fighting about Knoxville and Maryville, Tennessee, in 1788. Ridge was about seventeen years of age at this time. (See Mooney, *Myths, op. cit.,* p. 65.)

11. Properly *Tălǐkwă;* in Oklahoma, *Tahlequah.* It was the name of several Cherokee settlements at different periods: (1) Great Tellico, at Tellico Plains, on Tellico River, Monroe County, Tennessee; (2) Little Tellico, on Tellico Creek of Little Tennessee River, in Macon County, North Carolina; (3) A town on Valley River about five miles above Murphy, Cherokee County, North Carolina; (4) Tahlequah, established as the capital of the Cherokee Nation, Indian Territory, in 1839. The meaning of the name has been lost (Mooney, *op. cit.,* 533).

12. The white man's name of *Na'ts-asûñ'tlûñyĭ* (abbreviated *Na'ts-*

asûñ'tlûñ), " Pine footlog place," from *na'tsĭ*, " pine " ; *asûñ'tlĭ*, or *asûñtlûñ'ĭ*, " footlog," " bridge " ; *yĭ* the locative. This was formerly a Cherokee settlement on Pinelog Creek in Bartow County, Georgia (Mooney, *op. cit.*, p. 527).

13. This was the affair in September, 1793, at Cavitts Station, a small blockhouse a few miles west of Knoxville. The building at the time contained only three men, with thirteen women and children, who surrendered on promise that they would be held for exchange, but Doublehead's warriors fell upon them and put them all to death except a boy. This bloody work is attributed directly to Doublehead, the other chiefs having done their best to prevent it.

The Cherokee name of this chief is *Tăl-tsúskă'*, " Two heads," from *tă'lĭ*, " two," and *tsúskă'*, plural of *usk'ă*, " (his) head." Haywood (*Natural and Aboriginal History of Tennessee*, 241, 1823) evidently refers to the same Indian as " Bullhead," one of the participants in the Creek war of 1813 (Mooney, *op. cit.*, pp. 75, 384, 532). He signed several treaties between 1791 and 1806.

14. Sevier's last campaign against the Creeks and Cherokee was in the autumn of 1793. The treaty referred to is that concluded at Philadelphia (then the seat of Government), June 26, 1794. " Chuquila-tague, or Double Head," was one of the signers, but not the first.

15. Spinning-wheels and looms were introduced among the Cherokee shortly before the Revolution. See Mooney, *op. cit.*, p. 212.

16. Compare note 12.

17. The clans of the Cherokee, as given by Mooney (*op. cit.*, p. 212), are here referred to. They were : Aní-Wá'ya, or Wolf ; Aní-Kawĭ', or Deer ; Aní-Tsískwa, or Bird ; Aní-Wâ'dĭ, or Paint ; Aní-Sahá'nĭ, Aní-Gâtâgéwĭ, Aní-Gilâ'hĭ. The names of the last three cannot be translated with certainty. Compare note 21.

18. The treaties signed by Ridge are as follows :—Tellico, October 25, 1805 (as Path Killer, or Nenohuttahe) ; Washington, March 22, 1816 (as Major Ridge) ; Chickasaw Council House, September 14, 1816 (name misprinted as " John Beuge " ?) ; Washington, March 14, 1835 (as John Ridge) ; New Echota, December 29, 1835 (as Major Ridge) ; supplementary treaty of March 1, 1836 (as Major Ridge). Of the last three treaties, he was the first signer in behalf of his tribe.

19. There were two creeks of this name in Georgia, but the one here referred to is evidently Ougillogy Creek of Oostanaula River, on which was situated a Cherokee town of the same name, *Uy'gilâgĭ*, abbreviated *Tsuyu'gilâ'gĭ*, " Where there are dams," *i.e.* beaver dams, near the present Calhoun, Gordon County, Georgia (Mooney, *op. cit.*, p. 545).

20. For John Ridge, see Volume II.

21. Inâ'lĭ, or Black Fox. He was chief in 1810, in which year (April 18) the Cherokee National Council formally abolished the practice of clan revenge. See Mooney, *op. cit.*, pp. 86, 522; Morse, *Report to Secretary of War*, App., 176, 1822.

22. Atálûñtískĭ, denoting one who throws some living object from a place, as an enemy from a precipice (Mooney, *op. cit.*, p. 511). He was a chief of the Arkansas band in 1818.

23. Correct Cherokee form, *Tágwădihĭ'* (abbreviated *Tágăwdĭ*), "Catawha killer," from *Atágwa*, or *Tágwa*, Catawba Indian, and *dihihĭ'*, "he kills them" (habitually). He was called Glass by the whites, through confusion of the name with *adakĕ'ti*, "glass," or "mirror" (Mooney, *op. cit.*, p. 533).

24. This was evidently in 1816, on March 22 of which year the Cherokee concluded with the Government the Treaty of Washington, and on the same day certain Articles of Convention, "Major Ridge" being the third Indian signer of each. Under this treaty the Cherokee agreed to quit-claim to the State of South Carolina all their lands within that State for the sum of $5000.

25. See note 13. Judging by the treaties, the height of this Indian's influence in the tribe was during the years 1791-1806, and it was probably in the latter year that he was killed. For the circumstances that lead to this execution, see Royce in *Fifth Report of the Bureau of Ethnology*, pp. 183, 193, 1888; and Mooney, *op. cit.*, p. 85.

26. Strictly *U'stănáli* (from *u'stănaláh'ĭ* or *unistănálă* (a plural form), denoting a natural barrier of rocks across a stream)—occurring in several places in the old Cherokee country, and variously spelled Eastinaulee, Eastanora, Estanaula, Eustanaree, Istanare, Oostanaula, Oostanalee, Ostinawley, Ustenary, etc. One settlement of this name was on Keowee River, below the present Fort George, in Oconee County, South Carolina; another seems to have been somewhere on Tuckasegee River, in western North Carolina; a third, prominent during and after the revolutionary period, was just above the junction of Coosawatee and Conasauga Rivers, to form the Oostanaula, in Gordon County, Georgia, and adjoining New Echota. Other settlements of the same name may have been on Eastanollee Creek of Tugaloo River, in Franklin County, Georgia, and on Eastaunaula Creek, flowing into Hiwassee River, in McMinn County, Tennessee (Mooney, *op. cit.*, p. 543).

27. Evidently *Kúsăwetíyĭ* (abbreviated *Kúsăwetî*), "Old Creek place," a former important Cherokee settlement on the lower part of Coosawatee River, in Gordon County, Georgia (Mooney, *op. cit.*, p. 526).

28. Possibly the same Charley (*Tsáli*) who was shot for resisting the troops during the removal in 1838. See Mooney, *op. cit.*, p. 131.

29. Intended for Jesse Vann. This is a common family name among the Cherokee. David Vann (see Vol. III.) rendered aid to the early missionaries.

30. See *Tenskwautawaw* in this volume, p. 75.

31. See his biography in this volume, p. 261.

32. " Fort Mims, so called from an old Indian trader on whose lands it was built, was a stockade fort erected in the summer of 1813 for the protection of the settlers in what was known as the Tensaw district, and was situated on Tensaw Lake, Alabama, one mile east of Alabama River and about forty miles above Mobile. It was garrisoned by about 200 volunteer troops under Major Daniel Beasley, with refugees from the neighboring settlement, making a total at the time of its destruction of 553 men, women, and children. Being carelessly guarded, it was surprised on the morning of August 30 by about 1000 Creek warriors led by the mixed-blood chief, William Weatherford, who rushed in at the open gate, and, after a stout but hopeless resistance by the garrison, massacred all within, with the exception of the few negroes and half-breeds, whom they spared, and about a dozen whites who made their escape. The Indian loss is unknown, but was very heavy, as the fight continued at close quarters until the buildings were fired over the heads of the defenders. The unfortunate tragedy was due entirely to the carelessness of the commanding officer, who had been repeatedly warned that the Indians were about, and at the very moment of the attack a negro was tied up waiting to be flogged for reporting that he had the day before seen a number of painted warriors lurking a short distance outside the stockade."—Mooney, op. cit., p. 216.

33. The name of this chief of the Upper Creeks is a common title in the tribe. Each town had a *miko*, or town chief, next to whom in rank were three *tastŭnŭ'gi*, or "warriors," who formed the chief's council which decided matters of public importance. One of these men was their nominal head and bore the title *tastŭnŭ'gi hlákko*, "big warrior" (Speck in *Memoirs Amer. Anthropological Assn.*, II., p. 113, 1907). The Big Warrior here mentioned was evidently the one who signed the treaty of Colerain, Ga., June 29, 1796 (as Tustunika Thlocco). He died in Washington, March 8, 1825. See Drake, *Aboriginal Races*, p. 409, 1880.

34. Tukabatchi was an Upper Creek settlement on the west bank of Tallapoosa River, in Elmore County, Alabama. It became a tribal centre, though it suffered much in wars with the Chickasaw, and it was here that Tecumseh met the Upper Creeks when he tried to incite them to war against the United States. In 1799 Tukabatchi could muster 116 warriors, and in 1832 it contained 386 houses.

35. See note 22, p. 103.

36. James White, Brigadier-General of Tennessee Volunteers (born Iredell County, North Carolina, 1737 ; died Knoxville, Tennessee, 1815). He led a successful attack on the Creeks at Hillabee Town in November 1813.

37. General Andrew Jackson, of course.

38. See note 4, p. 270.

39. General John Coffee commanded a volunteer regiment of cavalry.

40. "On account of the general looseness of Indian organization, we commonly find the credit claimed for whichever chief may be best known to the chronicler. Thus McKenney and Hall make Major Ridge the hero of the war, especially of the Horseshoe fight, although he is not mentioned in the official reports."—Mooney, *op. cit.*, p. 96.

41. One of these was the treaty of March 22, 1816 (see note 24). The only other treaty negotiated by the Cherokee tribe at Washington during Monroe's administration (1817-1825) was that of February 27, 1819, which does not bear Major Ridge's signature, although he signs as "Pathkiller" an appended document, dated Cherokee Agency, January 6, 1817.

42. See note 2, p. 143. Ross (see Volume III) became assistant chief in 1827, and chief in the following year, holding the latter position until his death, August 1, 1866. The Cherokee Constitution was adopted July 26, 1827.

43. For the details, consult Mooney, *op. cit.*, and the authorities cited by him.

44. This was due to the policy of Jackson, who believed the Indian had no rights that the white man was bound to respect, even after the United States Supreme Court had decided the contrary.

45. For an account of the general removal of the Cherokee to Indian Territory, beginning in October 1838, and ending in March 1839, with the awful sufferings *en route*, see Mooney, *Myths of the Cherokee* (p. 131 *et seq.*), on which excellent work we have drawn so largely for details bearing on the life and surroundings of Major Ridge. On their arrival in the Territory, "jealousies developed in which the minority or treaty party of the emigrants, headed by Ridge, took sides with the old settlers against the Ross or National party, which outnumbered both the others three to one. While these difficulties were at their height, the nation was thrown into a fever of excitement by the news that Major Ridge, his son John Ridge, and Elias Boudinot—all leaders of the treaty party—had been killed by adherents of the National party, immediately after the close of a general council, which had adjourned after nearly two weeks of debate, without having been able to bring about harmonious action. Major Ridge was waylaid and shot close to the Arkansas line, his son was taken from bed and cut to pieces with hatchets, while Boudinot was treacherously killed at his home at Park Hill, Indian Territory, all three being killed on the same day, June 22, 1839." In his report of the case, the agent said Major Ridge left a white wife, and that both he and his son were rich.

"About three weeks afterward," writes Mooney, "the National Council passed decrees declaring that the men killed and their principal confederates had rendered themselves outlaws by their own conduct, extending amnesty on certain stringent conditions to their confederates, and declaring the slayers guiltless of murder and fully restored to the confidence and favor of the community " (pp. 134-135).

That Ridge's portrait was painted at Washington during one of the subject's numerous visits on behalf of his people, there seems to be no doubt, but neither the painter nor the date is known. Judging from the portrait itself, it was painted not many years prior to Ridge's death —perhaps when he was in Washington in 1835. It is not listed in the Rhees *Catalogue* as one of the Indian Gallery pictures, nor does it appear in the list of Inman copies in the Peabody Museum.

LAPPAWINSOE

(A DELAWARE CHIEF)

THE preceding engraving, and the one which follows it, are taken from the original portraits, in the possession of the Historical Society of Pennsylvania. They were presented to that body by Granville Penn, Esq., of Stoke Park, England, a worthy descendant of the illustrious founder of the State which bears his name.[1] These portraits are highly interesting to the antiquarian, because they preserve to him the only likenesses which exist of the famed Lenni Lennapi[2] tribe of Indians.

All that is known respecting their originals is contained in a report made by Mr J. Francis Fisher and Mr Job R. Tyson, in the course of the last year, to the Historical Society, and published in the last volume of the Society's *Transactions*.[3]

The portraits were painted just a century ago (1737), and even the name of the limner would now be a subject of curious but uncertain speculation. If a native, his work would show the skill employed and attention bestowed at that time, in British America, upon this department of the arts. Mr Tyson and Mr Fisher suggest that the portraits were probably painted either by one Swede, named Cecilius, who executed a likeness of James Logan, or a later artist, named R. Feke, whose name appears on a picture of the year 1746.

408

The fame of Lappawinsoe, whatever it was, has not been transmitted to us. James Logan[4] speaks of him as an honest old Indian; and his name, "He is gone away gathering corn, nuts, or anything eatable," according to Heckewelder's translation, implies the character of an honest old hunter.[5] He was a chief, and is ranked by the last-named writer among those of the Forks of the Delaware. The act by which Lappawinsoe is chiefly known is, signing, at Philadelphia, the celebrated Treaty of 1737, commonly called *The Walking Purchase*. The character and effect of this negotiation are adverted to in the succeeding article.[6]

NOTES

1. Granville Penn (1761-1844) was the son of Thomas, the son of William the founder by his second wife. Granville was the author of a biography of his great-grandfather, Admiral Sir William Penn. He left several sons at his death in Stoke Pogis, all of whom died without issue, so that his pension descended to the family of his sister, Sophia Margaret, who married William Stuart, Archbishop of Armagh. Granville Penn visited Philadelphia in 1834, bringing with him the portraits of Lappawinsoe and Tishcohan for presentation to the Historical Society of Pennsylvania. Buck says: "They had probably been long in possession of his family. From the Penn accounts we derive sufficient information to believe that they were painted by Hesselius, a Swedish artist, by order of John or Thomas Penn, while in this country."

Of these two paintings, which are still in possession of the Society, practically nothing is known beyond what is here recorded. Each measures 24 × 32 inches, and is attributed to Hesselius (not Cecilius) or Feka. The committee appointed to report on the portraits consisted of Roberts Vaux, J. Francis Fisher, and Job R. Tyson, who say: "Of Lappawinzo we have been able to discover no further notice in history. James Logan [see note 4] speaks of him in 1741 as an honest old Indian. Tishcohan seems to have moved to the West, and was met by [Christian] Frederick Post, when he made his first journey to visit the Indians on the Ohio, in July, 1758. Such is the whole result of the inquiries of this committee, although they have examined all the documents printed and manuscripts within their reach. They have only to regret that they have been able to give so little interest to their report, and that so little has been handed down to us of the history of the only

two chiefs of the Lenni Lenape whose portraits have been preserved."
See *Memoirs of the Historical Society of Pennsylvania*, Vol. III., 1836, pt. 2,
pp. 211-212; and W. J. Buck in *Pennsylvania Magazine of History and
Biography*, VII., 1883, pp. 215-218. For the Journal of Post's first tour,
in which the name of Tishcohan appears as *Tasucamin* (one of the forms
used by McKenney and Hall), signed to a speech delivered to Post, see
[Thomson] *An Enquiry into the Causes of the Alienation of the Delaware and
Shawanese Indians from the British Interest*, London, 1759, pp. 130-184,
reprinted Philadelphia, 1867; Proud, *History of Pennsylvania*, Philadelphia, 1798, II., App., pp. 65-95; Craig, *The Olden Time*, I., 99-125;
Rupp, *Early History of Western Pennsylvania*, Pittsburgh and Harrisburg,
1846, App., pp. 75-98; *Pennsylvania Archives*, III., 520-544, and *Early
Western Travels*, edited by R. G. Thwaites, Cleveland, 1904, I., pt. 3.

On the face of the canvas of the Lappawinsoe portrait the name
Lapawinsa is painted, but *Lapawinze*, meaning "Getting provisions,"
seems to be the more nearly correct form. Heckewelder's translation,
referred to later in the text, is from his "Names which the Lenni
Lenapes or Delaware Indians . . . had given to Rivers, Streams, Places,
&c., &c." (*Transactions of the American Philosophical Society*, n. s., IV.,
p. 386, Philadelphia, 1834), although instead of "He is gone away,"
Heckewelder gives "He is gone again."

In a good photograph of the original picture of Lappawinsoe in
possession of the Bureau of American Ethnology at Washington, the
facial decoration, strongly noted in the accompanying illustration, is
hardly discernible.

2. These are the Delawares, as has been seen (note 1), formerly one
of the most important of the Algonquian tribal groups. They consisted
of three tribes—the Munsee, Unami, and Unalachtigo—and at the time
of William Penn's first treaty, in 1682, had their chief council fire at the
site of the present Germantown, a suburb of Philadelphia. They were
gradually driven westward by the colonists, settling on the headwaters
of the Alleghany in 1724, and in eastern Ohio by 1751. About 1770
they settled between the Ohio and White River, Indiana, and in 1789, by
permission of the Spanish Government, a part of them removed to
Missouri, and afterward to Arkansas. By 1820 these with some
Shawnee found their way into Texas, where the two bands numbered
about 700. By 1835 most of the tribe had been gathered on a reservation in Kansas, whence they were removed in 1867 to Indian Territory,
and incorporated with the Cherokee. Another band, now numbering 95,
is affiliated with the Caddo and Wichita in Oklahoma. About 260
Munsee are with the Stockbridges in Wisconsin, and about 45 with the
Chippewa in Kansas, while in Canada there are about 625, known as
"Moravians" and Munsee, living chiefly on the Thames. The total
Delaware population is about 1900, probably only a small proportion
of their number in colonial times.

The Delawares call themselves *Leni-lenápe*, equivalent to "real men,"
"native, genuine men."

3. For the report, see note 1.

4. James Logan the statesman, of Scotch-Irish parentage, born County Armagh, Ireland, October 20, 1674; died near Philadelphia, October 31, 1751. He came to America in 1699 as the secretary of William Penn, and remained in Philadelphia on the return of the founder to England in 1701. He held several positions of trust in the colony, and in various embassies gained such high esteem and confidence of the Indians that the celebrated Logan was named after him. He was impeached in 1707 and went to England, but returned five years later. In 1715 he was commissioned a Justice of the Court of Common Pleas, Quarter-Sessions, and Orphans' Court, and in 1723 became Judge of the Common Pleas, and in the same year Mayor of Philadelphia; from 1731 until 1739 he served as Chief-Justice of the Supreme Court, and in 1736-38 acted as Governor. The later years of his life were spent at "Stenton," his country-seat, now within the city, devoting his time to science and literature. Logan was the author of numerous works, including an annotated translation of Cicero's *De Senectute,* with notes and a preface by Benjamin Franklin, who printed the first edition (Philadelphia, 1740), which is regarded as the finest production of Franklin's Press. Logan bequeathed to Philadelphia a library of more than two thousand volumes, which in 1792 were transferred to the Library Company of Philadelphia, founded by Franklin in 1731, and are still preserved as the "Loganian Library."

5. See note 1.

6. Buck, in his article above cited (note 1), gives all the available information respecting both Lappawinsoe and Tishcohan. It is here quoted, practically in full:

"At a treaty held at Pennsbury, May 9, 1735, with John and Thomas Penn the proprietaries, Lappawinzo distinguished himself as the principal orator. On this occasion Nutimus, Tishcohan, Lesbeconk, and others were present. Another meeting was agreed upon in Philadelphia, which was accordingly held on August 24 and 25, 1737, in the presence of Thomas Penn, and on the latter day Lappawinzo, Manawkyhickon, Tishcohan, and Nutimus signed the release for the Walking Purchase, witnessed by fourteen whites and twelve Indians. Barefoot Brinston acted as the leading interpreter for the respective parties. According to his portrait, Lappawinzo is represented as a stout Indian of about forty years of age. A few black marks are painted on his forehead and cheeks. His hair is long and brought to the back part of his head, with a blue blanket thrown around him, and a pouch on his breast fastened to his neck. This will answer as a description of this chief, transmitted to us on canvas more than two years before the Walk.

"From Edward Marshall's testimony, taken in 1757, we learn that on the night of the first day's Walk they lodged near an Indian town called Hockendocqua, and that early next morning Nicholas Scull,

Benjamin Eastburn, and another person went to said settlement and spoke with Lappawinzo, who lived there, to send some other Indians to accompany the walkers for the remainder of the distance; when he replied 'that they had got all the best of the land, and they might go to the Devil for the bad, and that he would send no Indians with them.' He further stated that about eight weeks after the Walk he was again at the said town, when the same chief said that 'they were dissatisfied with the Walk, and that they would go down to Philadelphia the next May, with every one a buckskin, to repay the proprietor for what they had received from him and take their land again.' He also complained that the Walk was not fairly performed, and should not go the course fixed on by the proprietors, but should have gone along the Delaware or by the nearest Indian path as the proper direction. Alexander Brown, in his evidence, chiefly corroborates the aforesaid.

"It was Lappawinzo that Moses Marshall had reference to in his reminiscences taken down by John Watson, Junior, in a visit to him in 1822, in which 'an old Indian said "no sit down to smoke, no shoot a squirrel, but *lun, lun, lun,* all day long."' By this it would appear as if he had been pretty well on in years. I have been unable to trace him as living to a later period than the year of the Walk. Heckewelder says that his name signifies *going away to gather food.* It would seem by some of the statements as if he had been chiefly instrumental in the selection of John Combush, Neepaheilomon, *alias* Joe Tunean, who could speak English well, and his brother-in-law, Tom, the three young men appointed on the side of the Indians to be present as deputies to see that the Walk was fairly performed for the Delaware nation. James Le Tort, an Indian trader, mentions dealings with Lappawinzo in 1704, if not earlier.

"From an affidavit made by William Allen in 1762 we learn that whilst on visits to the Durham iron works (one of the owners of which he was), after 1727, he became personally acquainted with 'Tishecunk, who was always esteemed and reputed to be an honest upright man,' and with "Nutimus had always been regarded the chief original owner of the land in and about the Forks of Delaware and adjacent lands above Tohiccon.' This, coming from this great land speculator, is pretty good evidence that they had recognised rights there, and that any dissent on the part of either as regards unfair dealings in obtaining said lands must be of some weight. By his own oath, Allen has further implicated himself with the Penns in depriving at least those Indians of a considerable portion of their lands, long before they had obtained any right to them either through purchase or treaty.

"By appointment, Tishcohan and Nutimus, in October, 1734, had met John and Thomas Penn at Durham, in relation to a treaty and sale of lands, and also in May, 1735, at Pennsbury; but no particular business was accomplished, except to have the trial walk secretly performed in order to have things in readiness for the signing of the release for the Walking Purchase, which was duly concluded in

Philadelphia in the presence of Thomas Penn, William Allen, James Logan, and others, August 25, 1737, and to which Tishcohan, Nutimus, and two other Delaware chiefs affixed their marks. The walk was performed at such speed the 19th and 20th of the following month by Edward Marshall, that Solomon Jennings and James Yates, who were selected his associates by the proprietary party, were compelled to succumb before the termination of it, having made, according to the testimony of several of the witnesses present, *the first thirty miles in six hours*. According to the evidence of Ephraim Goodwin, we learn that at this time Tishcohan was an aged man and lived at the Indian village called Hockendocqua, near which the walkers and company staid over night on their first day's journey.

"Like nearly all Indian names, that of Tishcohan has been variously spelled or called, as Teshakomin, Tiscoquam, and Captain John Tishekunk, perhaps according to the fancies of the several writers. In his portrait, which is nearly the size of life, Tishcohan is represented with a Roman nose, a large mouth, and several deep wrinkles reaching nearly across his forehead. He appears no bad-looking man, of a stout muscular frame, and about forty-five or fifty years of age, and (what is singular for an Indian) has a bunch of hair growing from his under lip and chin. He has a blue blanket around him, and a squirrel-skin pouch hanging on his breast, fastened by a strap around his neck, in which is stuck a Plaster-of-Paris pipe, proving it to be his tobacco-pouch, and that he was a consumer of 'the weed.' His hair is so long as to be gathered together on the back of his head." *

---

* *Memoirs Hist. Soc. Pa.*, Vol. III., pp. 215-218.

LAP-PA-WIN-SOE
A Delaware Chief

TISHCOHAN

(OR, HE WHO NEVER BLACKENS HIMSELF)

OF Tishcohan, Tasucamin, Teshakomen *alias* Tishekunk, little is known, except what is contained in Mr Fisher and Mr Tyson's report.[1] His name occurs in Heckewelder's *Catalogue*, and means, in the Delaware language, "*He who never blackens himself.*"[2] We may note, on referring to the likeness, the correctness of the description, in the absence of those daubs of paint with which the Indian is so fond of deforming himself.

Tasucamin and Lappawinsoe were both signers of the celebrated *Walking Purchase* of 1737. By this treaty was ceded to the proprietaries of Pennsylvania an extensive tract of country, stretching along the Delaware from the Neshaminy[3] to far above the *Forks* at Easton,[4] and westward "as far as *a man can walk in a day and a half.*"[5] This transaction has been stigmatised by Charles Thomson[6] as one of the most nefarious schemes recorded in the colonial annals of Pennsylvania. It appears that the white men employed to walk with the Indians, performed the task with a celerity of which the Indians loudly complained. They protested against its manner of performance as opposed to the spirit of their contract, and an encroachment on their ancient usages. They alleged that it had been usual, on other occasions, to walk with deliberation, and to rest and smoke by the way, but that the walkers,

so called, actually *ran*, and performed, within the period,
a journey of most unreasonable extent.

This purchase has been differently viewed by different
writers. Logan claims the land for the proprietaries, on a
twofold title, independent of the treaty. He claims it
under a Deed made in 1686 with the predecessors of the
Indians, who asserted a right to it in 1737. He claims it
under a Release from the Five Nations, in the year 1736,
who, at that time, exercised over the Delawares that
insolence of superiority which the code of all nations has
accorded to conquest. This duple right, the same
excellent writer seeks further to confirm and establish
by denying to the Indians, with whom the Walking Treaty
was concluded, any original title to the territory ceded, on
the ground that they were new settlers from Jersey.

On the other hand, Charles Thomson disputes the
antecedent right of the proprietaries, under the Deed
of 1686, and the Release of 1736, and places the whole
question upon the honesty with which the stipulations of
the contracting parties were performed in the *Walking
Purchase.* And does it not at last repose here? The
terms of the original Deed are not known. Its authenticity rests only on tradition, and several authoritative
legal writers speak dubiously of its ever having existed.
One thing is certain, even if it did exist—*it had never been
walked out.*[7]

The Release from the Five Nations[8] can scarcely be
thought to impart validity to a title which is defective
without it. The peculiar subjugation to which the
vanquished tribe submitted, could only give to their
conquerors *the right of personal guardianship*, not the
power of *expatriation*. Besides, it is justly contended,
that any territorial rights acquired by the Five Nations
were confined to the land on the tributaries of the

Susquehanna, and never extended to the waters of the Delaware.

We may, therefore, return to the Treaty of 1737, and examine into the manner it was executed. If the Indians contracted with had no rights, why was a treaty entertained with them at all? When the proprietaries entered into a compact with the Indians, they gave to them a right to inquire into the fidelity with which it was performed, and pledged their own honours for its faithful observance. Was the speed of *running* a literal or honourable execution of a treaty *to walk?*

It was this departure from the terms and spirit of the contract which filled the Indians with so much dissatisfaction and heart-burning. The execution of the treaty was viewed by them as a piece of knavery and cunning, and concurred with other potent causes of estrangement in bringing about the most unhappy results. The minds of the Indians became alienated, embittered, inflamed; and a perverse and heartless policy on the part of their white neighbours made the breach irreconcilable.

But this people, even when goaded to desperation by acts of high-handed oppression and cruel selfishness, did not forget the days of William Penn, and were sometimes induced by the recollection to abstain from visiting upon his successors that degree of retaliation which would have been just, according to their ideas of retributive justice. It was this same people, in the days of their valour and martial glory, that lived on terms of cordiality and friendship with that great man and his followers, in conferring and receiving benefits, for a period of forty years! It was this people so actively kind, so unaffectedly grateful towards the unarmed strangers who sought refuge from persecution in their silent forests, that suffered from the descendants of these strangers, those keen griefs arising from a deep sense of unmerited injury, joined to a perception of meditated and the certainty of ultimate annihilation.   Contemporaneously with the date of the portraits from which the two foregoing engravings are reduced, the amity and good neighbourhood which had subsisted between the colonists of Pennsylvania and the Delaware Indians gave way to a state of feeling which ended in the departure of these sons of the soil from their long-enjoyed inheritance, to seek an abode in some distant wild, some unappropriated solitude of the western country. After the indignity they received from Canassatego in 1742,[9] they retired to Wyoming and Shamokin, and finally penetrated beyond the Ohio, where the survivors live but to brood over their wrongs, and transmit them to their descendants.   Pursued from river to river, they at last grew tired of retreat, and, turning back upon their pursuers, inflicted upon them all those cruelties which are prompted by resentment and despair.

NOTES

1. See *Lappawinsoe*, note 1, for information concerning this report, and for further details respecting the subject of the present sketch, see also *Lappawinsoe*, note 6.

2. Heckewelder (*Transactions of the American Philosophical Society*, n. s., IV., p. 387, Philadelphia, 1834) gives: "Tasucamin : Tasúcka-mend, he who never blackens himself." The forms Teshakomen and Tishekunk, given by McKenney and Hall, are evidently derived from the treaty of August 25, 1737, otherwise known as the "Walking Purchase" (see C. S. Keyser, *Penn's Treaty with the Indians*, Philadelphia, 1882, p. 28). In the treaty itself, printed in *Pennsylvania Archives*, Philadelphia, 1852, I., 541-543, the name appears as "Teeshakomen, *alias* Tisheekunk."

3. Neshaminy Creek, which flows into Delaware River between Philadelphia and Bristol, Pennsylvania.

TISH-CO-HAN, *or* HE WHO NEVER
BLACKENS HIMSELF
A Delaware Chief

4. At the mouth of the Lehigh, in Northampton County, fifty miles north of Philadelphia.

5. The quotation is in error and thus lessens somewhat the weight of the argument, which bears the style of Judge Hall. The wording of the treaty is: ". . . doth extend itself back into the Woods as far as a Man can goe in one day and a half, and bounded on the Westerly Side with the Creek called Neshameny, on the most Westerly branch thereof, So far as the said Branch doth extend, and from thence by line to the utmost extent of the said one day and a half's Journey, and from thence   to the aforesaid River Delaware, . . . " (Treaty of August 25, 1737, in *Pennsylvania Archives*, I., 541, Philadelphia, 1852. Compare Thomson, *Enquiry*, cited below, p. 34). Nevertheless, there is no doubt that the good Quakers of the City of Brotherly Love covertly swindled the Delawares of their lands.

6. See *An Enquiry into the Causes of the Alienation of the Delaware and Shawanese Indians*, etc. (London, 1759), by Charles Thomson, the patriot (*b.* County Derry, Ireland, 1729; *d.* Montgomery County, Pennsylvania, 1824). Thomson, who became a man of remarkable veracity, was brought to America by his father in 1740, the father dying in sight of land. When the Delawares adopted him into their tribe, he was called by a name meaning "Man of truth," and Ashbel Green in his auto-biography says that it was common to say that a statement was "as true as if Charles Thomson's name was to it." In 1774 he was unanimously chosen secretary of the First Continental Congress, and is spoken of as having been "the soul of that political body," retaining the position through every Congress until 1789. Among his works is *The Holy Bible, Containing the Old and New Covenant*, etc., in four volumes (Philadelphia, 1808), which contains the first English version of the Septuagint, con-sidered by contemporary biblical scholars as reflecting high honour on American scholarship. The manuscript of his *Critical Annotations on Gilbert Wakefield's Works* is in the Historical Society of Pennsylvania.

7. The original of the first Deed from the Indians to William Penn in 1682 is in possession of the Historical Society of Pennsylvania. In addition to Thomson's *Enquiry*, above cited (note 6), consult *Pennsylvania Archives*, 1st series, Vol. I., *op. cit.;* Drake, *Aboriginal Races*, 15th ed., New York, 1880, p. 528; Keyser, *Penn's Treaty, op. cit.*; Duponceau and Fisher in *Memoirs Historical Society of Pennsylvania*, III., pt. 3, 141-207, Philadelphia, 1836.

8. This release of the "lands on Susquehanna" was effected by the treaty with the Iroquois (Onondaga, Seneca, Oneida, Tuscarora, and Cayuga, the Mohawk not being represented by their own tribesmen) at Philadelphia, October 11, 1736. See *Pennsylvania Archives, op. cit.*, I., 494-497.

9. This refers to the council at Philadelphia with reference to the dispute between the Delawares and the Pennsylvania government con-

cerning the tract at the forks of Delaware River. Evidently pursuant
to a preconcerted arrangement between the Governor and Canasatego,
an Onondaga chief, and after easing the conscience of this Indian with
"a present from the Province, to the value of three hundred pounds, and
what more from the proprietor is uncertain," Canasatego, addressing the
Delawares, said :   "How came you to take upon you to sell Lands at
all ?   We conquered you ; we made Women of you :   You know you are
Women, and can no more sell Land than Women ; nor is it fit you should
have the Power of selling Lands, since you would abuse it.   The Land
that you claim is gone thro' your Guts ; you have been furnished with
Cloaths, Meat, and Drink, by the Goods paid you for it, and now you want
it again like Children as you are.   .   .   .   You are Women.   Take
the advice of a wife Man, and remove immediately.   .   .   .   Don't
deliberate, but remove away, and take this Belt of Wampum."   The
choice of the Shamokin and Wyoming was granted and the Delawares
yielded (Thomson, *Enquiry*, 45-47).

TOKACOU

(OR, HE THAT INFLICTS THE FIRST WOUND)

The character of this brave is indicated by his name, which means, *He that inflicts the first wound,* and expresses the idea that he is foremost in battle.[1] He is of the Yankton tribe of the Sioux nation, and is one of two persons who officiate as a kind of conservators of order within the village or encampment of the band. This office is never executed except by warriors of high repute, who can command respect and obedience in consequence of their personal influence. Among savages mere rank gives little authority unless it be sustained by weight of character. In each band of the Sioux several distinguished warriors are appointed, whose duty is to maintain order, and to notice every departure from the established discipline. These duties are not sufficiently well defined to enable us to describe them with any particularity; they are of a discretionary nature, and depend much upon the temper and character of the individuals who discharge them, and who, to some extent, make the rules which they enforce. As those over whom it is necessary to exert their authority are chiefly the unruly and the young, the ill-trained, rapacious, and idle, who hang loosely upon the community, the women, the children and the stranger, they usually execute summary justice upon the spot, according to their own notions of propriety, and inflict blows without scruple when they deem it necessary. In case of resistance or refusal to obey, they do not hesitate to put the offender to death.[2]

Tokacou and his colleague have long maintained the reputation of strict disciplinarians, and their authority is greatly respected by their people.   This is especially observable on the arrival of a white man, or a party of whites, at their village.   If these persons take the strangers under their protection, no one presumes to molest them : if the sword or the war-club of one of them is seen at the door of the white man's lodge, the sign is well understood, and no Indian ventures to intrude.

NOTES

1. The name appears as *Tokacon* in former editions, evidently through misprint.   According to the Rhees *Catalogue* (No. 85; see Introduction, p. 1), the portrait, which was painted by Cooke in 1837, bore the label "To-ca-cou, He that gives the first wound. Sioux of Missouri."   From Riggs we have *oo* (pronounced as two distinct *o's*), "wound"; *to-ka', to-kah*, "at the first"; *tokaheya*, "first"; *to'-ka*, "enemy" (*Grammar and Dictionary of the Dakota Language*, Washington, 1851).   The portrait is not listed by name in the manuscript catalogue of Inman copies in the Peabody Museum.

Tokacou signed the following treaties: Fort Lookout, June 22, 1825 (as "To-ka-oo, the one that kills"); Prairie du Chien, July 15, 1830 (as "To-ka-oh, wounds the enemy"); Washington, October 21, 1837 (as "To-ka-can, He that gives the First Wound").   The next treaty with the Yankton, that of Washington, April 19, 1858, was not signed by him.

2. On this question of punishment among the Dakota, Riggs (*Dakota Grammar, Texts, and Ethnography*, Washington, 1893, p. 220) says: "The only real punishment existing among the Dakota, having the sanction of law or immemorial usage, comes under the name of 'soldier-killing.'   This is carrying out the customs of the braves or warriors. The shape it takes is the destruction of property, cutting up blankets or tents, breaking guns, or killing horses.   But the same immemorial custom places an estoppage on this power.   A man who has killed more enemies than anyone else in the camp cannot be 'soldier-killed' by anyone else.   Or if he has killed an enemy in more difficult circumstances than the others, as, for instance, if he has climbed a tree to kill one, and no other man has performed a like feat, no one has a right to execute on him any decree of the 'Soldier's lodge.'   In this way he is placed above the execution of law."

TO-KA-COU
A Yankton Sioux Chief

MOU-KA-USH-KA, *or* THE
TREMBLING EARTH
A Yankton Sioux Chief

MOUKAUSHKA

(OR, THE TREMBLING EARTH)

THIS portrait represents a young man of the Yankton tribe, of the Sioux nation, who, but a few years ago, occupied an obscure and menial rank. The distinction of grade seems to be a law of human nature, and occurs to some extent even in the least artificial state of society. It is observable among all the Indian tribes. The sons of chiefs and distinguished warriors stand aloof from menial employments, and are early trained to the exercises of war and hunting, while the offspring of indolent or inefficient men receive less consideration, and are apt to be thrown into degrading offices. But in either case, the individual, on arriving at maturity, becomes the artificer of his own fortune, because, in a state of existence surrounded by danger and vicissitude, where boldness, cunning, and physical qualities are continually called into action, he must rise or sink in the proportion that he displays the possession or the want of those qualities.

Moukaushka, or *The Trembling Earth*,[1] while a boy, was employed as a cook, horse guard, etc., and had not met with any opportunity to distinguish himself, until near about the time when he arrived at manhood, when he forced himself into notice by a single act. A small party of young men, of the Yankton tribe, fell in with an equal number of *voyageurs*, who were travelling through the prairies from Saint Louis to some trading establishment in the interior of the Indian country. One of the Yanktons requested permission to ride on the same horse with one of the whites, which the latter declined, as his horse was much fatigued, and the journey was still far from being finished. The Indian, being offended, resolved, with the capricious resentment of a savage, to take revenge upon the first opportunity, and shortly after shot an arrow through the unfortunate white man. The remainder of the party fled in alarm, and reached the Yankton camp on the next day.

When the news of this outrage reached the Yankton village, Moukaushka, though a mere youth, declared himself the avenger of the white man. The Indian rule is, that the nearest relative of the deceased may put the murderer to death, but he must do it at his peril. If there be no relative who will take up the quarrel, a friend may do it; and in this instance, whatever may have been the motive of the young Indian, the act was according to their notions highly generous, as he took up the cause of a deceased stranger, without the prospect of reward, and at the risk of his own life. He was, however, laughed at by his companions, who did not give him credit for the courage necessary to carry out such a design, and supposed that he was only indulging in an idle boast. But he was in earnest; and, having loaded his gun, he deliberately walked up to the offender, when he entered the village, and shot him dead.

The impunity with which such an act might be done, would depend much on the manner of its execution. Had not the most determined intrepidity been displayed throughout the whole proceeding, it is probable that the deed would have been prevented, or avenged. Although done under colour of an acknowledged usage, it was not required by the Indian rule, and might have been considered an exception from it. The injured party was a stranger, and there was no tie of consanguinity or friendship which authorised Moukaushka to claim the office of his avenger. It might even have been an odious act to volunteer on such an occasion. It is most likely that a latent spirit that had been suppressed by the circumstances under which he had grown up, was glowing within him, and that he grasped at an opportunity, thus fortuitously presented, to emancipate himself from his humble condition. The occasion would recommend itself to a mind thus situated, by its novelty, and would make a greater impression than a commonplace achievement, which required only an ordinary effort of courage. If such was the reasoning of Moukaushka, it showed a sagacity equal to his spirit; and that it was, is rendered probable by the successful event of the affair. He rose immediately to distinction, and, having since shown himself a good warrior, is now, although a very young man, one of the chief persons in his tribe, and was sent to Washington in 1837, as one of their delegates. During their stay in Washington, Moukaushka became ill. He was suffering under the influence of fever when he sat for his portrait—but recovering a little, he was supposed able to proceed with the delegation on their tour to the East.[2] On arriving at Baltimore, however, it was found impracticable for him to proceed farther. He was left in charge of a faithful interpreter, and, although surrounded by all that was required for his comfort, he gradually sank under his disease, and, after a few days of suffering, died.

NOTES

1. The name Moukaushka is derived from *maka shkaṇshkaṇ*, "earth-quake" (Riggs, *Dakota Grammar and Dictionary*, 297, 1851). The name in the Omaha language, according to information furnished by Miss Alice C. Fletcher, is "Moṇkáshkoṇ."

2. His portrait was painted by G. Cooke in the year named, as appears from the Rhees *Catalogue* (No. 81 ; see Introduction, p. 1), in which it is recorded as "Mou-ka-ush-ka, Trembling Earth. Sioux of the Missouri ; died in Baltimore, October 25, 1837." The name does not occur in the list of Inman copies in the Peabody Museum.

Moukaushka signed the treaty of Washington, October 21 (three days prior to his death), his name appearing as "Mau-ka-ush-can, The Trembling Earth."

SHA-HA-KA, *or* THE BIG WHITE
A Mandan Chief

SHAHAKA

(OR, THE BIG WHITE)

THIS portrait is not included in the Indian Gallery at Washington City, but is of an older date, and equally authentic with those contained in the National Collection. It was kindly pointed out to us in the hall of the American Philosophical Society, in Philadelphia, by the venerable and accomplished librarian of that institution, John Vaughan, Esq., who permitted us to take this copy. Our information concerning the original is chiefly gleaned from the travels of Lewis and Clark, a work compiled with singular fidelity, and replete with valuable information.[1]

In the ascent of the Missouri, in the year 1804, the enterprising travellers above mentioned halted at the Mandan villages,[2] situated far beyond the frontier settlements, and at a point to which but few white men had penetrated. They were kindly received by the Mandans, who, having had no direct intercourse with the white people, had not experienced the oppression which has ever fallen upon the weaker party, in the contact of the two races. The leaders of the exploring expedition were so well pleased with their reception, that, finding they could not proceed much farther before their progress would be arrested by the excessive cold of this high latitude, they determined to spend the winter among the hospitable Mandans. Huts were accordingly erected, and they remained here, during the inclement season, enjoying an uninterrupted interchange of friendly offices with the natives.

On their first arrival a council was held, at which, after smoking the pipe of peace, a speech was delivered, explaining the objects of the exploring party, and giving assurances of friendship and trade. " This being over," says the narrative, "we proceeded to distribute the presents with great ceremony : one chief of each town was acknowledged by a gift of a flag, a medal with a likeness of the President of the United States, a uniform coat, hat and feather : to the second chiefs we gave a medal representing some domestic animals, and a loom for weaving; to the third chiefs medals with the impression of a farmer sowing grain." The account proceeds : " The chiefs who were made to-day are : Shahaka or Big White, a first chief, and Kagohami or Little Raven, a second chief of the lower village of the Mandans, called Matootonha," etc.[3] The making a chief, alluded to in this sentence, consisted simply in recognising that rank in those who previously held it, by treating with them in that capacity, and giving them presents appropriate to their station. On a subsequent occasion, we find this individual noticed in the following manner : " The Big White came down to us, having packed on the back of his squaw about one hundred pounds of very fine meat : for which we gave him as well as the squaw some presents, particularly an axe to the woman with which she was very much pleased."[4] If the measure of this lady's affection for her lord be estimated by the burthen which she carried on her back, we should say it was very strong.

On the return of Lewis and Clark to the Mandan villages, after an interval of nearly eighteen months, during which they had crossed the Rocky Mountains, and pene-

trated to the shores of the Pacific Ocean, these enterprising travellers were cordially received by the friendly
Indians with whom they had formerly spent a winter so
harmoniously. Anxious to cement the friendly disposition
which existed into a lasting peace, they proposed to take
some of the chiefs with them to Washington City, to visit
the President. This invitation would have been readily
accepted, had it not been for the danger to which the
Indians imagined such a journey to be exposed. Between
them and the United States frontier, were the Arickaras,
their enemies, whose towns must of necessity be passed
by the descending boats; the roving bands of the Sioux
also frequently committed depredations along the left
shore of the Missouri, while the right bank was accessible
to the Osages; and although the American officers
promised to protect those who should accompany them,
and to bring them back to their homes, they could not
overcome the jealous and timid reluctance of any of the
chiefs, except *Le Grand Blanche*, or the Big White, who
agreed to become their companion. Our gallant explorers
have unfortunately given a very brief account of their
journey after leaving the Mandan villages, on their return
voyage, and we find no record of the conduct of the Big
White under such novel circumstances. It would have
been very interesting to have heard from those gentlemen,
who had just visited the Indians in their own abodes, an
account of the remarks and behaviour of an Indian chief
under similar circumstances. We, however, only know
that he visited our seat of Government, and returned in
safety to his friends.[5]

NOTES

1. There are many writings on this expedition, but the definitive work is the *Original Journals of the Lewis and Clark Expedition, 1804-6,* 7 vols. and atlas, edited by Reuben Gold Thwaites, New York, 1904-5. To this most excellent work the student is referred for details respecting the important undertaking of which it treats.

2. The two Mandan villages (Metutahanke and Ruptari) in 1804 were on opposite sides of the Missouri River, about four miles below the mouth of Knife River, in the present North Dakota. In 1837 the tribe was visited by small-pox, which carried away all but 125 to 145 of a population of about 1600. They have almost doubled in numbers since that time, the population in 1906 being 264, on the Fort Berthold Reservation. The Mandan belong to the Siouan stock.

3. Metutahanke, meaning "Lower Village."

4. Extracted from the *History of the Expedition under the Command of Captains Lewis and Clarke,* prepared for the press by Paul Allen, Dublin, 1817, vol. I., pp. 150-151, 158-159.

5. Shahaka is more commonly called *Gros Blanc* and Big White in the Lewis and Clark journals. He was principal chief of Metutahanke, the "Lower Village" of the Mandan, and rendered friendly service to Lewis and Clark while at their Fort Mandan in the winter of 1804-5, in recognition of which he was given a medal. Brackenridge described him as "a fat man, not much distinguished as a warrior, and extremely talkative, a fault much despised amongst the Indians." When the expedition returned to the Missouri from the Pacific, Lewis and Clark persuaded Shahaka to return with them to St Louis, with a view of making a visit to President Jefferson, and Jefferson later invited Lewis to visit his home, "Monticello," with Shahaka, for the purpose of showing the latter his collection of Indian objects from the North-West. Shahaka remained in the East for a year, and while there, evidently in Philadelphia, Charles Balthasar Julien Févre de Saint Mémin, then visiting America, made a portrait of him with the aid of a physionotrace, the original of which still belongs to the American Philosophical Society of Philadelphia. Shahaka left St Louis for his home in May 1807, the party, consisting of himself and his interpreter, René Jessaume, with their wives and one child each, escorted by two non-commissioned officers and eleven privates under the command of Ensign Nathaniel Pryor, who, as a sergeant, had accompanied the expedition of Lewis and Clark. There ascended the Missouri at the same time a deputation of twenty-four Sioux, including six children, who were provided with a separate escort ; and also two trading parties, one of which, consisting of thirty-two men under Pierre Chouteau, was designed to traffic with the Mandan. The expedition proceeded slowly up the Missouri, reaching the lower Arikara village on September 9, where it was learned that the Mandan and the Arikara were at war. The demand of the chief of the upper Arikara village that Shahaka go ashore with him being refused, the Indians became insolent and aggressive, and afterwards opened fire on the boats, which was returned. Pryor then ordered a retreat down-stream, but the Indians followed along shore, killing one of the Sioux, mortally wounding one of Chouteau's men, and wounding several others, including Jessaume. Pryor now proposed to Shahaka that they attempt to cover the rest of the distance—about three days' journey—by land, but this the Mandan refused to do on account of the incumbrance of the women and children, and the wounded condition of their interpreter, whereupon the party returned to St Louis. By an agreement entered into with the Missouri Fur Company in the spring of 1808 for the safe conduct of the Indians to their home, another expedition, consisting of about 150 men, having Shahaka and his companions in charge, started from St Louis about the middle of May 1809, and although the Sioux at first showed a disposition to be troublesome, the Arikara were found to be friendly, and the party reached its destination September 24. In addition to the *Original Journals of the Lewis and Clark Expedition,* consult Chittenden, *American Fur Trade,* 1902 ; Coues in *Annals of Iowa,* 3rd ser., I., 613, Des Moines, 1895 ; Brackenridge, *Views of Louisiana,* 1814.

INDEX

A

"Absentee Shawnees," 43 (*note* 8)
Adams, John Quincy, succeeded by President Jackson, xviii
Adams, Mrs, and Tshusick, the Chippeway woman, 360
Ahyokah, daughter of Sequoyah, 139
Alexander, Mrs Mary Louisa, xxix
Algonquian family, tribes of, 42 (*notes* 2 and 8), 405 (*note* 2)
Alphabet, the Cherokee, 138, 141
Anacamegishca ("Foot Prints"), 344-346
Apushimataha. See Pushmataha
Arikara, Caddoan tribe, 230 (*note* 7)
Atkinson, Henry, concludes Fort Atkinson treaty, 221 (*note* 4)
Autossee, massacre of Creeks at, 261

B

Barbour, James, Secretary of War, appoints Colonel McKenney to treat with the Choctaws and Cherokees, xvi, xxiii
Barbour, Lucy Cornelia (Tshusick), 353, 365 (*note* 3)
Battles of—
  Autossee, 261, 270 (*note* 2)
  Black Hawk War, 147, 153 (*note* 2)
  Bladensburg, viii and *note*
  Braddock, 236
  Camp Defiance, 270 (*note* 2)
  Delawares, 40, 41, 405 (*note* 2)
  Fort Duquesne, 99 (*note* 8)
  Fort Massac, 34, 42
  Fort Meigs, 107
  Horseshoe Bend, 261, 262, 270 (*note* 4), 391
  Knoxville, 372, 373
  Lundy's Lane, xxiv
  Point Pleasant, 39, 43 (*note* 7), 170 (*note* 2)
  Pontiac, 99 (*note* 8)
  St Croix, 51
  Thames, the, 61 (*note* 13), 97, 100 (*note* 11)
  Tippecanoe, 96

427

Beasley, Major Daniel, massacred at Fort Mims, 400 (*note* 32)
Bellevue, 221 (*note* 4)
Benton, Senator, and abolishment of Superintendency of Indian Trade, xviii
Biaseka ("The Wolf"), Shawnee chief, 246
"Big Axe." See Inthehone
"Big Elk." See Ongpatonga
"Big Kansas." See Choncape
"Big Kaw." See Choncape
"Big Neck." See Moanahonga
"Big Thunder," 126; at Lake Traverse and Pembina, 126, 129; killed by the Chippewa, 129 (*note* 6)
"Big Tree," signs Fort Harmar Treaty, 186
"Big Warrior" of Tuckabachee, 390; requests United States assistance to quell the "Red Sticks," 390; signs treaty of Colerain, 400 (*note* 33); death of, *ibid.*
"Big White." See Shahaka
"Birchen Canoe," Schoolcraft's poem, 254
"Black Bird." See Washinggusaba
"Black Fox." See Enolee
Black Hawk War, 147, 153 (*note* 2)
"Black Hoof." See Catahecassa
Black Snake Hills country, 313, 317 (*note* 6)
Blackwell, Robert, state printer, xxv
Bladensburg, battle of, viii; General Ross and Admiral Cockburn in command of British forces, *ibid.*; quoted by McKenney, viii, *note*
Boudinot, Elias, 369; biography of, 396 (*note* 4); editor of *Cherokee Phœnix* and *Cherokee Advocate*, *ibid.*; writes *Poor Sarah; or, the Indian Woman*, in Sequoyah's syllabic characters, *ibid.*; murder of, *ibid.*
Bowles ("The Bowl"), chief of Western Cherokees, killed by Texans, 336, 338, 342 (*note* 6)
Boyd, Mrs, and Tshusick, 355
Braddock, battle at, 236

Chilly McIntosh, 266

Chinnubbee, or Chinnaby, Creek chief, attacks Knoxville, 372; his "fort" at Ten Islands on Coosa River, 397 (*note* 9)

Chippeway, or Ojibwag, tribe, xiii, 197, 198 (*note* 1), 199, 344, 346; Red Lake, 122 (*note* 1)

Choctaw, a tribe of the Muskhogean family, 62, 71 (*note* 2); their agriculture and civilisation, 62, 71 (*note* 2); habitat and settlement, 62, 71 (*note* 2); intermarriage with white traders, 62; missionaries among, 62; number of tribe in 1906, 71 (*note* 2); one of the Five Civilised Tribes, 71 (*note* 2); treaty with, xii, 72 (*note* 6)

Choncape, "Big Kansas" or "Big Kaw," 218; account of, by J. T. Irving, 221 (*note* 4); family of, 221; signs treaties at Fort Atkinson, Prairie du Chien, Otto Village, Bellevue, 221 (*note* 4); portraits of, by King and Neagle, 222 (*note* 5); visits Washington, 222 (*note* 4); fights against the Americans, 226, 227

Chonmonicase, 156

Clan revenge (Cherokee), 398 (*note* 21)

Clark, General William, Governor of Missouri Territory, and Superintendent of Indian Affairs, xii, 72 (*note* 6), 290, 293 (*note* 4), 303, 312, 319

Clark and Lewis Expedition, 421, 424

Clinton, De Witt, on "Red Jacket's" eloquence in Council, 18

Cockburn, Admiral, in command of British forces at battle of Bladensburg, viii

Coffee, General John, at battle of Horseshoe Bend, 392

Cole, Robert, successor to Pushmataha, 72 (*note* 6)

Colerain, treaty of, 400 (*note* 33)

Cooke, G., Indian portrait painter, xxxvi, xlvi-liii; his portrait of Moukaushka, 417, 420 (*note* 2); of Tokacou, 416 (*note* 1)

Coosa River, 397 (*note* 9)

Coosa Wathla, Cherokee settlement, 399 (*note* 27)

Cooweescoowee (John Ross), celebrated Cherokee chief, intimate friend of Col. McKenney, ix, 394

Copper, virgin, specimen of, 57, 61 (*note* 10); story of, 349

Corcoran Art Gallery, 4 (*note* 2)

Cornplanter, or Kiontwogky, Seneca chief, 18, 174, 180; signs treaties at Fort Harmar and Fort Stanwix, 18, 30 (*note* 12), 185, 191 (*note* 10); visits England, 174; death of, 180; General Putnam in council with, 182; Governor Mifflin presents tract of land to, 183; letters of, to Governor of Pennsylvania and President of United States, 186; his son Henry Obeal, 188; Matlock's portrait of, 188

Council Bluffs. See Fort Atkinson

Coweta town, 270 (*note* 1)

Cradle, Indian, 249

Crane gens, 50

Crawford, Colonel, birth of, 99; burned at the stake, 80, 99 (*note* 8); in expedition to Fort Duquesne and Pontiac war, 99 (*note* 8)

Creeks, at Broken Arrow, 263; and treaty of Indian Springs, 264, 265; reservation, 271 (*note* 13); in battle of Horseshoe Bend, 391-393

Crowell, Creek agent, xvi; and treaty of Indian Springs, 264, 265, 271 (*note* 7)

Cusick, Indian artist, his famous picture of "The Treaty," 7; its moral truth, 8

D

Dacotah (Dakota) nation, character and habitat of, 106, 107, 225, 226; their law of punishment, 416 (*note* 2)

Dances—the "Begging," "Greencorn," "Peace," "Pipe," "Mourning for the Dead," the "Sun," and the *Wabana*, 1, 2, 3, 227, 230; "Medicine," 387

Dearborn, General, Secretary of War, 169, 171 (*note* 6)

Decatur, Commodore Stephen, and Algiers Expedition, xxiv

Delawares, wars of the, 40, 41; settlements and number of, 405 (*note* 2). See also under Lenni Lennapi

Detroit, siege of, 203

Dexter, Mrs Cornelia, presents portrait of Nawkaw, Winnebago chief, to the Peabody Museum, 153 (*note* 5)

Dinsmore, Colonel Silas, American Government agent in Cherokee country, instructs Indians in use of plough, spinning-wheel, and the loom, 376

"Disputed Shot, The," Stanley painting, 4 (*note* 2)

R

S